Shaping Places

Shaping Places explains how towns and cities can turn real estate development to their advantage to create the kind of places where people want to live, work, relax and invest. It contends that the production of quality places which enhance economic prosperity, social cohesion and environmental sustainability require a transformation of market outcomes. The core of the book explores why this is essential, and how it can be delivered, by linking a clear vision for the future with the necessary means to achieve it. Crucially, the book argues that public authorities should seek to shape, regulate and stimulate real estate development so that developers, landowners and funders see real benefit in creating better places.

Key to this is seeing planners as market actors, whose potential to shape the built environment depends on their capacity to understand and transform the embedded attitudes and practices of other market actors. This requires planners to be skilled in understanding the political economy of real estate development and successful in changing its outcomes through smart intervention. Drawing on a strong theoretical framework, the book reveals how the future of places comes to be shaped through constant interaction between State and market power.

Filled with international examples, essential case studies, colour diagrams and photographs, this is essential reading for undergraduate and graduate students taking planning, property, real estate or urban design courses, as well as for social science students more widely who wish to know how the shaping of place really occurs.

David Adams holds the Ian Mactaggart Chair of Property and Urban Studies at the University of Glasgow, where **Steve Tiesdell** was Senior Lecturer in Public Policy until his death in 2011. They worked together for over a decade, first at the University of Aberdeen and then at Glasgow, sharing a mutual interest in state-market relations in land and property, and applying this to research and teaching on planning, public policy, real estate development, urban design and urban regeneration. Before moving to Aberdeen, Steve worked at the Universities of Nottingham and Sheffield, while David was previously at the Universities of Reading and Manchester. *Shaping Places* represents the culmination of their mutual endeavour and builds on previous joint publications, including their edited book *Urban Design in the Real Estate Development Process* (2011).

David and Steve have each researched and published widely in their respective fields. Steve's previous books include *Revitalising Historic Urban Quarters* (co-author 1996), *Public Places – Urban Spaces: The Dimensions of Urban Design* (co-author 2003 and 2010) and *The Urban Design Reader* (co-editor 2006). David's previous books include *Urban Planning and the Development Process* (author 1994), *Greenfields, Brownfields and Housing Development* (co-author 2002) and *Planning, Public Policy and Property Markets* (co-editor 2005).

Shaping Places

Urban planning, design and development

David Adams and Steve Tiesdell

Routledge
Taylor & Francis Group

LONDON AND NEW YORK

First published 2013
by Routledge
2 Park Square, Milton Park, Abingdon, Oxon OX14 4RN

Simultaneously published in the USA and Canada
by Routledge
711 Third Avenue, New York, NY 10017

Routledge is an imprint of the Taylor & Francis Group, an informa business

British Library Cataloguing in Publication Data
A catalogue record for this book is available from the British Library

Library of Congress Cataloging in Publication Data
Adams, David.
   Shaping places: urban planning, design, and development /
   David Adams and Steve Tiesdell.
      p. cm.
   Includes bibliographical references and index.
   1. Cities and town—Growth. 2. Real estate development.
   I. Tiesdell, Steven. II. Title.
   HT371.A33 2013
   307.76—dc23   2012003739

ISBN: 978-0-415-49796-1 (hbk)
ISBN: 978-0-415-49797-8 (pbk)
ISBN: 978-0-203-10566-5 (ebk)

Typeset in FS Albert
by Keystroke, Station Road, Codsall, Wolverhampton
Printed and bound in India by Replika Press Pvt. Ltd.

To Judith, Daniel and Eleanor Adams and to Ian, David, Tina, Paige and Mason Tiesdell

STEVE TIESDELL (1964–2011)

Steve Tiesdell, who died on 30 June 2011, was one of the UK's leading academic urban designers and, to those who knew him, an exceptionally supportive colleague, friend and teacher. Educated at the University of Nottingham, and professionally qualified as both an architect and planner, Steve held academic posts successively at the Universities of Nottingham, Sheffield and Aberdeen before moving to the University of Glasgow as Senior Lecturer in Public Policy in 2005.

Throughout his career, Steve was at the forefront of re-interpreting and re-energising urban design as a means to transform people's lives for the better by creating places in which they could thrive. He always remained incredibly passionate about urban design. What made this passion so intellectually powerful, however, were his inherent curiosity and his enthusiasm for scholarship. These marked him as possessing an unusual keenness to reach out well beyond his own discipline and build numerous bridges to those with other academic and pro-fessional interests. He was keenly committed to seeing those in practice equipped with stronger design skills and appreciation, and was equally at home speaking to practitioners as to students. He was a fervent advocate of multidisciplinary approaches and a powerful critic of what he called 'silo-based' thinking.

Steve was a highly effective communicator, whether in the lecture room or, as he loved to do, guiding a party of students or visitors around the cities in which he lived and worked. As one former student said, Steve 'had the rare gift of being able to convey the common-sense nature of urban design in such a way that was inherently memorable and intuitive'. He could readily capture and retain audience attention by the enthusiasm he always conveyed for his subject. With his voice resounding across the lecture theatre or in the open air, it was never hard to hear what Steve said or to appreciate the importance he attached to saying it.

Despite the greater commitment needed, Steve always believed strongly in the importance of publishing books, even though he also wrote numerous conference and journal papers, both individually and jointly. As his career developed, he increasingly saw the importance of effective delivery to urban design, which led to his growing interest in real estate development as well as policy and governance. Steve's architectural background proved no barrier to developing an ever stronger knowledge of these fields – indeed by drawing on design language he was often able to communicate key policy concepts more effectively.

Although passionate about academic enquiry, he never took himself too seriously – his self-deprecating sense of humour was frequently used to good effect. His widespread popularity among colleagues and students alike reflected his own generosity of time and his keenness to share and debate ideas. So many people have remarked how much they enjoyed their lively discussions with Steve and will long remember those chances to share a drink or a meal and appreciate his company. He was indeed an outstanding academic, and a much valued friend to many.

David Adams

Contents

CONTENTS

Illustrations

Figures

Figures without accreditation are copyright of the authors

Tables

Boxes

Preface

This book is intended for all those who will help to create the places of tomorrow, whether in education, practice or the wider community. Although written primarily as an academic resource for those studying planning, design and development, especially in the later years of university education, *Shaping Places* is also meant to contribute to and, indeed, provoke that wider debate about the quality of the built environment which takes place well beyond academia. Its purpose is to demonstrate what can be, and often is, achieved when those in positions of influence – developers, landowners, planners, funders, professional advisers and, above all, politicians – work together to make and remake places that are sustainable, resilient and successful.

Shaping Places emerged from conversations between Steve Tiesdell and myself about updating and considerably extending *Urban Planning and the Development Process*, which I had published in 1994. We had planned this in some detail and, indeed, agreed the contract with Routledge before Steve was taken seriously ill in July 2010. For nearly a year, Steve and I regularly talked about the chapters I was writing and his valuable insights and comments continued to inform the book. Since Steve died, I have used and interpreted the material he left to help complete the remaining chapters in such a way that I trust the finished product is as much a joint effort as was originally intended.

David Adams
University of Glasgow
December 2011

Acknowledgements

Much of the content of this book was developed in research and teaching that Steve and I have undertaken over the past few years. The encouragement and feedback from all those colleagues and students who helped us explore the many different dimensions of *Shaping Places* has been much appreciated. Particular thanks are due to those who collaborated with us on specific research projects or papers in recent years, including Rob Croudace, Chris De Sousa, Alan Disberry, Tim Dixon, Norman Hutchison, Chris Leishman, Garry MacFarlane, Craig Moore, Thomas Munjona, Sarah Payne, Georgiana Varna, Craig Watkins and George Weeks.

In writing the book, I have particularly appreciated the support of friends and colleagues at Glasgow and, in the wider academic community, those who have been willing to comment on emerging drafts, especially Alastair Adair, Phil Allmendinger, Matthew Carmona, Trevor Davies, Martin Dixon, John Henneberry, Chris Leishman, Danny Mackinnon, Kevin Murray, Sarah Payne, Libby Porter, John Punter, Steven Tolson, Craig Watkins and George Weeks. Their input has been invaluable, but they are of course absolved from any responsibility for what has finally emerged. I am also grateful to those who have provided illustrative material for the book, which is acknowledged as it appears. The thorough and systematic work of Maggie Reid in compiling the index has also been greatly appreciated.

Finally, the Routledge team of Alex Hollingsworth, Nicole Solano and, especially, Louise Fox, our editorial adviser, deserve particular thanks for encouraging us to get started, for constructive comments as the book progressed, and for their support at difficult times.

David Adams

PART I

THE DEVELOPMENT CONTEXT

1 Introduction

Places matter

In 2009, the then UK Government published its strategy for improving place quality. This declared that 'Good quality of place should not be seen as a luxury but as a vital element in our drive to make Britain a safer, healthier, prosperous, more inclusive and sustainable place' (UK Government 2009: 2). The document set seven strategic objectives:

- to strengthen leadership on quality of place at the national and regional level;
- to encourage local civic leaders and local government to prioritise quality of place;
- to ensure relevant government policy, guidance and standards consistently promote quality of place and are user friendly;
- to put the public and community at the centre of place shaping;
- to ensure all development for which central government is directly responsible is built to high design and sustainability standards and promotes quality of place;
- to encourage higher standards of market-led development;
- to strengthen quality of place skills, knowledge and capacity.

Although published towards the end of the life of a Labour Government that had by then dominated British political life for the previous twelve years, the strategy reaffirmed messages from the Urban Task Force (1999), the Sustainable

Communities Plan (OPDM 2003) and other earlier documents that place-making is as important as plan-making. It also echoed the call of Sir Michael Lyons (2007), in his wide-ranging review of local government, for place shaping in its broadest sense to be at the heart of local council concerns.

Since evidence from Europe (see, for example, Cadell *et al.* 2008, PRP *et al.* 2008) pointed to a stronger culture and practice of place-making on the Continent, the strategy generated important questions around the purpose and effectiveness of long-standing British approaches to managing spatial change. By that time, however, the UK economy was in severe trouble after more than a decade of continuous economic growth, and those involved in the development process were concerned more with their own survival than with the creation of great places for the future. It was therefore not the best time to make the perfectly reasonable claim that 'Good quality development does not have to be more expensive than poor quality – and in the longer term the savings will be significant' (UK Government 2009: 2). Within a year, the Labour Government had left office, to be replaced by a new coalition of parties with a very different agenda. A wave of public service cuts then threatened the capacity of local authorities to deliver even basic services, let alone place transformation, with Britain heading towards an era of economic austerity.

The main message of this book – that places matter and that shaping places is an essential governance activity – is not necessarily one that appears to match the state of Britain in 2012. Yet, the issues addressed here are so fundamental to delivering long-term sustainability that, in reflecting on recent experience, it is important to put down markers that can inform policy directions and likely achievements in the years to come. How place is interpreted and managed is crucial to balancing economic prosperity, social cohesion and environmental protection, which will become increasingly central to the task of governments over coming decades. Indeed, global concerns around climate change, rapid urbanisation, peak oil and economic restructuring put urban management among the most pressing issues likely to face governments of the future.

As Figure 1.1 shows, the factors that constitute 'quality of place' at the local level make a significant contribution to what might be construed within a broader understanding of the quality of life. As place is multi-dimensional, it is essential to emphasise that its physical and environmental characteristics are important in their own right, while also providing a platform for effective social and economic interaction. Moreover, if planning is about 'promoting ways to advance the liveability and sustainability of daily life environments, not just for the few but for the many' (Healey 2010: 20), it becomes important to consider all its various dimensions, including the economic, within the broader concept of human flourishing in a sustainable context.

Indeed, a host of debates around, for example, access to employment opportunities, educational achievement, neighbourhood quality, service delivery,

FIGURE 1.1

Local area factors contributing to good quality of life. (UK Government, 2009)

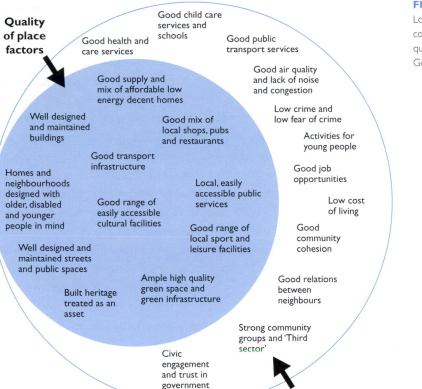

Quality of place factors

Good child care services and schools

Good health and care services

Good public transport services

Good supply and mix of affordable low energy decent homes

Good air quality and lack of noise and congestion

Well designed and maintained buildings

Good mix of local shops, pubs and restaurants

Low crime and low fear of crime

Good transport infrastructure

Activities for young people

Homes and neighbourhoods designed with older, disabled and younger people in mind

Local, easily accessible public services

Good job opportunities

Good range of easily accessible cultural facilities

Low cost of living

Well designed and maintained streets and public spaces

Good range of local sport and leisure facilities

Good community cohesion

Ample high quality green space and green infrastructure

Good relations between neighbours

Built heritage treated as an asset

Strong community groups and 'Third sector'

Civic engagement and trust in government

Other factors

mobility and community safety have consistently shown that place matters. This is why 'The way places and buildings are planned, designed and looked after matters to all of us in countless ways. The built environment can be a source of everyday joy or everyday misery. It is an important influence on crime, health, education, inclusion, community cohesion and well-being. It can help attract or deter investment and job opportunities. Planning, conservation and design have a central part to play in our urgent drive to reduce greenhouse gas emissions and protect biodiversity' (UK Government 2009: 2).

The purpose of this book is not to delve into each of those debates in any detail but, rather, to explore the process by which more successful places can be delivered, especially in a physical and environmental sense. This focus acknowledges the importance of the social and economic, while concentrating on what can reasonably be covered in a text of this length. Although the conception of place presented here is inevitably part of a broader picture, it is important enough to deserve clear focus. By reflecting on recent experience in shaping places, both within and well beyond the UK, the book aims to speak to those who, in the years ahead, will be centrally involved in such activity.

The search for future policy solutions is likely to prompt a fundamental reappraisal of how governments should seek to shape places and of how this will influence those beyond government whose impact on place is equally important. This highlights the importance of state–market relations, since places of real quality are generally delivered neither by the state nor by the market alone, but by some form of interaction between them. We argue that the nature and effectiveness of this interaction is at the core of understanding how places change over time and how they might be delivered more successfully.

Some schooled in the British hierarchical mode of governance (see Chapter 6) may well regard our interest in markets as indicative of a neo-liberal approach that has created places simply to satisfy the demands of the well-off, while ignoring the needs of those with limited market power. Yet, because the poor and the less mobile are often those most trapped by poorly designed and poorly integrated environments, creating well-designed and inclusive places is as much about social justice as it is about economic prosperity or environmental sustainability.[1] Those who really delve into the book will therefore find strong criticism of what has come to be known as 'market-led planning' and discover instead something of the theory and practice of 'plan-shaped markets'. Our essential argument is thus that effective place-making involves a style of market engagement in which city authorities are sufficiently skilled and knowledgeable to turn real estate markets to their advantage in seeking to create the kind of places in which the many can live, work or enjoy themselves. We now explain how this argument develops, as we outline the main themes of the book.

Themes of the book

Four main themes are explored in this book. The first investigates what makes places successful and, by implication, what makes them less than successful. This takes centre stage in the next chapter, which identifies five characteristics of successful places. Specifically, these highlight the importance of people to place, of connectivity and permeability, of variability in use and form, of local distinctiveness, and of sustainability, resilience and robustness. These characteristics have considerable potential to make places more valuable, not only in a narrow financial sense but also in relation to their broader social, cultural and environmental attractiveness.

Illustrations throughout the book draw attention to specific places of varying success. One of the main concerns has been to highlight lessons that can be learnt more generally from successful places, especially those in Europe and the UK that are considered by many to be exemplars. Among such case studies presented are those developed by a far-sighted landowner (Newhall), an active municipality (Hammarby-Sjöstad) and a government agency (Upton). These experiences are used later on in the book to help to establish what is involved in 'the place production process' (see Chapter 11).

Such valued places can be contrasted with what we term 'default urbanism' – the kind of second-rate places that emerge spontaneously, when no one has consciously tried to do better. Here, we emphasise the lack of collective thought and action that tends to intensify the risks of development activity and produce more disintegrated outcomes across both time and space. Unfortunately, many people's everyday experience of place is represented by default urbanism, to the extent that those fortunate enough to live or work in more successful, sustainable or attractive places are considered the exception.

The contrast between successful and less successful places prompts us to explore how places come about, which is the second theme explored in the book. To understand the varied ways in which places originate, grow and evolve, we need to explore how the concept of place has been commodified, parcelled up and traded both as a financial asset in its own right and as the basis on which to exploit other economic opportunities. To investigate this, we analyse real estate markets, values and development processes in Chapters 3 to 5. Crucially, we see these as both socially and economically constructed and as highly diverse in their operation over time and space. This makes it difficult to predict, let alone manage, the kinds of places that emerge from market operations. Even so, it is apparent that the distinctive nature of real estate coupled with the unpredictability of the development process reinforces the tendency towards default urbanism.

Our third theme therefore concerns the need for collective action in place-making, and specifically the importance of governance arrangements that can promote and deliver more integrated forms of development. Chapter 6 thus examines different approaches that can be, and have been, taken towards the governance of place. Significantly, we do not assume that government intervention in real estate development necessarily produces more successful places than would market processes left to their own devices. Indeed, Chapter 6 illustrates the potential for government failure with some notable examples of where government interventions, undertaken at the time with the best of intentions, turned out to produce places of exclusion and neglect, which had subsequently to be remedied at significant public expense. *How* governments participate in place-making is thus just as important as *whether* they choose to do so in the first place. Issues around place leadership, stakeholder engagement and delivering capacity, all of which we explore in Chapter 6, are indeed critical to the potential success or failure of government attempts to reshape places.

The final theme thus concerns the interaction between public policy and private initiative, or what we call 'state–market relations' in land and property development. Such relations matter because places develop in a way that reflects both the dynamics of real estate markets and the dominant mode of governance at the time of their production. Significantly, we start this analysis in Chapters 7, 8 and 9 not with public policy, but by looking in turn at the strategies, actions and interests of developers, landowners, funders and investors, primarily in the private sector. This reveals widespread diversity in their performance and highlights the contrast between entrenched and more innovative behaviour.

On that basis, in Chapters 10 to 14, we review a range of relevant policy instruments, defined by their capacity to shape, compel, constrain or incite what market actors choose to do. This final theme thus emphasises that producing more successful places necessarily involves shaping, regulating and stimulating real estate markets, while building the capacity to do so.

The book views planners as market actors whose potential to shape the built environment depends on their ability to analyse and transform the embedded attitudes and practice of a range of other market actors. This challenges planners both to be skilled in understanding the political economy of real estate development and to be successful in influencing its outcomes. We trust that the four themes covered in the book will help current and future planners, wherever they work, to meet those challenges.

2 Successful places

Introduction

Places matter intensely to human experience. Where we live, and how far we can travel daily, conditions our personal activities and interactions. Alongside this, economic prosperity or reversal displays conspicuous expression in its differential treatment of different places. Increasingly, specific notions of place are invoked in confronting climate change, with more compact cities, for example, seen as central in reducing energy consumption and making development more sustainable. The social, economic and environmental importance of place thus makes it essential to understand why certain places appear to be more successful than others.

To answer this, some commentators point to the countless unconnected and spontaneous decisions of the real estate development process (see Chapter 5), which from time immemorial have fashioned cities as if by some physical equivalent of Adam Smith's 'invisible hand'. Yet others, well aware of urban history and political economy, know that places are also shaped by the powerful forces of state power and finance capital – sometimes conflicting with each other, but more often working in collaboration. Those who look can thus recognise a 'visible hand' that explains the way places develop. Too often, however, developments created by the visible hand of state power or finance capital have turned into places of exclusiveness and exclusion, showing how place can readily become a physical manifestation of prevalent power relations (see Figures 2.1 and 2.2).

The purpose of this chapter is to establish a normative concept of what is meant by successful places so as to provide a benchmark for influencing the visible

FIGURE 2.1
Red Road Flats, Glasgow, Scotland. Built between 1964 and 1968, Red Road Flats once housed 4,700 tenants in eight tower and slab blocks. Symbolic of social exclusion and now occupied mainly by asylum seekers, the blocks will all be demolished by 2016. (Amanda Vincent-Rous, used under the Creative Commons licence)

FIGURE 2.2
Gated community, River Run, North Tempe, Arizona, USA. Residents of the 112 homes behind these entrance gates enjoy well-maintained common areas, with access to community swimming pools, tennis courts and other private recreational facilities. (Nick Bastian, used under the Creative Commons licence)

hand of state power and finance capital as well as the seemingly unconnected and spontaneous decisions of the real estate development process. In other words, understanding what makes places successful is an essential prerequisite to creating places that function socially, economically and environmentally. This task is indeed as much about social justice as economic prosperity and environmental sustainability, since the poor, the less-mobile and those with limited market power can often find themselves trapped by poorly designed and poorly integrated environments, from which the rich and powerful are able to escape.

The next section explores what is meant by the concept of place and interprets urban design as essentially a place-making activity. The central part of the chapter then highlights five characteristics of successful places, suggesting that they are:

- places meant for people
- well-connected and permeable places
- places of mixed use and varied density
- distinctive places
- sustainable, resilient and robust places.

The penultimate section of the chapter explores the ways in which urban design has value (and especially financial value) as a place-making activity, while the final section concludes by identifying barriers that deter or inhibit successful place-making.

Places, design and place-making

The Dutch architect Aldo Van Eyck famously remarked that 'Whatever space and time mean, place and occasion mean more. For space in the image of man is place, and time in the image of man is occasion' (Smithson 1968: 101). So, in the same way that the occasion of a well-attended sports match brings an empty stadium alive, the presence of people turns the otherwise empty abstraction of an urban space into the warm embrace of a public place. Places thus derive their meaning and value from people, and without them, they would remain mere elements of space defined by physical characteristics alone. For, as Healey (2010: 18) commented, 'In our webs of relations, we are also socially and culturally "placed" in relation to others, and in places of dwelling and encounter. We value these places, as they give shape to our daily life flow, and as they collect meanings through the encounters of daily life and of special occasions and incidents . . .' In short, place is socially constructed. Our appreciation of particular places, while individually experienced, is thus characterised by our social interactions.

Healey's differentiation between places of dwelling and of encounter helps us to appreciate how different types of place are created or come about in different ways and for different purposes. Places where people live and work are those of daily dwelling or existence (see Figure 2.3), where the most important design task is often to integrate social, community, recreational, commercial and residential functions to ensure their effective operation. Places of encounter or experience (see Figure 2.4) are those to which people come for leisure, entertainment, shopping or social interaction. In this case, design helps to create a destination capable of attracting people from a distance. In postmodern cities, many places such as regenerated waterfronts act as places of both dwelling and encounter, drawing people from across the city for particular retail or leisure experiences, while offering new accommodation to those who seek to make their home there.

FIGURE 2.3

Places of existence: Java Island, Eastern Harbour, Netherlands. This popular residential area within Amsterdam's Eastern Docklands was redeveloped between 1994 and 2001. (Steve Tiesdell)

FIGURE 2.4

Places of encounter: Tallinn's Old Town Square, Estonia. Now on the list of UNESCO World Heritage Sites, the square has been the hub of the town for eight centuries. (Steve Tiesdell)

Places form the focus of this book, rather than specific developments, reflecting the importance of the urban experience as a whole. Indeed, successful places generally derive not from individual pieces of architecture, however well designed, but from explicit attention to the totality of the place. This means that well-designed and interesting 'backcloth' buildings that can contribute towards an overall sense of place are normally more important than occasional 'signature' pieces of architecture. Reflecting Tibbalds' (1992) analogy, successful places thus require a strong choir but not an excess of soloists. Indeed, what matters most is the overall quality of a place and how well it functions for the people who use it.

In this sense, urban design is best conceived as a place-making activity and, specifically, one of making better places through conscious acts of intervention than would otherwise be created. This contrasts with earlier conceptions that placed urban design in such categories as 'big architecture, small-scale planning, civic beautification, urban engineering, a pattern-book subject, just visual/aesthetic in its scope, (or) only a public sector concern . . .' (Carmona *et al.* 2010: 4). Indeed, according to an official UK definition 'Urban design is the art of making places for people. It includes the way places work and matters such as community safety, as well as how they look. It concerns the connections between people and places, movement and urban form, nature and the built fabric, and the processes for ensuring successful villages, towns and cities' (DETR and CABE 2000: 8). Although urban design is the widely accepted term, the activity is often better described as place-making.

Making successful places is a design challenge, in both product and process terms. Vitruvius' 'firmness, commodity and delight' can be taken as the basis of good design in product terms. Firmness is where a design achieves the necessary technical criteria, commodity is where it achieves the necessary functional criteria, and delight is where it has aesthetic appeal. In making places, a fourth criteria of 'economy' should be added, not merely in a financial sense of respecting budget constraints, but also in the broader sense of minimising environmental costs. The design challenge in process terms is to meet these multiple objectives simultaneously and within a context of uncertainty that requires designers to make trade-offs intuitively. For, as Kelbaugh (2002: 16) argues, 'the mark of a good designer, unlike a scientist, is the very ability to make good decisions without all the requisite information, because it is rarely all available at the proper time'.

Who is involved in the urban design process? 'An inclusive response is all those who take decisions that shape the urban environment. This includes not just architects, landscape architects, planners, engineers, and surveyors, but also developers, investors, occupiers, civil/public servants, politicians, events organisers, crime and fire prevention officers, environmental health officials, and many others. In this view, everyday users are as important as designers' (Carmona *et al.* 2010: 16). Nevertheless, there is a distinction, or more accurately a continuum, between those who consciously see themselves as urban designers, having usually gained urban design expertise through academic qualification and professional experience, and the much wider array of development actors, whose interventions affect design quality, even if by their unconscious acts. As a result, 'Today's city is not an accident. Its form is usually unintentional, but it is not accidental. It is the product of decisions made for single, separate purposes, whose interrelationships and side effects have not been fully considered. The design of cities has been determined by engineers, surveyors, lawyers, and investors, each making individual, rational

decisions for rational reasons' (Barnett 1982: 9). Such disparate and 'unknowing' designers have the potential to be place-breakers rather than place-makers (see Figure 2.5). An important responsibility of 'knowing' urban designers is thus to persuade and educate 'unknowing' designers of the significant impact of their individual decisions on overall urban quality and to promote a shared concern in working together to create a well-integrated and holistic urban environment.

This points the focus towards what designers, rather than simply design, can achieve. Essentially, urban designers bring creativity, ideas and innovation to the task of solving design problems. Drawing on their past experience and knowledge of technological possibilities, 'knowing' urban designers offer developers the expertise to achieve the effective configuration of complex development sites, including those at brownfield locations that may have to be knitted back into the urban fabric. Although many urban designers have developed their expertise from an architectural base, a qualification in architecture is no longer seen as the sole entry point into urban design. Successful urban designers thus help developers to negotiate tough regulatory regimes and increasing stringent environmental requirements. This takes urban design well beyond the scope of architectural aesthetics, since it is essentially about adding value through exploiting positive externalities, neutralising negative externalities and creating a much better sense of place than is normally produced by standard speculative development.

Place-making can be considered both a 'first-order' and 'second-order' design activity (George 1997). Our focus so far has been on 'first-order' design, where the designer is responsible for some particular project, such as a building, public space or element of street furniture. 'Second-order' design is about modifying the decision environments within which other development actors operate, including developers, investors, architects and surveyors. This can be achieved by means of design frameworks, plans and policies, supported where necessary by incentives and disincentives, including financial subsidies, discounted land or infrastructure provision. By setting design constraints and potential, second-order design can give policy-makers significant influence on first-order design. Second-order design is similar to planning and much contemporary governmental practice (see Chapter 6) in which public managers must devise incentive systems that obtain co-operation from actors over whom they have only limited control (Salamon 2002). Effective place-making thus requires second-order design to set an appropriate context for first-order design. We now turn to consider what we identify as the five characteristics of successful places.

Places meant for people

Successful places attract people, and encourage them to linger and return. People animate places by their very presence, both creating and reflecting urban vitality (see Figure 2.6). To achieve this, four factors are crucial: activity, scale, safety and comfort.

Activity draws people to places. The more diverse or complex the activities on offer, the more people are likely to be attracted to a place. So places are likely to appeal more widely if endowed, for example, with shops of varied size, type and cost, matched by theatres, restaurants and bars of different qualities and prices and placed within a setting that allows people to stop, chat and relax. Crucially, the engagement of such activities with the street matters as much as their variety.

FIGURE 2.6
Busy streets in Harajuku, Japan, showing how people both create and reflect urban vitality. (Steve Tiesdell)

FIGURE 2.7

FIGURE 2.7
Sheraton Hotel, Seattle, USA. This dominant blank façade was once named by Time Magazine as among America's 'worst offenders' in deadening street life. (Seattle Daily Journal of Commerce)

Doors and windows at street level create active frontages reinforcing urban vitality. Conversely, activities hidden behind blank façades interrupt the performance of the street and, if lengthy or spatially concentrated, drive people in other directions (see Figure 2.7). Since activities generate people flows, their variety and presentation to the street helps to fashion the places within which they are located.

Places work best when set at a *human scale*, where people feel neither hemmed in nor overwhelmed by the scale of the environment. Setting the pace of movement at the human scale involves giving greater priority to the needs of pedestrians than those of vehicles. People-friendly places work by expanding the space devoted to pedestrians relative to that of vehicles and by slowing down the speed of vehicles to a point that is harmonious with the presence of pedestrians.

The more enlivened places are by people, the *safer* they are likely to feel. Busy streets are generally more reassuring places than deserted parks. Occupied upper floors with windows overlooking the street can reinforce ground-floor activities with a stronger human presence. Residential uses above shops provide one important means to achieve this. Places with a lively evening economy will be populated for longer than those that rely merely on day-time trade. Nevertheless, where the concept of an evening economy is conflated simply with growth of alcohol-based establishments, it can undermine people's perceptions of safety.

Comfortable or restful places make people feel at ease, wanting to stay longer and return. Signage and visual identity can help people to identify with places better. Street furniture can provide the opportunity for chance or planned encounter, while water features or public squares with outside cafes may encourage people to wait a while and take in the activity round and about. An inclusive environment is one designed to be widely accessible to all users, including the disabled, the elderly and those with young children in pushchairs. Buildings create an important sense of enclosure, but their relative height and massing can impact directly on people's comfort within, and their enjoyment of, the space they enclose. Tall buildings, for example, while appropriate in certain circumstances, can create wind funnels or excessive shade. Places that offer some shelter from excessive summer heat or winter cold will also provide better comfort throughout the year, and function longer as a result. In summary, people are more likely to be attracted to vibrant and active places that are deemed safe, comfortable and reflective of the human scale, and which offer their own distinct sense of welcome.

Well-connected and permeable places

Places are more likely to be successful if they enable people to move in and through them easily, especially on foot or bicycle. Well-designed movement frameworks open up areas, connect locations and permit people to move between them by the most direct route. Well-trodden and readily visible routes that follow natural movement patterns make it easier for people to understand how places work, and turn walking and cycling into safer and more pleasant experiences. By improving connectivity across the city, layouts that facilitate through movement reinforce urban vitality, since most shops, cafes and leisure uses need to be well located within the strategic movement framework to take advantage of passing trade. Indeed, only the most significant activities are able to survive in more isolated locations as destinations in their own right (see Figure 2.8). Successful places also encourage and enable travel by public transport, by bringing fast and efficient

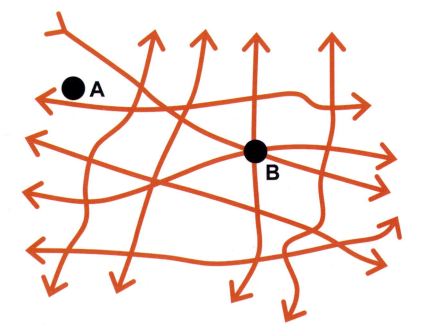

FIGURE 2.8

The importance of centrality. Destination A is off the beaten track and attracts only those who specifically choose to visit it. Destination B is centrally located and well placed for activities seeking to benefit from passing trade such as shops, restaurants or bars.

transit systems, such as light rail, close to where people want to go. In essence, 'The movement framework should, wherever possible and practicable, make it as easy and attractive to walk, cycle or take the bus, as it is to travel by car' (English Partnerships 2007a: 34).

How can connectivity and permeability be best achieved? According to the first volume of the *Urban Design Compendium*, 'The time-honoured way of achieving efficient connections is to create a grid, which provides a simple structure, allowing access throughout the area. The form may be orthogonal or more irregular; but its virtues are the same' (English Partnerships 2007a: 34). Grids maximise connectivity and promote a more even distribution of movement across an urban area than does the concept of road hierarchies. The latter were developed from the early twentieth century to separate movement from access and have subdivided the city into a series of closed cells or neighbourhoods. At their most extreme, hierarchical road systems reduce the city to a collection of specialised 'pods' (see Figure 2.9), with each use – shopping centre, school, business park, housing estate – conceived as a separate component with its own parking provision and usually enjoying its own individual, exclusive access to a collector or main distributor road. In contrast, sustainable urbanism seeks to integrate all such activities within a well-connected grid.

FIGURE 2.9

Sustainable urbanism contrasted with suburban 'pod-style' development. Activities in the upper part of the diagram take place in isolated pods, while in the lower part they are mixed together, with different implications for lifestyle and car dependency. (The Prince's Foundation for the Built Environment (2007), *Valuing Sustainable Urbanism*)

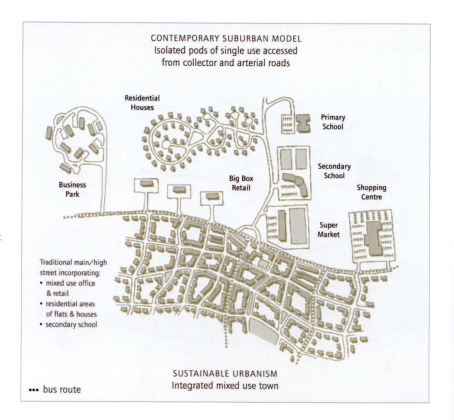

The return to interconnected street patterns is exemplified in the concept of 'traditional neighbourhood developments' promoted by the 'New Urbanist'[1] movement in the US. This thinking has significantly influenced contemporary development, especially where masterplanned on a large scale, creating a modern urban form that is street oriented and defined by urban blocks, usually of low- or medium-rise development. The urban form it produces stands in sharp contrast to the modernist view of setting buildings as individual 'objects in space' surrounded, at best, by landscaped parkland and, at worst, by extensive car parking and patches of poorly maintained 'leftover' land. Street-orientated blocks create a much denser urban fabric in which the continuous façade of buildings serves to 'define and enclose space' by setting a clear boundary between the public realm of the street or urban square and the private realm of the buildings themselves.

The width and depth of blocks can vary greatly, with the examples given in the *Urban Design Compendium* ranging from Portland in the US, where blocks are 65 metres by 50 metres, to Edinburgh New Town in Scotland, with its much larger blocks of 180 metres by up to 140 metres. As Jane Jacobs (1961) famously argued, small blocks engender urban vitality by offering greater opportunities for a variety of business users. Yet, real estate developers usually prefer larger blocks, as they are considered more efficient to construct and more likely to meet the requirements of large commercial users. Successful places may need to provide a variety of block sizes, some large and some small, to encourage diversity in both building type and use and to balance the needs of different interests (Love 2009, Love and Crawford 2011).

As the Edinburgh New Town example shows, successful blocks may supplement the 'primary mesh' intended for principal movement with a 'secondary mesh' of service lanes or alleys through the centre of the blocks, and even a 'tertiary mesh' for circulation within the blocks (see Figure 2.10). Crucially, the scale of buildings, especially fronting on to the principal streets, should bear some relationship to the width of the streets so that, as building height increases, so does street width.

FIGURE 2.10
Movement patterns within street blocks. This stylised plan shows three circulation meshes in James Craig's plan for Edinburgh New Town. The primary mesh is shown in red, the secondary in green, and the tertiary mesh in blue. In Edinburgh, the secondary mesh has become an important pedestrian thoroughfare, and the location for small shops, bars and restaurants.

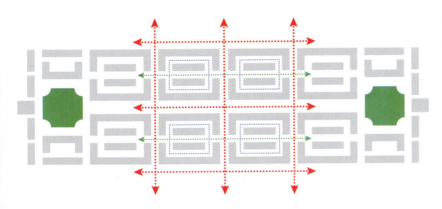

Whereas large-scale masterplanning provides an unrivalled opportunity to create well-connected and permeable places from scratch, making existing places more successful may well involve removing physical barriers to connectivity and permeability or 'healing' street patterns, when the chance of redevelopment arises. The *Urban Design Compendium* provided an excellent example of the former by showing how a new link has been punched through a railway viaduct to

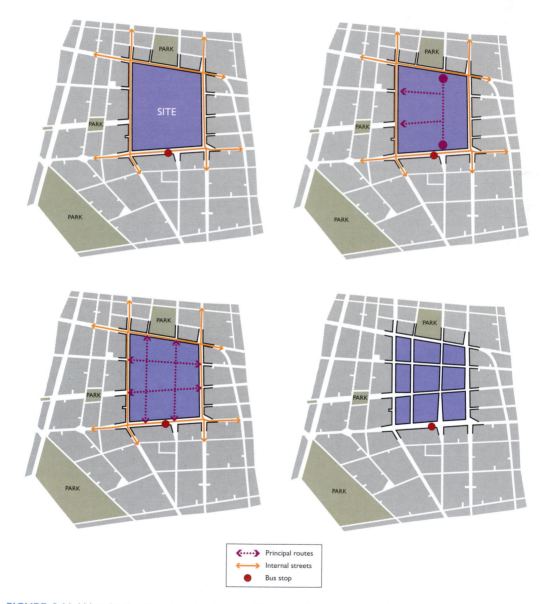

FIGURE 2.11 Urban healing through redevelopment. This redevelopment opportunity provides the chance to enhance connectivity throughout the area. The cul-de-sac layout in the second diagram creates an introverted layout and fails to achieve this. The third diagram offers pedestrian routes through the new development, while in the fourth reconnected streets form the basis of development blocks. (Willie Miller, adapted from English Partnerships (2007a), *Urban Design Compendium*)

FIGURE 2.12
Aerial view of Liverpool
One development,
England. This award-
winning scheme, built on
a 17-hectare site at the
edge of the city centre,
provides a mixture of
retail, leisure, commercial
and residential space.
Rather than a single
covered development,
Liverpool One comprises
30 separate buildings
based around an open
street design. (Grosvenor
Property Group)

FIGURE 2.13
Street view through
Liverpool One
development, England,
showing the retail and
leisure terrace. (Yellow
Book, used under the
Creative Commons
licence)

stitch together the city centre and riverfront in Leeds by taking out uses previously occupying the railway arches. Figure 2.11 shows diagrammatically how major redevelopment sites provide an opportunity to 'stitch back' interconnected street patterns and restore the connectivity of the urban fabric.

The award-winning Liverpool One development provides another good example of how this principle has been applied in practice (see Figures 2.12 and 2.13). As the Chief Executive of Liverpool City Council explained: 'Liverpool One will not be perceived as one large development but six districts of varying individuality, each having its own distinctive character, knitting the heritage and streetscape of the past with the modern urban fabric we need today' (Hilton 2007: 28). As this shows, recreating traditional street patterns within established locations can be crucial to successful place-making.

Places of mixed use and varied density

The more varied a place, the more active it is likely to be. Essentially 'The mix of uses (whether within a building, a street or an area) can help to determine how well-used a place is, and what economic and social activities it will support' (DETR and CABE 2000: 31). This is because, as Jane Jacobs (1961) argued, the overlapping and interweaving of activities crucially impacts on the vitality of urban neighbourhoods. To encourage what she termed 'exuberant diversity' within a city, Jacobs considered that a district must serve at least two primary functions, of which providing places of residence and employment are the most significant. It is often argued that mixed-use development has benefits well beyond promoting urban vitality and creating a more active street life (English Partnerships 2007a). Socially, mixed development is often thought by policy-makers to provide greater opportunities for social interaction and help to create socially diverse communities, although this claim is highly contested among researchers (see, for example, Bridge *et al.* 2011 and Cheshire 2006). Environmentally, it can offer more facilities within convenient distance, cut down on travel, minimise journey-to-work congestion and enable more efficient use of space and buildings, with improved energy efficiency. Economically, by locating more customers close at hand, mixed development can make local businesses and services more viable, while offering consumers a greater choice of lifestyle, location and building type.

Towns traditionally grew and developed as a patchwork of mixed activities and uses. Left to their own devices, that pattern would have continued through small-scale, incremental changes. Two driving forces, however, came together to separate out uses and create the mono-functional development so characteristic of today's urban environment. Modernist urban planning, which divided uses into separate zones so as to enhance amenity, efficiency and safety, was the first of these. Its partner was the second: modernist real estate development. Significantly, from the developer's perspective, single-use developments are generally easier to create, simpler to manage and more readily understood by potential investors. To create successful places involves challenging the combined resistance of modernist planning and modernist real estate development to mixed use (Leinberger 2009).

In planning terms, this requires careful attention to the precise mix of uses proposed in any development so as to 'maximise synergy and minimise conflict' (English Partnerships 2007a). Although some uses (such as residential apartments and car dismantling) will never be good neighbours and should not be placed together, correct building design and specification, coupled with modern business technology, provide much greater scope than in the past to accommodate a variety of uses in close proximity. Broader planning approaches may include setting intermediary uses between those likely to be incompatible as direct neighbours, or using small urban parks to do likewise.

In development terms, it may prove hard to change the embedded cultures of institutional investors and like-minded major developers who concentrate on substantial single-use developments built for blue-chip tenants on large blocks in prime locations. But it is possible to make the development process more competitive by opening up opportunities for what Guy *et al.* (2002) identify as locally based independent developers who can make smaller lot sizes, multiple tenancies and mixed uses work to their advantage. To create successful places thus requires diversity in block and plot sizes so as to facilitate involvement by a wider range of potential developers (see Chapter 11). This is why mixed use is not simply about mixing activities and land uses, but must also involve diversity in development form, tenure, market segments and density (English Partnerships 2007a).

By its very nature 'Mixed-use development can make the most of opportunities for higher densities and intensive activity at locations with good access to public transport' (DETR and CABE 2000: 31). Higher urban densities are an essential feature of the compact city, which has long been argued to provide a more sustainable form of urban development as a result of lower transport and energy usage. As Newman and Kenworthy (2000: 113) contend, 'achieving a more sustainable urban form inevitably involves the development of densities that can enable public transport, walking and cycling to be viable options'.[2] Nevertheless, significant concerns have been raised that undue concentration on density alone may well produce a form of 'town cramming' that proves counter-productive in the context of ever-increasing consumer preferences for more space. The over-development of high-density blocks of small one- or two-bedroom apartments in many English city centres in the first decade of the twenty-first century provides a case in point, especially since these suffered disproportionately in value and occupancy when the housing market fell into recession. Such development has been much criticised as a result of its poor design and architecture, restricted social mix, limited energy efficiency and inadequate management and amenities (Punter 2009).

Nevertheless, as REAL Associates remind us in the second volume of the *Urban Design Compendium* (English Partnerships 2007b: 91) 'Higher density does not mean building smaller units. Generous space can be accommodated at higher densities through good design and a creative use of volume, light and outdoor space.' Tall buildings provide only one way to achieve this, for, as Figure 2.14 shows, similar densities can be achieved using a variety of building types and forms (see also Martin and March 1972). As this suggests, on larger development sites there is much merit in creating graduated densities across the area with, for example, higher densities concentrated along the main roads and at neighbourhood centres, with lower densities along minor routes.

Mixed use is often misinterpreted as the subdivision of a major development area into different parcels for different uses. Although such mixed-use neighbourhoods are certainly better than separating uses wholly into different zones in

FIGURE 2.14

Ten different ways to achieve the same density. This diagram shows how exactly the same density can be achieved in different ways by varying building height, block size and building depth. (Image courtesy of studio REAL architects and urban planners)

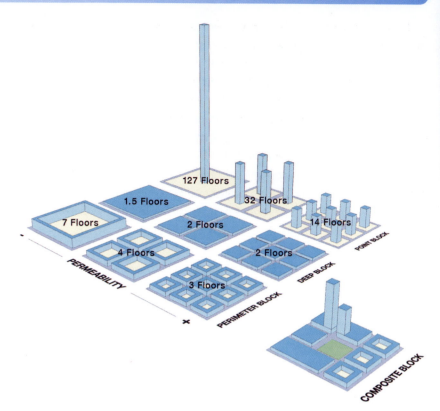

different parts of a city, they do not produce the same benefits for urban vitality as does mixing uses horizontally within a street or vertically within a building (Montgomery 1998). With the benefits of mixed use now better understood, real estate developers are increasingly prepared to promote mixed-use neighbourhoods, especially when masterplanned as part of a major development scheme. Yet, successful places demand a more fine-grained approach to mixed use that requires developers to be persuaded of its merits below the scale of the neighbourhoods and to blur the distinctions between uses at the scale of the street and building.

Distinctive places

The twentieth century witnessed an ever-growing standardisation of place as local development processes were subordinated by national and global pressures for conformity. In the UK commercial sector, according to the New Economics Foundation (2005: 1), 'Real local shops have been replaced by swathes of identikit chain stores that seem to spread like economic weeds, making high streets up and down the country virtually indistinguishable from one another.' This is alleged to have created 'Clone Town Britain', evident in 'the march of the glass, steel, and concrete blandness of chain stores built for the demands of inflexible business models that provide the ideal degree of sterility to house a string of big, clone town retailers' (New Economics Foundation 2005: 1).

In the residential sector, much the same could be argued about standard house types replicated across the UK by speculative housebuilders, which produce new homes built by national companies in Scotland that are essentially the same as those produced in the south of England (see Figure 2.15). Such trends are economically and socially driven, since they reflect the economies of scale that are thought to be achieved by managing the development process at a national (and even global) scale rather than at the local level. However, they are reinforced by the increasing importance of mass brands, mass culture and mass marketing. Inevitably, they produce what Relph (1976: ii) was amongst the first to characterise as the phenomenon of 'placelessness', which he defined as the 'casual eradication of distinctive places' and the 'making of standardised landscapes'.

In contrast, successful places tend to display distinctiveness. At the local level, this involves highlighting and enhancing whatever can draw out the particular identity and authenticity of that location. Such local balance can counter the prevailing national, and indeed global, drive towards place uniformity. Yet, there can be no single formula to achieve local distinctiveness. In some places with a strong historical character, it may be appropriate to emphasise, or to reinterpret, local building materials and traditions (see Figure 2.16). Elsewhere, on greenfield sites or at brownfield ones where there is little left from the past, there may be real opportunities to create new and memorable places in a contemporary idiom. In many locations, however, the real challenge is to blend the old and the new in a way that responds to the natural terrain and respects the inherited pattern of buildings, streets and spaces. Symbolic skylines or emblematic waterfronts, for

FIGURE 2.15
Standard speculative house types at Cambusbarron, Scotland. This newly completed housing estate could be almost anywhere in the UK but it is actually just outside Stirling. (David Adams)

FIGURE 2.16

Newly built traditional housing close to the centre of Durham, England. Drawing on local vernacular traditions, this development creates its own distinctive environment which contrasts strongly with the standard house types generally used elsewhere. (Steve Tiesdell)

example, can contribute significantly to place distinctiveness, and are often worthy of special protection. New iconic buildings can help to mark the uniqueness of a place, but need to be well integrated into the urban fabric so as to be place-making, rather than just place-signifying.

According to Kevin Lynch (1960), five key physical elements – paths, edges, districts, nodes and landmarks – help to establish an individual's image of the city. Each of these provides an opportunity to reinforce place distinctiveness. *Paths*, such as the streets, walkways and transit lines that people use to travel through the city, can serve as or open up important vistas across an area (see Figure 2.17). Where urban *edges* are continuous and visually prominent (see Figure 2.18), they can help to symbolise place character. In many cities, certain *districts* have developed an identity of their own that marks them out from surrounding areas and helps to establish something different about the city as a whole (see Figure 2.19). Dominant *nodes* such as important urban squares serve as both activity 'concentrations' and 'junctions' that have functional and physical significance (see Figure 2.20). The key aspect of *landmarks* (see Figure 2.21) is their 'singularity' that makes them 'unique or memorable in their context', whether seen at a distance and from many angles (as in the case, for example, of towers, spires and hills) or encountered only at specific points (as with, for example, works of art or landscaped features). Urban design can exploit each of Lynch's five elements to create stronger images for places, which enhance local distinctiveness.

Here the challenge is to create what Florida (2002) calls authentic places that offer unique and original experiences which permit, facilitate and reward participation. He contrasts what he considers real places with those that replicate each other by linking place distinctiveness to active involvement in the urban experience: 'You can do more than be a spectator; you can be part of the scene . . . to choose the mix, to turn the intensity level up or down as desired, and to have a hand in creating the experience rather than merely consuming it.' In contrast, 'A chain theme restaurant, a multi-media-circus sports stadium or a pre-packaged entertainment-and-tourism district is like a packaged tour' (Florida 2002: 232). In this sense, successful place-making is about creating urban experiences to be

FIGURE 2.17
Buchanan Street, Glasgow, Scotland. Illustrative of Kevin Lynch's paths, this busy thoroughfare is at the heart of Glasgow city centre. (Steve Tiesdell)

FIGURE 2.18
Hong Kong's waterfront and central business district. Illustrative of Kevin Lynch's edges, this view remains the enduring image of modern Hong Kong. (Lee Snider)

FIGURE 2.19
Montmartre, Paris, France. Illustrative of Kevin Lynch's districts, the distinctive character of Montmartre makes an emblematic contribution to the image of Paris. (Steve Tiesdell)

FIGURE 2.20
Columbus Circle, New York, USA. Illustrative of Kevin Lynch's nodes, this is where Broadway meets Eighth Avenue at the edge of Central Park. (David Adams)

FIGURE 2.21
Sydney Opera House, Australia. Illustrative of Kevin Lynch's landmarks, Sydney Opera House is instantly recognisable, even in the background, as an internationally known symbol of the city. (Jimmy Harris, used under the Creative Commons licence)

savoured and remembered, rather than readily forgotten as indistinguishable from the formulaic repetition so beloved of global capital.

Sustainable, resilient and robust places

According to the European Union (2004: 39), 'Sustainable urban design is a process whereby all the actors involved . . . work together through partnerships and effective participatory processes to integrate functional, environmental, and quality considerations to design, plan and manage [the] built environment.' Carmona (2009a), having reviewed this report and twelve other sources on sustainability and urban design published between 1984 and 2009, concluded that it is possible to draw out ten universal principles of sustainable urban design. These can be applied in different ways to the different scales of the buildings, spaces, quarters and settlements. Four of these principles – promoting diversity and choice through mixing uses and facilitating movement by other than simply car; encouraging local distinctiveness; designing places at the human scale to meet human needs; and encouraging more compact urban forms – have already featured in this chapter. The other six concern resource efficiency, pollution reduction, biotic support, self-sufficiency, stewardship, robustness and resilience. These will now each be briefly discussed in turn.

Resource efficiency, and especially energy efficiency, is increasingly seen as a core element of sustainable urban design. Actions include those that seek to minimise energy use through better design, promote communal energy systems and invest more in public transport. Pollution reduction includes sustainable urban drainage systems, increased recycling and greater control over private motorised transport. The principles of both pollution reduction and resource efficiency demonstrate how successful places seek to limit their overall demands on the Earth's ecosystems, or their 'environmental footprint'. The growing importance of biodiversity as a sustainability issue is reflected in the principle of integrating biotic support within urban design, for example, through respecting natural features, creating new habitats, supporting indigenous species and developing networks of open space. Self-sufficiency is about enabling people and communities to make sustainable urban design a reality, for example, by providing the necessary facilities and infrastructure to facilitate cycling and walking, and more generally through ensuring consultation and participation in decisions around design and future visioning.

As the principle of stewardship highlights, 'successful places are safe, well maintained and well managed' (English Partnerships 2007b: 171). To achieve this, initial design must therefore be informed by knowledge of how a place will be maintained and managed in future. This is especially important in relation to the public realm, where future maintenance arrangements need to be built into the design choice.

Although resilience and robustness are often used interchangeably, the former refers more to the ability of a place to 'bounce back' from unexpected external change, while the latter concerns its internal flexibility to accommodate change without excessive physical disruption. Both reflect the principle that places which are designed to adapt to future change have better sustainability prospects. This is more likely to be achieved by a fine-grained form of development, working, for example, with existing street patterns, that facilitates small-scale incremental changes over a long period of time. Indeed, quite ordinary buildings that endure over time will often accommodate different uses or different intensities of use during their lifetime. In contrast, 'megastructure development', such as large out-of-town shopping malls or major single-purpose industrial plants, may be quite hard to adapt to different uses. Despite their perceived economic benefits at the outset, they may well store up within themselves the seeds of large-scale blight and dereliction when no longer required for their original use.

As this suggests, too much change at any one point in time has the potential to be as detrimental to place sustainability in the long term as is an inability to change. With great foresight, Jane Jacobs (1961: 383) therefore suggested that successful places were characterised by a gradual flow of money for new development that behaves like 'irrigation systems, bringing life-giving streams to feed steady continual growth', rather than a cataclysmic flow that behaves 'like manifestations of malevolent climates beyond the control of man – affording either searing droughts or torrential, eroding floods'. We return to the importance of this insight in Chapter 9. In the meantime, the design challenge for places experiencing substantial transformation at any one time is to make allowance for gradual future adaption, enabling component parts to evolve in different ways and at different speeds. Successful places are thus resilient and robust enough to survive future change.

The value of urban design

According to research undertaken by Carmona *et al.* (2001: 8), 'good urban design adds value by increasing the economic viability of development and by delivering social and environmental benefits'. However, 'value' is a multi-dimensional concept which requires careful interpretation in relation to urban design. Drawing on Macmillan (2006), we can identify six different categories of value, each of which can be enhanced by good design:

- *exchange value*, revealed by the price at which buildings are traded;
- *use value*, evident in the appeal of places to occupiers, reflected in their contribution to productivity, profitability and competitiveness;
- *social value*, reflecting the extent to which places help to connect people,

enhance social interaction, reinforce civic pride, encourage social inclusion and promote neighbourly behaviour, while reducing vandalism and crime;

- *environmental value*, shown by the degree of adaptability, flexibility and robustness and reflecting concern for intergenerational equity and bio-diversity;
- *image value*, demonstrated in the contribution that places make to corporate identity, prestige, vision and reputation;
- *cultural value*, apparent in the relationship of a place to location and context, and its contribution to the rich tapestry and broader patterns of historical development of the town or city in which it is situated.

So far, this chapter has focused on how successful places add to social, environmental, image and cultural value. This discussion could readily be expanded to consider how better design improves the use value of real estate for both immediate occupants and the broader economy. Yet, the prime driver of real estate development is exchange value. So, 'What matters is whether the quality of a scheme's design will enhance its financial viability to the developer, not whether it will make the wider balance of economic costs and benefits more positive' (Henneberry *et al.* 2011: 220). This section therefore considers how better design and successful place-making can improve development viability, reviews its actual impact on exchange value, explores how these benefits may be perceived differently by different actors in the development process, and reflects on what institutional changes might be necessary as a result.

In principle, better design and successful place-making have considerable potential to enhance the financial viability of real estate development. These include:

- Making more efficient use of the site, by enabling development to take place at higher density or simply by achieving a higher proportion of net marketable floorspace within a given development. In one example at Portishead near Bristol, the developer was more than able to offset a 10–20 per cent increase in build costs at a mixed-use development by using external architects to produce a high-quality and higher density scheme (English Partnerships 2007b).
- Fashioning a design image to bestow a competitive marketing advantage. The major Brindley Place development near the centre of Birmingham provides a good example of this. Here, the developer saw quality design as an important factor in attracting good tenants, commenting that: 'This has started conversations for us; quite often leading to lettings . . . Good development gives us something to be proud of, even if there is a gap in the letting. People feel it will help their business' (quoted in English Partnerships 2007b: 107).

- Exploiting the financial potential of the site, by designing any development to take full advantage of any distant or immediate features or views. Luttick (2000) found that proximity to parks or stretches of water can increase house prices by 6–11 per cent, while Dunse *et al.* (2007) suggested that the price premium for close access to a park can be as much as 20 per cent, depending on house and park type.

- Protecting the financial potential of the site, by designing any development to reduce the negative impact of any bad neighbours.

- Creating bespoke solutions for problematic sites to open up new markets and/or facilitate access to grant funding. For example 'High quality design is proving instrumental in the regeneration of East Manchester, where a major regeneration initiative is transforming the urban landscape . . . Doing "ordinary" development in New East Manchester seems not to have been an option. There has been a recognition that new development in East Manchester needs to be that much better to attract people back to the area and choose to live there' (NWRA and RENEW Northwest 2007: 54–55) (Figure 2.22).

- Offering potential occupants greater scope to adapt the development in future and reduce long-term expenditure on energy, management and maintenance.

According to an early study of one traditional neighbourhood development in the US designed by Andres Duany and Elizabeth Plater-Zyberk, house purchasers

FIGURE 2.22
Waterside canal apartments, East Manchester, England. Designed by Will Alsop and known as 'Chips', this apartment building is intended to set the standard for future design quality in what was previously a run-down part of the city. (Steve Tiesdell)

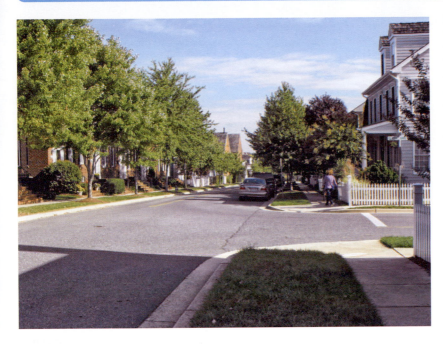

FIGURE 2.23
New Urbanist housing at Kentlands, Maryland, USA. Tu and Eppli's research found that house purchasers were prepared to pay a 12 per cent premium to live in this type of development. (Steve Tiesdell)

in Kentlands (Figure 2.23) were prepared to pay on average an extra 12 per cent to live in a community with New Urbanist features (Tu and Eppli 1999). In the UK, research undertaken for the Prince's Foundation compared three exemplars of 'sustainable urbanism' with standard new developments nearby and with old urbanism in the same locality. It discovered that, in each case, the end value of 'sustainable urbanism' was much higher than standard urbanism, and in two cases, higher also than old urbanism (Figure 2.24). Significantly, the end-value advantage of sustainable urbanism made it possible to accept higher building costs, which would have had to increase by 46 per cent at one location, 75 per cent at another and a highly unlikely 120 per cent at the third before that advantage was totally wiped out. In another study, this time of largely town centre and mixed-use development, it was found that good urban design can increase rental and capital value by 15–20 per cent, as well as increase sales and letting rates (NWRA and RENEW Northwest 2007). From his experience as a US real estate developer, Leinberger (2009) argues strongly that what he calls 'walkable urbanism' offers better long-term investment prospects than suburban growth that depends on mobility by private car.

   In an extensive review of evidence around value creation through urban design, Hack and Sagalyn (2011) argue, from North American experience, that urban designers who set out to create value can do so to the benefit of the developer and purchaser and of the intrinsic quality of the development. Significantly, for this 'win-win' result to be achievable, they call for urban designers to be become skilled in 'understanding markets and financial models, acquiring knowledge of legal arrangements for parcelling rights to land and facilities, learning about innovative

FIGURE 2.24

Comparing the market value of sustainable, standard and old urbanism. In each of the three areas studied, newly built sustainable urbanism achieved a higher market value per hectare of buildings than newly built standard urbanism and, indeed, well-established old urbanism. (The Prince's Foundation for the Built Environment (2007), *Valuing Sustainable Urbanism*)

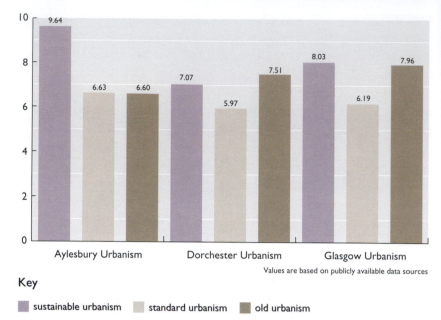

Values are based on publicly available data sources

Key

■ sustainable urbanism   ■ standard urbanism   ■ old urbanism

precedents for complex public-private arrangements, and mastering the skills of negotiation to reach successful agreements' (Hack and Sagalyn 2011: 280). In other words, the extent to which better design improves development viability is in part determined by the skill of designers.

Some have expressed concerns that such evidence about the financial value of urban design is over-dependent on case studies or simplistic hedonic analysis (Henneberry *et al.* 2011). However, one passionate advocate of better urban design proclaims the rallying call 'Let's dispel the myth that we don't know enough about whether or not good design adds value', since published studies 'present an overwhelming set of arguments to justify the hypothesis that good design sometimes (but not always) costs more initially, but that it adds value' (Simmonds 2006: 11). For any remaining sceptics, Simmonds highlights the case of a badly designed housing estate in East London, intended to last for at least 60 years, but which had to be demolished and rebuilt after only 20 at a cost of £92 million. Calling for a methodology to predict and measure the costs of bad design, he argues that bad design produces significant negative external costs in the form, for example, of poorly laid out housing estates and public open spaces that remain deserted, which eventually have to be remedied at public expense.

Nevertheless, evidence of the financial value of urban design, even if it is as strong as Simmonds believes, may not be enough to change developer behaviour. Here, the institutional structure of real estate development presents a fundamental problem, since, as Henneberry *et al.* (2011: 221) explain, 'for reasons of market structure, most of these various streams of value are not captured by the developer'. Put simply, a trader–developer who moves on from one scheme to the next, always selling out on completion, has no long-term interest in the value of the development, but must instead be able to generate a return from better design in the initial sale. While the Portishead example, referred to above, demonstrates how that can be achieved, the culture of trader–developers is dominated by concern with short-run costs and returns. So even if better urban design pays as well as its advocates argue, institutional change is likely to be essential to ensure its more widespread adoption. Here, four particular issues need to be explored: the policy environment, the appraisal process, the diffusion of innovation and the relations between actors in real estate development and investment.

Some contend that a much stronger *policy environment* would make developers take urban design more seriously, and that this would actually be in their own best interests. This is certainly Hall's (2011) view of policy shift towards more stringent design standards in Chelmsford which, he argues, enabled certain developers to become more profitable as well as to produce better-designed development. This is matched by evidence from Vancouver, where strong urban design guidelines worked precisely because they were well known, consistently operated and thus factored in the value that developers paid for land (Hack and Sagalyn 2011).

According to the Prince's Foundation (2007), the *appraisal process* can discriminate against sustainable urbanism because it is inherently backward looking and fails to anticipate the likely uplift in value that such developments eventually generate. This means that technical deficiencies can matter as much as information deficits. Here Henneberry *et al.* (2011) demonstrate what might be achieved by linking a simplified form of CAD through to viability analysis so as to enable the financial implications of successive design iterations to be instantly tested.

Despite the reluctance of many trader–developers to embrace the design agenda, it is clear that there are important exceptions. One good example is Igloo Regeneration (see Chapter 9), whose development of an award-winning business and residential development focused on creative and digital media in the inner city of Leeds was explained by the Chief Executive in the following terms: 'If we developed "contractor design" (as we call it), we would just be creating a poor building in an off-centre location, and we could only let it to an average tenant. Instead we commission and deliver great design to attract dynamic, design-led independent creative business occupiers' (quoted in English Partnerships, 2007b: 108). It is here that considerable potential and indeed appetite may exist for what Bell (2005) calls 'developer learning' in the sense of encouraging the *diffusion of innovation* among developers through better sharing of experience. As Symes and Pauwels (1999) contend, the willingness of implementation actors to accept and embrace innovation in urban design is crucial to the delivery of sustainable urbanism.

In the end, however, to deliver the full financial benefits of successful places, it may be necessary to restructure the *relations between different actors* in real estate development and investment. For example, as Savills (2007) suggest, new models may be needed to bridge the gap between short-term developers and long-term investors. These could include greater emphasis on shared ownership and shared equity in new housing. This would have the dual advantage of making housing more affordable and ensuring that developers retain a stake in the value and sustainability of homes over the long term.

Another approach might be to encourage a clear split between the role of land or master developer and that of building developer (as already happens in many countries). This would mean that the building developer's short-term interest in one component of a much larger project is kept in check by the land or master developer's long-term interest in the project as a whole (see Chapters 5 and 7). This is particularly relevant in the case of major development areas, where the value of urban design often derives from the whole's being worth considerably more than the sum of the parts. As Carmona *et al.* (2001: 11 explain): 'Delivering good urban design seems to some extent to rely on delivering the critical mass needed to support it. New public spaces, infrastructure improvements, mixing uses and so forth all rely on the realisation of developments large enough to fund their delivery. This suggests an important role for the public sector in assembling larger sites.' We return to this concept in Chapter 11, when we explore the importance of excellent design quality to the delivery of strategic transformation.

Conclusions

This chapter has suggested that places which are designed with people primarily in mind, which are well connected and permeable, of mixed use and varied density, which have their own identity and distinctiveness, and which are intended to be sustainable, resilient and robust, are more likely to be successful over time than those which are not. In principle, such characteristics are equally relevant to places of experience and existence, although the manner in which they apply will vary from place to place. The chapter has portrayed urban design as the crucial task of creating successful places so as to help achieve social justice and environmental sustainability, as well as economic prosperity. Before moving on, it is important to consider why successful places are not created more often, and why many places that are created turn out not to be successful. Here, three main reasons can be identified, which we respectively term cultural, institutional and procedural.

Although there are many excellent examples of successful place-making, they generally do not happen by chance but require determination and commitment over a lengthy period of time. In short, successful place-making is the visible outcome of an ingrained place-making culture. This culture, which is evident in the desire to understand, apply and refine what really makes places successful, privileges long-term quality over short-term expediency. It challenges accepted ways of thinking and emphasises reflective learning. Such a culture depends on clear leadership from the top, but also requires embedded commitment throughout an organisation. Since successful place-making represents a powerful challenge to standard forms of development and easy means of delivery, its potential is constantly under threat from interests who profit most from short-term expediency or who prefer quick and simple methods of implementation. Without a strongly ingrained place-making culture, it is all too tempting to give way to those who see no personal benefit in creating places for long-term success. This demonstrates the need as much for effective leadership and governance within the public sector as for greater commitment to place quality within the private sector (see Chapter 5).

The absence of a place-making culture is often linked to the second explanation for why successful places are not created more often, which derives from the institutional fragmentation of real estate development. This highlights the need for a shift in the power relations of development so as to tip the balance in favour of sustainable urbanism. As already intimated, some trader–developers see no benefit in investing in long-term place quality, even though this would be advantageous to subsequent occupiers and investors. Yet, this is but one example of a 'producer–consumer' gap in real estate development. Demarcation is still strongly evident within the development professions, with the link between quality and value not always understood, especially as the former tends to be the prerogative of the designer, while the latter is the responsibility of the financial appraiser. This is why place-making is such an integrative activity. It calls on all those involved in the development process to leave behind their own particular silos and work collectively towards a common aim of creating quality development and successful places. While much may be achieved by negotiation and compromise, fundamental institutional change may well be needed in the processes of real estate development in order to ensure that those who benefit most from long-term quality have greater input at the initial design stage and to prevent professional barriers from impeding successful place-making.

To bring about successful places more often may require procedural and indeed political reform, as much as cultural commitment and institutional change. Here, there is often an urgent need to integrate decision-making, so that any particular procedural requirement, for example, on street design, does not invalidate the overall intention to create a place of some quality. This is about ensuring that procedural decisions are so well integrated that the task of place-making is neither delayed nor deterred by procedural conflict within the processes of governance. As we contend in Chapter 11, it is essential for those in place leadership both to put in place effective spatial development frameworks and to take responsibility for their subsequent delivery.

While many might argue with some of the qualities of successful places set out in this chapter, there is now much greater consensus among both commentators and practitioners about what needs to be done to deliver the quality places of the future. Much has been learnt from the failure of earlier Modernist experiments in urban planning and design. Indeed, there is now real understanding of how the timeless essentials of urban vitality and resilience can be fused with contemporary forms of development. Yet, to deliver the cultural, institutional and procedural change outlined above, and produce places with strong potential for success, requires a particular form of state–market relations in development, with an inherent policy emphasis on shaping, regulating and stimulating development activity, and indeed on building the capacity so to do. It is to these themes that we return as the book progresses.

3 Real estate markets

Introduction

Real estate markets are central to the way places are created and evolve over time. Successful places are valued by people as attractive environments in which to live, work and enjoy themselves. Value, in this sense, is about much more than visual appeal – it is measurable by how much people are willing to pay to locate in such places. Real estate markets both express society's financial view of different locations and channel resources to enable the creation and subsequent management of places considered to be of value. Conversely, they drain resources away from places that are considered unattractive or hard to manage. In reflecting on the power of real estate markets, it is important to regard them not as some abstract force beyond human control, but rather as a channel for human interaction which reflects society's rules and conventions. Since real estate markets are socially constructed, it follows that they can be shaped by human intent. Shaping markets to make them more economically efficient, socially just and environmentally sustainable than they might otherwise be is thus integral to shaping places. Doing so enhances their capacity to produce places of social, and not merely private, benefit.

This chapter provides a framework to help those involved in shaping places to understand real estate markets. Its starting point is to appreciate the particular commodity traded in such markets, namely property rights. It then moves on to consider how real estate markets are structured and, especially, how they are subdivided in various ways. What becomes important here is to understand how market activity, rules and conventions may well vary significantly from one sub-market to the next. The chapter therefore explores how real estate markets work in practice, with different theoretical perspectives used to shed varying light on market operations. It concludes by highlighting the distinctive nature of real estate as a commodity and reflecting on the implications of this for place-making.

Property rights

The concept of property rights

For centuries, how places changed, how land was used and what buildings were constructed or demolished were almost always determined by those who held the rights of property to particular plots of land. Essentially, rights of property are socially constructed, since they frame relationships between people, specifying, for example, who can enter or who can be excluded from the particular land or property. They are meaningless unless protected by a system of law with the power and intent to evict anyone who has no right to enter. Real estate markets enable the legitimate and peaceful exchange of property rights precisely because these are embedded in processes of law and governance. It is thus false to regard markets as some natural creation by which people abide, irrespective of the society within which they live.

Although many countries have now introduced planning systems, these too operate as permitted by law and, crucially, interact with, rather than replace, systems of property rights. Indeed, unless a planning system can turn the power of land and property to its advantage or, in exceptional cases, remove it altogether by compulsory purchase action, what it can achieve may be quite limited. That is why it is important that planners understand and work within, and around, systems of property rights.

Property as a concept differs sharply between Continental Europe and countries with an Anglo-Saxon legal tradition, such as England and the US (see Needham 2006: 30–51 for a detailed explanation). Briefly, in much of Continental Europe, land and property is considered capable of full ownership in much the same way as any consumer good. Any lesser rights that exist in the same property do so by permission of the owner and cannot be considered a form of property on their own. In the Anglo-Saxon tradition, what is technically owned is not the land and property itself, but a set of rights to the property. This implies that a bundle of rights can exist to the same property, the ownership of which can be divided between different people and organisations. We now illustrate this by reference to English land law.

Land ownership in English law

Since the Norman Conquest, the basis of English land law has been that the absolute ownership of all land is vested in the Crown. The Crown itself occupies only a very small proportion of the nation's land. According to the doctrine of tenures, all other land is nominally held under the Crown. Over time, all forms of feudal tenure from the Crown were transformed into freeholds, with the freeholder's right to possession not restricted by any feudal burdens. This makes the right to possession, rather than some abstract concept of ownership, central to English land law. Today, the word 'tenure' is applied in a different sense to the relationship between a landlord and tenant. This particular relationship, which is not feudal in origin, is governed by the doctrine of estates.

Whereas the doctrine of tenures refers to the manner in which land is held, the doctrine of estates refers to the duration or period of time over which land is held. Under the Law of Property Act 1925, only two types of legal estate now exist. These are the fee simple absolute in possession, commonly called the freehold estate, and the term of years absolute, commonly called the leasehold estate. Each of these will now be explained.

The freehold estate

The freeholder is entitled to use the land without restriction, unless so prevented either by statute or by other estates and interests in the same land. The most valuable proprietary rights are those that allow the freeholder to develop, sell, transfer or create lesser interests in the land, without needing to obtain the consent of anyone else. The Town and Country Planning Act 1947, which nationalised the right to develop in the UK, was one of the most far-reaching statutory restrictions placed upon the rights of freeholders. Although the freeholder retains the right to use agricultural land for the grazing of cattle and the right to use retail premises for the sale of goods, the traditional right to build shops on grazing land and sell goods can now be exercised only if planning permission is given.

The leasehold estate

A leasehold estate or a term of years absolute is defined as any period of time which is of fixed and certain duration. The landlord in a leasehold estate lets the tenant into exclusive possession of the land or property for a specified period, usually in return for either an initial payment (known as a premium) or a periodic rent, or a combination of both. The landlord and tenant enjoy separate rights in the same land or property. At any time, the landlord is entitled to sell the freehold estate, irrespective of the existence of any leasehold estate. This does not affect the existence of the leasehold. One landlord or property investor simply replaces another. In the meantime, tenants are entitled to sublet for any period shorter than their own lease or tenancy, unless expressly forbidden by the lease. If a sublease (or underlease) is created, the original freeholder becomes the head landlord, the original tenant becomes the head lessee or sublessor, while the tenant under the sublease becomes the sublessee. A whole chain of subleases can be created. More than one leasehold estate may therefore exist in the same land or property. Each estate may be valuable.

For example, a tenant may occupy premises on a 15-year lease entered into 10 years ago. If the lease contained no provision for periodic rent reviews, the rent payable under the terms and conditions of the lease (known as the passing rent) may be substantially less than the current full letting value (known as the rack rent). The tenant could therefore sublet the premises at the rack rent, while continuing to pay only the passing rent to the head landlord, thus making a profit on the difference between the rack and passing rents. Alternatively, unless prohibited by the lease, the tenant could transfer (or assign) the remaining five years of the lease and receive a capital sum to take account of the difference between the rack and passing rents. This explains the paradox 'lease for sale'.

Building land may be sold freehold or let on a ground lease. Ground leases may be for any duration but, in commercial development, terms of 99, 125 and 150 years are common. A ground lease enables a freeholder, as ground lessor, to exercise control over the type and quality of development constructed. Once it is finished, the developer will let the property to tenants on rack rents. Any developer who chooses not to remain as ground lessee will sell the leasehold estate to a property investor. In due course, tenants who wish to move will either assign their leases or create subleases. At the end of the specified period of 99, 125 or 150 years (or whatever term is agreed), any buildings that remain revert with the land to the freeholder. No compensation needs to be paid for such buildings, unless agreed in the original ground lease.

Interests in land

Apart from the two types of legal estate, all other rights and entitlements in land and property are known as interests in land. Whereas the word 'estate' refers to rights over one's own land, 'interests' normally refers to rights over the land of another. There are four specified categories of legal interest, each of which is usually granted on a commercial basis for money or other valuable consideration. All other estates, interests and charges in or over land now take effect as equitable interests, most of which are created within families on a non-commercial basis. Whereas legal interests are enforceable 'against all the world', equitable interests are potentially less secure. This is because an equitable interest, if not registered, cannot bind someone who purchases a legal estate in good faith for valuable consideration if that purchaser was unaware of the existence of the equitable interest at the time of purchase. However, since it is estimated that around 85 per cent of all registrable titles, whether legal or equitable, are now registered, this distinction is much less important than it once was.[1]

Important examples of legal estates include restrictive covenants, mortgages, easements and options. A restrictive covenant, for instance, may arise when part of a large garden is sold for residential development. The original owner may wish to prevent the use of the dwellings for non-residential purposes, and will therefore impose a restrictive covenant to this effect at the time of sale. This enables the vendor's use and enjoyment of the original house to continue, without the fear of commercial or industrial activity taking place on the land that has been sold. The rights of those buying new dwellings are thus limited by the restrictive covenant imposed for the benefit of the original freeholder. Easements are rights exercised by one person over land belonging to someone else, such as a right of way or right of light. Options to purchase may be granted by a freeholder for a specified period, normally in return for payment. They enable developers to reserve the right to purchase land while seeking planning permission (see Chapter 7).

Licences

A licence is not a property right, but merely a personal permission given by an estate owner to allow the licensee to do what would otherwise be a trespass. For example, permission may be given to allow someone to exercise dogs on private land. Where a development site is due to be made available on a ground lease, the developer may initially enter the site under a building licence or contract. The ground lease itself will commence only when construction is complete.

Who is the landowner?

It is apparent that, in any one parcel of land, there may be several estates and interests. For example, a farm may be held freehold by an investor but let to a tenant. The tenant may have sublet one of the fields to the local pony club for show jumping. The investor may have mortgaged the land to a bank, who took out a legal charge. A developer may have obtained an option on part of the farm. Who owns the farm? None of the parties can claim exclusive ownership of the land, but each enjoys particular rights or entitlements in the land. Each of these rights is capable of being traded. None of the parties is entitled to violate the rights or entitlements of the others. If, for example, the developer obtains planning permission and acquires the freehold, the tenant and the subtenant are entitled to remain for the duration of their leasehold estates. Development cannot proceed immediately unless the developer is able to buy out such existing rights and entitlements and clean up ownership of the land.

We can therefore think of rights in land as existing in 'bundles' (Denman and Prodano 1972). The greater part of the bundle held by one individual or organisation, then the better placed is that individual or organisation to control the present use and future development of the land. However, unless otherwise stated, the word 'landowner' is used in the remainder of this book to refer to the owner of the highest form of property right in English law: the freehold estate.

The structure of real estate markets

Markets and submarkets

A market exists when buyers and sellers involved in the production and consumption of a single commodity come together to undertake transactions. Some markets, such as those for fruit and vegetables, have a clearly identifiable location. In contrast, rights in land and property are exchanged through informal and decentralised networks. Most communication between buyers and sellers (or normally between their respective agents) takes place by e-mail, phone or letter, rather than face to face. However, the absence of a specific location or of face-to-face communication does not prevent the existence of a market.

Effective real estate markets are fundamental to economic development, since economies that facilitate exchange of property rights create a safer environment for credit and investment. That is why international development policies emphasise the need to create property information systems, register land ownership, apply common valuation practices and adopt even-handed planning and land taxation measures (Dale *et al.* 2010). As this suggests, the effectiveness of real estate markets depends on their institutional context. We can therefore regard markets as 'a set of social institutions in which a large number of commodity exchanges of a specific type regularly take place, and to some extent are facilitated and structured by those institutions' (Hodgson 1988: 174). Understanding this institutional context is particularly important in explaining how real estate markets work.

Since real estate is a highly diversified product, there is no single market, but a series of separate but connected submarkets which arise in three main ways: sectorally, geographically and by motive of acquisition. Each of these will now be considered in turn.

Sectoral submarkets

Real estate thinking tends to subdivide markets according to use or proposed development. There are five traditional sectors of the market – agricultural land, residential, retail, office and industrial – and two more recent ones: business space and leisure, which we review below. Shaping places often involves challenging ingrained customs within the real estate industry which assume that developments should cater for only one sector. Despite strong policy backing, the concept of mixed use, especially of individual buildings, has still to be widely accepted.

Agricultural land

Agricultural land is divided between owner-occupied and tenanted. Land sold with vacant possession is usually much more valuable than tenanted land. Agricultural owners able to obtain planning permission for urban use can reap very substantial development gains. In the case of Oxford, for example, residential building land is worth about 500 times the value of agricultural land on the urban fringe (see Chapter 10).

Residential property

Almost 70 per cent of dwellings in the UK were owner occupied in 2009. This sector is highly specialised, with apartments, terraced housing, semi-detached and detached houses each forming a particular submarket. New development is usually targeted at particular niches of the market, such as for first-time buyers, executive housing or retirement accommodation. Private renting remains a minority sector, despite significant recent expansion of 'buy-to-let' apartments, especially in city centres (Leyshon and French 2009). Residential building land is subdivided into urban sites usually for apartments, small sites of less than two hectares and bulk land for mass production. Bulk land is generally cheaper on a per hectare basis.

Retail property

Until the late 1960s, the retail market was concentrated in city centres and district or suburban centres. Many of these traditional locations remain vibrant, with substantial development having taken place in recent decades. However, three waves of retail decentralisation have occurred in the past 40 years. These trends reflect fundamental changes in the structure and organisation of retailing, and in

FIGURE 3.1

Meadowhall regional shopping centre, Sheffield, England. Built some three miles north-east of the city centre on the site of a former steelworks, Meadowhall has 140,000m² of shopping floorspace and over 280 individual stores. Its close proximity to the M1 motorway means that it attracts car-borne customers from across the north of England. (Alan Disberry)

the behaviour and priorities of consumers. Superstores and hypermarkets, which formed the first wave, were developed from the late 1960s. Retail warehouses, developed from the mid-1970s, were the second wave. Regional shopping centres, which first caught public attention in the mid-1980s, became the third wave. These centres, which now include the Metrocentre in Gateshead, Bluewater in Kent and Meadowhall in Sheffield (Figure 3.1), offer the complete range of convenience and comparison shopping in purpose-built, undercover accommodation of at least 50,000m². National planning policy subsequently turned against out-of-town retailing and no further approvals have since been given for regional shopping centres.

Office property

The office market is heavily concentrated in the South East, with the City and West End of London acting as traditional market leaders, but with Canary Wharf exemplifying the emergence of the London Docklands as an important decentralised location. The main provincial centres, such as Birmingham, Edinburgh, Glasgow, Leeds and Manchester, have also seen substantial recent office development, mainly due to the growth of the financial services sector. Decentralised locations have been promoted in some provincial centres, such as at Salford Quays in Greater Manchester.

Industrial property

As companies grow, they prefer to expand on their existing sites. If this is not possible, a move up the property ladder may be necessary. The foot of the ladder consists of small workshops (from 50m²) and nursery units (from 250m²). Standard terraced units on industrial estates, commonly known as sheds, are normally constructed at between 1,000m² and 3,000m². At the top of the ladder, units of 10,000m² and above are constructed on self-contained sites. Beyond this, companies tend not to rent space, but to purchase or develop premises for owner occupation.

Business space

Business space emerged as a separate real estate sector in the late 1980s as a result of planning changes that abolished the official planning distinction between most office and light industrial uses. This led to the development of low-density out-of-town business parks that may include some research or light assembly uses, but tend to be dominated by offices.

Leisure property

Growing affluence and more leisure time have helped to create a specialist leisure market. The market includes health clubs, restaurants, multiplex cinemas, golf courses and theme parks. Many new shopping centres now incorporate a leisure element. The leisure market is highly volatile and, in comparison with other sectors, the value of property is more closely linked to the profitability of particular occupiers' business.

Geographical submarkets

A computer might reasonably be expected to sell for roughly the same price across the whole of a country, and even perhaps across several neighbouring countries. In contrast, national housebuilders may construct an almost identical house in different parts of a same country but sell it at very different prices. This illustrates how real estate markets are subdivided geographically, with important differences between regions, cities and even within cities.

There has been extensive research to identify real estate submarkets, especially within housing (for a detailed review, see Jones and Watkins 2009: 51–89). This has challenged the mainstream economic view of a single, unitary housing market spanning the whole of a large metropolitan area. What emerges instead is a series of local housing market areas, the boundaries of which may or may not coincide with those of municipalities or the built-up area as a whole. Prices of virtually the same property will often differ between such areas, and price movements may take place at different speeds. The distance people are willing to move when looking for a new house is crucial in identifying local housing market areas. Housing submarkets are important, although problematic for planners seeking to shape places, since new housing provision is best related to local market areas, rather than to administrative boundaries. Thinking on geographical submarkets has been applied to other types of property (see, for example, Dunse and Jones 2002 in relation to offices), but research here is much less advanced than it is in relation to housing.

Submarkets by motive of acquisition

Users, investors and developers acquire land and property for different motives. The user rents or buys space in the user market. The user is interested in use value, and especially in matters affecting business productivity and operating costs. The developer aims to exploit development value created by opportunities such as building sites, or redundant premises suitable for renovation, available in the development market. The investor buys and sells existing or recently completed property in the investment market. The investor is interested in the income flow from user rents, capitalised into the exchange or investment value of the property.

FIGURE 3.2
The Aurora office building, Glasgow, Scotland. This 16,000m² city-centre office building was completed in 2006 by the developer, Commercial Estates, and let to prime office users, including Barclays Bank, BNP Paribas and Burness Solicitors. The total rent passing was approximately £4.7 million. In 2008, the building was sold to an investor, Credit Suisse, for £92 million, representing an initial yield of about 5 per cent. (David Adams)

Although an individual or organisation may combine these roles, they help us understand how real estate is marketed through a linked series of user, development and investment markets (see Figure 3.2).

The user market

Users evaluate the accessibility, specification and tenure of potential accommodation against their own particular needs. Accessibility and location are critical to almost all users. Specification requirements vary between users, with some concerned only with practicality and others interested also in image. Users have tenure choice, since they can rent or buy property. Most rented premises are constructed to a standard specification in order to appeal to a wide variety of potential tenants. Users retain greater flexibility to move by choosing to rent, subject to the terms of the lease.

The development market

Developers seek to minimise development costs and maximise development revenues in order to maximise development returns or profits. They look to the user market to determine rental values and the investment market to set yields. Unsatisfied user demand provides developers with an opportunity to gain from the development process. In the literature, developers are often portrayed as impresarios, orchestrating the development performance by bringing together capital, labour and property rights to create the right product in the right place at the right time (see Chapter 7).

The investment market

Property is a cost to the user but an investment to the owner. A property investor seeks a return from holding real estate over a period of time. A real estate portfolio normally consists of standing investments, which are buildings already occupied by tenants, offering the investor a known present income in the form of rent, with the prospect of future capital appreciation. Some investors may also look to fund development, especially when standing investments are in short supply.

An ideal investment combines three essential qualities: security, liquidity and profitability. The more secure an investment, then the lower the risk that the capital invested will be lost or the expected income not paid. The more liquid an invest-ment, then the easier it is to sell, either in whole or in part. Liquidity depends on the existence of potential purchasers, on the costs of transfer, on the overall size of the investment and on the extent to which it is capable of subdivision for the purposes of sale. Profitability may refer to either income or capital growth, or to both combined in the form of overall returns. In the long run, capital growth and high overall returns will depend upon the prospects for income growth.

No investment offers complete security, perfect liquidity and guaranteed profitability. Indeed, the balance between security, liquidity and profitability varies from one investment to another. Each investment represents a different com-bination of these attributes, with investors able to play off security, for instance, against profitability. Higher expected returns would therefore be required from higher-risk investments. This is expressed by the concept of yield. Initial yield is defined as the annual income at the date of purchase as a percentage of the capital value. Other things being equal, investors expect a higher initial yield from riskier investments, on the same basis that dangerous employment commands higher pay.

Property investment has traditionally been considered to provide a real asset which, at its best, offers an attractive combination of security, liquidity and prof-itability. Nevertheless, property investment involves considerable risks. A building may remain unlet for a considerable period, with no income received. In the long term, expensive maintenance or refurbishment may be necessary. Management expenses may be high, particularly when a single building is let to many tenants. Liquidity may be poor, especially in the case of very large buildings which become unfashionable. Property returns are also more frequently affected by changes in legislation than are returns from the other forms of investment.

The most important investors in UK commercial property have traditionally been major insurance companies and pension funds, known as the main 'financial institutions', who tend to invest the most secure, liquid and profitable types of property, termed 'prime property'. Their investment strategies are discussed in more detail in Chapter 9.

The operation of real estate markets

We now turn to investigate how real estate markets actually work. As one might expect, economists differ significantly in the way they understand real estate markets. There is often fierce debate between those who take an orthodox view, grounded in the economic 'mainstream', and those who have developed a 'heterodox' position, which aims to introduce more social and cultural factors into the study of real estate. We take the view that those interested in creating better places can learn something from each of five main perspectives reviewed below, since what matters most in understanding real estate markets may well vary from place to place.

Perspectives from neo-classical economics

Neo-classical economics is primarily concerned with how the price mechanism brings the quantity supplied and the quantity demanded into equilibrium. At its core is the concept of 'perfect competition' – the more markets accord to the conditions of perfect competition, the better they work. Where markets work well, outcomes can be explained and indeed predicted graphically, and often mathematically. Such analysis presumes that each individual, household or firm makes its own financial decisions on the basis of rational calculation and independently of those of other individuals, households or firms. Neo-classical economics thus discounts any potential social influence on economic behaviour and attributes outcomes simply to the sum total of the separate or atomistic decisions taken by individual agents.

Real estate markets have been extensively analysed from the neo-classical perspective. Standard textbooks are littered with graphs that demonstrate, for example, how shortages of space cause rents to rise (Figure 3.3). More advanced research papers construct sophisticated mathematical models connecting rents, yields and other real estate variables with broader economic and demographic statistics to predict future movements in real estate markets. How far do such perspectives help us to understand the reality and, indeed, complexity of real estate markets? To answer this, we need to know how well such markets meet the conditions of perfect competition and decide whether, and to what extent, any failure to meet those conditions invalidates the neo-classical approach.

Markets that are perfectly competitive must meet five central conditions:

1. The number of buyers and sellers must be large enough to ensure that no single buyer or seller can influence the market price.
2. The products exchanged should be homogeneous so that in all respects, apart from price, buyers should not prefer the qualities of any one product above another.

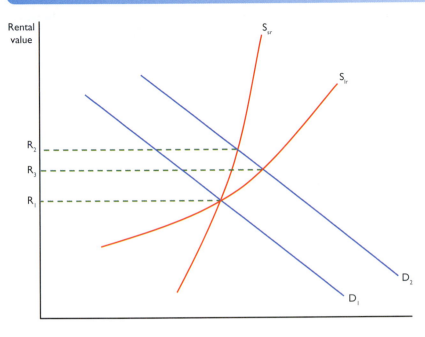

Rental value

S_{sr}

S_{lr}

R_2

R_3

R_1

D_2

D_1

FIGURE 3.3
A basic neo-classical model of rent determination. The red lines represent the capability of markets to supply space. The steeper of the two lines (with subscript sr) represents the short run – in other words, the ability of markets to supply space without any new construction. The long-run supply curve (with subscript lr) represents the ability of markets to respond to demand through new construction as well from within the existing stock. A rise in demand is shown by a shift in the demand curve from D_1 to D_2. Following a rise in demand, rents increase from R_1 to R_2 because this additional demand must be accommodated from within the existing stock, without any new construction. Once new construction has occurred, the rise in rents becomes less significant and is shown as R_3.

3. There should be ease of entry and exit, enabling buyers and sellers to enter and leave the market at will.

4. Transactions should be frequent enough to ensure rapid elimination of surpluses or shortages.

5. Full information should be available so as to ensure that buyers are aware of all the prices asked by sellers, and sellers of all offers made by buyers, so that each can make rational choices.

In practice, the perfectly competitive market does not exist – it is simply a theoretical ideal against which the extent of market imperfections can be measured. Such imperfections occur when the conditions of perfect competition are violated *within* the market. Some have argued that real estate markets are so riddled with market imperfections that they are among the least efficient of all (Balchin *et al.* 1988). It is easy to understand this point of view. For example, the market for most real estate products, apart from standard houses and flats, is often dominated by few buyers and sellers. Far from exchanging homogeneous products, every real estate transaction is different, since, at the very least, its location is unique. (Some products may be close substitutes, although substitutability of apparently similar commodities may diminish with age, location and tenure.) High transaction costs attributable to bespoke marketing and legal work involved in trading property, along with the costs and disruption associated with relocation, deter entry and exit. Real estate is a bulky, capital good that most buyers acquire infrequently, rather than frequently. Finally, market information is sporadic, limited, and notoriously asymmetric in the sense that sellers often know much more than buyers and indeed may adopt strategies to restrict the information available to buyers. If market conditions are indeed so imperfect, why does neo-classical economics retain such a powerful hold on intellectual thought about real estate markets? There are four main answers to this question.

The first is the simple elegance of the neo-classical perspective. It helps to demonstrate with classic simplicity what people know to be true – for example, when few houses are on the market, but people are keen to buy, prices do rise rapidly. At a rudimentary level, the neo-classical perspective thus helps to explain and predict market outcomes. Secondly, modern 'orthodox' microeconomics is built on the mathematical potential of neo-classical analysis. Consequently, those who come to real estate from a broader economic background see an opportunity to apply complex techniques developed in financial markets, where conditions are much less imperfect. Thirdly, it can be argued that, over time, property market imperfections have been reduced as new developments have become more standardised and better information systems created (especially with the growth of the internet) and as property research has grown into a well-established profession. Finally, and perhaps most fundamentally, those now at the forefront of neo-classical study of real estate markets increasingly regard the conditions of perfect competition as a benchmark against which departures can be measured, rather than an essential prerequisite of analysis. Indeed, pioneering work in the neo-classical tradition now recognises and allows for market imperfections.

As an example, Hendershott *et al.* (2002) have modelled short-run disequi-librium in UK regional retail and office markets to find out how long it takes for significant imbalances between supply and demand to be corrected. As intimated earlier, this type of work has been matched by much greater understanding of the spatial differentiation and operation of real estate submarkets. According to Ball *et al.* (1998), rational expectations, transaction costs and asymmetric information are all that neo-classical economics now assumes in seeking to explain property market behaviour. Since neo-classical theory no longer depends on such assump-tions as perfect competition, full information and instant equilibrium (Maclennan and Whitehead 1996), Ball (1998) warns us not to construct neo-classical economics as a straw man, fashioned in a form that can be readily knocked down. Despite widespread market imperfections, we therefore need to be careful not to reject neo-classicism, but instead to think critically about what it reveals and what it keeps hidden, and to be open to other perspectives that take our understanding of real estate markets beyond neo-classical economics.

Perspectives from welfare economics

Welfare economics is essentially concerned with resource efficiency and is regarded by many economists as a subset of the neo-classical approach. This is because it presumes that individuals are narrowly self-interested and make rational choices. It thus conceptualises overall welfare not in relation to any external standard of social provision (such as quality healthcare or education, for example) but merely in terms of an economy's efficiency in satisfying individual preferences. Whether an economy considered efficient in this narrow sense produces outcomes that are unethical or inequitable is not an explicit concern of welfare economists. Indeed, some welfare economists may implicitly take it as given that an efficient resource allocation implies an equitable resource distribution, however it is defined (Carrithers and Peterson 2006).

Although neo-classical and welfare economics are both part of the 'economic mainstream' and share common methodological ground, the specific focus of welfare economics on market failure merits separate treatment in relation to real estate. Market failure occurs as a result of distortions that arise *externally*. These can prevent even the perfectly competitive market invoked in theory from delivering resource-efficient allocations. Efficiency in this sense refers to the important concept within welfare economics of Pareto optimality, in which resources cannot be reallocated to make one person better off without making someone else worse off.

Certain types of markets are more prone to failure than others, with externalities, under-provision of public goods and lost opportunities (each of which we discuss below) endemic within real estate markets. This means that creating better places may necessitate government intervention to make real estate markets more efficient (let alone more equitable or sustainable). Of course, government intervention carries the danger of government failure, so it becomes important to consider whether the outcome is better than that which would have been produced by market processes alone. Nevertheless, many economists see a strong rationale in welfare economics for government intervention to improve property market efficiency and enhance economic welfare (see Evans 2004a, Cheshire 2009). This does not discard consumer choice but recognises instead that 'in given circumstances market processes are unable to produce outcomes which do fully respect individual preferences' (Oxley 2004: 54). Welfare economics has thus been highly influential in planning thought and planning, especially through its application in urban and environmental economics (see, for example, Balchin *et al.* 1995, Garrod and Willis 1999, Pavlov 2004, Willis 1980).

Externalities

An externality arises when the production or consumption of a commodity creates social costs or benefits which market mechanisms are unable to transmit into private costs or benefits. Externalities therefore create beneficial or harmful effects for which no payment is either made or received by producers and consumers. For example, if the owner of a derelict site undertakes reclamation and landscaping, it may enhance the value of the neighbouring properties. However, if the site is

FIGURE 3.4
Scrapyard adjacent to River Plym, Plymouth, England. Not the most attractive of neighbours! Uses such as this have a negative externality impact on development potential in their immediate locality. (Graham Richardson, used under the Creative Commons licence)

subsequently brought back into use for car dismantling, property values in the neighbourhood may decrease (Figure 3.4). Since individual owners take little or no account of such social costs or benefits, real estate markets tend to produce an under-provision of beneficial externalities and an over-provision of harmful ones.

Pearce *et al.* (1978) define three types of externality which may affect real estate value. Producer–producer externalities occur, for example, where a riverside brewery is dependent upon the quality of the water supply. If another firm up stream begins to dump waste into the river, then the brewery will be faced with the additional cost of water purification. A factory chimney that pours black smoke on the washing of nearby residents provides a classic example of a producer–consumer externality. Consumer–consumer externalities often occur in the housing market. A substantial extension built on one house may shade a neighbouring house and cause its value to fall.

Developers normally compare the private costs of development with the private benefits. Unless unusually altruistic, a developer is not particularly interested in the social costs that a development may inflict on the community, nor in the social benefits that it may create. Left to the private market, the development process thus tends to encourage highly individualistic behaviour, with attention concentrated on the production of individual developments rather than on the creation of the broader urban environment to which they contribute and from which they potentially benefit.

Public goods

A public good, once produced, can be enjoyed by more than one consumer at the same time, without diminishing the utility of any other consumer. Indeed, no consumer who wishes to benefit from a public good can usually be excluded, creating the classic problem of 'free riders'. Since access to public goods cannot be controlled, no charges can be levied at the point of consumption. This makes it impossible to organise their supply through normal market mechanisms. Although public goods are often supplied by the public sector, the definition of a public good is dependent on its distinctive qualities rather than on the means of supply. Urban infrastructure such as roads and public space are quasi-public goods, so these tend to be heavily used but under-produced, even when supplied by the public sector.

Lost opportunities

Opportunities to use real estate more efficiently may be lost if individual action is dependent upon common agreement. All the householders in an older area may be keen to spend time and money in renovating and modernising their own properties. However, no single householder will want to be the first to start, unless there is a guarantee that others will follow suit. On that basis, no one would take any action and the area would continue to deteriorate. All the householders are trapped in what is known as 'the prisoner's dilemma', since each is unable to act in their own best interests without knowing the intentions of the others. Another 'lost opportunity' is where development is frustrated by multiple or fragmented ownership. This happens where a site has no single owner but is divided between two or more freehold owners. In a private market, the last owner to settle is in the strongest position to drive a hard bargain with any developer who has already bought out all other owners. Without state intervention, development cannot proceed unless agreement is reached with each owner. This is why developers seeking to assemble redevelopment sites through private transactions often proceed gradually and operate through third parties (see Chapter 5).

Perspectives from new institutional economics

New institutional economics represents an important recent addition to the economic mainstream. It can be traced back to Coase's (1937) seminal paper on 'The Nature of the Firm' in which he first introduced the concept of transaction costs as a means to explain whether firms contracted work out or undertook it themselves with hired labour. Transaction costs include those of information search, contract bargaining and contract enforcement. Transactions require governance structures or 'rules of the game' (called 'institutions') to determine how they are organised, of which systems of property rights are among the most important. Over time, such institutions should evolve to help to reduce transaction costs and minimise uncertainty in human interaction. As Samuels (1995: 578) thus explains, new institutional economics 'works largely within neoclassicism, and shares its rationality, maximisation, and market or market-like orientation and likewise tends to seek, though with less formalisation, the conventional determinate, optimal, equilibrium solutions to problems'.

According to Keogh and D'Arcy (1999) the property market operates as a three-level institutional hierarchy (Figure 3.5). The institutional environment at the top level, defined by the political, social, economic and legal rules by which society is organised, sets the market context. The market itself sits in the middle of the hierarchy as an institution in its own right, since it operates as a network of rules, conventions and relationships. At the bottom level, attention is focused on how important property market organisations are structured and change over time. Although institutions are designed to reduce uncertainty, Keogh and D'Arcy (1999) argue that they reflect prevalent power and influence. As a result, they may succeed in reducing transaction costs only for those groups who are most powerful in the market or most successful in lobbying policy-makers. It should not therefore be assumed that property markets are always moving towards greater efficiency and lower transaction costs.

In a second seminal paper, entitled 'The Problem of Social Cost', Coase (1960) challenged the implicit assumption in welfare economics that market failure should necessarily be addressed by government intervention. He argued that such failure could not be intrinsically ascribed to the existence of externalities but was due to high transaction costs that undermine attempts to allocate ownership over

FIGURE 3.5

The institutional hierarchy of property markets. (Keogh and D'Arcy, 1999)

such externalities. In this case, governments may well be able to deal with market failure more effectively by creating a stronger system of private property rights that would enable externalities to be internalised. For it to work in practice, however, any externalities need to be concentrated on relatively few people, who might be willing to exercise their property rights, rather than spread over many individuals, none of whom might see enough personal benefit in negotiating an externality contract. Nevertheless, new institutional economics calls on governments to assign stronger property rights to private decision-makers and create institutional arrangements designed to promote greater market certainty.

In recent years, there has been much interest among planning theorists in applying ideas from new institutional economics. Alexander (2001) emphasises that, by assigning development rights, planning helps to create a more stable institutional environment for real estate markets. He points to planning's potential to reduce the transaction costs of development by managing neighbourhood effects and bestowing greater certainty about the future. In this context, Webster and Lai (2003) contrast markets as institutions that potentially reduce *individual* transaction costs with government policies and regulations that potentially reduce *collective* transaction costs. However, Dawkins (2000) highlights the increased transaction costs that private developers actually incur as a result of lengthy delays in planning approval. Looking for reform, van der Krabben (2009) contends that compensation rules could be devised to replace regulatory planning as a means of tackling externalities caused by out-of-town retail developments. These might oblige developers to compensate existing retailers for loss of trade attributable to such developments.

Perspectives from behavioural economics

Do market participants actually behave as neo-classical theory might expect – rationally thinking through all possible alternatives before deciding what is in their own best interest? To answer this, economists have increasingly looked to insights from psychology and have experimented to find out what financial decisions people actually take when faced with particular choices. From this has blossomed the rapidly growing study of behavioural economics, whose often surprising insights are producing a drastic rethink of how markets operate in practice.

At the heart of behavioural economics is the concept of bounded rationality, which means that limits exist to the information people can access and take in before making any decision. Since the world is highly uncertain, people tend to resort to rules of thumb, habits of practice and even emotions in deciding what transactions to make. This introduces bias into market decision-making and takes market operations well beyond the cool rationality presumed in original neo-classicalism.

Behavioural research has spread right across economics, and its extensive experimental work is reviewed in detail by DellaVigna (2009). He considers that this experimentation helps to explain three main types of behavioural deviation from what might be predicted by standard economic models. The first is that people's actual preferences cannot be explained merely by rational self-interest – for example, they take up unfavourable credit card offers, fail to put enough money away for retirement and give to charity. The second is that people act on beliefs that turn out to be manifestly incorrect. Managers, for example, are often over-confident about their own abilities and the likely future performance of their companies, and so invest in too many projects and pay more for mergers than they should. This may be aggravated by herd behaviour, where entrepreneurs pay too much attention to what other entrepreneurs are doing, rather than to market fundamentals. Third, people's decision-making turns out to be not as expected in economic theory. This is shown, for example, when they ignore shipping costs in deciding how much to bid on e-Bay or pay excessive attention to peer pressure or purchases made by others.

Among those who have sought to apply these ideas to real estate are Pryce and Levin (2008: 16), who define behavioural economics as 'the study of the social, cognitive and emotional biases that cause economic decisions to deviate from rational calculations'. Pryce and Levin illustrate three important principles from behavioural economics with real estate examples in order to show how transactions can be 'framed' to influence the behaviour of participants. Framing in this context refers to the manner in which information affecting the transaction is presented. First, estate agents may use an unjustifiably high asking price as an 'anchor' or reference point to persuade potential purchasers to make higher offers than they otherwise would. Second, 'prospect theory' suggests that people are prepared to spend more to improve their chances of market success, and so, in a buoyant market, agents are able to talk the market up by encouraging people to 'bid as high as you can to make sure you get the house'. Third, behavioural economics suggests that peoples' system of mental accounting will affect how much they are prepared to pay for property. According to Pryce and Levin, this is one reason why some housebuilders target middle-aged couples moving from large family houses into small, easily managed flats, since such couples are likely to have surplus funds in their notional housing account and so be less concerned with finding a bargain.

As these examples suggest, the way in which information is presented to consumers can make an important difference to what they decide to buy. Applying this principle to public policy-making, Thaler and Sunstein (2008) argue in their bestseller, *Nudge*, for policy-makers to work with human nature to encourage behavioural change, for example, by making people fully aware of their daily energy use. To some, however, this particular interpretation of behavioural economics smacks of the efficiency-enhancing approach of mainstream economic theory and underplays important social and cultural factors that mould aspirations and frame choices (Ferrari *et al.* 2011). Such factors come to the fore in exploring the social construction of markets, to which we now turn.

Perspectives on the social construction of markets

A recent and more radical view of real estate markets views them as a 'social construct . . . understood as part of the system of social relations' (De Magalhães 2001: 106). This approach implies that people are strongly influenced in their economic decisions by their social context and by what others decide. It challenges the mainstream view that economic agents individually make self-interested decisions on the basis of rational choice. Instead, it holds that market transactions, like social interactions, are highly conditioned by humanly devised rules, norms and regulations and reflect dominant powers and interests. As Smith *et al.* (2006: 81) explain:

> Of late, there has been a paradigm shift at the interface between economy and society. Markets, the core concept of classical economics, have been taken for granted throughout the modern period. Now, for the first time in half a century, social researchers are challenging the economic essentialism invested in these and in other 'stylised facts' of economics. Terms like supply, demand, information, competition, efficiency, price and value have all been opened to scrutiny. [. . .] Instead, research is emphasising the social and power-filled character of markets: their diversity and complexity, their sensitivity to context, their passions as well as their 'rationality' and their part in the social construction and performance of the economy.

These insights can be linked to those from the cultural economy perspective (see Amin and Thrift 2003, Amin 2005), for, as Christie *et al.* (2008: 2291) emphasise, 'markets are saturated with all kinds of emotions, sometimes calm and predictable, sometimes wild and out of control, sometimes dependent on aggressive behaviour, but also infused with humour, warmth, affection, even love'. This chimes with work on the York housing market undertaken by Wallace (2008), who draws attention to the intuitive side of market making, with many agents and developers repeatedly referring in interviews to their 'gut feeling' and their innate ability to just 'know the market'.

This highlights the importance of market makers or intermediaries in understanding market operations. As Amin (2005: 14) explains, 'there has been a turn to explaining the rules of the markets – from price formation through to actor rationality and investor behaviour – as a performance involving many intermediaries to get actors to think and act in certain ways'. De Magalhães (2001) demonstrates the importance of international property consultants in incorporating Madrid and Milan into transnational property investment networks from the late 1980s. Smith *et al.* (2006), who provide a fascinating insight into the role professional intermediaries played in scripting the performance of the Edinburgh housing market in the late 1990s, draw specific attention to the potentially destabilising impact of property agents, arguing that their activities might actually amplify market volatility.

These insights into market construction produce strongly disaggregated views of market structures, with each local market reflective of its own routines, procedures, distinctive relations, social culture and other institutions. Those who regard markets as socially constructed thus take a very different view of what drives market operations from that of neo-classical economists, reported earlier.

Conclusions

This chapter has outlined some of the key features of real estate markets that are of particular relevance to those who wish to shape, rather than merely regulate, places. It has sought to challenge the dichotomous distinction between planning and the market, often promoted by mainstream economists, and has instead explored markets as socially constructed and shaped by public policy. Of the many points covered in the chapter, three stand out as of critical importance to the themes developed in the book. First, it is clear that real estate is a quite distinctive commodity that is not readily analysed in the same way as other commodities. This is evident both in the concept of property rights and in the evidence of market imperfections and failure. Second, it is actually erroneous to refer to 'the real estate market', since there are numerous different submarkets, each with its own relationships, conventions and modes of operation. This makes it essential to grasp the fundamentals of any particular submarket(s), and not presume that what happens in one submarket is necessarily transferable to another. Finally, the complexity, dynamism, unpredictability and, indeed, the passions that drive real estate markets should not be underestimated.

Those keenly interested in shaping places thus find it important to understand how real estate markets work and to discover how far they might constrain or facilitate the creation of successful places. This is an intensely practical matter, for it concerns the malleability of real estate markets from a policy perspective and, specifically, the extent to which those who wish to shape places can turn markets to their advantage so as to help create the kinds of places where people genuinely want to live, work and visit. Indeed, working through markets and shaping their operations for public benefit is now generally considered a more effective approach to the governance of place than seeking to achieve policy aims simply through state actions and directives (see Chapter 6). The next step towards shaping places is thus to understand what creates and destroys real estate value and to investigate how far this can be influenced by public policy. We turn to this in Chapter 4, as a basis for investigating three different levels at which the market impact of planning actions can be analysed.

4 Real estate values and the state

Real estate markets are characterised by energy, dynamism and turmoil precisely because of their constant, but often elusive, search to create and capture value. Shaping places involves seeking to turn this search to broader advantage. Since successful places command real estate value, the prospect of value enhancement can potentially be harnessed to attract the investment necessary to help them succeed. Planners who ignore real estate value will, at best, fail to exploit what is perhaps the most potent force in determining whether their plans be implemented or not. At worst, they run the risk of creating places of little value that turn out to be unloved and unwanted by those for whom they are intended. This applies as much to less-prosperous locations as to affluent ones. For, as past experience has told us, leaving poorer locations to unfettered markets or even to public-sector domination does not necessarily create better places.

In this chapter, we first unpack the main components of real estate value and challenge those who lazily argue that 'location, location, location' is all that matters in real estate. We suggest instead that, despite the importance of location, it needs to be matched by careful attention to product and timing. The chapter then moves on to categorise the market impact of planning actions in three ways: macroeconomic, urban economic and microeconomic. Such understanding is essential in order to discover the intended and often unintended consequences of planning actions, enabling the task of shaping places to be recast (see Chapters 10 to 14) as one of conscious and carefully chosen interventions in market processes.

The context for this analysis is that provided by the five main perspectives on the operation of real estate markets, set out in the previous chapter. These perspectives each interrogate market interventions in different ways and cause us to ask five distinct questions about the market impact of planning actions. Specifically:

- Drawing on neo-classical economics, we might ask how far planning directly affects the overall quantity of market supply and demand.
- Drawing on welfare economics, we might ask how far planning can overcome market failure.
- Drawing on new institutional economics, we might ask how far planning reduces or, indeed, increases market transaction costs.
- Drawing on behavioural economics, we might ask how far planning can nudge markets towards more beneficial outcomes.
- Drawing on the social construction of markets, we might ask how far planning can transform market cultures and practices.

These questions set a demanding agenda for any form of intervention in real estate markets, and one that is rarely directly addressed by policy-makers. They nevertheless highlight the diverse ways in which the task of shaping markets can be interpreted and the varied expectations placed on the planning system from the different interests it seeks to serve.

The creation of real estate value

Since the word 'value' is used in varied ways, it is important to specify its meaning in relation to real estate. By 'value', we mean a more substantial and fundamental quality than the price asked or paid in a particular transaction. Values represent more subjective perceptions or expectations of what land or property might really be worth. The more efficient the market, the more likely is value to correspond to price. We can identify three types of value. *Use value* represents the utility or profitability that property affords to a particular user in a particular use. *Exchange value* represents the expectation of what that particular property would fetch, if it were to be offered for sale. People often spend money improving the use value of their homes, without enhancing exchange value. Attractive places may also benefit from features, such as a fountain, that have use value but no immediate exchange value. However, shaping places first seeks to enhance overall exchange value, from which it becomes easier then to fund welcome features that may have no immediate exchange value. *Open market value* is a term commonly used by professional valuers for exchange value, since it is an estimate of the best price at which property might reasonably be expected to be sold, given certain assumptions.

There is a common misperception that what creates real estate value is 'location, location, location'.[1] This mantra reveals only part of the picture, and should be rephrased as 'location, product and timing'. In this section, we explore the importance of each of these factors and reflect on how they are often socially constructed and open to policy influence.

Location

Location has achieved a privileged position in real estate thinking, primarily because it is central to neo-classical marginalist models of urban land use (see Balchin *et al.* 1995: 50–56). In short, these assume that accessibility confers the advantage of lower costs and thus enables users to bid more in rent. In the long run, a competitive land market will therefore allocate the most accessible locations to the activities able to pay the highest rents. This explains why offices are congregated in central business districts within traditional cities and at motorway junctions within the modern edge city. As this example illustrates, the point of maximum accessibility may change over time and is often determined by public rather than private investment, in this case by motorway construction. What primarily confers accessibility is the opportunity for maximum social and economic interaction, so agglomeration economies which encourage complementary uses to co-locate are important. Moreover, since the locational aspect of real estate value is essentially created by the broader community rather than by private individuals or firms, it can be argued that any private value enhancement attributable to public infrastructure provision should be captured to help fund such provision. Yet, despite the theoretical attraction of this argument, it has proved hard to devise a fair and efficient means to achieve this in practice.

Significantly, locations exist as much in the mind as in physical space. This makes it possible for real estate developers to enhance real estate value by extending locations perceived as desirable into areas considered less attractive areas. In Glasgow, for example, since a 'Merchant City' address commands a premium, developments to the east are increasingly marketed as 'within the Merchant City', creating the perception that the area has moved eastwards (Figures 4.1a and 4.1b).

Product

One reason why locations fall out of favour is that the products they contain become obsolete, physically, functionally or, more often, economically. Moreover, some developments fail fully to exploit the advantage of their location, owing to poor design. So value depends on matching the product to the location and not thinking that location alone brings success. That is one reason why 'hedonic' models are increasingly used to analyse the value of real estate products. Unlike

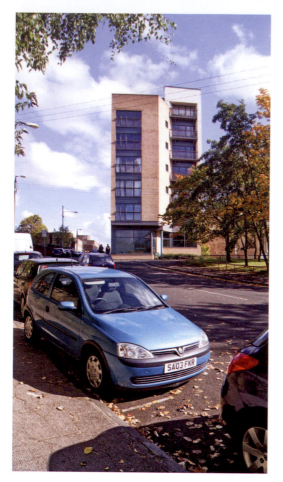

neo-classical marginalist models, hedonic analysis sees each real estate product as a bundle of different attributes, so that house purchasers, for example, are really buying a certain number of bedrooms, a particular size of garden, proximity to a park, and the chance to send children to a specific school etc., all of which can be valued separately. Some aspects of the bundle may be directly determined by public policy, such as school quality, the extent of local open space and so on. Hedonic analysis, which is the focus of much innovative research, helps to indicate how important parts of the bundle are socially constructed.

The dynamic nature of human needs and desires also means that real estate products are notoriously fickle and open to significant culture influence. So, over the past two decades, what earlier generations may have dismissed as outdated industrial premises with bare brickwork, exposed pipes and floorboards become exactly the right setting for the new fashion of 'loft living' (Zukin 1989). Since product demand in real estate is socially as well as economically determined, those involved in creating new places can often exploit their advantage of flexibility by responding to, and indeed promoting, new forms of demand generated by emerging social choices.

FIGURE 4.1

Moving the Merchant City, Glasgow, Scotland. The apartment block shown in Figure 4.1a is located within an industrial area roughly 300 metres beyond the traditional eastern boundary of Glasgow 'Merchant City'. In 2006, in an attempt to capture a popular address and extend its location, it was marketed as 'A striking new development of 1 and 2 bedroom apartments *in* Glasgow's Merchant City' (Figure 4.1b). (Figure 4.1a: David Adams, Figure 4.2b: Steve Tiesdell)

Timing

The third important influence on real estate value is that of timing. Here it is important to distinguish between real estate stock and flow. What moves real estate markets is not the total stock of built property, but the flow available to buy or rent at any one time. This flow is not readily replenished by new development. As real estate is a capital good, purchased infrequently, new supply is notoriously volatile, with pronounced booms and slumps in development activity (see Chapter 5). This means that value is dependent not simply on location and product, but on the time when the particular property comes to the market. Developers who miss the top of a boom may well find it necessary to offer substantial price discounts in order to avoid lengthy vacancy periods until the market recovers. Those serious about shaping places recognise the importance of development upturns, for they provide 'windows of development opportunity' that may require concentrated action from planners to achieve results before the window closes.

In summary, real estate value is multi-faceted, with product and timing as important as location. What commands value is both socially and economically driven, with public policy often equally as important as private decision-making in determining the quality of the various attributes that make up the real estate bundle. We therefore explore policy matters in more detail in the next section.

The market impact of planning actions

Most accounts of how markets work see planning as quite distinct from the market, and portray planners as external agents who make specific interventions from off the field of play. This is not what happens in practice, where the relationship between planning and the market is one of continuous and dynamic interaction. As a result, planners essentially operate as 'market actors' in the sense that they are intricately involved in framing and reframing real estate markets and so become a significant constitutive element of such markets (Adams and Tiesdell 2010). Since other market actors seek to anticipate and influence what planners might do (and planners do likewise of other market actors), over time it becomes problematic to ascribe outcomes either to planning or to the market, since what happens in practice derives from rich and complex interconnection between the two. With this in mind, we can identify three powerful, but not exclusive, themes around which much debate has taken place on the market impact of planning.

The first of these concerns the impact of spatial planning on a country's overall economic performance. Relevant questions here include whether spatial planning redistributes welfare between areas and/or socio-economic groups and, especially, whether it impedes or facilitates economic growth, for example, by increasing or reducing the costs of space occupancy. We label such issues 'macroeconomic' in the sense that they are concerned with the broad impact of planning on wealth creation and distribution. The second theme is more local and concentrates on the immediate impact of planning actions on the patterns of land values in any locality. Relevant contributions here have concentrated on the extent to which spatial planning may create, destroy or modify local land value patterns. We use the label 'urban land economic' to describe such issues. Finally, much controversy has been generated by claims that planning intervention has rendered particular developments 'unviable', especially by increasing their costs or delaying their delivery. We label this theme 'microeconomic', since it is conducted at the level of individual projects or firms, with specific examples often highlighted to fan the controversy.

Macroeconomic impacts

Planning and housing markets

What is the economic impact of restrictive planning policies on house prices, wealth distribution and labour flexibility? Economists have studied this in depth over the past two decades. Despite important methodological differences, they generally agree that planning restrictions reduce the number and size of homes built and lead to higher house prices and higher residential densities (see, for example, Cheshire and Sheppard 1989, Evans 1991, Bramley 1993a and 1993b, Meen 1998, Monk and Whitehead 1999, Bramley and Leishman 2005, Cheshire 2008 and 2009). This makes house production less responsive to price changes (known technically as a lower 'price elasticity of supply'), which exacerbates booms and slumps in the housing market and thence in the wider economy. In distributional terms, it becomes harder to 'get on the housing ladder', so first-time buyers and other new entrants must wait longer until they can afford to buy, and then borrow more to do so.

In contrast, reflecting the regressive nature of planning constraints, those already in owner occupation may gain significantly, along with those with land to sell for development. As such constraints bite harder in more prosperous regions (such as South East England), this makes it even more difficult to move from a less-prosperous region and find a similar quality house, so impeding labour mobility. Where planning restrictions are most intense, teachers, nurses and other key workers may be priced out of the local housing market. All these problems seem to have got worse in the UK since the early 1990s, when a 'plan-led' system was introduced (Whitehead 2009).

Restrictive planning policies also mean that the fiercest competition between housebuilders occurs during land purchase, rather than in selling newly built homes. This has made the industry 'land focused' not 'consumer focused' (Barker 2004). Where competition for land is intense, builders cannot make winning bids for sites unless they assume the highest possible sale prices. They know that, if successful, they can then 'drip feed' the release of new homes in order to achieve these projected prices, primarily because the planning system has limited potential competition in the locality. Unambitious building rates thus result (Adams *et al.* 2009b).

Do the environmental benefits of planning restrictions such as reduced urban sprawl and protected countryside justify these various costs? Economists have avoided this question (because it is not easily answered) and concentrated instead on developing ever more-sophisticated means to measure the economic costs of planning restrictions.

By 2003, the UK Government had become so concerned about the macro-economic impact of planning restrictions that it appointed Kate Barker to conduct a fundamental review of housing supply (Barker 2003 and 2004). She found that UK house price inflation over the 30 years to 2001 ran at an average of 2.4 per cent per annum, compared with 1.1 per cent across Europe. She attributed this to the UK's failure over that period to build enough new homes, which she considered was due mainly to planning restrictions. Her remedy was precise: to reduce UK house price inflation to the European average would require an extra 120,000 new homes to be built for sale in England each year (on top of the 125,000 completed in 2002/03), and in order to eliminate house price inflation altogether, an extra 200,000 would need to be built.

The then Labour Government responded enthusiastically to Barker's proposals, while shifting the focus from house price inflation to affordability. This involved creating an econometric model to quantify, region by region, the impact of different levels of housebuilding on affordability (ODPM 2005a). Eventually, the government set a total housebuilding target for England of 240,000 new homes each year (DCLG 2007) and made significant changes to the planning system in an attempt to achieve this. Ironically, this policy switch came just before the near-collapse of the private housebuilding industry as a result of the recession of 2008–9.[2] When a new Conservative–Liberal Democrat Coalition Government took office in 2010, it scrapped the regional housebuilding targets that had been thought necessary to deliver the Barker agenda, prompting fears that the economic costs of planning restrictions would, in due course, again be keenly felt in the housing market.

There is international evidence of the economic costs of planning restrictions, especially in the US, where Glaeser and Gyourko (2003) attribute high house prices, where they exist, to zoning and other land-use controls. Cheshire (2009) argues that Germany and the Netherlands have a much better track record in housing production than does England, with proportionately more homes built and with a stock that is of higher quality and significantly cheaper relative to incomes. This he ascribes to planning approaches that are more certain than those in the UK and that require local authorities to ensure that there is no shortage of available building land. However, according to Oxley *et al.* (2009: 6), what really matters is that 'Proactive policy-driven land assembly and land supply processes in the

Netherlands, Germany and France contrast with a more passive and reactive approach in England.' They argue that applying the European experience of local authorities with significant development promotion functions is more likely to increase UK housebuilding than is relaxing the planning system. We explore this particular theme further in Chapter 11.

Planning and business space

Although business interests have often drawn attention to the transaction costs of the planning system (see CBI Scotland 2004 and CBI 2005), an answer is still awaited to the important macroeconomic question posed earlier by Healey (1992b: 13), namely, 'Do plans stabilise land and property markets, creating greater certainty, thereby reducing transaction costs and, by limiting the potential for "over-building" in a property market, producing greater efficiency in the relation between supply and demand in land markets?' Since habit persistence tempts developers to start new projects even when market conditions begin to deteriorate (Antwi and Henneberry 1995), in recessionary times many of them will be thankful in retrospect for the planning delays that prevented such development starts.

The impacts of planning on business space have received only limited attention, compared to housing. This is partly because most local authorities, even in prosperous areas, are keen to attract new employment and thus so make generous allocations of land for business development. This explains why Bramley and Kirk (2005) found average annual take-up rates for available employment land in Central Scotland to be only 4 to 5 per cent, compared to between 13 and 20 per cent for housing land.

An initial econometric model of the main UK commercial and industrial property markets, produced by Henneberry *et al.* (2005), found that restrictive planning policies caused the supply of local business space to fall, resulting in higher rents. More detailed econometric work by Cheshire and Hilber (2008) sought to estimate the property cost implications of supply constraints upon commercial office development in fourteen major locations in the UK and eight in Europe, and to compare the results with earlier but similar work in Manhattan, undertaken by Glaeser *et al.* (2005). These development constraints are largely due to policies intended to restrict building height or massing, or to protect conservation areas. According to Cheshire and Hilber, their results show that British office markets are considerably more supply constrained by regulation than are those in Europe, which are in turn more supply constrained than those in Manhattan. Interestingly, they argue that legislation which prevents British local authorities from benefiting directly from additional property tax revenues from new offices is primarily responsible for councils' unenthusiastic attitude to commercial development.

Nevertheless, such work has been subject to severe criticism on both theoretical and methodological grounds (Wong and Watkins 2009). Theoretically, it is argued that Cheshire and Hilber's conception of planning intervention as a regulatory tax that distorts competitive markets deliberately narrows the reality of planning in practice, while disregarding important market constraints such as the structure and capacity of the development industry. Methodologically, data omissions and limitations are considered to lead to over-reliance on proxies and poorly specified equations, exacerbated by a tendency to generalise from weak statistical relationships. Such flaws may serve significantly to overestimate the impact of planning on the cost of business space, especially as 'The reality is that it is not easy to strip away the institutional effects' or 'to adequately construct a counter-factual "policy-off" position' (Wong and Watkins 2009: 484).

Planning and retail space

Although the market impact of planning policy on retail property has again been little studied, two important papers by Jackson and Watkins (2005 and 2007) challenge the negative perception of planning so far portrayed in mainstream economics. Three key conclusions emerge from their work. First, economists who reduce planning simply to development control are mistaken, since by taking account of only town centre management activities and public realm improvements etc. (Figure 4.2) is it possible to evaluate the full impact of public policy on retail property. Second, using econometric analysis, they suggest that even a restrictive policy regime has little negative impact on retailer rents, primarily because strong competition among national retailers to locate in all the major centres is a far more powerful influence. Third, active planning intervention to

FIGURE 4.2
Belmont Street, Aberdeen, Scotland. This image illustrates Aberdeen City Council's long-standing commitment to town centre management and public realm improvements and demonstrates that retail planning is a much broader activity than just development control. (Steve Tiesdell)

manage and improve the retail core of cities helps to attract real estate investment, since it enhances retail capital values and yields.

Since the mid 1990s, planning policies have generally sought to concentrate retail development within town and city centres. As part of a wider investigation of grocery retailing, the Competition Commission (2008) took a particular interest in whether, by restricting the sites considered suitable for new superstores, the planning system acted as a constraint on competition in the grocery sector. While the Commission accepted the overall thrust of planning policies, it eventually took action to prevent retailers from using restrictive covenants to impede their competitors' access to potential development sites in the same area (Competition Commission 2010).

Urban land economic impacts

Much of the debate around the impact of planning on urban land markets has been conducted in relative terms, with the mistaken presumption made that, while planning policy may redistribute value around the city, its overall impact is neutral. This approach can be traced back to the Uthwatt Report (1942), which developed the concepts of floating and shifting values.

Applying these concepts, Uthwatt believed that if a steadily expanding city is surrounded on all sides by agricultural land, all owners within the surrounding area will hope one day to be able to sell their land for development at a price higher than its value in agricultural use. In practice, only a small proportion of owners would actually find their land in demand for development, even if no planning system existed. Development value thus 'floats' over an extensive area, but eventually settles on only part of it.

When urban planning is introduced, planning permission will be granted in some locations but refused at others. As a result, any potential development value lost on land that is refused planning permission is considered to 'shift' to land that is granted permission. However, since the collective expectations of all owners in the wider area had been unduly raised by floating value, the value gained on those sites granted permission is felt to be outweighed by that perceived to have been lost by owners of sites refused permission. Uthwatt (1942) argued that the actual, rather than the perceived, gains and losses cancel each other out and that planning intervention has a neutral market impact. This conclusion was significant because it led in the UK to successive statutory attempts in 1947, 1965 and 1974 to appropriate development value for the community, none of which lasted for any time.

Uthwatt's theory has since been much criticised, owing to its unrealistic assumptions and static, rather than dynamic, understanding of land price determination. For planning in practice does not simply shift values around a city but critically affects the utility or profitability of the uses from which the demand for land is derived. Indeed, if 'bad' planning produces a less efficient allocation of land uses by making users locate sub-optimally, thus reducing utility and profitability, users will lower their bidding prices for land and value will be lost and not merely shifted. In contrast, if 'good' planning produces a more efficient arrangement of land uses, improving accessibility within a city, it will increase utility and profitability and enable users to make higher bids. Furthermore, if planning overcomes market failure by regulating negative externalities, encouraging the smooth provision of public goods and opening up opportunities that would otherwise be lost, resources will again be allocated more efficiently. Urban planning can thus cause higher or lower bidding prices to be made for land, depending on whether it increases or decreases overall welfare.

As Balchin *et al.* (1995: 107) thus argue, 'planning can be seen as a means of increasing the values of private and profitable uses of land'. In some cases, this involves what Healey (1992b) describes as 'creating markets' through a strategic development or regeneration framework, which rescues weak local property markets through public-sector vision and investment that then breeds confidence and co-ordination among private landowners and developers. However, such intentions need to be exercised with care, for, as the recent apartment building boom demonstrated in many British city centres, stimulus policies can encourage short-lived financial speculation, rather than the creation of sustainable urban property markets (Unsworth 2007).

Microeconomic impacts

At the level of the firm, the impact of the planning system on financial appraisals has generated increasing interest in the policy community. The Scottish Government's (2009) guide to development viability, expressly prepared to inform the work of local planning authorities, highlights the financial impact of regulatory delays, uncertainties and additional planning requirements. In the case of three hypothetical residential examples, which illustrate specific planning requirements for lower density, better materials, community benefits and even a bat survey, development profits are shown to be reduced by up to 31 per cent. This comes on top of the £400,000 considered as a typical sum needed to prepare a planning application for 100 new homes, once account is taken of all necessary professional and technical work. If these are important transaction costs imposed by the planning system, what financial benefits does planning provide in compensation at the microeconomic level?

Here, much depends on the extent to which planning acts as a risk-reduction or risk-intensification measure through making the future more or less certain. As Adair *et al.* (1998: 16) comment in relation to urban regeneration, 'Reduction of risk is a key issue with the result that private-sector investment depends on the facilitating role of the public sector.' As yet, there is little substantive research to enable the risk implications of planning intervention to be evaluated at a micro-economic level, so it is perhaps not surprising that risk reduction is rarely seen as an explicit purpose of planners.

Summary of the market impact of planning

As this section has demonstrated, research undertaken on the market impact of planning has concentrated more on its costs than on its benefits. This is partly a methodological issue: it is easier (although still challenging) to assess the costs of planning, since, unlike the benefits, they tend to be specific and more readily attributable to identifiable individuals or organisations. Alongside this, however, planners themselves have been reluctant to engage in debate on the market impact of their activities, leaving mainstream economists to dominate the field. Take, for example, the 'house price inflation/affordability' turn, which tends to produce one of two reactions from the planning profession. Denial of responsibility, with the finger pointed elsewhere is the first of these (see RTPI 2007). Disinterested resignation, reflected by the view that constraining supply is an essential part of planning, even if it leads to higher house prices, is the second. Crucially, both reactions demonstrate the profession's failure to understand the very macroeconomic analysis that proved so influential on government policy. What remains missing from the debate is rigorous economic analysis of whether and how different planning approaches might contribute more to revenues than costs and thus generate higher value added. Such detailed investigation must be an important research priority.

Conclusions

According to Hamilton's (1932: 84) classic definition, an institution is 'a way of thought or action of some prevalence, which is embedded in the habits of a group or the customs of people'. In this book, we argue that planners already serve as market actors, shaping, regulating and stimulating market activity. But, crucially, planners do not always see themselves playing this role, with the result that their market influence is less effective than it might otherwise be. The institutional change that, in Hamilton's terms, is required is thus not for planners to *become* market actors, but rather to *realise* that they already are market actors, intricately involved in framing and reframing real estate markets, and to think and act accordingly.

Understanding what creates real estate value is an important prerequisite for planners seeking to exploit that value in creating more successful places. As this chapter has shown, economists already identify many varied ways in which planning actions impact on market outcomes, even if this analysis is not always welcomed by planners. Yet, planners who think consciously about the market impact of their actions will be better placed to take advantage of market operations where this is possible, and to challenge those operations where they undermine effective place-making. With this in mind, attention now turns to the development market, and specifically to the process by which real estate development comes about.

5 The real estate development process

Some places change gradually over many years, while others experience rapid transformation in a short space of time. Whether the pace of change is slow and almost unnoticed, or rapid and highly disruptive, a production process is at work to shape and reshape the built environment. This form of production is known as the real estate development process. There are many similarities between real estate development and other production processes, such as car assembly. As with other production processes, real estate development requires complex organisational systems to bring together the necessary inputs at the correct time so as to create a desirable finished product. Alongside capital and labour, however, real estate development consumes extensive quantities of another factor of production – land – which makes it distinctive from most other forms of production. Indeed, the potential of real estate development to transform place is crucially dependent on its capacity to source land from real estate markets and combine it successfully with capital, labour and raw materials sourced from other input markets.

While the 'developer' is often portrayed as the impresario who orchestrates this development performance, its successful outcome depends on effective collaboration between a range of actors with different interests in, and commitment to, the specific project. The complexity of this performance, and the variety of actors involved, may not be immediately apparent to members of the public who daily pass development sites and gradually witness their transformation into completed buildings. Indeed, the public often equates the process of development with the process of construction, remaining unaware of the extensive preparatory work necessary 'behind the scenes' before construction starts. Such work may take place over several years, in anticipation of eventual development.

The purpose of this chapter is to explain what is involved in real estate development from inception to conclusion, identify the roles played by different actors, consider the extent to which they enjoy freedom of manoeuvre, and enquire whose interests are best served by the prevailing structure of real estate development. The chapter therefore falls into two main parts. The first part concentrates on the sequence of events typically involved in a development project. It explores how pressure for new development builds up, how development feasibility is then tested and how implementation is subsequently managed. An important related issue then explored is that of 'development failure', evident in the extent of vacant land and buildings to be seen in many urban locations.

The second part of the chapter focuses on actor relations in real estate development by considering whether actors are free to innovate and able to break away from established practices or, alternatively, whether they find themselves hemmed in by powerful economic, social and political forces. If, as can be argued, the real estate development process does not automatically produce successful places, nor distributes its benefits in a socially equitable way, it becomes essential to know how far it can be fashioned to produce outcomes that might be more socially or environmentally desirable. Crucially, then, the chapter seeks to explain both *how* development happens (by identifying its sequence of events) and *why* development happens (by exploring its power relations).

Models of the development process

To help understand what is involved in real estate development, it is useful to create a simplification or diagrammatic representation of its essential components. This can be termed a 'model' of the development process. A good model is more than descriptive, since it also acts as a framework for ideas or concepts of how development actually operates. A model may specify, for example, the contribution of particular actors, the significance of specific events, the nature of relationships that make development happen or some combination of these. Its prime purpose is to reduce the complexity of real estate development so that we can think about it in a logical and ordered way.

Over the years, numerous models of the development process have been produced. Early reviews by Gore and Nicholson (1991) and Healey (1991) identified some fifteen different models. According to Healey (1991), these fell into four main types, each of which involved different ways of thinking about real estate development. These were:

* *equilibrium models*, which reflect the neo-classical economist's concern with balancing supply and demand for new development;

- *event-sequence models*, which seek to specify the various stages of a development project and identify the order in which they take place;
- *agency models*, which focus on actors in the development process, the roles they play and the interests which guide their strategies. Some of these highlight how different actors cluster around different events in the development process;
- *structure models*, which derive from urban political economy and which try to identify the driving forces that power the development process.

An ideal model would successfully combine these various perspectives. Yet, despite Healey's (1992a) valiant attempt to construct an all-inclusive institutional model of the development process, that goal remains largely elusive. As highlighted in both Hooper's (1992) and Ball's (1998) critiques of the Healey model, it is remarkably difficult to summarise all the different aspects of real estate development in a single model that is both operationally accurate and conceptually convincing. The task will therefore not be attempted in this chapter. Instead, two different models are presented. The first concentrates on the events or stages of the development process, while seeking to link them to the drivers of development. This is explained in the next three sections, which focus respectively on development pressure and prospects, development feasibility and implementation. After exploring the related concept of 'development failure', the chapter then sets out an alternative model of the development process, which explores the relations between development actors.

Development pressure and prospects

Although the real estate development process involves many different activities, they can be broadly grouped into three main sets of events, represented by the three sides of the development triangle shown in Figure 5.1. This event-sequence model of the development process is based on the seminal development pipeline originally constructed by Barrett *et al.* (1978), but revised and simplified to reflect more recent thought and practice. As in Barrett *et al.*'s original model, development sites make their way round the triangle from the top, as development pressure builds up, feasibility is tested and implementation takes place. While events may well take place in a different order from that shown within each side of the triangle, the essential requirements of each side must be completed before moving on to the next. This means that a clear development concept must be articulated by the end of the first side and a firm development commitment must be secured by the end of the second side. The implication is that at any point prior to making that commitment, potential projects may be abandoned or significantly revised. Although members of the public may become aware of intended development only when they see a start on site (at the beginning of the third side of the triangle), with enough information, the point(s) reached by every potential

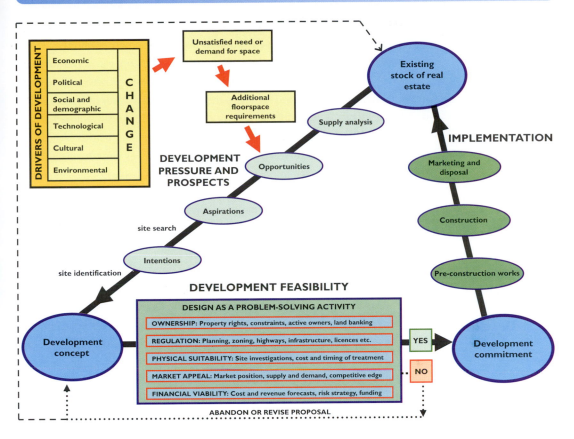

DRIVERS OF DEVELOPMENT
- Economic
- Political
- Social and demographic
- Technological
- Cultural
- Environmental

CHANGE

Unsatisfied need or demand for space

Additional floorspace requirements

Existing stock of real estate

Supply analysis

IMPLEMENTATION

DEVELOPMENT PRESSURE AND PROSPECTS

Opportunities

Marketing and disposal

Construction

Aspirations

site search

Intentions

Pre-construction works

site identification

DEVELOPMENT FEASIBILITY

DESIGN AS A PROBLEM-SOLVING ACTIVITY
- OWNERSHIP: Property rights, constraints, active owners, land banking
- REGULATION: Planning, zoning, highways, infrastructure, licences etc.
- PHYSICAL SUITABILITY: Site investigations, cost and timing of treatment
- MARKET APPEAL: Market position, supply and demand, competitive edge
- FINANCIAL VIABILITY: Cost and revenue forecasts, risk strategy, funding

Development concept

YES

NO

Development commitment

ABANDON OR REVISE PROPOSAL

development site on the first or second side could be plotted. This would give a more accurate picture of the true extent of development interest across a city than would focusing just on construction activity.

It is conspicuous that developments begin and end at the same point of the triangle, since they emerge from the existing stock of real estate as sites or redundant buildings ripe for (re)development, and return to that stock as finished products. This has two main implications. First, it suggests that even pristine, newly completed developments may deteriorate and become obsolete over time, raising the possibility of eventual demolition, with the cleared site then re-entering the development pipeline. Second, as each new development emerges from the pipeline, it reshapes, in some small way, the urban landscape as a whole. Although shown two-dimensionally as a triangle, the pipeline operates in reality as a three-dimensional spiral, producing a fresh pattern of land use at the end of each cycle. Over time, the urban landscape is thus transformed, sometimes imperceptibly, sometimes unmistakably, by the products of the development process. However, since the uncertainties experienced internally within the pipeline are matched by constant shifts within and between the factors driving development externally (shown in the box at the top left hand of the model), actual development outcomes remain inherently unpredictable.

FIGURE 5.1

An event-based model of the real estate development process.

As Figure 5.1 indicates, development is driven externally by economic, political, social/demographic, technological, cultural and environmental change. These factors, which explain how development pressure builds up, may operate independently or in combination with each other. Economic growth and decline, internationally, nationally and locally, is the most obvious driver of development activity or inactivity. Development may also be politically determined where governments decide themselves to invest in particular real estate projects or subsidise investment by others through taxation incentives. Beauregard (2005), for example, highlights the impact on New York of the Liberty Bond programme, enacted by the federal government after the 2001 attacks on the World Trade Center, which made $1.6 billion available in triple-tax-free bonds to stimulate private residential development for both rent and purchase.

Social and demographic change is most evident in the ageing population and growth of single-person households in many advanced countries, increasing demand for smaller dwellings and elderly people's accommodation. Technologically, the IT revolution has transformed development requirements, especially for commercial floorspace, and encouraged more decentralised business development. As Fisher's (2005) study of Newcastle City Centre shows, technological change can have important local impacts, encouraging new development in one area, but accelerating obsolescence in another.

Cultural drivers reflect human perceptions of where development is likely to prove successful and what form it should take. Although implicit and often fleeting, the cultural perceptions held by important development actors can open up or close down development opportunities. Some developers, for example, may restrict their activities to what they consider to be prime locations, while others may be willing to develop in apparently secondary locations (Guy *et al.* 2002). In recent years, environmental drivers have become ever more important, as governments and development actors have prioritised sustainability, with indicators such the US LEED-ND rating system[1] and the UK Code for Sustainable Homes achieving much prominence.

These external drivers prompt development activity once it becomes apparent, from analysis of existing supply, that the need or demand for built space cannot be fully satisfied by what is available at that time for sale or rent. Specific requirements for additional floorspace generate development opportunities, initiating activity within the first side of the development pipeline. Such opportunities may seek to meet either social need in the public sector, or market demand in the private sector, or, indeed, some combination of the two within a joint development framework. As opportunities give rise to specific development aspirations, the search is instigated for suitable development sites, if these are not already available. Once a site has been identified, a broad development concept can be articulated, expressed either as indicative drawings or as a written or verbal statement of the kind of scheme the promoter(s) wishes to see implemented. Only the second side of the triangle will determine whether this broad development concept can be translated into a firm development commitment.

The first side of the triangle warns planners not to assess development potential superficially. It is inappropriate, for example, to allocate sites for specific types of development simply because the sites appear ideal in physical terms. Instead, it is essential first to consider whether the relevant external drivers are likely to generate sufficient need or demand for the development proposed in the locations identified. Similarly, effective property professionals should avoid excessive focus on immediate demand for real estate and concentrate instead on the broader drivers of development.

Development feasibility

Development concepts must be tested and refined to determine whether or not they are feasible. Five specific tests of feasibility must be passed, each of which is explained in detail in this section. These are shown as five parallel streams on the second side of the triangle, each relating to a particular set of constraints or influences. All five streams must be successfully negotiated if development is to occur. It requires only one stream to be blocked for the development concept to prove unfeasible and for it to be abandoned, or at least to require substantial revision. The model neither implies a particular sequence of events within or between streams, nor infers that any one stream is more important than another. This varies from one development to the next.

For the developer, testing development feasibility is not some detached investigation to be watched dispassionately from the side-lines. On the contrary, successful developers seek to make development happen by tackling constraints and pushing away whatever impedes feasibility. Where advantageous, developers will draw on professional expertise to help achieve this. Most developers retain only limited professional staff in-house and instead appoint an external professional team for each development. Some team members may be commissioned early to help explore development feasibility, while others will not be required until implementation is assured. A full professional team comprises design, financial, legal, managerial and technical expertise (Box 5.1). Since appointing a full professional team is a significant expense for the developer, it needs to be justified by the scale and complexity of the development. On smaller or more standardised developments, professional involvement will be more limited, especially where the developer can claim appropriate expertise, such as on project management.

This section has a particular interest in how design expertise can help to establish development feasibility, while not denying the potential contribution of other professional experts. At the start of the second side of the triangle, the designer will fashion the broad development concept into an appealing vision of the future that can capture popular imagination and command professional

BOX 5.1 Professional roles in the development process

Design roles

- Architect
- Interior designer
- Landscape architect
- Planning consultant
- Urban designer

Financial roles

- Accountant or financial consultant
- Property market analyst or economic consultant
- Construction economist or quantity surveyor
- Valuation surveyor/estate agent

Legal role

- Solicitor

Managerial role

- Project manager

Technical roles

- Civil engineer
- Mechanical and electrical engineer
- Structural engineer

attention (Figure 5.2). The design challenge over the second side is to work up what starts as primarily concept sketches into construction drawings capable of implementation.

The term 'designer' is here used as shorthand for a skilled and talented designer with professional experience in at least one of the design roles specified in Box 5.1. Our argument is that design is essentially a problem-solving activity (rather than one narrowly focused on architectural aesthetics, for example), since it seeks to minimise and resolve development constraints, while maximising development potential. A skilled designer will combine technical knowledge with creative thinking to achieve this, with the best-known architects, such as Will Alsop or Norman Foster, all exploiting their reputation to drive projects through regulatory

FIGURE 5.2

Visualisation of Princes Dock development, Liverpool, England. Illustrative of a broad development concept, the image shows part of a £6 billion redevelopment project known as 'Liverpool Waters', proposed by the Peel Group in 2011. (Courtesy of Rust 3D)

systems. Each test of development feasibility is now examined in turn, with specific reference made to design issues as appropriate.

Ownership control

As Chapter 3 explained, a variety of property rights may exist in the same land. A developer must acquire or respect all such rights. Rights of way across a development site, for example, must not be infringed without consent. Where development is unable to proceed because the required ownership rights cannot rapidly be acquired through normal market processes, an ownership constraint can be said to exist (Adams *et al.* 2001a). Such constraints derive from the distinctiveness of land as a commodity, the imperfect nature of the land market, the behavioural characteristics of landowners and the institutional context for land ownership, exchange and development (for more detail, see Chapters 3 and 8 and Adams *et al.* 2001a: 454–60).

As Box 5.2 shows, there are five main types of ownership constraint, each of which can be further subdivided into more precise categories:

- Ownership itself may be unknown or unclear.
- Ownership rights may be divided: the power of freehold owners to sell development land with immediate vacant possession may be restricted by lesser rights in the same land.
- Ownership of separate land parcels may need to be assembled in order to create a suitable development site.

BOX 5.2 Typology of ownership constraints

Ownership unknown or unclear

- Title deeds incomplete or missing
- Ownership in dispute

Ownership rights divided

- Land held in trust
- Land subject to leases or licences
- Land subject to mortgages/other legal charges
- Land subject to restrictive covenants
- Land subject to easements
- Land subject to options or conditional contracts

Ownership assembly required for development

- Ransom strips
- Multiple ownership

Owner willing to sell but not on terms acceptable to potential purchasers

- Restrictive terms or conditions of sale
- Unrealistic expectations of price

Owner unwilling to sell

- Retention for continued current use for occupation
- Retention for continued current use for investment
- Retention for continued current use for making available to others on non-profit basis
- Retention for control or protection
- Retention for subsequent own development
- Retention for subsequent sale: indecision
- Retention for subsequent sale: postponement
- Retention for subsequent sale: uncertainty
- Retention for subsequent sale: speculation
- Retention for no specified purpose: inertia

For further explanation of each category and analysis of its significance in practice see Adams *et al.* (2001a)

- Owners may be willing to sell, but not on terms acceptable to potential purchasers.
- Owners may be wholly unwilling to sell.

From an investigation of eighty large redevelopment sites in four British cities, Adams *et al.* (2001a) found that such ownership constraints disrupted plans to use, market, develop or purchase sixty-four of the sites between 1991 and 1995. Although divided ownership rights emerged as the most prevalent form of constraint, multiple land ownership was the most disruptive. This proved hard to resolve without the prospect of lucrative commercial development and/or state intervention. In the UK, the latter may potentially take the form of compulsory purchase (known as eminent domain in the US).[2] However, as Chapter 13 explains, even if empowered to initiate compulsory purchase action to overcome ownership constraints, British local authorities may be reluctant to do so.

To achieve development feasibility, it is essential to resolve ownership constraints and achieve ownership control. This usually requires a transfer of land into active development ownership (see Chapter 8). So, for example, as a strategic response to the inherent uncertainty of speculative residential development, UK speculative housebuilders aim to control and 'bank' land at least two or three years before it is needed, usually by entering into options or conditional contracts with 'pre-development' owners (Bramley *et al.* 1995).[3] Commercial developers seeking to promote urban redevelopment may take several years to assemble suitable sites and may succeed only by operating covertly through third parties. Even then, seemingly large amounts must sometimes be paid out in order to persuade the last few owners to sell. In the end, however, developers may need to work round ownership constraints by employing skilled designers to maximise the potential of awkwardly configured sites that would have been easier to develop if more land could have been acquired.

Regulatory consent

Real estate development is a highly regulated industry, with a variety of government consents normally required for each project. Planning approval is often considered the most important, since it establishes the principle of development. In the UK, planning applications are assessed individually against established policies, of which the statutory development plan is considered the most important. While development proposals may be submitted for approval in full, it is also possible first to seek 'outline approval' or 'approval in principle' of the broad development concept, before investing time and resources on subsequent 'reserved matters' application(s). The latter are intended to cover more detailed issues such as access, external appearance, scale, layout and landscaping. The discretionary scope of the UK planning system means that local planning authorities retain considerable flexibility on how they determine individual applications, even though appeal processes exist for disappointed applicants. Additional consents may also be required from planning authorities in the UK for developments that affect conservation areas or buildings listed as having historic or architectural interest. In many European countries and in many parts of the US which operate zoning systems, developments that accord with the statutory plan or zoning ordinance have the benefit of automatic consent, with individual applications required only for developments that appear to conflict with the relevant plan or ordinance.

Politicians and the public usually equate regulatory consent with planning approval, since the planning process provides an important channel for democratic debate around development proposals as well as a means to secure community benefits through planning gain (see Chapter 12). As this implies, developers should undertake 'political market research' in order to assess the likely political risks to their proposals and to enable them to anticipate and handle red tape and potential neighbourhood opposition (Graaskamp 1970, Ciochetti and Malizia 2000). In this context, developers increasingly see value in direct engagement with affected communities, for instance through 'charrette-style' exercises (see Condon 2008, Walters 2007), to reduce potential local opposition, especially to major development proposals.[4]

For developers, planning approval is often the most important, but by no means the only consent required to make development feasible. For example, in the UK, construction standards, building safety and energy efficiency are covered by building regulations, while highway design and construction standards for new streets intended to be taken over and maintained at public expense are specified by highway authorities. Infrastructure connections to water supply and sewerage systems require the consent of the relevant utility provider. A local authority licence will also be needed if it is intended to sell alcohol or offer public entertainment from the proposed development.

Different aspects of any development may thus require regulatory consents, typically under different legislation and often from different bodies. As explained in Chapter 12, regulatory approvals are usually sequential rather than integrated, with considerable potential for conflict between different requirements. This has been aggravated in recent decades by the fragmentation and 'hollowing out' of the state (see Chapter 6). In general, the more complex the development, the more numerous are the regulatory requirements and the greater the potential for conflict between them.

The designer's challenge is to join together what separate regulatory bodies keep apart by anticipating and co-ordinating all the regulatory requirements likely to be imposed on the development. This often involves seeking to negotiate and trade off the demands of separate regulatory bodies so as to ensure that overall design quality and integrity is not compromised by the temptation to settle for the lowest common denominator able to satisfy different regulatory requirements.

Here, the mark of effective design is its ability to turn a broad development vision into a specific development proposal capable of securing planning consent, while also meeting other regulatory requirements.

Physical suitability

A developer must ensure that the identified site can physically accommodate the intended development. Site surveys will thus be undertaken to record ground levels, investigate soil structure and check for the extent and severity of contamination. Any constraints that impede connections to the foul or surface-water sewers, water supply systems or gas, electricity or telecom networks must be identified. Any need for on- or off-site highway improvements should also be specified well in advance.

There are few physical constraints (apart from the obvious exception of nuclear waste) that present an absolute barrier to development (Urban Task Force 1999). Instead, uncertainties about the cost and extent of treatment, and around the attribution of legal liabilities for the past and in the future, must be resolved if development is to prove feasible. In the US, for example, liability for past contamination has proved 'the most contentious of all brownfield issues' (De Sousa 2008: 13), with more money spent on legal action to determine who should be responsible for clean-up than on the clean-up itself. In the UK, following the Environmental Protection Act 1990, a clearer legal framework has been established on the responsibility for, and treatment of, contaminated land (Syms 2004). A good recent example of high-quality development on previously contaminated land is shown in Figure 5.3.

What is essential at this stage in the development process is to gather as much information as possible about likely physical and infrastructural constraints. If the

FIGURE 5.3

Gasworks Business Park, Belfast, Northern Ireland. For 150 years until 1985, this was the site of Belfast's main gasworks. The heavily contaminated site was subsequently purchased by Belfast City Council with government assistance. It was reclaimed and developed from the 1990s with European Union funding to provide a major hotel and business park, now employing around 2,500 people. (William Murphy, used under the Creative Commons licence)

treatment considered necessary to resolve any physical constraints (whether attributable to contamination or to other reasons) can be established with some confidence, the crucial issue for the developer becomes whether the proposed development will generate enough end-value to pay for the cost of treatment. The more reliable the information gathered, the easier it becomes to contract out necessary treatment to a specialist contractor or remediation company and factor that cost into the development appraisal.

For development to prove feasible, it is essential to identify all physical and infrastructural constraints well in advance and to devise technically proven and cost-efficient means for their resolution. Here, expert design can help to resolve constraints at lower cost, for example, by introducing sustainable urban drainage systems (see Figure 5.4) to reduce the need for off-site surface water drainage, and by facilitating on-site treatment of contaminated material rather than expensive off-site disposal. Failure fully to anticipate physical constraints runs the risk that construction will be interrupted and completion delayed if unexpected problems are subsequently discovered. Any such delay can have serious consequences for development viability if market conditions change or interest charges have to be paid for longer. To avoid time and cost overruns, necessary remediation and infrastructure works therefore need to be well programmed, usually in advance of the main construction contract.

FIGURE 5.4
Sustainable urban drainage system (SUDS), Upton, Northampton, England. This drainage channel, intended to reduce and manage surface water run-off, has been deliberately designed to enhance overall development quality. (Steve Tiesdell)

Market appeal

As stated earlier, economic, political, social/demographic, technological, cultural and environmental change combine to generate development pressure and enhance development prospects. The operation of these important drivers may seem to be taken for granted on the first side on the development triangle, as events move through to the specification of a broad development concept. Their impact therefore needs to be well researched on the second side of the triangle to ascertain the propensity of the proposed development to serve social need or meet market demand (see Figure 5.1).

Although a social needs assessment might, in theory, help in assessing this aspect of feasibility for public-sector development, what really matters in practice is a government funding commitment to the development, evidence of which is normally taken as a proxy for social need. The comparative test for private-sector development is that of market appeal. This means that there should be enough evidence that demand for space in the development's target market sector is likely to exceed supply sufficiently to ensure speedy take-up at the time when the development is expected to be finished. Market appeal has both a quantitative and a qualitative dimension.

Quantitative forecasts of future supply and demand conditions are never easy, but need to be undertaken as accurately as possible. A two-stage approach is recommended. The first stage requires a shrewd assessment of how the development is likely to be positioned within the market as a result of its location, product mix and timing. Locationally, the accessibility and size of the proposed site will highlight whether it represents a local or more strategic opportunity. In product terms, the target market sector(s) (for example, residential) and the intended market niche (such as first-time buyers, executive housing etc.) need to be clearly identified (see Chapter 3). Here, the merits of a single-product development should be compared to those of a mixed-product range. On timing, a realistic assessment should be made of the earliest likely completion date for the development.

Once it is 'positioned' in the market, supply and demand analysis can be undertaken for the proposed development. Supply analysis aims to identify likely competition from within the existing stock as well as from other planned developments 'in the pipeline'. Demand analysis collates relevant information on people, businesses and real estate:

- Drawing on census data and statistics on consumer expenditure, employment etc., *people-based* research identifies potential users and customers of the development and provides forecasts of their disposable income.
- Drawing on economic trends, financial market data, measures of business confidence and announced investment decisions, *business-based* research interrogates national, regional and local economic trends to identify which economic sectors are likely to grow and shrink.

FIGURE 5.5
Overgate Shopping
Centre, Dundee City
Centre, Scotland.
Originally built in the
1960s, this centre was
partly demolished and
rebuilt in the late 1990s.
High-quality contemporary
design has been carefully
used to reposition the
centre's image, with the
main entrance located in a
way that readily draws in
custom from the
surrounding pedestrian
area. (Steve Tiesdell)

- *Real estate* research seeks to connect these broader development drivers to future trends in rents, prices, yields, vacancies etc.

Such quantitative analysis of market appeal needs to be matched by a qualitative appreciation of how quality design can be used to differentiate the product and maximise its competitive appeal to its intended target sector (Figure 5.5). Since market conditions can alter rapidly over even a short space of time, successful design will also provide flexibility to adapt the development, even when under construction, to market change. As this implies, since market appeal is ephemeral in nature, it needs to be monitored continuously as development proceeds.

Financial viability

The final feasibility test links information from the previous four into a financial appraisal of the proposed development. For private-sector development, this aims to discover whether expected revenues are likely to exceed expected costs by enough to produce the developer's desired rate of profit. Costs can usually be forecast with much greater accuracy than revenues, and cover land acquisition, construction, professional fees, marketing and interest payments on working capital. Revenue depends on market demand upon completion, which may be up to four years ahead. Its estimate requires rental forecasts based on user market data and yield forecasts based on investment market data. Although developers may undertake a simple residual valuation, or even a 'back of the envelope' calculation, to determine their initial interest in a development proposition, a full development appraisal, using discounted cash-flow analysis, is essential in order to determine financial viability.

Development appraisal and design refinement are intricately linked. Although quality design cannot retrieve a development that is fundamentally unviable, design refinements can maximise uses likely to produce most revenue and min-imise those likely to produce least revenue. Design can also assist financial viability by phasing development so as to bring forward high revenue generators and put back low revenue generators. Where appraisal indicates the need for more floor-space so as to make development viable, the design challenge will be to deliver that requirement without undermining development quality or endangering regulatory consent. Viability is reassessed each time design is refined.

Advanced development appraisal uses computer software to generate a range of potential financial outcomes, specifying the degree of risk attached to each. As a general principle, developers expect to be better rewarded for higher-risk projects. This means that development risk may be seen as a welcome opportunity by some developers, even if regarded as an unwelcome threat by others. Risk management involves selection of an appropriate strategy to avoid, reduce, transfer or retain risk so as to produce a lower, narrower and more stable range of potential financial outcomes (Fisher 2010).

Important changes may take place in economic activity, interest rates or the availability of competing accommodation between the commencement and completion of development. Unless a prospective occupier is secured in advance, there may be significant risk that demand at the time of completion will not be strong enough to make development viable. When a lease is signed before development has commenced, it is known as a pre-let. Development is unlikely to commence in fragile markets without a pre-let. Pre-lets are common as the development cycle takes off, when they most help to reduce development risk and enhance lender confidence (Fisher 2010). Even in a robust market, a prudent developer with no pre-let will allow for a void period of at least six months, when the development may remain unoccupied following completion.

If development appears viable, external sources of funding will be sought, unless a developer has sufficient internal reserves. Short-term finance will be needed to provide working capital during construction and long-term finance will be required on completion. The main sources of development finance are discussed in Chapter 9.

Implementation

Once ownership control, regulatory consent, physical suitability, market appeal and financial viability are achieved, a development commitment can be made and implementation can begin. Although the core members of the professional team may have been commissioned to help test development feasibility, any remaining appointments will need to be made early in the implementation stage. Implementation involves three key components: pre-construction works, construction and marketing/disposal. Once implementation begins, developers find their freedom of manoeuvre much reduced and must concentrate on managing risk and balancing speed, cost and quality in delivery. Any discovery of unexpected ground conditions or any significant alterations to the design, for example, can render the construction process highly problematic.

Pre-construction works

Pre-construction works may be required to prepare the development site for the main construction programme. On brownfield sites, for example, buildings may have to be demolished and contamination may have to be treated. Larger development sites may require advance infrastructure provision, including off-site connections to highway, water supply or drainage networks.

Construction

Some developers, such as UK housebuilders, undertake their own construction work, but most rely instead on building contractors. Although developers can devise whatever forms of contract they wish, two main forms are in common usage (Havard 2008). Under the first, the development is designed by the developer's professional team. Tenders are normally invited from around six contractors, on the basis of the drawings and specifications prepared by the team. The lowest tender is usually selected, unless there are particular reasons for not doing so. In the UK, a standard form of contract prepared by the Joint Contracts Tribunal (known as the JCT contract) is common. The professional team is responsible for the supervision of the contract and for ensuring that the development is constructed in accordance with the approved drawings and specification. Liability for any subsequent faults rests with the professional team, provided that the contractor has faithfully executed the contract.

Design and build is the second form of contract, in which the contractor takes responsibility for all design and construction work. A performance specification is drawn up which sets out the quantity and quality of the accommodation required by the developer. On this basis, normally two or three firms specialising in design and build packages are invited to tender. The firm chosen is responsible for the way in which the performance specification is achieved and for obtaining all necessary statutory consents. Liability for any subsequent faults rests with the contractor. Contractors will normally adapt their standard package for different types of development, which makes design and build comparable to the purchase of existing property. It is normally cheaper and quicker than a JCT contract and is particularly advantageous for simple or standard forms of development.

The fortunes of the construction industry are especially susceptible to the development cycle. Tenders may be unexpectedly low for any development commenced during a slump. In contrast, contractors may be unable to cope with the volume of work offered in a boom. At such times, lengthy delays may occur in obtaining materials and considerable difficulties may be experienced in recruiting and retaining skilled labour.

Marketing and disposal

The developer's profit is realised only when the development is transferred into occupation and ownership. Where the occupier also acquires ownership (more usual with housing), the developer's task is complete. Where occupiers simply rent space (more usual with retail and office development), the developer must seek an investment sale once the development is fully let, unless it is intended to retain the development as an investment. In any event, the developer's ultimate aim of producing a marketable development that proves attractive to potential tenants and/or purchasers colours decisions throughout the development process.

Marketing campaigns thus often begin as part of testing development feasibility. Some developers (such as UK housebuilders) conduct their own campaigns, often with an on-site sales presence, but many rely on national and local property agents both to market the development and to conduct any negotiations about sale or lease terms. As well as more conventional brochures and mailshots, marketing campaigns increasingly involve electronic communication and an internet presence.

Where developments are subdivided into various components for separate disposal to different tenants and/or purchasers, some mechanism needs to be devised alongside disposal so as to ensure proper management and after-care of the common parts. If occupiers take space as tenants, it is normal practice to require payment of a service charge, usually to the landlord on top of the rent, to cover common maintenance. If the development is subdivided between different owner-occupiers, the position is potentially more complex unless enforceable and effective contracts are put in place to compel all owners subsequently to contribute to a common fund or collective management arrangements. Developers who do not pay heed to this at the time of disposal are liable to create developments that prove hard to maintain and experience faster deterioration.

Once the development is constructed, marketed, disposed and occupied, a full cycle in the development process has been completed. In due course, the property may become obsolete, fall vacant and be demolished, with the site again entering the first side of the development pipeline (Figure 5.6). Demolition and replacement of commercial property is induced primarily by external economic pressure rather than by physical deterioration or obsolescence (Bourne 1967). Buildings are likely to be sold for redevelopment once they are worth more as cleared sites.

FIGURE 5.6
Demolition of Carlton Towers housing estate, Leeds, England. These local authority flats were built in the 1960s close to the city centre on the site of what had previously been back-to-back and terraced housing. The flats were demolished by the council in 2010 to pave the way for yet another round of housing redevelopment, which is due to start in 2012. (James W. Bell)

Redevelopment will occur sooner in areas where rents are rising than in areas where they are falling (Evans 1985). However, in many locations, vacant land and buildings are not redeveloped but remain idle. The chapter therefore now turns to consider this common experience of 'development failure'.

Urban land vacancy

Since 2001, the UK Government has published annual statistics on the extent of vacant and derelict land and buildings in England. The total area affected by such vacancy and dereliction fell from 41,130 hectares in 2001 to 33,390 hectares in 2009, primarily as a result of concerted government action to concentrate new development on brownfield land. If the 33,390 hectares recorded in 2009 were all developed for residential purposes, some 660,000 additional new homes could be built at current densities, without touching a single greenfield site (Homes and Communities Agency 2010). Although it is quite unrealistic to expect all vacant and derelict land to be used for housing, or to believe that the stock of vacancy could ever be wholly eliminated, these figures dramatically illustrate the scale of brownfield land still remaining in England after a decade of significant policy attention, and point to the existence of what might be termed 'development failure'.

While government statistics now provide much better information on the extent of vacant land and buildings, they offer few clues as to why vacancy remains such a serious problem. Here, it is useful to distinguish between frictional, demand-deficient and structural vacancy (Cameron *et al.* 1988, Couch and Fowler 1992). Land that is frictionally vacant may be making its way round the development pipeline, only to be blocked by constraints at the feasibility stage. If those constraints can be identified and overcome by supply-side action, development is likely to take place. Demand-deficient vacancy primarily results from the operation of development cycles, which are discussed in more detail later in the chapter. Sites in this category have development potential but await the next upturn before beginning their journey around the development pipeline.

Structural vacancy, defined as land rendered permanently surplus to requirements by changes in technology or in the nature of demand, is especially characteristic of deindustrialised locations left behind by economic change. In this case, the prospects of sites even entering the development pipeline are slim without substantive policy intervention to change the structural character of the land and its surrounding area. Most such cases fall into the categories of 'hard-core' vacancy or dereliction (Figure 5.7), defined by English Partnerships (2003) as sites that have remained in that condition for ten or more years. In 2003, some 16,000 hectares of hard-core vacant and derelict land were identified in England. Even so, research by Dixon *et al.* (2010) on Manchester and Osaka, Japan highlighted the potential for policy intervention to remake structurally weak markets and stimulate the redevelopment of hard-core brownfield sites.

Making the development process work better can certainly help to resolve the 'development failure' that is evident in sites blocked by development constraints. However, urban land vacancy is often more intractable than this, and analysis of demand-deficient and structural vacancy suggests it is essential to look beyond the

FIGURE 5.7

Hardcore vacant site of the John Brown Shipyard, Clydebank, Scotland. During a 130-year period, some of the world's most famous ocean-going liners and warships were built at this site. In private ownership, and now vacant for over a decade, it presents a highly problematic regeneration challenge for the west of Scotland. (Steve Tiesdell)

pipeline itself and consider how the drivers of development might be influenced to create greater market interest in locations that still suffer from long-term vacancy and dereliction.

Actors and market relations

Whereas the pipeline model helps to explain the sequence of events involved in real estate development, it only hints at the importance of individuals and organisations. Despite the significance of development drivers, feasibility and implementation, real estate development is an intensely social process in which relations between people, often nurtured over many years, matter intensely in determining outcomes. Such relations are inherently time and place specific, so that the particular mix of what is considered possible in development is highly dependent on the exact combination of individuals and organisations in dominant positions at that particular time and in that specific location. This makes it harder to map out a people-based model of the development process than an event-based one, since the relative importance, and indeed the very presence, of cate-

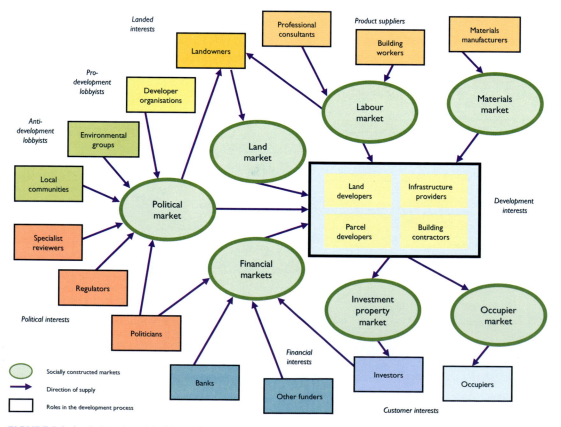

FIGURE 5.8 A role-based model of the real estate development process.

gories of participant may vary significantly from development to development. Nevertheless, Figure 5.8 presents a broad framework of development roles in relation to their specific market involvement.

The distinction between actors and roles in the development process is crucial to understanding Figure 5.8. Actors are named individuals and organisations, such as specific development companies, financial institutions or local authorities. Some writers refer to actors as agents, or even as agencies. Roles are the parts that actors play in the development process, such as those of landowner, regulator, occupier, investor or developer. Figure 5.8 identifies roles, not specific actors, since any single actor may play more than one role within a development project and, crucially, these separate roles may conflict with one another. A classic example is where a local authority acts as landowner, developer and regulator for the same development.

The prime reason for concentrating on roles in Figure 5.8 is because it is intended to provide a generic account of relations in the development process. However, for any single development, it could be adapted to show the actual individuals and organisations involved. Indeed, by tracing how particular roles are combined within a particular case study, it would offer a clearer sense of the extent of role conflict or integration in the case study and more fully reveal the significance of power relations between different actors in explaining how the development process plays out in practice.

Successful development depends on co-ordination between roles. Crucially, this involves cultivating networks of trust between actors (see Adams *et al.* 2012b for evidence of networks operating in the UK housebuilding industry). Taking forward the view expressed in Chapter 3 that markets are socially constructed networks of rules, conventions and relationships, Figure 5.8 identifies seven essential markets for real estate development. Five of these are what we might regard as input markets, in the sense that they create opportunities for development interests to access the necessary inputs of materials, labour, land, finance and political support. To some, it may seem strange to identify a political market in which development interests compete to acquire regulatory consents. However, there is a distinguished theoretical tradition that applies economic analysis to political decisions through a focus on how incentives motivate politically engaged behaviour (see Pennington 2000 for a review of this tradition and a provocative application to the UK planning system). The other two markets identified in Figure 5.8 trade the outputs of the development process, namely completed buildings ready for occupation or investment. In practice, these two output markets overlap, so that with owner-occupied housing, for example, the occupier is also the investment purchaser.

The seven markets act as vital network hubs for development interests, since they enable relations with other key participants to be fostered and, where necessary, mediated and negotiated. Four types of development interest are identified in the model. The land developer (often called the master developer) operates at a strategic level to masterplan and then to subdivide a development area into smaller parcels, each of which may be assigned to different parcel developers. The infrastructure provider is responsible for provision of roads, sewers and other major investment requirements across the development area as a whole, while the building contractor constructs the actual houses, shops, offices etc. It must be stressed that these four development roles are not necessarily undertaken by four different actors, which is why they are contained within a single box in Figure 5.8. For example, speculative housebuilders in the UK usually integrate all four roles within a single organisation. Whether and how the four roles are combined varies from one development type to another and from one country to another.

Apart from development interests, other roles in the development process fall into seven further categories. These start with product suppliers at the top right hand of Figure 5.8, from whom developers source materials and labour. Labour includes both building workers and professional consultants, each of whom might be employed either directly or indirectly. Indirect employment through subcontracting or outsourcing is common in construction. The land market provides a largely informal network through which developers acquire ownership rights from landowners. More active landowners may seek to obtain regulatory consent from the political market with the assistance of professional consultants drawn from the labour market before selling their land to developers for a higher price. This is one of the issues explored in Chapter 8, where the role of the landowner is considered in more depth.

As already demonstrated in the event-sequence model, regulatory consent is a crucial development input. This needs to be sourced from the political market, which developers see as highly complex and unpredictable. As the diagram indicates, the complexity of the political market arises from the scale and variety of roles that seek to influence its decisions. Political interests include elected politicians who may delegate the role of regulator to appointed officials. Specialist (and usually independent) reviewers may also have significant influence on decisions supplied by the political market. These may include design review panels, normally established on a permanent basis to offer some external expertise on design quality (Punter 2011), and major national policy reviews, such as the Barker Review of Housing Supply (2003 and 2004), which resulted in fundamental change in the political market for new housing in the UK.

Importantly, the political market also provides the arena within which those for or against development proposals can engage in debate about regulatory decisions. Here, significant contributions may be made by local communities, environmental groups and representative developer organisations. This is discussed in more detail in Chapter 6. While development interests are essentially concerned to gain regulatory consent from the political markets, they are normally well aware that individual consents relate to the broader policy framework generated by the political market. In this context, development interests will make full use of the resources gained from the labour, land and financial markets in attempting to influence decisions in the political market.

As Chapter 9 explains, developers depend extensively on the financial markets to provide both debt and equity capital for development. A variety of banks, investors and other funders channel finance for development through these markets. Since the state often acts as lender of last resort to financial institutions, politicians are portrayed in the model as an important potential contributor to the financial markets. Ironically, significant state support granted to major UK banks in 2008 was necessary mainly because those banks had overstretched themselves in lending on real estate. The customers of the development industry who occupy and/or invest in newly completed building comprise the final set of interests shown in the model.

Although seemingly static, the role-based model is energised as resources and political decisions flow, often unevenly and unpredictably, to development interests. As intimated below, power relations between and within interests ebb and flow, depending on the state of the development cycle. Significantly, as Carmona *et al.* (2010) point out, many development roles have only a transient concern with the particular project. As a result, only a minority of participants may be interested in high-quality urban design, while developers may see little point in specifications that promise long-term value, if they are not reflected in short-term sale prices. This is because 'while high quality, low maintenance materials increase initial development costs, reduce long-term occupation costs and enhance long-term functionality, the costs are borne by the developers but the benefits accrue to the occupier' (Carmona *et al.* 2010: 286). One solution to such producer–consumer gaps in real estate development would be to encourage individual actors to combine development roles. The potential for this is well illustrated in Chapter 7, where the strategies of developers who also act as investors are compared with the strategies of those who simply act as traders.

Power relations in development

Development cycles

The real estate development process is boom prone and crisis prone, experiencing much more dramatic fluctuations than the economy as a whole (Edwards 1990). Two cities, London (see Barras, 1984, 1985 and 1994) and Dublin (see Dubben and Williams 2009, MacLaran *et al.* 1987, MacLaran 2003 and 2010) provide powerful evidence of how the production of commercial office floorspace is highly volatile and uneven, as waves of new development are followed by subsequent dearths of production. MacLaran has tracked how five development booms since the early 1970s have transformed the urban environment of Dublin, with

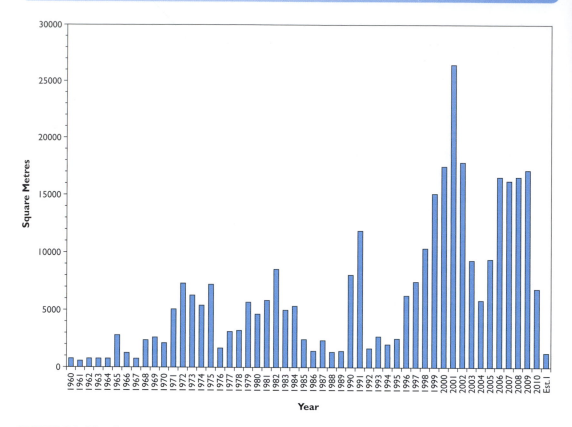

FIGURE 5.9 Office floorspace completed in Dublin, Ireland, 1960–2011. (Andrew MacLaran, Centre for Urban and Regional Studies, Trinity College, Dublin and Savills, Dublin)

FIGURE 5.10

FIGURE 5.10
Office development at Spencer Dock, Dublin, Ireland. Taken in 2009, this image shows parts of what its promoters describe as 'the most ambitious example of urban regeneration ever undertaken in Ireland'. Built on former freight yard, the 20-hectare Spencer Dock scheme will comprise the Dublin Convention Centre, 300,000m^2 of commercial office floorspace, a dozen apartment blocks, along with restaurants, bars and retail units. (William Murphy, used under the Creative Commons licence)

disruptive market consequences for both real estate and the wider economy (Figures 5.9 and 5.10). In Dublin's case, government policies often exacerbated development volatility, with taxation incentives and public–private partnerships used to stimulate commercial development (Dubben and Williams 2009).

According to MacLaran (2003), the 'anatomy' of a development cycle has five stages:

1. *Upturn and acceleration*: when demand increases, rents and prices rise rapidly, as supply cannot respond immediately.
2. *Boom*: more and more developers plan or begin construction, often in locations normally considered far too risky.
3. *Investment-driven development*: as capital values rise, investment capital flows into real estate, stimulating further development beyond that justified by user demand. The first signs of impending trouble are ignored, as individual developers believe their own schemes will fare better than those of their competitors. Significantly, 'Property development is like steering a supertanker at sea; it is impossible suddenly to slam on the brakes and stop' (MacLaran 2003: 52).
4. *Over-supply*: too much completed development means that developers find it increasingly hard to attract tenants. Rents and prices eventually plummet.
5. *Bust*: with falling capital values, investor interest wanes and investment funds are switched into equities or gilts. Completed buildings remain vacant and half-built schemes may be temporarily abandoned. Only when the excess supply has finally been absorbed does the upturn begin again.

Power relations within the development process vary significantly between boom and bust. At boom times, power generally flows in the direction of supply shown in Figure 5.8. This is because development interests have to pay more for inputs (materials, labour, land, regulatory consents) when they are in short supply, but can expect to receive more from investors and occupiers for outputs in the form of completed developments. With the bust, power generally flows against the direction of supply, since the limited number of occupiers and investors still interested in new development can secure beneficial terms from developers. At the same time, developers, if able to secure a pre-let and commence a new project, can take advantage of the slackness in most input markets to drive hard bargains with suppliers. As an exception to the general rule, financial power tends to flow counter-cyclically, exacerbating development cycles with a flood of finance capital in the boom but a severe shortage in a slump.

As all this implies, development activity is concentrated in 'windows of oppor-tunity' which open with the upturn but effectively close once it becomes evident that too much development is underway. A comparison of development activity and land vacancy in Aberdeen and Dundee (Adams *et al.* 1999) demonstrated how such windows open later but close sooner in regeneration locations than in prosperous ones. Developers are more likely to succeed if they are ready to start on site as soon as the window opens than if they still have extensive preparations to complete. The crucial importance of timing to development success thus makes it essential to use development downturns for preparatory work, especially in regeneration locations. This important example of how development interests can turn broader forces to their advantage opens up a wider discussion of how structure and agency relate in the development process.

Structure and agency

As the development process is so volatile, it is relevant to ask whether it is controlled by people or driven by powerful forces beyond the control of individuals and organisations. According to Healey and Barrett (1990), if we wish to discover why development takes specific forms in specific places and at specific times, we need to set the strategies, interests and actions of individuals and organisations within the context of broader social, economic and political processes. Drawing on Giddens' (1984) theory of structuration, Healey and Barrett (1990) therefore explore how 'structure' and 'agency' relate to each other in development.

Agency is a term used to embrace the entire manner in which actors in the development process define and pursue their strategies, interests and actions. For example, as Chapter 8 reveals, particular landowners may choose to take an active or passive approach to development opportunities. Agency represents the capacity of individuals and organisations to act independently and make their own free choices. To a greater or lesser extent, however, the performance of each actor is linked to that of others. More importantly, actors define and pursue their strategies, interests and actions within a broader socio-economic, political and cultural context. Known as structure, this represents the external forces that seem to limit individual choice.

Healey and Barrett (1990) argue that the structural framework for land and property development is neither fixed nor free from challenge, but, rather, that continuous interaction takes place between structure and agency. People are not simply driven by powerful forces wholly beyond their influence or control. Although actors define and pursue their strategies, interests and actions in the context of a structural framework, structure itself is established, re-established or replaced as the resources, rules and ideas by which it is constituted are deployed, acknowledged, challenged and potentially transformed through agency behaviour. What people can achieve is not simply determined by powerful forces, since, over time, such forces themselves are continuously shaped and changed by what people achieve. This highlights the 'duality of structure', in the sense that external constraints on social action exist because they are produced and reproduced by the innumerable decisions of individuals and organisations.

While Giddens' theory of structuration has been much debated and indeed contested by social theorists, its application to land and property development by Healey and Barrett (1990) has generated significant interest and critique. This has centred on the precise relationship between structure and agency. The strategies and actions of one 'upper level' actor, for example, may impose a structural constraint upon 'lower level' actors, while certain structural constraints may have less impact on a group of actors working collectively than if they were each to operate individually. Ball (1998) goes so far as to claim that agency behaviour cannot produce significant structural change, while arguing that it is conceptually problematic to offer structural explanations of the existence and roles of agencies. This prompts him to contend that Healey and Barrett's approach does not actually dissolve the dichotomy between structure and agency in property research. Indeed, 'The separation of structure and agency faces insuperable problems of identification, which other theories manage to avoid by the simple device of not having the difference' (Ball 1998: 1513).

To resolve such criticisms, we need to know how structure and agency are constituted in specific contexts and by what means they interact with each other. Here, the strategic relational approach developed by Jessop (1996, 2001 and 2007) is particularly helpful. Jessop's concern is to develop a more nuanced account of the relationship between structure and agency and so to move beyond the theoretical separation between the two, which Ball (1998) and others criticised. Jessop pinpoints the problem as what he calls the 'bracketing' of structure and agency, by which he means that, at any one time, Giddens' structuration approach concentrates on structure while temporarily ignoring agency, or concentrates on agency while temporarily ignoring structure. This 'tends to relate structure and agency in a rather mechanical fashion' (Jessop 2001: 1223) and to produce what Jessop calls a 'dualism masquerading as a duality'.

Jessop's response is to 'to examine structure in relation to action and action in relation to structure, rather than bracketing one of them' (Jessop 2001: 1223). What this means in practice is that the same element of structure may have different impacts on different actors at the same time, or on the same actors at different times. So any abstract or generalised view of the relationship between structure and agency needs to be stripped away in favour of one that is context specific and highly dependent on the particularities of time and space. In short 'a given structure may privilege some actors, some identities, some strategies, some spatial and temporal horizons, some actions over others' (Jessop 2001: 1223) while, crucially, those actors who realise this through their 'strategic-context analysis' and 'feel for the game' will adopt strategies and tactics that enable them to take advantage of 'conjunctural moments'. These comprise those structural elements that can be modified by a particular actor pursuing a particular strategy at a particular time, and contrast with 'structural moments' that cannot be so modified. Of course 'the self-same element can operate as a structural constraint for one agent (or set of agents) and as a conjunctural opportunity liable to transformation by another agent (or set of agents). It also implies that a short-term structural constraint for a given agent (or set of agents) could become a conjunctural opportunity over a longer time horizon or even within the same time horizon if there is shift in strategy' (Jessop 2007: 42).

From this brief summary of Jessop's approach,[5] it is clear that he offers a more fine-grained understanding of the relationship between structure and agency than that originally developed by Giddens (1984), and as subsequently applied to land and property by Healey and Barrett (1990). Instead of a 'dualism masquerading as a duality', Jessop claims to have reached a 'dialectical duality' in which structure has been transformed into 'structurally inscribed strategic selectivity' and agency into 'strategically calculated structurally orientated action'.

What has all this to do with the practicalities of real estate development, on which most of the chapter has been focused? At the start of the chapter, we asked whether actors are free to innovate and able to break away from established practices, or whether they find themselves hemmed in by powerful economic, social and political forces. Structure and agency theory helps us to work towards an answer to that important practical question. It does not deny the existence of powerful external forces and so remains sceptical of those who think that they can succeed in development by virtue simply of their talents or good fortune. Instead, it calls for development actors to have a thorough understanding of structural constraints, a realistic appreciation of when 'structural moments' constrain their freedom of manoeuvre and a resolute mindset to anticipate and take advantage of conjunctural opportunities by altering their strategies and tactics to do so. In short, it is quite possible to 'break the development mould', but only if the time and place are chosen strategically in response to the changing impact of powerful external forces.

Conclusions

Since the real estate development process has a significant impact on how places change over time, it behoves those interested in shaping places to understand the complexity of events and actors involved in making development happen. As we argue in Chapter 10, the risks inherent in real estate development can often result in a disintegrated built environment as participants each separately pursue what is in their own immediate interest. It would thus be unrealistic to rely on the real estate development process alone to produce successful, well-integrated places and, even more ambitiously, to produce them consistently over time and space. For real estate development is primarily driven forward by those who regard it as a lucrative business opportunity, rather than by those who might see within it a potential to enhance environmental sustainability or social justice. This raises the important question of how far it might be feasible to adjust the development process to meet such broader concerns, rather than sweeping it away (if that were possible) and starting afresh with a new model of development provision.

As a preliminary response, it is evident from much of the material in this chapter that the development process is intrinsically time and place specific, with significant variation apparent in its operation at different times and in different places. The immense variety in the product range delivered by the process suggests that there is scope to learn how more successful places come about and to apply the conclusions to moderating the operation of the development process more generally. It is from this point that we turn in the next chapter to explore the role of governance in place-making and to highlight the range of policy interventions that might be used to mould the development process so that its potential contribution to creating well-integrated and successful places is more fully realised.

6 The governance of place

Introduction

As Chapter 2 showed, what makes places successful and sustainable is now much better understood. Yet, too often, this knowledge is not put to good use to create places of real quality. According to one influential and independent group of economists, much of what has recently been built in Scotland, for example, 'is a missed opportunity and of mediocre or indifferent quality. There are a few examples of new or regenerated places which are well thought out, some fine new buildings and smaller projects that are to be welcomed but they are the exception rather than the rule' (Scottish Government Council of Economic Advisers 2008: 44). Such comments could also apply in many other countries across the world. We need to understand why successful places are not created more consistently, especially since doing so is economically, as well as socially and environmentally, advantageous.

Despite the intrinsic value of successful places both to immediate occupiers and to the broader community, real estate markets and development processes alone cannot be relied upon to produce them, at least not frequently enough. The inherent risks and complexity of the development process, for example, militate against quality and innovation in design and encourage disintegration in the production of the built environment. Too many development actors are trapped in the classic prisoner's dilemma, even if all would profit from enhanced co-operation. Each individual actor may be fearful of potential disadvantage if they alone champion sustainable place-making while others are allowed to pursue immediate self-interest.

This highlights the need for some effective form of institutional arrangement or higher authority to encourage or impose greater spatial co-operation between development actors and so secure the benefits of collective action. Many see this as an essential task of governance in general, and a clear justification for planning in particular. The focus of this chapter is thus on how governments can help to create more successful and sustainable places, especially by acting to remedy perceived market weaknesses.

There are three main parts to the chapter. The first explores how the concept of government has evolved into one of governance and considers the implications of this for place-making. It considers how three modes of governance – hierarchies, markets and networks – have each produced different types of places. This shows how places can be considered to reflect an interaction between the dynamics of real estate markets and the dominant mode of governance at the time of their production.

Since the governance of place rarely involves a wholesale state takeover of the real estate development process, but is normally characterised by specific inter-ventions within it, governments must wrestle with the inherent tension between what they might ideally want to achieve and what they actually can achieve without taking over development projects directly. In this context, 'planning' is often portrayed as an exercise in spatial governance, responsible for co-ordination between all stakeholders involved in charting an area's future. This causes us to reflect on what spatial planning now means in practice and on how this contrasts with earlier concepts of planning.

The middle part of the chapter concentrates specifically on governance capacity. Urban leadership is a central theme here, since urban leaders who articulate and carry through a well-developed vision of how places can be transformed for the better are likely to have far greater impact than those who do not. Yet, leadership must be connected to capacity for effective delivery. This involves marshalling the necessary powers, resources and expertise to make a real difference to places, while recognising the increasing importance and benefit of stakeholder engagement. Nevertheless, these factors cannot automatically deliver better places, since they depend on the context and spirit in which they are deployed.

The final part of the chapter concentrates on the tools or instruments by which governments can intervene in market or development processes to create more successful and sustainable places. We contend that such instruments are best classified by looking at their impact on the constant interaction between structure and agency in development, and especially on how they affect the scope for autonomous action by individual development actors. We therefore set out a fourfold typology which categorises relevant policy instruments by their intent in seeking to shape, regulate or stimulate market behaviour or in building the capacity so to do. Crucially, we argue that creating better places normally requires some combination of these policy instruments, chosen to reflect the specific development challenge. This section thus lays important foundations for Chapters 10 to 14, in which each type of policy instrument is examined in turn.

In the conclusions, we contend that the stakes are high in the sense that much can be changed, either for better or worse, through government intervention in the development process. This is why the issues raised in the chapter reach to the heart of debates around the nature and importance of democratic governance at the urban level.

Government and governance

Successful places come about through effective co-ordination between the many different actors involved in their production and consumption. This task is essentially one of governance, which in its widest sense is defined as 'the various ways through which social life is co-ordinated' (Heywood 2000: 19). Governance differs from government, which instead refers to 'the formal and institutional processes which operate at the national level to maintain order and facilitate collective action' (Heywood 2000: 19), such as the executive, legislature and courts. This suggests that governance can take place without any direct involvement of government, as happens with private sports clubs or in the business sector, where the term 'corporate governance' is now widely used. Within the built environment, gated communities provide an example of the private governance of place, where relations between residents are managed through private contracts (see Blakely and Snyder 1997, Le Goix and Webster 2008, and Webster 2001 and 2002 for detailed explanation of their extent and operation).

Nevertheless, since most places have an inherent public dimension, government in the formal sense is usually involved in some way in their governance. This is why Healey (2010: 48–49) 'includes government as part of the overall deliberate collective activity involved in place management and development', while acknowledging that globally 'The role of formal government in the governance arrangements of urban areas is very variable'. This chapter thus focuses on the critical role that governments play in the governance of place and does not explore private governance arrangements any further. Significantly, the governance of any particular place may well involve more than one scale (central, regional, local etc.) or component (elected bodies, appointed commissions etc.) of the government machinery in that country. This can well create potential for conflict or confusion around how places should be managed and developed.

There are three commonly recognised modes of governance, each seeking to achieve co-ordination in different ways. These are hierarchies which function through command, markets which operate through exchange, and networks which depend on co-operation and trust. These are, of course, theoretical distinctions, since in practice any particular governance arrangements may well involve a combination of these three. These modes of governance can span both the public and private sectors, so the state may rely on market-based competition or networked relationships as much as on bureaucratic hierarchies to achieve its objectives.

Crucially, as we explore below, each mode may have different implications for the way in which both conceptions and realities of place are constructed and reconstructed. This is why the chapter is not directly concerned with specific government structures (such as the particular format of the UK planning system at the present time) but looks instead at how particular modes of governance open up or close down opportunities to shape places. In other words, if we wish to understand how places came about, we need to investigate how the dominant mode of governance at the time interacted with the dynamics of real estate markets. As we explore hierarchies, markets and networks in turn, it will also become apparent how their relative popularity as modes of governance has shifted over time.

Governance through hierarchies

Hierarchies concentrate power at the top and pursue co-ordination through the authority that decision-makers at each level hold over those at levels below them. A fundamental principle of UK governance has long been the 'sovereignty of parliament' in the sense that ultimate power is highly centralised at Westminster, and that other sources of government power, such as devolved or local government, exist only as permitted by the Westminster Parliament.[1] In this unitary model, parliamentary support enables the UK Government to exercise hierarchical power through its control of the government bureaucracy. Although democratic parliamentary elections mean that political control changes hand intermittently from one party to another, sometimes generating significant policy changes, the government bureaucracy in the UK serves whoever is in power. As Rhodes (1996: 653) comments: 'Bureaucracy remains the prime example of hierarchy or co-ordination by administrative order and, for all the recent changes, it is still a major way of delivering services in British government.'

As a form of governance, hierarchies operate on the expectation that those at lower levels will adhere to rules set at the top, such as laws, statutory regulations and government circulars. Resource availability may also be strictly controlled from the top in order to reinforce compliance with those rules and limit freedom of manoeuvre at lower levels. In practice, even hierarchies must allow some measure of local discretion to take account of local circumstances. Yet, in a unitary state such as the UK, the extent of local discretion is determined more by political expediency and the distribution of political power than by any managerial view of how responsibilities could be best divided. In recent decades, UK governments of both political persuasions have sought increasingly to centralise important decisions around the governance of place (Allmendinger 2011). The Coalition

Government, elected in 2010, pledged to reverse this trend, but it remains to be seen whether this will actually happen.

The creation of the British welfare state immediately after the Second World War initiated the heyday of hierarchical bureaucratic governance in the UK, which lasted well into the 1970s. The welfare state was epitomised by free access to health, education and other social services delivered directly by government and paid for out of general taxation. This was the era of big government, in which the state assumed ever greater responsibility for social organisation and economic activity. The broad agenda of social reform also included government action to transform places where people lived or interacted with each other. It was characterised by extensive public-sector housebuilding programmes and by the physical reconstruction of Britain's towns and cities. This was all driven forward by the widely held belief that it was the responsibility of governments to ensure that places were created where people could flourish. Indeed, at the time, many people believed that capitalist development processes were so flawed that creating better places required their wholesale replacement by government action.

In this context, the British new towns programme, initiated as part of the postwar reforms, showed how democratic governments can plan and build entire new settlements without reliance on private-sector initiative (Figure 6.1). Between 1946 and 1970, some twenty-eight new towns were designated across the UK, with the intention of eventually housing some 2.8 million people (Alexander 2009, Hall and Ward 1998). To implement this novel, state-led approach to place-making, a public development corporation, directly answerable to the relevant minister, was established for each new town and endowed with the necessary powers and resources to acquire land, provide infrastructure and undertake building construction. Although, as time passed, the private sector became more involved in the delivery of the new towns programme, 'the British Treasury made an unusual departure from its traditional effort to minimize government spending, arguing that publicly funded development corporations rather than private developers should build town centers in New Towns so as to reap returns from property development' (Heim 1990: 903).

In 1947, the Labour Government nationalised development rights in land, matching its nationalisation of the coal, steel and power industries. It established a nationwide system of development plans, to be produced by local planning authorities under the hierarchical control of central government. Even though most development was expected to be undertaken by the public sector, individual planning permission was required for each development project. The subsequent Conservative Government, elected in 1951, largely retained the inherited planning system, but concentrated its attention on delivering a rapid increase in housing production.[2]

The sheer determination of Harold Macmillan, as housing minister in the early 1950s, pushed housing production to a record of 354,000 new dwellings com-

FIGURE 6.1
Stevenage town centre,
Hertfordshire, England.
Stevenage New Town
was designated in 1946,
with the pedestrianised
town centre, shown
here, opened in 1959.
Construction of the new
town was driven forward
by the public sector
through a powerful
development corporation.
(Picture reproduced by
kind permission of Nick
Hawkes, Shefford,
Bedfordshire, taken on
7 March 2010)

pleted in 1954 as central government marshalled the necessary powers and resources to maximise public-sector output, while also reviving private-sector production (Jones 2000). Although many of the homes built in Macmillan's time as housing minister remain well regarded today, in time, central government's obsession with driving forward housing completions through hierarchical directive led to the extensive production of high-rise public housing estates in the 1960s and 1970s. Many of these turned out to be so badly planned and badly constructed that they degenerated all too quickly into places of neglect and exclusion. The eventual demolition of many of them (Figures 6.2a, 6.2b and 6.2c) was widely seen as a powerful symbol not only of housing failure but also of an entire mode of governance.

By the mid-1970s, concern began to be expressed that government in Britain (and indeed in the US) had become overstretched and overloaded (King 1975). It was alleged that as the bureaucratic hierarchy had grown ever bigger, it proved increasingly ineffective and inefficient, while at the same time 'crowding out' private enterprise with mounting fiscal demands generated by enhanced expectations of what government could and should deliver. The worldwide economic slowdown in the 1970s, which followed the 1973 oil crisis, served to increase the appeal of these arguments. Growing community and environmental protests against housing demolition and motorway construction also highlighted how top-down decisions were increasingly challenged from the bottom up. As Healey (2010: 53) comments: 'The governments of the twentieth century, with their sectoral organisation, did not find it easy to address issues surrounding place qualities, especially where such governments were large and centralised.'

FIGURE 6.2

Demolition of Hilltown flats, Dundee, Scotland. At 12.30 pm on Sunday 31 July 2011, these four multi-storey tower blocks – the Maxwelltown, Carnegie, Jamaica and Wellington – which had stood in Dundee for 43 years, were demolished in a matter of seconds by controlled explosion. Such demolitions have been commonplace in the UK. Their very public spectacle, usually organised at the weekend and watched by large crowds, encapsulates the decline of large-scale state housing provision. (Courtesy and copyright The Courier, D.C. Thomson & Co. Ltd, Dundee, Scotland)

By the late 1970s, the call to slim down 'big government' found voice in the election of Margaret Thatcher as UK Prime Minister in 1979 and Ronald Reagan as US President in 1980. Over the next decade, the impact of 'Thatcherism' and 'Reaganomics' fundamentally changed the mode of governance in their respective countries by introducing market-based competition into what had previously been bureaucratic hierarchies. As is discussed next, this new mode of governance, epitomised by the term 'neo-liberalism' (see Brenner and Theodore 2002), had far-reaching implications for the types of places that were developed and for relations between the state and the real estate development industry. Although neo-liberalism subsequently spread widely across the western world, it should be remembered that governments in many parts of the globe still adhere to the hierarchical approach to place-making – formulating development plans, acquiring land and overseeing implementation. So while the UK Government no longer builds entire new towns, the hierarchical model of public sector-led development is alive and well elsewhere, as illustrated by the cases of Hammarby-Sjöstad in Sweden and IJburg in the Netherlands, discussed in Chapter 11.

Governance through markets

According to Heywood (2000: 68) 'The principal neo-liberal goal is to roll back "the frontiers of the state", in the belief that unregulated market capitalism will deliver efficiency, growth and widespread prosperity . . . This is reflected in a preference for privatisation, economic deregulation, low taxes and anti-welfarism.'[3] Responding to the alleged failures of 'big government' and the perceived inefficiencies of sprawling bureaucracies, neo-liberalism sought both to free markets from undue state interference and to instil market-based thinking into policy-making. It represented a fundamental shift towards governance through markets in both the privatisation of significant activities previously undertaken by the public sector and, wherever possible, the marketisation of activities that remained in the public sector.

Under neo-liberalism, the role of the state changed from that of direct provider of collective goods and services to that of strategic enabler of alternative provision by the private and voluntary sectors. In the UK, for example, Thatcherism brought a virtual end to local authority housebuilding programmes, encouraged the extensive sale of existing council houses to their tenants and tried to fill the supply gap, to varying degrees of success, by subsidising voluntary housing associations and freeing up constraints on speculative housebuilders. This illustrates how the neo-liberal state sought to pursue its objectives through light-touch policy direction rather than the heavy muscle of direct provision, turning the job of government, in Osbourne and Gaebler's (1992) famous analogy, from that of 'rowing' the boat to merely 'steering' it.

However, according to Rhodes (1994), the capacity of government even to steer was undermined by what he called the 'hollowing out of the State'. A key tenet of neo-liberalism was to close down parts of the state that appeared hostile to governance through markets and open up alternative agencies that would embrace its market-led philosophy. So in the UK, for example, the Greater London Council and the six metropolitan county councils, responsible for strategic planning across England's largest conurbations, were abolished in 1986, while some eleven urban development corporations, directly responsible to central government, were set up during the 1980s to encourage private-led regeneration in inner-city areas. In London Docklands (Figure 6.3), for example, the development corporation pursued a planning approach characterised by Carmona (2009b) as 'incremental opportunism'. This remains the strategy still followed there, even though planning powers have long been returned to the local authority.

In time, greater competition within the UK public sector meant that schools were encouraged to compete with each other for pupils, hospitals for patients and urban areas for regeneration resources, through competitive bidding arrangements. Such competition within and across the public sector, now itself reduced in scale and scope through privatisation, made it increasingly hard to achieve 'joined up' thinking at a local level. Indeed, what was left of municipal government in the UK often had to depend on securing agreement between the many local partnerships and agencies now responsible for the delivery of services that once had all been the responsibility of the town hall. This problem was exacerbated because the administrative city rarely coincided with the functional city, whether expressed in economic or in physical terms (Parr 2007). Such institutional fragmentation at the local level was matched by reduced capacity of national politicians to co-ordinate spatial policies across the UK, as a result of the devolution

FIGURE 6.3
London Docklands Light Railway, England. Redevelopment of the London Docklands epitomised a neo-liberal style of planning. Driven forward by private developers from the early 1980s with the backing of a public development corporation and the benefit of taxation incentives, individual projects were developed in a piecemeal fashion with little thought given to long-term infrastructure needs. The Docklands Light Railway shown here was never intended to cope with the eventual scale of development and has struggled to provide enough capacity, especially at peak times. (Steve Tiesdell)

FIGURE 6.4
City Lofts, Salford Quays, England. Property-led urban regeneration in action: exclusive, upmarket apartments on the site of former Manchester Docks. (Steve Tiesdell)

of powers to Scotland, Wales and Northern Ireland and the increasing influence of the European Union over aspects of domestic policy.

Across the US and the UK in particular, neo-liberalism transformed the managerial state into the entrepreneurial state (Harvey 1989a) as cities increasingly saw themselves competing against each other to attract economic activity in what became portrayed as global 'place wars'. Governance through markets thus produced its own distinctive places – convention centres, luxury hotels, executive apartments, up-market shopping malls and places of entertainment – designed to attract the urban rich and reinforce the image of the city as an enthusiastic participant in the new global prosperity (Figure 6.4).

Urban transformation at the height of neo-liberalism was essentially property led, with little thought often given to the effective provision of urban infrastructure such as transport systems, or even to co-ordination between individual developments. Municipalities were stripped of their capacity to influence the development process, as planning powers were reduced, fiscal constraints imposed and public land sold off to developers, often at subsidised prices. Design was portrayed merely in aesthetic terms and considered as a matter of private taste, not public debate.

At its worst, neo-liberalism was seen to create what became known as the revanchist city (Smith 1996), which turned on the homeless and the destitute, deliberately designing and managing urban spaces to exclude those whose social characteristics did not match the new urban lifestyle. Instead, neo-liberalism enabled and encouraged real estate developers to profit substantially from well-chosen redevelopments to such an extent that Weber (2002: 537) claims that

'Neo-liberal redevelopment policies amount to little more than property spec-ulation and public giveaways to guide the place and pace of the speculative activity.'

Although many of its worst excesses have been tempered, at least in the way places are now conceived and developed, neo-liberalism remains a powerful political philosophy which aims to limit state intervention in the development process and promote a market-led approach to urban planning and development. Its misplaced faith in the capacity of markets alone to produce successful places demands direct challenge by evidence of what can be achieved when the state seeks to re-orientate the behaviour of real estate actors, either through hierarchical systems of planning or, as next discussed, networked modes of governance.

Governance through networks

While neo-liberalism challenged the control that top-down bureaucracies had exerted over place management and development, its legacy of institutional fragmentation proved ill equipped to enhance urban quality (other than in quite limited locations) or to deliver more sustainable forms of development. To overcome the break-up of governance structures engendered by neo-liberalism, collaborative approaches began to emerge in order to enable all relevant stake-holders across the public, private and voluntary sectors to work together to achieve common ends. Such collaborative attempts to co-ordinate social life came to be termed 'network governance' (Rhodes 1997).

According to Heywood (2000: 19) 'Networks are "flat" organisational forms that are characterised by informal relationships between essentially equal agents or social agencies.' Since networks depend on trust, reputation and voluntary collaboration, they indicate how deeply economic and political life is often embedded in social relations. In theory, networks organise themselves, have no requirement for a dominant leader and embody Rhodes' (1997) concept of 'governance without government'. While such informal networks may well co-ordinate different aspects of social life and exist well beyond the 'steering' reach of government, their influence on policy can readily be overstated. As Hudson and Low (2009: 168) contend, the idea of 'governance without government' risks 'overemphasising the decline of the State, which remains hugely powerful. Rather than having diminished, its role has changed and it is clear that networks are often created by government rather than emerging from outside it.'

Network governance has indeed often been deliberately promoted by gov-ernments as a means to overcome the organisational fragmentation of the state created by neo-liberalism. Skelcher (2000) argues that neo-liberalism deliberately transferred responsibility for many public services that could not be privatised from primary and multi-purpose governmental bodies to secondary and single-purpose agencies. Over time, the proliferation of such agencies created what Skelcher

(2000: 12) termed the 'congested State', which he defines as 'an environment in which high levels of organisational fragmentation combined with plural modes of governance require the application of significant resources to negotiate the development and delivery of public programmes'. In other words, an important consequence of the congested state is the need to establish a tertiary level of government in the form of mediating partnerships to manage, integrate and steer the activities of all agencies in any one area. As this implies, the congested state reflects how 'a complex of networked relationships between public, private, voluntary and community actors have created a dense, multi-layered and largely impenetrable structure for public action' (Skelcher 2000: 4).

As a decongestant, governments thus have promoted and encouraged the rapid spread of partnerships to re-integrate urban policy (Cowell 2004). Recent examples include Local Strategic Partnerships in England and Community Planning Partnerships in Scotland, which bring together main service deliverers in the public sector (health, education, police etc.) with key voluntary agencies and representatives of the private sector to create a more 'joined up' approach to long-term governance and planning. At its best, network governance can create a strong coalition of local interests capable of articulating a powerful vision of the future. Nevertheless, although networking may have become pervasive in modern governance (Rhodes 1997), some argue that excessive reliance on partnerships as a mode of governance can make regeneration even more complex, protracted and bureaucratic, resulting in frustration, disappointment and even the breakdown of trust among participants (Ball et al. 2003). Network governance is thus no panacea, since much depends on the power, resources and approach of the particular network.

One useful example of the kind of places that emerge from network governance comes from Stirling in Scotland, and specifically concerns the work of the Raploch Urban Regeneration Company (URC), established by the Scottish Government in 2004. Although originally settled in the fifteenth century, Raploch had been largely developed from the 1920s onwards as a local authority housing estate (Robertson et al. 2008), reflecting the hierarchical mode of governance described earlier.

By the end of the twentieth century, Raploch had fallen on hard times and was characterised as 'one of the country's most deprived neighbourhoods, plagued by crime, unemployment, poor health and low opportunity' (Kelbie 2008: 25). Under hierarchical governance, it would probably have been redeveloped entirely for local authority housing, but with little community engagement. A neo-liberal approach would probably have recognised the strategic position of Raploch at the foot of Stirling Castle, within two miles of the city centre and train station, and taken advantage of its location to clear away the old community and redevelop the area for up-market private housing. In Raploch's case, a network mode of governance resulted in a quite different redevelopment process and product.

The planned regeneration of Raploch (Figures 6.5 and 6.6) will involve about £120 million of public and private investment to be spent over a ten-year period from 2004. This will create a mixed community of about 6,000 people, compared to 3,800 at the outset, by demolishing many existing properties and building 900 new, energy-efficient homes, of which 250 will be socially rented and 650 available for owner occupation. Sale prices are modest, with a two-bedroom apartment initially available at £90,000, as compared to twice that figure two miles away. New homes are to be matched by extensive environmental, leisure and public realm improvements and by a new community education campus at the heart of Raploch, containing two primary schools, a special-needs school, nursery, youth club, adult learning centre and other community facilities. Emphasis within the regeneration programme on health improvement and youth training reflects its holistic approach, compared to the property-led schemes of neo-liberalism.

Although formally incorporated as a company limited by guarantee, Raploch URC is effectively a partnership network between the local council, three different agencies of the Scottish Government responsible for health, housing and economic development and the Raploch Community Partnership (RCP) (Shiel and Smith-Milne 2007). The latter acts as an umbrella body bringing together all community groups and voluntary organisations in the area. The URC has been strongly committed to community engagement, involving local people in initial masterplanning weekends and including the Community Partnership in developer selection. While the private sector is not formally part of the URC, two private housebuilders are working in partnership to deliver the owner-occupied homes, while a local housing association is responsible for the social rented homes.

FIGURE 6.5

View towards Raploch's village square, Scotland. Newly built private-sector apartments frame this approach to Raploch's new village square and Community Education Campus. (David Adams)

FIGURE 6.6
Newly built social rented housing in Raploch, Scotland. (David Adams)

Although the economic recession of 2008–9 slowed the progress of redevelopment, Raploch demonstrates how a constellation of different actors working in partnership across the public, private and voluntary sectors is creating a quite different place from the mass public housing estates delivered by hierarchical governance or the exclusive property-led schemes of neo-liberalism. In 2009, the transformation of Raploch was recognised as the UK Social Regeneration Project of the Year and heralded as an exemplar project within the Scottish Sustainable Communities Initiative. For the purposes of this chapter, it again demonstrates the importance of understanding how particular types of place emerge from particular modes of governance.

Spatial planning as spatial governance

The scope of spatial planning

'There are stories from across the world of people mobilising to improve and protect the qualities of the places they live in, work in and care about' (Healey 2010: 1). Such struggles represent the origin of what Healey describes as the 'planning project', which during the twentieth century 'moved from the advocacy and experimentation of activists into a significant activity of formal government' (Healey 2010: 10). While the planning project takes many different forms and relies on varied types of legislation across the world, 'The focus of this broad field of ideas and practices is on deliberate, collective attempts to improve place qualities, as a contribution to the management and development of places' (Healey 2010: 8). Such attempts can be conducted across large or small geographical areas – hence 'planning' may be prefaced by terms such as regional, urban, local or neighbourhood. Planning has also focused at certain times on managing the two-dimensional arrangement of activities in space, especially at the local level (often termed 'land use planning'), and, at others, on achieving some three-dimensional conception of how places should look and function (often termed 'civic design' or 'big architecture').

Since planning is centrally concerned with the distribution and redistribution of value, whether conceived in narrow financial or broader environmental terms, it is an inherently political activity, prone to controversy and political calculation. Politicians do not always accept the recommendations of planning professionals. Indeed, those professionals who base their advice to politicians on what may seem to them rational expert analysis can become highly frustrated if such advice is regularly ignored and political ideology or short-term electoral advantage drives planning decisions.

One critique of planning, whatever its precise form, is that it is readily subverted by powerful interest groups. Pennington (2000) draws on public choice theory to argue that political markets, such as that created by the planning system, are endemically prone to special-interest capture. In the UK, according to Pennington, four main interest or lobby groups have benefited most from the planning process, primarily by exploiting public consultation opportunities for their own ends. These are the housebuilding lobby, the agricultural lobby, the local amenity/ environmental lobby and the professions that service the system. Controversially, he argues that other interest groups 'suffer in silence', including home buyers and those crammed into tightly developed urban areas. Others identify different winners and losers, with Healey (2010: 15) reminding us that the planning system is often seen as 'little more than a creature of business elites driven by capitalist profit making rather than concern for the wider collective interest'. Moreover, the identification of that wider collective interest presents a particular problem, especially since the concept of a public interest has long been considered vague and elusive (Sorauf 1957).

An alternative approach has been to regard planning as a form of mediation between conflicting interests. Yet, taking on the role of neutral referee is precisely why planning often appears so impotent to prevent the most powerful from winning the game. According to Albrechts (2003), it is not enough for planners to be skilled in communicative, people-centred practices. Crucially, they must also be shrewd strategic actors, understanding the dynamics of the wider strategic context. So one important issue in thinking about the institutional design of any planning system is to ask: 'How can governance practices and cultures develop with the capacity to prevent such subversion' (Healey 2010: 15).

Much of what now comprises the planning project is about making places for people and is essentially concerned with delivering the five characteristics of successful places set out in Chapter 2. Alongside the 'making of place', planning is equally concerned with the 'mediation of space'. These come together to create a focus on what is increasingly called 'spatial planning' (RTPI 2001). Yet, even this term has evolved in meaning over the past decade, to the extent that it is usually taken to represent a particular approach to spatial governance, which we now explore.

Spatial planning emerged within the European Union in the late 1990s as a term used to signify a deliberative departure from traditional land-use zoning or regulation practised in many European countries. Although the term 'spatial planning' may be new, the concept is not, for, as Healey (2007: 14) comments: 'The history of spatial planning in the twentieth century can be read as a repeated cycle.' In this context, Healey sees constant friction between those who wish to narrow the place agenda and box it up within a localised focus around the right to develop land and property and those who want to break out of this box with place-focused strategic energy. So, according to the RTPI (2003: 3), the essential idea around spatial planning is that of 'critical thinking about space and place as the basis for action or intervention.' Among those who have sought to explore what this means in practice are Albrechts (2006), Allmendinger and Haughton (2007), DCLG (2008), Haughton *et al.* (2010) Healey (2007 and 2010), Morphet (2011), RTPI (2001), UCL and Deloitte (2007) and Vigar (2009). These varied sources suggest that spatial planning has four crucial attributes which help to distinguish it from traditional land-use zoning or regulation: it is meant to be visionary, integrative, inclusive and action orientated. Each of these is now considered in turn.

Spatial planning as visionary

Spatial planning often starts by creating an image or vision of what an area might become in the future. Essentially, this concentrates attention on the intended point of arrival rather than departure, so that the 'planning journey' becomes a purposive series of steps towards an intended target, rather than a meander from, or even around, the current state of affairs. Scenario planning (Docherty and McKiernan 2008) is often used to achieve this. Nevertheless, imaginative, but realistic, planning visions do not simply emerge from the thoughts of planners. Instead, collective visions representing the shared thinking of all those with an interest in the future of the area are likely to be both more robust and more able to capture commitment for implementation.

To draw out such collective wisdom and commitment often requires some form of visioning exercise (Grant 2007). However, throughout any spatial planning exercise, visions need to be founded on evidence-based analysis, rather than on the whims of the participants. Increasingly, planning visions emphasise achieving more sustainable futures and promoting the comparative advantage of the areas, or the local distinctiveness of the places with which they are concerned. Importantly, planning visions then need to be translated into achievable objectives, strategies, policies and proposals.

Spatial planning as integrative

When spatial planning is characterised as integrative, one or more of three meanings are usually intended. The first is what might be termed scalar integration, in the sense that spatial planning seeks to co-ordinate and link what is intended to happen at different geographical scales, whether at the neighbourhood, urban, regional, national or even transnational levels. The second involves the integration of physical planning with that for other sectors, such as economic development, education, health, regeneration and transport. In other words, what is put forward for any particular site or place reflects not simply its physical characteristics but what are seen as broader social and economic requirements. Inevitably, this depends on the third aspect of integration, which involves co-ordinating the work of all the various agencies across the public, private and voluntary sectors, whose otherwise independent plans might impinge detrimentally on the prospects for places. It is here that the task of spatial planning most approaches that of spatial governance, especially in relation to the creation, and indeed the leadership, of a network of different agencies who need to be brought together to have a beneficial impact on place quality, and to avoid a detrimental one. As can be imagined, whatever meaning is implied by the phrase 'integrated planning', it is usually much harder to deliver in practice than to advocate in theory.

Spatial planning as inclusive

Spatial planning is intended to be inclusive in two main aspects. The first concerns the planning process, in which advocates of spatial planning argue for the widespread involvement of all stakeholders in collaborative decision-making, often through innovative methods of community engagement. Some, however, believe that planning processes have an inherent tendency to privilege the powerful and well-informed – an issue to which we return below. The second aspect concerns the inclusive nature of the planning product, and the extent to which plans produce different outcomes than markets, in the sense of giving voice to the dispossessed and socially excluded and acknowledging the extent of difference, whether of gender, faith or otherwise, within what might superficially appear a homogeneous society. Again, it is relatively easy for spatial plans to claim to be inclusive, but much harder to grapple with the difficult trade-offs that determine the extent of inclusivity in practice.

Spatial planning as action orientated

Finally, as Albrechts (2006: 1161) points out, in the end 'Strategic spatial planning relates to action, to implementation – things must get done!' This means that planning is essentially about acting in the world, about changing outcomes that would otherwise be produced, were place governance to be left entirely to markets. What matters, then, is not so much the plan, but what is eventually delivered through the planning process. As Albrechts (2006: 1162) comments further: 'This stresses the need to find effective connections between political authorities and implementation actors (officers, individual citizens, community organizations, private corporations, developers, and public departments).' To achieve this, we argue below that spatial planning must have access to, and where appropriate deploy, the full armoury of instruments intended to shape, regulate and stimulate markets, while also building the capacity to do so.

It remains to be seen whether this will prove to be the case with spatial planning, or whether, as in earlier attempts to broaden the ambit of planning, high ambitions will flounder if the implementation tool-box is found to be rather limited. For, as Mark Twain is reported to have said, 'If your only tool is a hammer, all your problems are nails.'[4] Planners with access only to regulatory instruments must confine themselves to land-use regulation, and indeed may come to regard regulation as the essence of planning. A true test of whether spatial planning is really action orientated and significantly different from traditional land-use planning is whether it is bestowed with the necessary tools to shape and stimulate markets, rather than simply to regulate them. As a precursor to exploring this further, we now turn to the issue of governance capacity.

Governance capacity

There are some excellent examples across the world of government leadership to help create successful and sustainable places. In Korea, for instance, Seoul's much-acclaimed Cheonggye waterfront has replaced an urban expressway with a linear urban park of flowing water and sensitive landscaping (Figure 6.7). In Germany,

FIGURE 6.7

Cheonggye linear park, Seoul, South Korea. Until 2003, the Cheonggye stream in the centre of Seoul, South Korea was submerged and hidden under a four-lane expressway. At a cost equivalent to almost US$300 million, the expressway was removed and a water-based linear urban park created in its place. (Sarah Kim, http://www.flickr.com/photos/sarahkim/)

FIGURE 6.8
Streetscene at Vauban, Germany. Vauban has been expressly promoted by Freiburg City Council as a model sustainable district, with community-based energy-efficient housing and priority given to pedestrians, cyclists and public transport. (Steve Tiesdell)

FIGURE 6.9
Granville Island, Vancouver, Canada. Granville Island, the festival shopping and food market complex housed in former industrial buildings on the south side of False Creek, is one of Vancouver's prime attractions for residents and tourists alike. The spectacular backdrop is provided by the residential towers of the Downtown South neighbourhood in which the twin towers of the 888 Beach Avenue block (right) epitomise the townhouse/apartment perimeter block with slim corner towers, human-scale street and lushly landscaped interior communal space, that is the Vancouver contribution to high-density and high quality-urban design. (Hisakazu Watanabe, used under the Creative Commons licence)

Freiburg City Council's purchase of 40 hectares of former military barracks in the early 1990s enabled it to drive forward the development of Vauban, now widely recognised as an exemplar of sustainable urbanism (Figure 6.8). In Canada, Vancouver's strong commitment to urban design over several decades helped to establish its reputation as one of the best-planned cities in North America, with development of consistently high quality (Punter 2003) (Figure 6.9).

As such examples demonstrate, discovering the right balance, in any particular context, between private initiative, voluntary commitment and public direction is crucial to delivering successful places. Over the years, however, government intervention in urban development has been the focus of substantial and sustained criticism. It has variously been alleged, for example, that such intervention slows down development and restricts economic growth (Evans and Hartwich 2007), raises property prices and distorts housing markets (Cheshire 2008 and 2009), produces a more mundane built environment, hindering innovation and creativity (Dawson and Higgins 2009) and reinforces social divisions by benefiting the rich at the expense of the poor (Pennington 2000). But need this always be so? Despite such evidence that government intervention in development can have detrimental consequences, is 'government failure' inevitable?

In this section, we argue that, while governments have an essential role to play in shaping the built environment, whether they do this well or badly depends upon their chosen intent, their capacity and determination to act, and the approach they adopt in pursuit of their objectives. In other words, while it is possible to make out a strong case in theory for government intervention in the development process, what really matters is how this works out in practice in specific places. Our specific focus is therefore on the extent to which the state, in seeking to make a real difference to places, is able successfully to provide place leadership, engage with stakeholders and communities and deploy appropriate powers, resources and expertise. Drawing on the experience of hierarchical, market and network modes of governance, we identify pointers to the kind of governance approach likely to be most conducive to creating better places.

Place leadership

Successful place leaders are able to articulate and communicate their vision of a more efficient, equitable and sustainable city. They recognise the economic as well as the social and environmental importance of place quality. Effective place leadership cannot simply be privatised, as implied by neo-liberalism; centralised, as attempted by bureaucratic hierarchies; or dissipated, as often experienced under network governance. Capable leadership matters in place-making because it drives forward action, breeds confidence, reduces risk and widens participation. Only rarely does the private sector provide overall place leadership, even though it might take the lead on particular development projects. Instead, the stronger the local democratic mandate accorded to place leaders, the greater their legitimacy and potential influence. Four particular tasks, discussed below, characterise successful place leadership: promoting a place-making culture, charting a vision for the future, influencing and motivating people, and mobilising resources.

Promoting a place-making culture

Place-making is easily ignored by urban leaders. It is complex, normally offers no short-term electoral advantage and, unlike service delivery or regulatory decision-making, does not clamour for immediate daily attention. Moreover, the institutionalised processes of place governance, such as issuing development permits or making development plans, can be misinterpreted as all that is necessary to chart the future of an area, encouraging many local leaders to think that place-making as a governance activity is already well in hand somewhere within their organisations. Indeed, such complacency makes it all too tempting for political leaders, especially those of a neo-liberalist persuasion, to believe that speeding up such governance processes should mark the limit of their interest in how their cities develop in future.

Such neglect promotes what might be described as a 'place-breaking' culture. In such circumstances, although municipalities may go through the motions of regulating development, remarkably little difference is actually made to what would be delivered anyway. As a result, the built environment becomes increasingly characterised by what we later term 'default urbanism' (see Chapter 10) – the kind of second-rate places that emerge spontaneously, when no one has consciously tried to do better. Regulation alone may well achieve minimum standards, but cannot create a place of real quality.

As this suggests, many of those who emerge as place leaders, and come to understand the critical difference they can make to the long-term well-being of their cities, usually find that their first task is to challenge an embedded 'place-breaking' culture within and beyond their own organisations and instead instil a 'place-making' culture. This means championing the message that quality of place matters and can be achieved by determined collective action. It requires a strong sense of civic values and involves an essentially political appeal to hearts as well as minds. In certain circumstances, it may still be necessary for the new political leadership to make changes in personnel or senior management so as to ensure that place-making becomes embedded within the organisational culture (Hall 2011). Once place-making is seen as central to the dominant political agenda, it then becomes harder for those working within the municipality to continue to adhere to the previous 'place-breaking' culture.

Charting a vision for the future

A place-making culture creates fertile ground in which to articulate a long-term vision of how a city can be transformed over a ten- or twenty-year period. Successful place leaders are able to articulate what the city, at its best, can become; and how this relates to what its people, at their best, can achieve. This means that place vision extends well beyond intended design and development quality, to convey a powerful image of how a more efficient, equitable and sustainable city will open up social and economic opportunities for its citizens.

Such place visions are not primarily concerned with improving real estate development prospects (even though this may be among their consequences), but rather are intended to bring together a much wider range of civic interests to contribute to, and share in, the urban vision, for which place leaders act as an important focal point. In Barcelona, for example, the restoration of democratic government in the 1980s produced a new emphasis on enhancing the quality of the city centre, improving the public realm and creating a more urban ambience in the expanding periphery (Marshall 2004, Healey 2010).

Influencing and motivating people

Once established, such a vision needs to be communicated with passion and conviction, which is the next important task involved in effective place leadership. This involves motivating and inspiring a broad range of people across the city to believe that what is initially seen as visionary is achievable, given their own commitment and provision of the requisite delivery capacity. It may be necessary to reach out and bring on board apathetic members of the business sector or hostile local communities. Coalitions of interest and support must be created to ensure that it becomes increasingly difficult to return to the place-breaking habits of old. This does not imply unquestioned acceptance of whatever is proposed by urban leaders. Indeed, unlike the model of hierarchical governance, effective place leaders today are willing to welcome the input of 'critical friends', for example from local professional networks, who can usefully sharpen up urban visions through careful review and discussion.

Strong relations must also be built between political leaders and their senior professional advisers, with both being equally committed to the delivery of the intended place vision. It has to be understood that what is involved in the effective governance of place is far removed from more even-handed forms of governance (such as the regulatory management of taxi licences), since place-making involves deliberate value-laden intervention to confront socially damaging behaviour and promote socially beneficial behaviour. Communicating place visions may therefore involve persuading stakeholders to abandon what they may find easy to achieve alone, and encouraging them instead to strive together to achieve what may be more difficult but yet more worthwhile.

Mobilising resources

None of these leadership tasks will bring about improved place quality unless connected to delivery capacity, as discussed below. An essential part of urban leadership is thus to mobilise the necessary resources to bring about the intended vision. Here, it is important to maintain long-term direction while handling short-term concerns and crises decisively, without giving way to vested or sectional interests. This means that what starts out as a visionary concept of the future must be translated into a robust delivery strategy capable of exploiting emerging opportunities and riding out difficulties.

The responsibility of leadership

As Lyons (2007: 177) argues, 'Leadership of place is an inherently political role, involving the setting of clear priorities and making difficult choices, resolving conflict and balancing differing demands and views.' He sees 'place-shaping as capturing the central role and purpose of local government, defining it as the creative use of powers and influence to promote the general wellbeing of a community and its citizens' (Lyons 2007: 174). While Lyons takes a broader view of place and place leadership than is espoused here, it is important to recognise the contribution that a quality environment can make to all the other social, economic and environmental improvements that politicians seek. Despite recent trends that see urban mayors as encapsulating the essence of urban leadership (see Sweeting 2002), Lyons argues that a variety of leadership models can engage local people with energy and enthusiasm. It is important, then, not to reduce place leadership simply to single individuals, but to realise the importance of collective and embedded commitment to place transformation over a long period of time.

Stakeholder engagement

Effective place leaders consider stakeholder engagement as an essential part of creating a shared vision for the future. Stakeholders comprise those who participate in the development process, directly or indirectly, such as landowners, developers and infrastructure companies, those who advise them professionally and, importantly, those affected by or interested in what happens to their neighbourhoods, towns or cities. The latter include civic and community groups, amenity and environmental societies, resident associations and local people themselves. While the hierarchical mode of governance tends to downplay stakeholder engagement, in the conviction that those at the top know what is best, neo-liberalism privileges the development sector and tends to ignore other stakeholders, who may be portrayed as standing in the way of progress.

A network mode of governance is, by definition, more inclusive, but here the key challenge is to turn extensive stakeholder engagement to advantage, and not to remain marooned in endless debate that is never brought to a conclusion. To avoid this, those within government must approach stakeholder engagement with a certain sense of humility, recognising that stakeholders not only have the right to comment on what is intended for their areas, but may actually bring some valuable

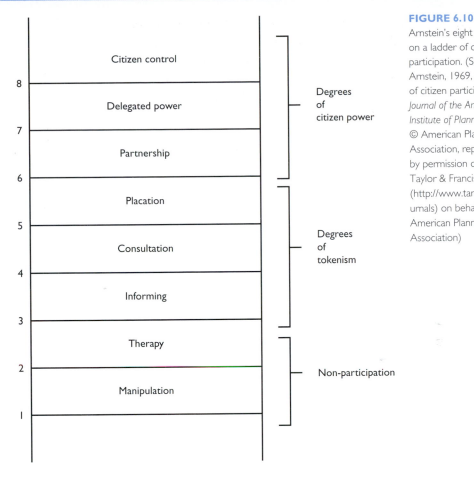

8	Citizen control
	Delegated power
7	
	Partnership
6	
	Placation
5	
	Consultation
4	
	Informing
3	
	Therapy
2	
	Manipulation
1	

Degrees of citizen power

Degrees of tokenism

Non-participation

FIGURE 6.10
Arnstein's eight rungs on a ladder of citizen participation. (Sherry Arnstein, 1969, 'A ladder of citizen participation', *Journal of the American Institute of Planners* © American Planning Association, reprinted by permission of Taylor & Francis Ltd (http://www.tandf.co.uk/journals) on behalf of the American Planning Association)

insight or information to the planning process that may well improve intended outcomes. The message to place leaders, at least from the *Urban Design Compendium* (English Partnerships 2007b: 55), is clear: 'Do not underestimate the value of public involvement.' This is why effective stakeholder engagement moves beyond the degrees of tokenism on Arnstein's ladder (Figure 6.10) and regards stakeholders as partners in a shared task of governance.

According to the *Urban Design Compendium* (2007b: 49), 'Resolving conflicts and making the most of the contribution of local people depends on providing the means for the community to become involved, being clear about the objectives of the engagement process, and ensuring that events are appropriate to the scale and stage of development.' This calls for innovative approaches to stakeholder engagement instead of more traditional and often one-directional methods of involvement, such as public meetings and exhibitions. Charrette and design workshops[5] which actively involve people in working out planning solutions for themselves, rather than simply responding to proposals put forward by municipalities or developers, provide a good example of this.

At Upton in Northamptonshire, for example (see Chapter 11), the Prince's Foundation and English Partnerships promoted the concept of 'Enquiry by Design', in which all relevant stakeholders helped to masterplan a sustainable urban extension through an intensive process of discussion, site visits and design workshops (Adams *et al.* 2011b). This approach brought together landowners, local authorities, community representatives and local people at two such events held in 1999 and 2001. With the assistance of an international team of planners, highway engineers, architects and surveyors led by independent designers/ facilitators, it proved possible for conflicts of interest to be addressed and co-operative solutions to emerge. According to participants, the process proved simultaneous and interactive, in contrast to the normally sequential and reactive nature of the statutory planning system.

At Vauban in Germany, Freiburg City Council deliberately embarked on an extensive citizen engagement process soon after it had acquired a 40-hectare former military site in the early 1990s. Forum Vauban, a non-profit-making local community organisation, applied to co-ordinate this, and, in 1995, the city council made it the official body for the consultation process. From 1999, Forum Vauban also became responsible for community development within the new neighbour-hood. Combined with a publicity campaign, the participation process mobilised prospective residents to meet, to contribute their ideas and to form housing co-operatives. Citizen engagement was promoted through a series of workshops and study visits as well as through newsletters and general public activism. Forum Vauban thus acted as joint place promoter, offering critical support to the city council, with its energy and activism pushing officials and politicians further than they might otherwise have gone.

Of course, stakeholder engagement does not readily overcome intense conflict of interest, whether attributable to development interests simply concerned to maximise their own profits or to amenity interests seeking to protect cherished environments. However, as the NHPAU (2010) discovered, support for new development may be much higher than is often thought, provided that new homes are matched by investment in new schools, health facilities and so on. Through the processes of negotiation or mediation which acknowledge that development interests often have broader motives than immediate profit making and that community or environmental interests are not always self-interested NIMBYs, it may well be possible to reach an agreed solution.

One relevant case study which shows how, with time and patience, mediation can apply to even the most controversial of cases, concerns Vienna International Airport (Participation and Sustainable Development in Europe 2005). Proposals for a third runway generated intense controversy from 1998 onwards, especially around noise pollution. A mediation forum was established in 2001 on which fifty stakeholder groups were represented, with a respected independent lawyer acting as mediator. Despite initial suspicion on both sides, open dialogue, including sharing of technical information, helped to rebuild trust and confidence. It then took another four years of careful mediation before the substantive issues of noise amelioration and environmental safeguards were resolved in 2005. In the end, only one stakeholder group refused to sign up to the agreement. Of course, development proposals cannot normally afford the luxury of such a lengthy mediation process, which is another reason why stakeholder engagement needs to be built into the process from the outset.

Delivery capacity

Although successful place governance requires effective leadership with a genuine commitment to stakeholder engagement, places cannot be transformed for the better without the necessary delivery capacity. Powers, resources and expertise are all essential here. In political analysis, power is often seen as 'the ability to influence the behaviour of others in a manner not of their own choosing' (Heywood 2000: 35). In his seminal study of the Aalborg Project, Flyvbjerg (1998) argues that it is essential to investigate how power is exercised, rather simply to identify who holds power and why they do so. Power cannot therefore be reduced to a matter of political supremacy or legislative authority, important as these might be. The enlightened governance of place depends on the creative and combined exercise of different sources of power to persuade, cajole and require development actors to participate in collective action.

Resources are an essential power support. While financial resources are often necessary to reinforce place-making ambitions, this does not imply mere subsidy of private-sector development. In most cases, public finance can play an important investment role, for example in infrastructure provision, but the opportunity for an investment return depends on the effectiveness of institutional arrangements to recoup consequential increases in land value. Another important resource that reinforces the exercise of power in place-making is the extent and quality of information held by the public sector, for example on the strategies and actions of private development actors.

Expertise refers to creative professional knowledge and sound political judgement. Crucially, in shaping places, these must interact at a high enough level to ensure that the exercise of political power is linked to well-specified forms of intervention. In some cases, appropriate professional expertise can be externally sourced on a contractual basis, but even so, its recommendations usually need to be mediated by some high-level in-house specialist advice. Relegating skilled professionals to a lower tier is not conducive to developing strong place-making capacity.

In practice, powers, resources and expertise must be exercised through an appropriate delivery agency. In many parts of Europe, municipalities retain the necessary technical and financial capacity to enable them to play a powerful delivery role in place-making (Adams *et al.* 2011b). In the UK, special development agencies have often had to be established, many directly accountable to central government, in an attempt to stitch together the fragmented state. One explanation of the UK's limited achievements in place-making, compared to its promotion of real estate development, is the lack of democratic capacity and commitment at the local level to ensure the delivery of better places on a consistent, long-term basis. As we next explain, governance capacity is thus essential in order to ensure a proactive rather than reactive relationship with private development actors.

Policy instruments

Only rarely in democratic countries does the state wholly control and direct place production. The British new town experience, recounted earlier, represents the exception, rather than the rule. If the state wishes to see more successful and sustainable places created, it must find ways to influence and modify the behaviour of important development actors. In practice, since the state cannot 'enforce its will on the others over the long run . . . public managers must learn how to create incentives for the outcomes they desire from actors over whom they have only imperfect control' (Salamon 2002: 15). State–market relations are thus central to shaping places, with the state seeking to achieve its policies by modifying what might be termed 'the decision environment' of key development actors. In Chapter 2 we equated this to 'second-order' design. As a means of intervention in the real estate development process, spatial planning makes an important contribution to this. It can be particularly effective where linked to other development roles that the State can adopt (Table 6.1). Moreover, shaping places goes well beyond what has often been characterised as regulatory planning and requires the combined deployment of a range of policy instruments, carefully selected from those outlined in this section.

Possessing appropriate instruments

Elmore (1987: 175) argues that it is important 'not to equate the term "instrument" with the term "policy", lest people confuse elements with compounds'. While policies specify the ends that governments may wish to achieve, instruments are about the means. As Elmore (1987: 175) explains, 'policies are typically composed of a variety of instruments', sometimes stuck together by the logic of coalition politics, sometimes combined into a more coherent package that 'carries a distinctive message and considerable impact'. The 'tools approach' in public policy focuses on the range of tools, instruments, mechanisms and actions that policy-makers can deploy in response to particular problems and challenges (see, for example, Hood 1983, Hood and Margetts 2007, Howlett 1987, Vedung 2007).

TABLE 6.1 Potential roles of the state in the development process

Role	Example
Building contractor	The state may retain a direct labour force to undertake specific types of construction.
Funder	The state may fund development for its own occupation and for occupation by others if considered socially desirable, for example in the case of affordable housing.
Infrastructure provider	State agencies may provide roads and sewers to service potential development sites.
Investor	State pension funds may be invested in real estate.
Land developer	State agencies may subdivide large development sites into suitable parcels for sale.
Landowner	The state may market its own landholdings for development by others.
Occupier	Growth in the state bureaucracy can fuel demand for new offices.
Parcel developer	State agencies may construct or commission schools, hospitals, libraries etc.
Politician	Political leaders may introduce policies to stimulate the overall level of development, or development of particular types or in particular location.
Regulator	Development permits may be required from the state before construction can begin.

Although the terms 'tools' and 'instruments' are used interchangeably in the literature, we consider that the term 'instrument' implies greater precision, although we still refer to the 'tools approach'.

At the beginning of this chapter, we set out to understand why successful places are not created more consistently, especially since doing so is economically, as well as socially and environmentally, advantageous. Let us assume for the moment that governments would wish to see enhancement rather than deterioration in the quality of places, much as they would hope to promote improvement rather than decline in people's quality of life and standard of living. So, if the policy direction is clear, why is it not necessarily achieved? According to the 'tools approach', this may well be because the tool-box used by governments is in some way deficient or, even if complete, is not put to effective use. To test whether this is the case, we need to know what is, or what potentially could be, within that tool-box. In other words, classifying potential policy instruments helps governments to select the appropriate instrument(s) for policy delivery in addition to providing policy researchers with an analytical frame to evaluate policy effectiveness. Significantly, a well-constructed classification may reveal gaps in the government tool-box. This is important because, without knowledge of the full repertoire of potential policy instruments, governments tend to rely on those which are most familiar, whether they are successful or not. So if we really want to steer real estate development towards policy-shaped rather than market-led outcomes, it may well be necessary to broaden the range of policy instruments that governments deploy or have at their disposal.

Many classifications of policy instruments or actions start with government actions and work 'outwards' and 'downwards'. In other words, they begin with the actions, choices or resources that are available to government to address policy problems. In the planning field, previous classifications by Lichfield and Darin-Drabkin (1980), Healey *et al.* (1988) and Vigar *et al.* (2000) (see Adams *et al.* 2003: 49–53 for a detailed review) follow this approach by concentrating on how particular forms of state intervention seek to address market failure. These classifications present a valuable picture of what governments might imagine to be in their tool-box. However, as an alternative to this 'forward-mapping' exercise, which starts with government actions, Elmore (1987) suggests a 'backward-mapping' approach, which starts at the policy problem, considers the actors closest to that problem and then asks what policy instruments are available to shape, compel, constrain or incite their behaviour, choices and actions. This is the approach we now take in classifying what might really be in the government tool-box.

Selecting appropriate instruments

Applying Elmore's (1987) 'backward-mapping' approach to place-making high-lights the importance of classifying policy instruments by their impact on the decision environment of development actors, and specifically on the extent to which they open up or close down opportunities for autonomous action. For example, we may wish to enquire whether particular instruments operate by ensuring that actors *have* to provide better-quality development, *want* to do so or calculate that it is *worth* doing so. As this suggests, while some policy instruments may seek to change behaviour by coercive means, others may operate more subtly, through persuasion or remuneration. So, within an effective policy armoury, 'sticks' may need to be supplemented by 'sermons' and 'carrots' (Bemelmans-Videc *et al.* 2007, Vedung 2007). To understand the operation of policy instruments, we therefore need to look at how decision environments are constituted and reconstituted over time.

We suggested in Chapter 5 that real estate development can be conceptualised as a set of seven interconnected markets across which eight different types of interest operate (see Figure 5.8). These interests are essentially development roles, such as those of the developer, landowner and investor, which may be played separately or in combination. Actors do not have complete freedom to perform their roles as they themselves might wish, but are bounded by the resources to which they have access, the rules that they acknowledge and which constrain their actions, and the prevailing values and ideas that people hold about the built and natural environment (Healey and Barrett 1990). Rules, for example, may be imposed externally (for example, through planning requirements) or internally (for example, through a company's preferred balance between risk and reward). They may operate either as formal rules and sanctions monitored by a supervisory authority (termed 'regimes'), or informal, but widely held, customs and conventions (termed 'cultures'). For example, while statutory enforcement is an example of a regime, fear of bankruptcy may serve as a cultural restraint on actions.

Such structural forces delineate each actor's decision environment, which can be equated to their 'opportunity space' or scope for autonomous action. Of course, each actor is constantly pushing at the boundaries of their opportunity space and looking for innovative ways to enlarge it. As Healey and Barrett (1990) argue, what actors can achieve is not simply determined by structural forces, since, over time, such forces themselves are continuously shaped and changed by what people can achieve. However, as Jessop (2001) contends, the extent to which actors can challenge and break free from structural constraints can be highly variable over time and space, and indeed between different actors (see Chapter 5). We can compare policy instruments, and evaluate their effectiveness, by thinking how they frame this constant interaction between structure and agency.

The four main types of policy instrument

It is in this context that we have developed and tested an approach which classifies policy instruments into four types according to how they each impact on the decision environments of development actors (see Adams *et al.* 2003, 2005, 2009a and 2012a, Tiesdell and Adams, 2004, Tiesdell and Allmendinger 2005). Shaping places involves deploying these four types of instrument to shape, regulate or stimulate market behaviour or build capacity to do so (Table 6.2). Chapters 10 to 14 explain in detail how they can each be operated to deliver more successful and sustainable places. In this section, we provide a brief introduction to each type of instrument as a summary of our approach to state–market relations in place governance.

In reality, these four types of instruments are often brought together in packages to support particular policy objectives. Yet, the design and choice of such policy instruments, both generally and when applied to particular circumstances, is never a primarily technical exercise. Instead, as must be emphasised, the use of a particular policy instrument is an essentially political decision, and one that is often highly contested. Over time, particular instruments come into or fall out of favour, or are subject to significant modification in their use (see, for example, the discussion of development plans in Chapter 10 and of planning gain in Chapter 12).

TABLE 6.2 Classification of policy instruments

Types of instrument	Common components
Shaping instruments Shape decision environment of individual development actors by setting broad context for market actions and transactions	• Making clear what kinds of places governments wish to see developed, through the publication of plans, strategies, visions and similar documents • Restructuring the institutional environment of real estate markets, for example, by making changes to property rights or taxation systems • Delivering strategic market transformation in the sense of radically changing what market actors consider achievable in particular locations
Regulatory instruments Constrain decision environment of individual development actors by regulating or controlling market actions and transactions	• Choice between public regulation by statute or private regulation by contract • Choice between preventative regulation, restricting detrimental action or directive regulation, requiring desirable action • Choice between regulation of activities to restrict harmful impact or actors to restrict unlicensed production • Choice between sequential regulation of different aspects of same activity or integrated regulation of different aspects of same activity • Choice between seeking to manage activity or eradicate activity • Choice between elective or mandatory enforcement • Choice between regulation based on case-by-case assessment or on meeting common rules or standards
Stimulus instruments Expand decision environment of individual development actors by facilitating market actions and transactions	• Direct state actions to stimulate new development in locations that would otherwise be avoided by market actors, such as reclamation, infrastructure provision, land acquisition and assembly, and land disposal • Price-adjusting instruments impacting on projected costs and revenues in development appraisal, such as development grants, tax incentives and project bonuses • Risk-reducing instruments seeking to overcome negative risk perceptions in particular areas by ensuring accurate market information, policy certainty and stability, demonstration projects and environmental improvements, and holistic place management

Types of instrument	Common components
	• Capital-raising instruments to provide or facilitate access to development finance, including loan guarantees, revolving loan funds, and public-private development partnerships
Capacity-building instruments Enable development actors to operate more effectively within their decision environments and so facilitate the operation of other policy instruments	• Market-shaping cultures, mindsets and ideas – looking afresh at cultural perspectives or ways of thinking
	• Market-rooted networks enhancing relations across the development spectrum
	• Market-rich information and knowledge about how place quality can be influenced through market and development processes
	• Market-relevant skills and capabilities – developing human capital and enhancing the skills and abilities of key individuals and organisations

Policy instruments intended to shape market behaviour

The first type of policy instrument seeks to shape the decision environment of individual development actors by setting the broad context for market actions and transactions. They concentrate on modifying the behaviour of individual actors by changing the institutional 'rules of the game' by which they operate. As they interpret and respond to such rule changes, actors find that their decision environment is recalibrated and their scope for autonomous action is refigured.

In Chapters 10 and 11 we identify three main sets of shaping instruments that have been deployed as 'game changers' to help create better places through modifying the behaviour of market actors. The first makes clear what kind of places governments wish to see developed through the publications of plans, strategies, visions and similar documents. The second seeks to restructure the institutional environment of real estate markets, for example by making changes to property rights or taxation systems. The third aims to deliver strategic market transformation in the sense of radically changing what market actors consider achievable in particular locations.

Policy instruments intended to regulate market behaviour

The second type of policy instrument constrains the decision environment of individual development actors by regulating or controlling market actions and transactions. Regulatory instruments are those that seek to compel, manage or eradicate certain activities or aspects of those activities, so limiting actors' scope for autonomous action. Regulatory instruments are normally supported by enforcement procedures so as to ensure that regulatory intentions are achieved. In Chapter 12 we set out seven regulatory choices open to governments and consider their impact on development.

Policy instruments intended to stimulate market behaviour

The third type of policy instrument facilitates market actions and transactions by expanding the decision environment of individual development actors. Stimulus instruments increase the likelihood of some desired event happening by making some actions more (or sometimes less) rewarding to particular development actors. They thus impact directly on financial appraisals. In Chapter 13 we review four main sets of stimulus action that can be taken to encourage development. The first involve direct state actions to kick-start the development process, for example by resolving physical, infrastructural or ownership constraints. The other three are more indirect and seek to change the pattern of incentives that motivate the locations or types of development in which market actors are most interested. They achieve this by altering the outcome of financial appraisals of development through price-adjusting, risk-reducing and capital-raising actions.

Policy instruments intended to build capacity

Capacity building enables development actors to operate more effectively within their decision environments. Market-shaping, market-regulation and market-stimulus instruments are only as effective as the people and organisations charged with their delivery. Capacity-building actions are a means of facilitating the better operation of these other policy instruments. The effect of future regulation and stimulus actions, for example, may depend on an institutional and human capacity that does not presently exist – hence, appropriate capacity building is a condition of future success (Elmore 1987: 178). Chapter 14 concentrates on building planners' capacity in four crucial areas: market-shaping cultures, mindsets and ideas; market-rich information and knowledge; market-rooted networks; and market-relevant skills and capabilities.

Conclusions

This chapter has contended that, if we wish to understand how places come about, we need to investigate how the dominant mode of governance at the time of their production interacts with the dynamics of real estate markets. Place governance is a highly challenging activity with the potential to create much better places, but also to produce much worse ones. It is possible to look with dismay on some of the places produced by bureaucratic or neo-liberal forms of governance, yet still believe that governments can help to create more successful and sustainable places if they are well-equipped to tackle market weaknesses. Indeed, for many of those committed to bringing about better-quality places and higher standards of development, the essential question is not whether, but how, governments should be involved in place-making.

Although unsustainable places are still created all too often, important signs of hope can be recognised in recent debates around the governance of place. It is now understood, for example, that a visionary, integrative, inclusive and action-orientated approach to planning the future of places needs to replace mere reliance on land-use regulation. It is widely accepted that this must be supported by effective place leadership, by genuine stakeholder engagement and by the capacity and determination to act in transforming the decision environment of key development actors. To achieve this, it is recognised that a well-stocked box of policy tools or instruments needs to be available so as to enable policy-makers to select whatever combination is necessary for the circumstances, rather than find their ability to act constrained by a shortage of tools.

As all this suggests, creating successful and sustainable places, and indeed successful and sustainable cities, is a complex and demanding task which requires a reflective and flexible place-making culture. Where governments fail, it is often because they are tempted to adopt what appear at the time to be familiar and easy solutions. Where governments succeed, it is usually because they appreciate the innovative and complex nature of place-making and so match high ambition with realistic endeavour.

PART 2

MARKET ROLES AND ACTORS

7 Real estate developers

Introduction

In May 2009, a controversial North of England property developer with links to a then government minister attracted national press attention. According to one prominent story, the developer, Tahir Zaman, had left school with a couple of GCSEs, but by the age of 37 had built up a large property portfolio with around 100 tenants. However, a court appearance in which he pleaded guilty to letting out uninhabitable property damaged his reputation. Around the same time, he was also found to have contravened planning law. Although he was formally declared bankrupt in 2007, this was annulled a year later. Mr Zaman then retreated to spend much of his time in Dubai (Rayner and Gemmell 2009).

This story encapsulates much of what public imagination considers a property developer to be, with its narrative of the self-made entrepreneur with limited education whose business is characterised by financial duplicity, disdain for authority and contempt for tenants, and whose personal lifestyle is touched by the distant and exotic. Such images would be mere ingredients of legend and novel, were it not for intense political interest both in the products of the development industry and in the ability of politicians to shape, regulate and stimulate the development industry through the planning system and related forms of public intervention.

This chapter seeks to disentangle the reality of life as a developer from the more far-fetched myths, whether promoted by the press or generated from within the industry itself. It offers a critical account of the extent to which developers (or rather, different kinds of developers) are genuinely committed to delivering better-quality places, rather than merely extracting financial reward at the expense of place quality. As a starting point, it seeks to understand developers better, in relation to both their roles in the development process and their own particular characteristics. It moves on to compare the still largely distinct sectors of commercial and residential development and to investigate some of the strategies adopted by developers to make a success of their businesses. The chapter then seeks to assess the potential commitment of developers to place quality before concluding with a review of the extent to which industry priorities and practices are open to policy influence.

Understanding developers

Roles of the developer

As Chapter 5 explained, real estate developers can potentially play up to four different roles in the development process (Figure 7.1). These are:

- master developer (also known as the land developer) – operates strategically, planning and driving forward the overall development of a substantial area (see Box 7.1 for an example);
- infrastructure provider – ensures provision of roads, sewers and other major investment across the development area as a whole;

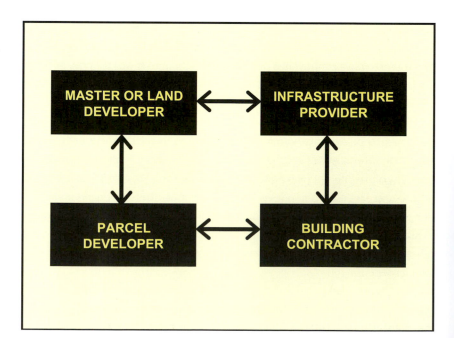

FIGURE 7.1
Four roles potentially played by real estate developers.

- parcel developer – organises the development of particular parcels or sites;
- building contractor – constructs the actual homes, shops and offices etc.

These are, essentially, conceptual divisions which help us to understand the range of tasks that may need to be undertaken in order to make development happen. There can be substantial variation from one development project to another, and indeed from one country to another, in how these four roles are carried out and which are considered necessary in particular circumstances. Such variations concern, for example:

BOX 7.1 Gallagher Estates

Gallagher Estates is one of the UK's largest master developers, with a land portfolio equivalent to 32,000 residential plots. Alongside Gallagher Developments, it forms half of Gallagher UK, a £450 million privately owned property development and investment company based in the West Midlands. Chairman Tony Gallagher was estimated by the *Birmingham Post* in 2010 to have a personal fortune of £500 million, placing him tenth of the region's 'rich list'.

Gallagher Estates oversees all aspects of the development process, including land assembly, masterplanning and strategic infrastructure provision. It is involved in about 50 projects at both brownfield and greenfield locations across the UK. As master developer, Gallagher Estates takes responsibility for delivering schools, health facilities, open space, affordable housing and other community facilities required for development. Parcel developers who buy land from the company are required by contracts of sale to follow the detailed design codes agreed with the relevant local authorities.

Two of Gallagher's biggest projects involve new settlements in English growth areas. At Northstowe just outside Cambridge, Gallagher Estates is working with the Homes and Communities Agency on plans for a sustainable new community of about 9,500 new homes. At a second location, Wixams, just south of Bedford (Figure 7.2), Gallagher entered into a joint venture partnership with landowner RWE npower to masterplan a new settlement of about 4,500 homes (25 per cent of which will be affordable). Gallagher will ensure delivery of employment land, schools, shops, open space, community facilities and a new rail station. Work at Wixams started in 2009, with housebuilders Bloor, Miller and Taylor Wimpey, along with Bedford Pilgrim's Housing Association, among those who bought development parcels.

FIGURE 7.2
Land development
underway at Wixams,
Bedfordshire, England.
(Richard Pool)

- the scale at which development is thought to require a master developer as well as individual parcel developers;
- whether the roles of master developer, infrastructure provider and parcel developer are played by the same or different actors;[1]
- whether the roles of parcel developer and building contractor are played by the same or different actors;
- the extent to which the state becomes directly involved in development, usually as master developer or infrastructure provider, but sometimes also as parcel developer and even as building contractor.

Actors are the individuals and organisations who carry out these roles, whether based in the private or public sectors. They include, for example, a private individual or development company concentrating on particular projects and a local authority or public development agency driving forward the development of a whole new urban quarter. Since those who act as parcel developers and/or master developers have considerable potential to shape the future of places, it is important to understand what drives their behaviour. For the sake of simplicity, we call these actors 'real estate developers', whether or not they themselves also act as infrastructure providers or building contractors. In the UK, on which this chapter is primarily focused, real estate developers are located mainly in the private sector and occasionally in the public sector. We therefore concentrate on the strategies and actions of those in the private sector and include those in the public sector only where we make explicit reference to them.

Developer characteristics

Real estate developers are considered by many to play a crucial role in the production of the built environment. Their expertise is seen to lie in spotting development opportunities (location), knowing the target market (product) and resolving constraints to make things happen when required (timing). As Chapter 4 thus explained, successful development is not solely about the old adage of 'location, location, location', but is instead concerned with the broader issues of 'location, product and timing'. Developers are thus often portrayed as impresarios, orchestrating the development performance by bringing capital, labour and rights in land together to create the right product in the right place at the right time (Marriot 1967, Ross Goobey 1992). Fainstein (1994: 218) takes up this analogy, arguing that 'the development industry resembles the entertainment business more than heavy manufacturing in having a profound cultural influence, in the singularity of each item produced, and in the process by which the elements of a project are combined'. Many developers would no doubt take pleasure in Fainstein's comparison of their business to that of film production, especially with its connotations of glamour and excitement, along with the promise of riches beyond measure for the best-known celebrities.

What personal characteristics distinguish the successful developer from the unsuccessful one? Millington (2000) lists ten qualities needed to make a successful real estate developer, of which four (thorough knowledge and understanding of markets, construction and finance along with management ability) relate primarily to the development process. The other six are essentially aspects of personality and consist of optimism, imagination and practical vision, judgement, decision-making ability, courage and a 'thick skin'. Interestingly, Millington recounts how, having presented his original list at a conference, he was approached by two prominent developers who suggested that the only relevant quality missing was 'a sense of humour'.

Such anecdotes emphasise the importance of individuality to successful development and suggest that the industry is exemplified by such atomised behaviour that anyone with the right frame of mind can make a success of the business. Certainly, as Coiacetto (2009) points out, development companies are often not large organisations, since one person with a phone and good contacts can be just as successful in orchestrating the development performance as a large corporation. However, if too much emphasis is placed on the individuality of developers, the significance of collective behaviour may be overlooked.

This is because a powerful 'herd instinct' often seems to drive activity within the industry. Many developers are reluctant to depart from standard development products until a market leader has successfully established a product innovation, at which point it is then widely replicated. The strong collective psyche among developers also has the potential to create waves of over-development at the height of an upturn. An important cause of this is over-reliance on trend extrapolation in inflating profit expectations (Henneberry and Rowley 2002). This implies that individual developers convince themselves, and indeed each other, that upward market trends are likely to continue for the foreseeable future. In such circumstances, it takes much wisdom and determination to stand out against the crowd. This is why some argue that, in order to survive and grow over the long-term, individual developers essentially require the necessary anticipation and common sense to avoid over-development in a downturn. Wellings (2006: 249), for example, places 'the judgement qualities of entrepreneurs at critical points in the housing cycle' alongside personal motivation, financial incentives and stock market pressures in explaining the growth and decline of individual housebuilders over time. In understanding how real estate developers help to shape places, it is thus important to recognise that what Guy *et al.* (2002) call 'development cultures' can be just as influential as the strategies pursued by individual developers.

The structure of the development industry

The tradition of sectoral distinctiveness

In the UK at least, there has been a long-standing distinction between developers who build new homes and those who concentrate on commercial, leisure and business property. From a North American perspective, Beauregard (2005: 2433) too points out that 'the disaggregation of property markets into sub-markets or sectors – also called property types – is so common as to be unquestioned and unexamined'. His explanation mixes the structural characteristics of a complex development market, in which 'developers and investors in one sector are likely to respond to market signals at variance with their counterparts in other sectors', with the agency need of individual developers to manage risk and contain their information requirements.[2]

Although Havard (2008) argues that the recent trend towards city-centre living has helped to break down some of the barriers between commercial and residential developers, he still maintains the importance of the distinction. Genuine and experienced mixed-use developers remain relatively rare in the UK, making genuine mixed-use development hard to achieve. With this in mind, we now concentrate on how the commercial and residential sectors have evolved and now operate.

The commercial development sector

A specialist commercial development sector, concentrating on the production of new shops and offices to rent, is reflective of the transformation of an economy from a manufacturing to service base. In the UK, the sector grew rapidly from the mid-1950s onwards, often partnering local authorities that were keen to transform run-down and war-damaged city centres through the development of pristine new shopping centres and office blocks. In a classic text, Marriot (1967) captures the spirit of the wheeler-dealer property tycoon of the 1950s, listing over 100 ordinary individuals each of whom became property millionaires in a few years. As companies founded in this period matured, they increasingly sought to retain completed developments as landlord, and so to create an investment portfolio comprised largely of properties they had themselves built. This highlights an important distinction which still persists within the commercial development sector between companies that are essentially dealers or traders (and that are usually of more recent origin) and those that combine development with investment (and that usually are longer established) (Adams 1994, McNamara 1983).

Dealing in real estate often precedes expansion into development of real estate. Pure dealers continuously buy and sell property on a short-term basis, without undertaking development. They profit by adding value between purchase and sale, for example, by restructuring a lease, improving a planning consent or assembling a development site. Dealers who begin to undertake development evolve into developer/dealers or trader–developers, moving on from one scheme to the next without retaining long-term interest (Box 7.2 and Figure 7.3). A trader–developer spots the development potential of a site, acquires the rights in land, commissions the design, seeks planning consent, lets the building contract, provides project management and, on completion, sells or lets the development. If the completed development is let to tenants, the trader–developer sells out as landlord to an investor. Profits are normally reinvested by trader–developers to produce rapid expansion. Such developers generally have a transient interest in place-making.

Indicative Masterplan

FIGURE 7.3
Gateway Park masterplan, Peterborough, England. Roxhill's masterplan attempts to soften the impact of large distribution units with extensive tree planting. (Roxhill Developments Ltd)

BOX 7.2 Roxhill Developments

Roxhill Developments demonstrates how quickly those with the necessary experience and contacts in real estate development can establish new companies and attract substantial business. Roxhill is a trader–developer concentrating on industrial and warehouse development that was founded in 2010 by David Keir, who, during 25 years of experience in the industry, had founded or co-founded three previous development companies that had then been sold on to larger organisations. To establish Roxhill, Keir gathered together a small management team, most of whom had previously worked for him, and persuaded two real estate finance and investment companies to partner the management team in investing £40 million of equity in the new company. This enabled the immediate acquisition of around 110 hectares of potential development land, which was supplemented by options, conditional contracts and management agreements on a further 330 hectares.

From his experience, Keir foresaw a shortage of high-quality distribution warehouses, especially for large retailers, and knew that only three or four other developers were active in the field. Roxhill's prospective development sites are almost all in the English Midlands, located close to motorways or major trunk roads, with some having rail freight facilities. As an exception, Roxhill has entered into a joint venture partnership with Moray Estates (see Chapter 8) and others to develop a business park at Inverness Airport. Roxhill's sites are capable of accommodating individual 'sheds' of between 5,000m^2 and 100,000m^2. Almost all of these are at greenfield locations, highlighting the importance of planning and infrastructure expertise, which the company claims amongst its strengths. Roxhill also specialises in fast-track construction and in sustainable design with high energy efficiency ratings. Completed developments will either be sold or let to occupiers, with the latter associated with an investment sale.

Roxhill's largest development is a 100 hectare strategic warehousing and distribution park located immediately adjacent to the A1M at Peterborough. Known as Gateway Park (Figure 7.3), it will accommodate a range of sheds up to 100,000m^2 within an unusual amount of landscaping for what is, essentially, an industrial estate.

Developer/investors typically hold and manage completed developments, retaining the full equity as a long-term investment (Box 7.3 and Figure 7.4). Such companies have grown and diversified over many years, often by taking over smaller firms in the process. They comprise the most influential and well-

BOX 7.3 Land Securities

Land Securities is the UK's largest commercial development and investment company, with a market capitalisation of over £5 billion. Founded by Harold (later Lord) Samuel in 1944, the company grew rapidly in the postwar property boom, focusing on the development of central London offices and provincial shopping centres. This created the base of a strong investment portfolio, which has enabled Land Securities to ride out subsequent booms and slumps with varying degrees of comfort. In 2007 it converted to become a Real Estate Investment Trust, but still remains listed in the FTSE 100 top UK companies.

Within London, Land Securities owns about 9.5 million square feet of office and retail accommodation valued at around £5.5 billion. Some 13 major development projects have recently been finished in London or are in course of preparation, reflecting the company's financial strength even in economically challenging times and its capacity to take advantage of lower construction costs and so have new space ready for the next market upturn. These include a £542 million shopping and office complex in the City of London, known as One New Change, and controversial proposals for a nearby 37-storey commercial office tower, again costing around £500 million and known colloquially as the 'walkie-talkie'.

Outside London, the company owns twenty-five shopping centres and twenty retail parks providing around 20.6 million square feet of accommodation and worth around £4.8 billion. Major shopping centres completed in recent years include St David's in Cardiff and Cabot Circus in Bristol (Figure 7.4).

Design quality is central to Land Securities' mission, as the tenants it seeks to attract are primarily global businesses, government departments and top retail brands. For example, an international architectural competition held to select the architect of One New Change was won by Jean Nouvel, one of the world's best-known modernist architects. The company's interpretation of design is focused on the architectural quality and environmental sustainability of its own developments, with interest in broader urban design largely confined to matters that can add value to its assets. As an investor, Land Securities is also constantly seeking to enhance the investment returns from its property portfolio, and to ensure that they outperform industry benchmarks, through both active asset management and strategic purchase and disposals of particular schemes.

FIGURE 7.4
Cabot Circus Shopping
Centre, Bristol City
Centre, England. Built at a
cost of £500 million, this
development provides
over 110,000m² of retail
and leisure floorspace,
with 140 shops, 25
restaurants, 250
apartments, offices,
student housing, a cinema
and a hotel. (Nick
Townsend, used
under the Creative
Commons licence)

established commercial development companies, many of whom now operate as Real Estate Investment Trusts (REITs).[3] The strength and reliability of investment income, protected even in a recession by long-term leases, shields developer/investors from the full force of a development downturn, to which trader–developers are exposed. To benefit from rental and capital growth, developer/investors concentrate on prime property built to the highest-quality design and specification, with subsequent occupancy restricted to tenants considered unlikely to default on rent payments. Developer/investors are matched in their strategies and actions by investor/developers who comprise those institutional investors (mainly insurance companies and pension funds) who, from time to time, undertake development themselves, rather than simply purchase completed projects from trader–developers.

As a general rule, the more established a development company, the greater its aversion to risk (see Chapter 5), whether in relation to product or location. For example, Guy *et al.* (2002: 1187) found that investors' own familiarity and proximity to 'all things London' appeared just as important as formal analysis in accounting for their disproportionate real estate investment in London and the South-East. Even when London-based capital was prepared to venture further north, to the regional capital of Manchester, its interest was largely confined to the well-established central office core, in contrast to independent local developers, whose collective culture encouraged innovative schemes in fringe locations.

As this suggests, shaping places may be dependent on different types of developer in different locations. Creating entirely new places or regenerating older ones can appear riskier than reinforcing already well-established locations.

This explains why trader–developers have generally been more involved in urban regeneration than developer/investors. Yet, policy-makers must also bear in mind that trader–developers are generally more fragile than developer/investors and that over-exposure to development risk can leave them prone to bankruptcy in a downturn.

The residential development sector

The growth of speculative residential development[4] can be traced to the early nineteenth century, when industrial methods of building replaced traditional craft production (Clarke 1992). Speculative housebuilding for rent, dominant throughout the nineteenth century, declined sharply in the decade before the First World War. After 1920, social and economic benefits encouraged the rapid expansion of speculative housebuilding for sale. With owner occupation increasing from 26 per cent of households in 1946 to 71 per cent in 2007, the post-Second World War period saw significant further growth in the industry (Wellings 2006). Speculative housebuilders are now responsible for much of the new urban form of Britain. Indeed, between 1990/91 and 2007/08, almost 2.95 million new homes across the UK were built by private developers, accounting for 85 per cent of all housing production (DCLG 2009).

Significantly, this new residential Britain was disproportionately produced by a small number of very large companies. Although there are about 18,000 housebuilders registered with the National House Building Council (NHBC), speculative production of new homes is dominated by only a few major companies, each with an annual output of 500 units or more. In 2000, for example, 71 per cent of all newly completed private homes across the UK were built by only forty-three 'major builders', each with an annual output of 500 or more units (Wellings 2001). The collective market share of the largest fifteen of these companies, each producing 2,000 or more units annually and classed as 'volume builders', had by then reached almost 50 per cent. By 2006, the ten largest companies were responsible for 58 per cent of output (Calcutt, 2007). Significantly, none of these companies succumbed to the economic downturn from 2008, although several required intensive support from their bankers to survive. However, by 2011, Persimmon (see Box 7.4 and Figure 7.5), the market leader in 2006, had returned to profitability, even though its production levels were still just over half of what the company had achieved at the height of the boom.

The increasing importance of large housebuilding capital was originally noticed by Ball (1983), who explained the relative growth of larger producers by their ready access to finance capital, often supplied by parent companies. In contrast, small and medium-sized producers were dependent for finance on the banks, which restricted the availability of capital, especially during cyclical downturns. According to Ball (1983), such financial constraints prevented small and medium-sized

BOX 7.4 Persimmon

Persimmon is one of the UK's top three housebuilders, which operates out of twenty-five regional offices across England, Wales and Scotland and is listed in the FTSE 250 top UK companies. It sold almost 9,500 new homes in 2010 from some 380 separate development sites. Its main Persimmon brand is augmented at the luxury end of the market by Charles Church Homes and in the social sector by Westbury Partnerships, which concentrates on building affordable housing in partnership with housing associations. The latter two brands account for about 20 per cent of output each, with the remaining 60 per cent coming from the main Persimmon brand.

The company was founded by Duncan Davidson in 1973 in York, where its headquarters are still based. It grew gradually until the mid-1990s, when its unit sales reached about 3,500. Successive acquisition of rival companies, including Ideal Homes in 1996, Beazer in 2001 and Westbury in 2006, took Persimmon's output to a record 16,700 units in 2006, making it then the UK's largest housebuilder. However, as John White, its chairman at the time, later admitted, 'One of the mistakes was that we were all sucked into this requirement for more new homes' (Kollewe 2011: 1). As the economic recession deepened and the housing market slumped, Persimmon's completions fell by 46 per cent between 2006 and 2009, reducing its annual revenue from £3.1 billion to £1.4 billion. A pre-tax profit of about £585 million in 2007 turned into a pre-tax loss of £780 million the following year, taking account of exceptional items including a £650 million write-down in the value of land and work in progress.

An agreement with its bankers at the start of 2009 provided new credit facilities of just over £1 billion and enabled Persimmon to restructure and survive the recession. Employment more than halved, to 2,400, while the company's debt was gradually reduced to nearly zero. By 2011, Persimmon was back in action, having spent around £290 million on land purchases the previous year and opening seventy new building sites in the first half of 2011. Its growth strategy is now focused on smaller, cheaper homes with an average price of just over £160,000. Although around 60 per cent of Persimmon homes are built on brownfield land, it has turned away from flats, which now account for only about 20 per cent of sales. With a current land bank of over 62,000 building plots (25,000 of which have been bought since the downturn) Persimmon is well placed to benefit from any upturn in the housing market. Its future development approach is likely to reflect a gradual evolution rather than a major change from the strategy that has accounted for the company's substantial growth over the past four decades.

FIGURE 7.5
Lomond Gate housing development, Dumbarton, Scotland. Persimmon commenced this brownfield development in 2011, demonstrating the company's confidence that the housing market had by then emerged from recession. These four-bedroom detached houses, which were marketed at £225,000, are symbolic of the standardisation of production in speculative housebuilding. (David Adams)

builders from taking advantage of booms and slumps in the same way as larger companies, which had the ability to acquire greenfield land cheaply during periods of slump and, as a result, were well placed to sell houses early in a boom. Golland and Boelhouwer (2002), who compared housing-market systems in the Netherlands and UK from 1975 to 1997, also emphasised the importance of land supply in explaining why the industry's structure and organisation differ significantly between the two countries. Whereas the public sector played the major role in land supply in the Netherlands, the UK speculative housebuilding industry has long depended on securing its own access to land.

Success in the land market is indeed crucial to the commercial prospects of any housebuilder. Yet, of all the raw materials required for housebuilding, land is the most problematic to source. It is used extensively, its quality is heterogeneous and its supply is fraught with uncertainty. It cannot simply be ordered 'off the peg' like bricks or other raw materials. Indeed, its sale may never be publicly advertised, let alone take place through open auction. Its successful acquisition requires both specialist expertise and significant resources. Most housebuilders try to secure their land supplies at least two to three years in advance, often by entering into options or conditional contracts with vendors, so delaying outright purchase until nearer the commencement of construction. To source land, companies maintain teams of land buyers and rely extensively on networks with landowners, planners and agents and other developers.

Networks matter in speculative housebuilding, since not all residential development land (or even perhaps a substantial proportion of it) is ever openly marketed. In any event, networks provide an opportunity to subvert market competition, since extensive personal contacts increase chances of acquisition. This is why, according to one volume housebuilder interviewed for recent research:

'the best way to buy current land is through contacts' (Adams *et al.* 2012b). Another claimed explicitly that 'the success of builders and their activities in the land market are determined by how strong their network is and how well they play that network'. Reliance on networks may not produce land any cheaper than perceived market values, but it reduces risk by protecting housebuilders from what they consider outrageously high bidding behaviour from competitors whose particular circumstances necessitate or favour bullish strategies.

There is little point in acquiring land unless planning permission for its development can eventually be secured. Since the early 1980s, housebuilders have adopted increasingly sophisticated strategies to minimise the risk of planning refusals (Adams *et al.* 1992). These focus on seeking to influence the relevant policy framework, instead of relying on an uncertain development-control system. Substantial investment in planning expertise, either retained in-house or commissioned from planning consultancies (and often with some previous experience of local authority employment) enables a wide range of potential development sites to be identified which might reasonably be expected to be considered by planning authorities for possible release over a period of up to 20 years. Land buyers then set to work to secure options or conditional contracts on as many of these sites as possible.

Such arrangements may last for up to ten or fifteen years, enabling housebuilders to press for the allocation of the sites for development at successive development plan inquiries. The potential rewards from such re-allocation make it worthwhile to reinforce planning expertise with specialist and experienced planning lawyers, who move from inquiry to inquiry, making a handsome return from what are essentially the transaction costs of the planning process. This model has evolved mainly to promote greenfield land release. The recent policy emphasis on brownfield development has reduced success rates at greenfield locations but, ironically, has ensured that those who succeed are even better rewarded.

Brownfield land acquisition presents speculative housebuilders with four particular challenges to these tried and tested methods. First, the very nature of brownfield sites, with their history of previous uses, often results in abnormal site preparation costs, making development appraisal more uncertain. Second, although options and conditional contracts are used to secure vacant land for future redevelopment (and even industrial buildings still in use – see Payne 2009), brownfield owners are less likely to allow developers lengthy periods of time to bargain with planning authorities. Third, if brownfield sites need to be pieced together from parcels in different ownerships, acquisition can be very protracted. Finally, the greater diversity of brownfield land demands more investment in building up the contacts and networks needed to succeed.

Developers and design quality

To what extent are real estate developers interested in design quality? Here, it is important to interpret design broadly, paying heed not simply to aesthetic criteria but technical and functional ones as well (see Chapter 2). Sustainable housing design, for example, is primarily concerned with reducing the 'carbon footprint' of new homes through ensuring more efficient energy usage and facilitating travel by public transport, for example, rather than necessarily with external appearance. Although some housebuilders equate design with improving the 'kerb appeal' of their products by attaching mock features to façades in order to give the pretence of individuality (Goodchild and Karn, 1997), design is a much broader problem-solving process with potentially significant impact on development viability. High-quality, low-maintenance materials, for example, may increase production costs, but over time, such investment should be rewarded by lower maintenance costs and/or higher capital value. However, the perceived costs and returns from better-quality design are not easily assessed by developers and, in any event, can be significantly affected by public policy.

In a classic cartoon, Louis Hellman (1995) portrays the products of the speculative housebuilding industry as having stood still for a hundred years, while all around, remarkable innovation has taken place in other consumer products (Figure 7.6). According to Ball (1999: 9) 'British housebuilding has an exceptionally poor record of innovation in designs and production methods', while Barlow (1999: 23) too chides the industry as 'notoriously slow to innovate'. Housebuilders still appear reluctant to embrace modern methods of construction (Pan *et al.* 2007), although there seems to be greater engagement with the broader sustainability and climate change agenda, especially among the most proactive companies (NextGeneration 2008).

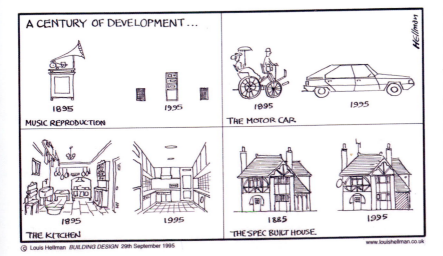

© Louis Hellman *BUILDING DESIGN* 29th September 1995

FIGURE 7.6

A century of development. Drawn in 1995, Louis Hellman's representations of the latest music reproduction, cars and kitchens of the time, compared to a century earlier, now themselves look dated. But speculatively built houses have still not changed that much – see, for example, those at Cambusbarron shown in Figure 2.15, which were built in 2010–11. (Louis Hellman, reproduced from Building Design, 29 September 1995)

Design quality and developer type

In a previous paper (Tiesdell and Adams, 2004), we argued that those who have a transient interest in what is built are likely to be less concerned with design quality than those who have an enduring interest. As a general rule, those who build and sell on new developments on completion will not want to invest in design quality unless it reduces production costs or increases selling prices by at least enough to justify that investment. As the Chief Executive of the British Property Federation commented, 'One of the shortcomings of the build for sale model is that the developer does not retain any interest once the sale is complete and the site is built out. There is therefore no particular incentive to design to any higher quality than that needed to achieve the initial sale: aspects such as public realm and long-term maintainability assume less importance than features such as a double garage' (Peace 2009: 59). In contrast, those who purchase and retain development over the longer term will be keener to see investment in design quality, especially if it is likely to reduce occupancy or later refurbishment costs. Yet, if the preferences of such long-term consumers of the built environment are not strong enough or sufficiently well signalled to its producers, design quality may fall through a production–consumption gap (see below).

This analysis explains why design quality is often (but not always) an important consideration in commercial development. Trader–developers usually find it hard to secure short-term finance for new shops or offices (except at boom times or in boom locations) unless they have already agreed an investment sale and thus a well-marked exit route (see Chapter 9). This creates a powerful bridge over any producer–consumer gap, since it enables the investor to influence design quality and ensures that it is evaluated on a long-term basis. Commercial development undertaken by developer/investors or investor/developers achieves much the same result, but in this case because the actor is both producer and consumer.

Producer–consumer gaps

The analysis also explains why design quality is generally seen as less important in speculative residential development. Extensive producer–consumer gaps arise in the residential sector because purchasers have little direct influence on design and, indeed, their precise identity is rarely known at the time of design. The availability of long-term mortgage finance for residential development is dependent on the income of the purchaser, rather than necessarily on the design quality of the product. Housebuilders may claim that what is built reflects what consumers want, but this is a circular argument that cannot really be tested when very similar products are offered by all the main housebuilders.[5]

Producer–consumer gaps in speculative housebuilding are further exacerbated by shortages of available building land, particularly at pressured times and locations, which has an insidious effect on the industry, making it inherently 'land-focused' rather than 'customer-focused' or 'community-focused'. As Barker (2004: 106) commented: 'When land is in relatively scarce supply, fewer per-missioned sites mean that there will be fewer competing housebuilders in any one area. This can reduce consumer choice. In such situations, competition focuses on land. Once land is secured, competitive pressures are reduced: to a large extent housebuilders can "sell anything".'

Standardisation and sustainability

Since producers rather than the consumers are dominant in housing development, (especially during market upturns, when mortgage finance is more readily available and people scramble to 'get on the housing ladder') mass house design tends to be relegated to a backroom activity undertaken by technicians rather than archi-tects, or increasingly by computer programmes overseen by technicians. Standard house types are thus widely used (Hooper and Nicol, 1999). These comprise two key elements: the structural footprint and the structural façade. By applying different façades to standard footprints, standard houses can be 'dressed' to match the requirements of any site and locality. Hooper and Nicol's detailed interviews with fourteen large housebuilders each producing at least 1,000 units per annum revealed that three companies employed 20–30 standard house types, five companies 30–40 types, another five 50–70 types, while one company used over 100 types. Companies were thus able to vary the standard product mix offered at each site according to the particular target audience. Standardised house types also enable blanket building-control approval, which further limits pre-construction costs and enables accurate cost forecasting when land bids are prepared.

In practice, most housebuilders are interested in better design only if it produces higher sales, wins planning approval more speedily or contributes to marketing strategies. In 2002, the Home Builders Federation (HBF) and the Commission for Architecture and the Built Environment (CABE) jointly established the 'Building-for-Life' initiative, which created a national standard for measuring sustainable and well-designed homes and neighbourhoods, through specifying twenty 'Building-for-Life' criteria that 'embody our vision of functional, attractive and sustainable housing'.[6] Although award-winning exemplars demonstrated commendable progress, the overall impact of the 'Building-for-Life' initiative was limited. Across England as a whole, only 18 per cent of new residential developments audited against the 'Building-for-Life' criteria by 2007 were rated as 'good' or 'very good', while 29 per cent were so poor that, according to CABE (2007), they simply should not have been given planning consent. In his foreword to this report, CABE's Chief Executive commented: 'The housing produced in the first few years of this new century is simply not up to the standard which the government is demanding and which customers have a right to expect. Our research indicates that some things are improving. But the improvement is too little and too slow' (CABE, 2007: 3).[7]

Opportunity space theory

In what circumstances are speculative housebuilders likely to invest in better design expertise, with its greater technical knowledge and its more creative, problem-solving skills? In simple terms, developers themselves will choose to invest in design only if they think it is 'worth it' to the extent of making development more viable. The developer's scope or potential to create a viable development can be visualised as an 'opportunity space'. The larger this space, the easier it becomes to create a viable development (Tiesdell and Adams 2004). As Figure 7.7 shows, the developer's opportunity space is framed by three contexts: the physical context of the development site and its immediate environment, the regulatory context and the market context.

The more constrained these contexts, the harder it becomes to create a viable development, and so the smaller the size of the developer's opportunity space. Of course, the boundaries or 'frontiers' of these contexts are best conceived as fuzzy rather than hard edged, since they ultimately depend on the negotiating abilities of the actors involved, the social dynamics of their relations and the institutional arrangements of the moment. Moreover, while relatively fixed at any time, opportunity spaces are open to transformation over time. This is why, alongside opportunity space, changing 'windows of opportunity' occur as real estate markets improve or deteriorate.

FIGURE 7.7
Developer's opportunity space. Three forces – the physical context of the development site, the regulatory context and the market context – press in and constrain the developer's room for manoeuvre or opportunity space. With few constraints, the space expands, so conferring more autonomy on the developer. In contrast, as sites become more problematic, regulation more demanding and/or markets more competitive, the space shrinks. If such forces eradicate the developer's opportunity space altogether, then development is not feasible at that point in time. (Adapted from Tiesdell and Adams, 2004)

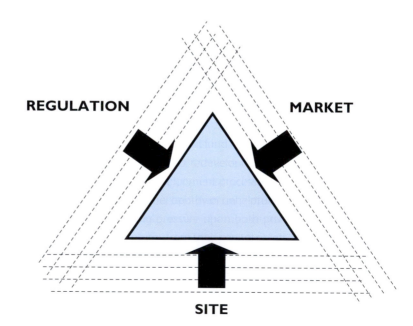

REGULATION   MARKET

SITE

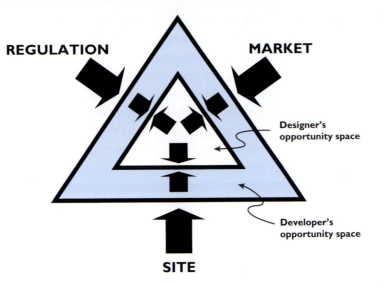

REGULATION

MARKET

Designer's
opportunity space

Developer's
opportunity space

SITE

FIGURE 7.8
Designer's opportunity space. The more challenging the design task, the more a developer needs design expertise in order to achieve a viable development. So, although contained within the developer's opportunity space, the designer's opportunity space is likely to expand as sites become more problematic, regulation more demanding and/or markets more competitive. (Adapted from Tiesdell and Adams, 2004)

In general, the more challenging the design task, the greater the developer's need to use skilled design expertise in order to achieve a viable development. As Figure 7.8 shows, the designer's opportunity space lies within that of the developer and is subject to similar defining forces, although mediated through the developer. The more demanding the site and the greater the challenge of putting the desired development on that site within the available budget, the more likely a developer will be to yield opportunity space to the designer. 'Good' design is able to exploit the site's positive features, while minimising the detrimental effect of its negative features. Equally, the developer may readily appreciate that opportunity space has to be yielded to the designer in order to obtain planning consent, overcome problematic site conditions and achieve a more marketable product.

As this implies, a tighter regulatory regime may well encourage developers to turn to skilled design expertise so as to ensure faster and smoother consents. Speculative housebuilders tend not to employ skilled designers at greenfield locations unless obliged by regulatory pressures, since neither the market nor the site context usually demand design expertise. Skilled designers are more likely to be employed at urban brownfield locations, since the market and site contexts are usually more demanding, irrespective of whether the regulatory context is tighter (Tiesdell and Adams 2004).

Of course, a larger opportunity space for the designer does not always translate into better design – designers may, for example, use it to impose their own 'heroic' view. Similarly, enlarging the developer's opportunity space does not necessarily enlarge the designer's opportunity, but could reduce it. To further their own interests, designers may seek to enlarge their opportunity space by outmanoeuvring developers. Indeed, designing and producing new development involves varied actors who have differing objectives, motivations, resources and constraints. This is a highly social process in which development actors variously 'negotiate, plot and scheme' in order to achieve their desired design and built form, in which process character, personality and interpersonal skills are crucially important (Bentley 1999). For developers, a key issue is thus the freedom they choose to give and the freedom they have to give to designers. For designers, it may involve knowing how far developers can be pushed towards their particular concept of better design.

Place and non-place entrepreneurs

Up to now, we have argued that developers, and especially speculative house-builders, turn to skilled designers only when their services are essential in order to resolve market, site or regulatory constraints. While this might be generally true, a small but far-sighted group of developers appear to have emerged in recent years who see real business opportunities in better design and in helping to create more sustainable places. In her study of brownfield development, Payne (2009) labels such developers as 'pioneers' in contrast to the more numerous 'pragmatists' and 'sceptics' who have long dominated residential development. The study concluded that 'Whereas pioneers were attracted or "pulled" by the market opportunity of brownfield sites, pragmatists and sceptics were driven or "pushed" away from greenfield sites by tighter policy constraints. Crucially, the research found that, while pioneers searched for innovative design solutions, both pragmatists and sceptics worked hard to transfer product standardisation as a key design solution from their greenfield experience to brownfield sites' (Adams and Payne 2011: 211). As regeneration specialists, pioneers have a strong competitive focus on brownfield development. Most, such as Urban Splash (Box 7.5 and Figure 7.9), are relatively small, although they include one of the UK's largest housebuilders, Berkeley Homes, which deliberately switched its production entirely to urban sites from the mid-1990s (Karadimitriou 2005).

These insights chime with Guy *et al.*'s (2002) view that the strategies pursued by locally based independent developers in Manchester were very different from those of London-based institutional investors. The independents concentrated their activities in locations on the fringe of the city centre and were willing to encourage mixed uses and multiple tenancies on smaller-sized development plots. Their close engagement with community-based networks and others in the locality enabled them to offset risks through collaborative ventures. Significantly, Guy *et al.* (2002: 1192) found that 'Independents also strive to add value through an emphasis on distinctive design, often with a preference for conservation of local vernacular styles through the re-use of former warehouses or department stores.' They quoted one independent developer interviewed for their research as commenting that: 'I believe that good design doesn't cost more money as it actually generates value.'

BOX 7.5 Urban Splash

Urban Splash is a remarkable and innovative mixed-use developer that has spent the last twenty years challenging commonly held perceptions of what can be achieved in run-down urban areas in the UK. Founded by Tom Bloxham and Jonathan Falkingham in 1993, the company built its reputation on the conversion of redundant mills and warehouses into 'loft' apartments with exposed brickwork and feature windows, along with associated commercial and retail floorspace.

At first, the premises were acquired relatively cheaply, allowing Urban Splash to invest in high-quality architecture with strong design images and sell apartments off-plan. The success of its initial conversions in Manchester and Liverpool enabled the company to expand rapidly, developing schemes in northern cities such as Bradford, Leeds and Sheffield, while moving further afield into Birmingham, Bristol, Plymouth, and Irvine in Scotland. Its conversion remit widened to include office blocks, decayed local authority housing estates and (at Plymouth) a historic navy dockland. Vacant land in and around these sites allowed Urban Splash to develop new buildings to set off the conversions, usually in strong contemporary architecture, and often designed by well-known architects. In many cases, the company worked in partnership with the public sector, taking advantage of the massive increase in regeneration spending under the 1997–2010 Labour Government. By 2010, Urban Splash had developed or was working on sixty separate sites, creating over £700 million of new residential accommodation and around 2 million square feet of commercial space.

Essentially, Urban Splash has built its success on identifying the potential of otherwise neglected areas, driving forward their regeneration and benefiting from the increase in value that this produces. The company has won over 300 awards for architecture, design and regeneration. As Chairman Tom Bloxham said in a 2010 interview 'My definition of regeneration is that it's about creating demand. Whereas property development is about fulfilling demand, regeneration is about creating it. What drives us is an interest in architecture and places and changing those places' (Branson 2010). On another occasion, he himself wrote 'I believe those of us privileged enough to work in the property industry have a duty not only to make profits, but also to try and make a difference. Our buildings will last longer than we do and I want them to make a positive impact on our towns and cities and that is what drives us at Urban Splash' (Bloxham, 2009).

To ensure Bloxham's continued control over the direction of Urban Splash, the company's expansion was largely funded by debt finance from the banks. As a result, he once said of himself 'I have a very good majority shareholder with 70 per cent equity and we rarely disagree' (Article 13, 2006). Nevertheless, Urban Splash initially struggled to cope with the 2008 credit crunch, having to scale back its operations and make some long-employed staff redundant. Its financial results saw a loss of £39 million in 2009, and one of £10 million in 2010. Nevertheless, it responded creatively by offering residential property for rent or shared ownership, as much as developing it for outright sale. This has the added advantage of matching its commercial investment portfolio with a residential one, thus ensuring less immediate reliance on development activity.

By 2011, Bloxham's main concern was that the withdrawal of government support for urban regeneration would lead to areas on the edge of city centres becoming increasingly poor and depressed. In a BBC interview that year, he said 'I do worry that unless positive action is taken, we will reverse the trend [of regeneration] and rather than see areas improve and great new places develop, we will see other places go into decline' (McGregor 2011).

FIGURE 7.9
Albert Mill, Manchester, England. Built in 1869, this Grade II listed building in Castlefield has been converted by Urban Splash into loft apartments and office space. In both cases, purchasers buy an empty shell and then subdivide it as they wish. (Urban Splash)

We can postulate a continuum from those developers who are more sensitive to the intrinsic value of place, and who seek development that respects and indeed enhances its location, and those who are less sensitive (Carmona *et al.* 2010). We can think of the first group as 'place entrepreneurs' and the second as 'non-place entrepreneurs', while acknowledging that many developers will occupy some midway point and will look to shift their strategies in either direction in response to shifting structural circumstances. In essence, place-based entrepreneurs are those who actively work with the grain of a city, responding to local factors, seeing added value in design, and taking a broader view of where development potential exists. They are typified by locally-based, relatively small-scale, independent entre- preneurs. Non-place entrepreneurs tend to ignore, undervalue or actively work against the grain of a city. They take a more limited view of where development potential exists and are generally risk averse. They are typified by externally based institutional investors.

Guy *et al.* (2002) make the argument that institutional investors base their strategies on the assumption that past trends will continue, while independent developers are at the forefront of creating a 'post-industrial script' around sus- tainable urban living. In the designer age, it is therefore tempting to ask whether the mass development of new homes will follow other forms of mass industrial production into oblivion and whether more bespoke and sensitive developers, smaller in size and focusing on particular niche markets, will determine how cities develop in coming decades.

Conclusions

Real estate developers play key roles in the development process and their activities are of central importance to the way cities evolve and develop over the decades. But not all developers are alike and there are certainly many whose strategies and actions challenge popular mythology. Alongside important differ- ences between commercial and residential developers, it is clear that attitudes to design and place-making also vary significantly.

Recent research into the Scottish Executive's understanding of developers suggested that 'it rarely seemed to acknowledge the entrepreneurial motives and risk-taking nature of many in the business. Instead, it portrayed the development industry as essentially an ally of the State whose objectives could be more closely brought into line by careful deployment of the correct policy tools. Significantly, private-sector development was seen as a lucrative source of funding for forms of community investment that in previous decades might have been met by the public purse' (Adams *et al.* 2009a: 17). While there are important signs of the policy responsiveness of the development industry, for example in taking envi- ronmental agendas more seriously and in moving production towards brownfield locations, it should not be presumed that such objectives are necessarily warmly embraced within the industry or that they would outlast any policy change. The widespread variation between developers in their attitudes and approaches to policy issues must again be recognised. As Figure 7.10 shows, for example, the sustainability performance of the top 20 UK housebuilders, according to analysis by the Worldwide Fund for Nature, varied from 85 per cent for the best-performing company to less than 10 per cent for the worst ones (NextGeneration 2008).

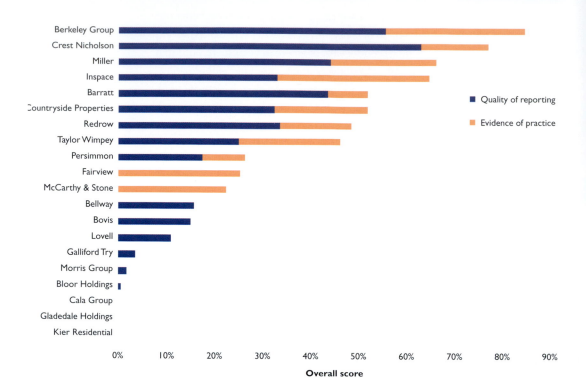

Quality of reporting

Evidence of practice

Overall score

One significant barrier to predicting how real estate developers might react to particular policies is that developers have not been as well researched as other important roles in development, such as regulators and landowners. This applies particularly to commercial developers. Despite obvious research appeal, the substantive academic account of what typifies the commercial real estate developer has still to be written. There are certainly some good anecdotal accounts, written mainly from inside the property industry, which reveal much about the behaviour and thinking of particular developers at particular times (see, for example, Marriot 1967, Ross Goobey 1992, Scott 1996). Occasionally, an attempt is made to provide a more reflective account of developer motives within the context of a rich understanding of process, of which Fainstein's (1994) classic account of property, politics and planning in London and New York is an excellent example.[8] Since then, however, it has been necessary to rely on the shorter and more focused journal contributions, which provide valuable insights but do not amount to a comprehensive study of commercial real estate developers. Although the residential development sector has been better served, for example by Ball (1983) and Wellings (2006), speculative housebuilders have not received the same concerted research attention as social housing providers, even though their output is now significantly greater. One important future aspect of shaping places must therefore be to ensure that up-to-date knowledge of the strategies and actions of a full range of real estate developers is readily available to policy-makers.

8 Landowners

Landowners potentially play a crucial role in the real estate development process. They can frustrate or facilitate the supply of what is often the most problematic of development inputs – land itself. They have considerable power to shape places by the extent and speed of land release and by any conditions they attach to land transfers. That power is at its most intense where pressures for urbanisation, or for the densification of existing urban areas, ensure that the demand for development land significantly outstrips its supply. Yet, as Goodchild and Munton (1985: 9) maintain: 'the motives and circumstances of landowners are extremely varied and as a consequence owners do not respond uniformly to the development opportunities open to them'. Some turn themselves into developers, or at least respond enthusiastically to the opportunities developers present to them. Others are more reticent to engage with developers, or even with other landowners, where parcels in different ownerships require amalgamation or co-ordination prior to development.

Many accounts of the development process underestimate the important contribution of landowners. There are two main reasons for this. First, a widespread misconception exists that planning has diminished the role of the landowner. In some countries, for example, the state allocates land for development in a plan, acquires the land from the owner and undertakes the development itself. This has never been the case in the UK (or indeed in most other countries) except in very special circumstances, such as the development of new towns or the reconstruction of obsolete or war-damaged city centres. Although the allocation of land is a public decision taken by planning authorities, the release of land to implement that allocation is normally a private decision left to landowners and developers.

The second reason is that the supply of land, at least in neo-classical theory, is considered to respond to demand pressure, enabling land to move into its most profitable use. As a result, the individual preferences of particular landowners have merited only limited attention from economists, who generally believed that such preferences were of little interest and were not amenable to general analysis (see Evans 2004b for a review). Although research reported below reveals that the strategies pursued by individual owners are highly diverse, it also challenges the notion that they are uniformly responsive to demand.

The variety and, at times, unpredictability in landowner behaviour is primarily due to the many different people and organisations who find themselves playing this key role in the development process. This chapter therefore begins by looking in more detail at the various actors who supply land into the development process. As a broad guide, we differentiate between former landed property, industrial landowners, financial landowners and statutory landowners. We then introduce the concept of land management and development strategies, which result from the interaction between contextual factors (such as land prices, taxation policy and planning policy), site characteristics and owner characteristics (see Goodchild and Munton 1985). Analysing such strategies highlights the distinction between active and passive owner behaviour in the development process, which is explored in the middle of the chapter. This prompts consideration of the extent of landowner interest in the design quality of what is eventually built. The chapter concludes by reflecting on the implications of varied owner behaviour for shaping places.

Understanding landowners

Landowner classification

The prime concern of this chapter is with what might be described as the 'pre-development landowner', in the sense of a particular individual or organisation whose original motive for acquiring ownership was not that of real estate development. Although this concept implies that development requires a transfer of ownership from the 'pre-development landowner' to the developer, this is not always the case. Certain landowners, on appreciating that their land has development potential, may make the conscious decision to transform themselves into developers. Moreover, investors in real estate, who retain the long-term ownership of completed developments, may operate as the 'pre-development landowner' when and if redevelopment eventually takes place.

We thus adopt a broad interpretation of the term 'landowner' to refer to those people and organisations, whether in the private or public sectors, who have the capacity to supply land for development. Within the private sector, Massey and Catalano (1978) identified three distinct types of landowner differing from each other in their role within the overall structure of social formation and, critically, by their function in the process of production. They termed these former landed property, industrial land ownership and financial land ownership.

Former landed property consists of the remaining holdings of the landed gentry and aristocracy, the monarchy and the church. In each case, extensive and largely rural estates are retained not purely for investment purposes, but as part of a wider social role. The 1,700 individuals who own about one third of British land, according to Norton-Taylor (1982), fall mainly into this category. As Massey and Catalano (1978: 79) contend: 'For the landed aristocracy (as for the gentry) landownership is not simply a question of owning land, but of owning specific tracts of land with which they have a historical and/or social connection.'

Nevertheless, landed owners are often keen to exploit any development potential, provided that this does not conflict with their wider role. Moray Estates, which manages the extensive holdings of the Earl of Moray in north-east Scotland illustrates this well. Most of the land was originally granted to Lord James Stuart, the 1st Earl of Moray in 1562 by his half-sister, Mary Queen of Scots. Today, alongside owning almost 7,000 hectares of farmland and around 4,000 hectares of commercial forestry, Moray Estates is actively involved in the development of a business park at Inverness Airport, a new championship-standard golf course at nearby Castle Stuart and, as discussed below, a new settlement to be developed at Tornagrain on New Urbanist principles.[1]

Industrial landowners consist of owner-occupier farmers and manufacturing industry, both of whom need to own land as condition of production. Conflict can arise between the desire of individual owner-farmers to benefit from the greatly enhanced value of land if it is sold for development and the policy stance adopted by their representative bodies to ensure the protection of at least the best-quality agricultural land. In 2011, the National Farmers Union, for example, urged the Coalition Government to agree that 'The importance of food production and the rural economy must be fully recognised in the new National Policy Planning Framework' (NFU 2011). Yet, given the opportunity, many individual farmers are often happy to enter into options or conditional contracts allowing housebuilders to test the development potential of their land. In recent decades, the decline of manufacturing employment within cities has created a rich source of brownfield development opportunities within cities. Despite potential contamination, such sites have attracted increasing interest from housebuilders, especially as supplies of greenfield land have diminished.

The main *financial landowners* identified by Massey and Catalano (1978) are the property companies, pension funds and insurance companies who hold real estate as a long-term investment asset. To these must now be added the overseas investors who, according to Dixon (2009), own about 15 per cent of UK commercial property. They have been attracted to the UK by institutional leases, financial deregulation, liberalisation and booming office markets. These financial landowners are the developer/investors and investor-developers mentioned in Chapter 7, whose activities often include the purchase and holding of secondary property, with the intention of eventual redevelopment.

Statutory land ownership was not discussed in any depth by Massey and Catalano (1978), even though they estimated that various state agencies at the time owned about 19 per cent of land in Great Britain. In the twentieth century, central and local government, the nationalised industries and statutory under-takers all became important landowners. Municipal land ownership grew rapidly from the 1950s to the late 1970s as slums were cleared, new houses built and new roads constructed. By 1982, for example, almost 58 per cent of land in Manchester was owned freehold by the city council, with a further 7.5 per cent owned by other public bodies (Kivell and McKay 1988).

Since the mid-1980s, statutory land ownership in the UK has shrunk, as a result of privatisations and land disposals. Nevertheless, much potential development land remains in statutory ownership. In Scotland, for example, it was estimated in 2009 that over 2,500 hectares of vacant or derelict land were owned by local authorities or other public-sector bodies (Scottish Government 2010b). The comparative figure for England that year was over 16,000 hectares, although this included potential brownfield redevelopment sites that were still wholly or partially in use (Homes and Communities Agency 2010).[2] The scale of brownfield land in public ownership north and south of the border highlights the significant role that local authorities and statutory development agencies can play in facilitating development through servicing and, where necessary, reclaiming brownfield land, and then making it available for development.

Land management and development strategies

Goodchild and Munton (1985) contend that individual owners perceive land management and development in a way that relates significantly to their own particular characteristics and circumstances. They identified six important owner characteristics – legal personality, occupancy status, sources of income and wealth, particular family and personal circumstances, knowledge of and attitude to risk, and motive for ownership – each of which are now discussed in turn.

The individual landowner can be distinguished from the company and the public body as different *legal personalities* owning land. In respect of *occupancy status*, owners of land or property that is tenanted are more likely to sell what they regard as an investment than are owner-occupiers who use land or property themselves. However, the presence of tenants may delay commercial redevelopment, since they will be entitled to remain at least until the expiry of any existing lease or tenancy agreement. Landowners may also be influenced in their behaviour by the extent of any *associate wealth* beyond their immediate land assets. Wealthy landowners with substantial income from a variety of assets are better placed to hold out for higher prices than are impoverished landowners in need of cash.

Family and personal characteristics may determine whether or not land is made available for development. This is illustrated by the case of a single dwelling in large grounds, owned by an elderly widow and located in a Surrey village. The property had been bought many years earlier by her husband and it held special memories of their married life. Despite its obvious development value, she had rebuffed numerous approaches from developers and had no intention of selling. As a result, the site was left unallocated in the local plan, despite its development potential (Adams and May 1991). Landowner behaviour is also conditioned by *knowledge of and attitude to risk*, as is evident in the relative willingness to undertake development directly, rather than sell out to a developer.

However, for many landowners, the *motive for ownership* is the single most important characteristic influencing behaviour. According to Goodchild and Munton (1985), the main motives for ownership are occupation, investment, making land available for others on a non-profit basis and control. Owner-occupiers are primarily concerned with use value, but may be tempted to sell by high exchange value. Investors who purchase land and property are likely to behave more consistently than those who inherit it. Benevolent owners, usually with extensive holdings, may be willing to make land available for non-profit-making organisations such as sports clubs. Some owners, such as manufacturing companies, may acquire land so as to control its future development. If land or property next door to an existing factory comes onto the market, acquisition ensures that it will be readily available if and when needed for future expansion.

Each of these six factors influences the particular land management and development strategies pursued by owners of land with development potential, whether consciously or unconsciously. These strategies are produced by the way in which owners respond, or fail to respond, to three basic decisions: if and when to develop land or sell for development, whether and how to relate to other actors, and how to manage land prior to development. These can be called, respectively, the financial, operational and management decisions. Those who own land with development potential but never consider these matters unconsciously pursue strategies that may affect the development process as much as those pursued by owners who energetically seek to exploit such potential.

Commenting on the financial decision, Goodchild and Munton (1985) maintained that virtually every owner of development land will eventually sell for capital gain. Although this may be generally true of farmland suitable for housing development, notable exceptions otherwise occur to this general rule, for example, where land is owned for control purposes. Operational decisions concern the relationship between landowners and other actors in the development process, particularly planners and developers. Once development potential is apparent, an owner must decide how best to manage land prior to its sale or development. Owners may be tempted to minimise their financial and legal commitments to any pre-development use, while seeking to maximise their opportunities for short-term earnings. Despite significant variety in the strategies pursued by different owners, there is a crucial difference between those who facilitate and those who frustrate the development process, to which we now turn.

Ownership behaviour in the development process

Active and passive behaviour

According to Cameron *et al.* (1988: 124–25), 'Major owners of urban land appear to utilise their land holdings in a variety of ways. In both the public and private sectors, some seek to maximise revenue by active participation in the land market releasing and buying surplus land as appropriate conditions arise. Others hold excess land as a measure of coping with future growth without the accompanying need for future land acquisition or relocation of production elsewhere. And others appear to have no explicit policy for their surplus land.'

This highlights the important distinction between active and passive ownership, which was first articulated in the British context by Goodchild and Munton (1985), who themselves drew on earlier North American work (Brown *et al.* 1982, Chapin and Weiss 1962, Kaiser and Weiss 1970, Weiss *et al.* 1966). The distinction between active and passive ownership was subsequently applied by Adams *et al.* (1988) to understanding the redevelopment process in six inner-Manchester wards between 1978 and 1984. This study revealed that almost 60 per cent of the 83 hectares of brownfield land that had been developed or brought into use for purposes other than public open space had required a change to active ownership as part of that process.

Further work by Adams and May (1991) into the role played by eighty-five landowners during the local planning processes in Cambridge, Greenwich and Surrey Heath in the mid to late 1980s suggested that landowner involvement in local planning was a useful early indicator of later activity by the same landowner in the development process. Of the sixty-six landowners considered to have played an active role in the development process, fifty-two had earlier been involved in the local planning process.

A related study of 120 industrial development sites in the Cheshire–Wirral corridor confirmed the importance of ownership behaviour in the development process (Adams *et al.* 1995). It found that active owners often play an important role in preparing land for development by tackling a broad range of development constraints. As a result, 'particular individuals and organisations were more successful than others in developing problematic sites. For example, manufacturing companies often went to tremendous lengths to develop well located but heavily constrained sites, especially where this enabled production to expand on to adjoining land, rather than having to relocate elsewhere' (Adams *et al.* 1995: 426).

We can therefore think of active landowners as those who develop their own land, enter into joint venture development or make their land available for others to develop. Active landowners may try to overcome site constraints in order to make land more marketable or suitable for development. This could involve applying for planning permission, appealing against a planning refusal or tackling problematic physical or infrastructural constraints. Active behaviour may be motivated by political concerns, or the prospect of financial reward, or a desire to meet their own land needs. Active owners who obtain planning permission, tackle development constraints or offer their land for sale without undue influence from developers make a significant contribution to the development process.

Historical patterns of urban development have been much influenced by active owner behaviour. As Kivell and McKay (1988: 170) state, 'there is a small, but impressive, body of literature within the mainstream of urban geography which stresses the importance of land tenure in determining the timing, direction and nature of urban morphology'. Yet, such influences are not merely historical, since active landowners continue to shape the development of towns and cities. For example, since 2004, Moray Estates has developed plans for a new settlement of around 10,000 people on land in its ownership at Tornagrain, midway between Inverness and Nairn. Having undertaken an extensive study tour of similar developments in the UK, Holland, Denmark and the US, it appointed Andres Duany to create a New Urbanist masterplan, which was refined through a charrette process held in 2006. The proposal was subsequently adopted by the Scottish Government as an exemplar scheme within the Scottish Sustainable Communities Initiative.

In contrast, passive landowners take no particular steps to market or develop their land, even though they may intend to do so in the distant future. They may respond, or fail to respond, to offers from potential developers, but otherwise they retain land without development. They rarely attempt to overcome constraints in order to make land more marketable or suitable for development. Passive owners therefore contribute little to the development process, and nothing at all if they refuse to sell land that has development potential. Indeed, as compulsory purchase is rare, owners of land with development potential who refuse to sell act as a constraint in the development process.

Exploring ownership behaviour in more detail

Although the distinction between active and passive behaviour is useful, it cannot fully reflect the diversity of landowner strategies and actions. Passive owner behaviour, for example, may range from that which is merely responsive to interest from developers to that which is openly hostile. More recent research by Adams *et al.* (2002) which examined the strategies, interests and actions of those owning land and property within eighty substantial redevelopment sites in four British cities sought to create a broader spectrum of owner behaviour. Two of these cities, Aberdeen and Nottingham, were chosen because they had experienced strong recent development pressure, while the other two, Dundee and Stoke-on-Trent, were selected because they had seen much weaker development pressure. Drawing on site development histories and owner questionnaires, the research developed a scaled measure of the extent to which 155 identified owners of vacant land and obsolete property within these eighty sites encouraged or discouraged redevelopment.

As the basis for this analysis, owners were considered to have significantly encouraged redevelopment if they had themselves sought to resolve at least the most important of the five established tests of development feasibility for that particular site, as previously identified by Barrett *et al.* (1978). These five tests relate to ownership, public procedures, physical conditions, market conditions and project viability and are very similar to those previously specified in Figure 5.1.

Owners who made some attempt to establish development feasibility but who did not themselves seek to resolve the most important feasibility test relevant to their site were considered to have encouraged rather than significantly encouraged redevelopment. Owners whose strategies and actions had made development feasibility harder to establish were considered to have discouraged redevelopment, while those who alone had rendered development almost unfeasible were considered to have significantly discouraged redevelopment. Allowance was also made for a midway ranking in which owners' strategies and actions were considered to have had neutral impact on development feasibility. The results are shown in Figure 8.1.

Most of the owners who had significantly encouraged redevelopment had pushed the process ahead energetically through such actions as assembling land, gaining planning permission, obtaining development finance and securing tenants. Those who had merely encouraged redevelopment intended either to complete necessary actions themselves at a later date or to pass the task over to others. Those whose impact was considered neutral were certainly not hostile to redevelopment. Indeed, most had either sold by 1995 or were open to offers, even if the site was not formally on the market.

In contrast, most owners considered to have discouraged or significantly discouraged redevelopment were either unwilling to sell or, if nominally willing, held unrealistic expectations of price, discounting special purchasers. A classic case of unrealistic price expectations concerned a former marl pit of 8.5 hectares in Stoke-on-Trent, half of which had redevelopment potential. It was on the market in 1997 for £860,000. At interview, it transpired that the owner believed its open market value to be £600,000, but would accept £500,000 if offered an immediate

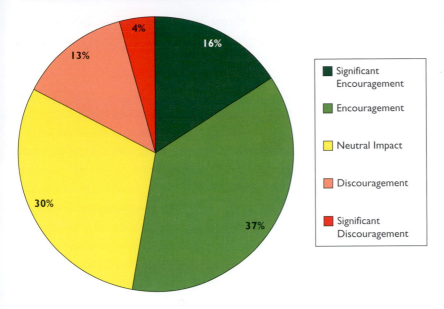

4%

16%

13%

30%

37%

- ■ Significant Encouragement
- ■ Encouragement
- ■ Neutral Impact
- ■ Discouragement
- ■ Significant Discouragement

FIGURE 8.1

Landowners' attitudes to redevelopment. This shows that just over half of the owners investigated in the four cities researched had encouraged or significantly encouraged redevelopment between 1991 and 1995. Another third had a neutral impact on redevelopment. Less than one fifth discouraged or significantly discouraged redevelopment.

cheque. This sum was calculated on the basis that it would cover original purchase price of £220,000 paid in 1987, the £220,000 spent in interest charges over the following ten years and approximately £60,000 of other expenditure. Yet, the owner admitted that a professional valuation of the land undertaken for his bank suggested that it was worth only £260,000. This reinforces earlier findings that urban land prices are 'revised downwards only slowly and reluctantly in response to lack of demand or excess supply' (Adams *et al.* 1985: 172).

Almost all of the unhelpful owners identified in the research regarded real estate development as either an occasional or an ancillary business. In some cases, they insisted on keeping land for operational use or for their own future development, even if it had lain unused or underused for some years. That others held on to sites speculatively in the hope of future retail planning permission was evident. Of course, it should not be presumed that strategies or actions that discouraged or significantly discouraged redevelopment were necessarily irrational from the individual owner's perspective, even if they frustrated public policies or private initiatives intended to achieve urban regeneration.

Public- versus private-sector ownership

The distinction between public- and private-sector ownership was investigated further to discover which type of owner was more likely to promote redevelopment. Much early work characterised vacant urban land as attributable primarily to poor land management in the public sector. While Nabarro and Richards (1980) argued that extensive areas of land remained vacant in the late 1970s as a result of large-scale passive ownership in the public sector, Moss (1981) suggested that local authorities rarely had the same commercial urgency as the private sector in land management. He contended that, in contrast to the private sector, which concentrated on projects that could be realised quickly, local authorities acquired land for schemes that they did not have the money to implement. It was suggested that such land failed to be released for development by others as a result either of procedural delays and organisational problems within local government (Cameron *et al.* 1988) or of local political reluctance (Chisholm and Kivell 1987).

This picture of neglectful public-sector but benign private-sector management of surplus landholdings has since been revised. By the late 1980s, it was generally agreed that a significant proportion of vacant urban land was in private ownership (Cameron *et al.* 1988, Chisholm and Kivell 1987, Civic Trust 1988). Within the public sector, a new urgency to rationalise landholdings became evident as a result of legislative changes, policy directions and, most importantly, pressure to maximise receipts from land sales in order to make up for lost revenue elsewhere. In a study of Strathclyde, for example, Llewelyn-Davies (1996) found that, despite the tendency of local authorities still to hold unrealistic or optimistic views of the value of housing sites in their ownership, there was a strong public commitment to working with private developers to ensure the re-use of brownfield sites for housing development.

The research in Aberdeen, Dundee, Nottingham and Stoke identified almost three times as many private-sector brownfield owners as public-sector ones. This imbalance in favour of the private sector runs counter to the popular perception that most brownfield land is in public ownership, although it partly reflects the privatisation of energy, transport and infrastructure companies during the late 1980s and early 1990s. The research discovered that 73 per cent of public-sector owners encouraged or significantly encouraged redevelopment, in comparison to 53 per cent of owners in the private sector. Local authorities and other statutory agencies, such as local enterprise companies, were usually keen to push redevelopment forward. Within the private sector, combined scores for significant encouragement and encouragement were recorded of 67 per cent for PLCs that had always been in the private sector, 55 per cent for private limited companies, 47 per cent for privatised PLCs such as British Gas and 33 per cent for trustees/private individuals.

In summary, most owners of vacant land and obsolete property investigated in the four cities actively pursued its redevelopment, while relatively few proved consistently hostile to the redevelopment process. This would suggest that earlier anecdotal evidence about owner apathy or unhelpfulness may need to be updated in the context of increasing pressure upon both private businesses and public authorities to maximise returns from their capital assets. In the public sector, local authorities and other statutory bodies appeared to be particularly enthusiastic about promoting redevelopment.

By moving beyond the earlier simple distinction between active and passive behaviour, it proved possible to categorise landowners according to the extent to which they encouraged or discouraged urban redevelopment over a five-year period. This more detailed approach is especially relevant to understanding the seventy-two owners who neither encouraged nor significantly encouraged redevelopment. Rather than label all these owners as merely passive, the research found that forty-six had a neutral impact of the redevelopment process and only twenty-six discouraged or significantly discouraged redevelopment. What this highlights is the need for innovative policy mechanisms that can rapidly channel brownfield land towards more active participants in the development process (Adams *et al.* 2001b).

Landowners and design quality

According to Goodchild and Munton (1985), an owner who wishes to maximise financial gain should sell for the highest sum offered as soon as planning permission is granted, unless at least one of four particular circumstances justify a delay. These are a likely favourable change in the rate of tax on the proceeds of sale, an expected significant increase in the value of development land in the short term, a shortage of alternative investment opportunities in circumstances where compulsory purchase would be unlikely, or the possibility of rapid growth in the income accruing from the land's existing use. The implication of this standard behavioural model is that landowners are primarily concerned with financial return and have little interest in the quality of what is eventually built. Three significant exceptions, which demonstrate how certain types of landowner are explicitly concerned to achieve sustainable and well-designed development, testify to the false dichotomy between financial return and design quality engendered by the standard model.

The first exception concerns landowners who retain a long-term investment interest in what is built on their land. Historically, the built form of much of central London, for example, can be attributed to the influence of the five great landed estates of Bedford, Cadogan, Howard de Walden, Grosvenor and Portman, who promoted the westward expansion of the city from the mid-seventeenth century onwards. According to an exhibition charting the past and current importance of these estates, 'The key to their success was the system of leasehold land tenure which was the basis of most of the capital's residential development. The landowner would let plots to the lessee – a developer or builder – on the basis that the lessee would build at his own expense a house or houses which, at the end of the period of the lease, would become the property of the ground landlord . . . Supervision by the developer and the estate surveyors would ensure the quality of elevations and finish . . . With most leases fixed at 99 years the estates were able to renew leases at increased rents or to redevelop the land at the end of the period' (New London Architecture 2006: 2–3).

The Grosvenor family, for example, built its fortunes on the development of 120 hectares of Mayfair and Belgravia (Figure 8.2), which the heiress Mary Davies had brought into the family in 1677 on the occasion of her marriage to Sir Thomas Grosvenor. Even now, this London estate remains the core asset of what has become the Grosvenor Group, an international property investment and development organisation with almost £11 billion of assets under its management, but still controlled by Sir Thomas's descendant, the 6th Duke of Westminster. Its recent award-winning Liverpool One development (see Chapter 2) demonstrates Grosvenor's continued faith in high-quality design as an essential contributor to long-term investment value.

The second exception concerns those landowners who see sustainable urban design as a core motivation for their involvement in the development process. The best-known British example is the Prince of Wales, whose Duchy of Cornwall estate promoted the development Poundbury (Figure 8.3) on the edge of Dorchester 'to demonstrate how traditional architecture and modern town planning could be used to create a thriving new community [where] people could live and work in close proximity' (Prince's Foundation for the Built Environment 2007: 45). Here, instead of selling off development parcels to individual housebuilders, licence agreements were used to ensure that builders adhered to the masterplan and design code, with the ownership of the completed dwellings then being conveyed directly by the Duchy to the end-purchaser.

Another less well-known but equally relevant example comes from Fairford Leys, a 200-hectare sustainable urban extension to Aylesbury in Buckinghamshire, developed from 1992 and now with 2,100 new homes and a mixed-use town centre (DCLG 2006a, Prince's Foundation for the Built Environment 2007). Here, the landowner was the Ernest Cook Trust, a charitable foundation interested in

FIGURE 8.2

Eaton Square, Central London, England. Built in Belgravia by the Grosvenor family in the eighteenth century and intended as a long-term investment, it still forms an important part of Grosvenor's London estate today. (Herry Lawford, used under the Creative Commons licence)

FIGURE 8.3
Poundbury, Dorset, England. Visually, Poundbury harks back to the architectural styling of an earlier age, reflecting the tastes of its patron, the Prince of Wales. In urban design terms, its interconnected pattern of streets and paths and its tightly knit urban fabric represent a very different type of development to that generally built in the UK over the last 100 years. (Steve Tiesdell)

architecture, conservation, design and community development. According to the Trust's website, it controlled the design and management of Fairford Leys 'to ensure community life would be central to the development, [and that] facilities such as a community centre, ecumenical church, leisure facilities, shops, offices and a primary school were provided. This has resulted in a vibrant community with a range of accommodation – Fairford Leys is always referred to as an exemplar of sustainable development.'[3] The Trust's intention in design terms 'was simply to increase quality over and above the volume housebuilder norm, in particular by controlling the quality of public space' (DCLG 2006a: 48). Development quality was achieved through including a requirement within the sale contracts for housebuilders to adhere strictly to the masterplan and design code for Fairford Leys.

The third exception represents an extension of the second and concerns landowners whose personal interest in design quality becomes the basis of a successful business model. Several of the most prominent examples of New Urbanism in the US were promoted by those who had inherited land and saw the potential to develop somewhere distinctive. Seaside in Florida (Figure 8.4) was founded by Robert S. Davis, whose grandfather had originally acquired 80 acres there in 1946 to build a summer camp for his employees. This intention was never fulfilled and the land instead became a holiday destination for the family, making an impression on the young Robert S. Davis. By the time he inherited the property in 1979, Davis was already a real estate developer, and one who saw potential at Seaside to revive 'Northwest Florida's building tradition, which had produced wood-frame cottages so well adapted to the climate that they enhanced the

sensual pleasure of life by the sea'.[4] He turned to Andres Duany and Elizabeth Plater-Zyberk to develop the masterplan and design code for what has become a model of New Urbanism.

A similar story lies behind the development of Prospect, the first New Urbanist development of any scale in Colorado, again designed by Duany and Plater-Zyberk. This was developed by John 'Kiki' Wallace on what had previously been a family farm, with the specific intention of building 'a distinctive project which would minimize negative impacts on the land'.[5] Like Seaside, the result has been a distinctive, award-winning development, in this case with narrow, tree-lined streets that connect homes of traditional and modern architectural styles to parks, public amenities, shops and offices.

A comparable UK example is Newhall in Essex, where the landowners, Jon and William Moen, whose family had farmed the land since 1925, were determined to see a high-quality urban neighbourhood created, rather than a standard suburban housing estate (Evans 2003 and 2008).[6] Newhall has been planned as a major greenfield extension to Harlow New Town and will eventually deliver 2,550 new homes, along with a neighbourhood centre, primary school, commercial space and leisure facilities. Significantly, the Moens believed that the best way to maximise the long-term value of the land would be to manage its gradual development themselves.

Operating as Newhall Projects Ltd, the Moens subdivided the first phase of just over 600 dwellings into six roughly equal development parcels. These were marketed on the basis that the winning developers would fulfil the requirements of the masterplan and design code, which were embedded into land transfers. To ensure greater diversity of urban form (Figures 8.5 to 8.7), each phase featured a different developer and different architects, with more than one architect employed on some of the parcels. Procurement methods gradually evolved over a five-stage learning process, which gave the Moens increasing control over the commissioning of designers and designs (Adams and Tiesdell 2011). Developers who wished to participate in Newhall found it impossible to use 'standard' designs and instead had to employ skilled designers who could successfully achieve the expectations of the masterplan and design code. The development has won numerous awards, both for overall place quality and for the design of individual housing schemes. These almost always feature adventurous contemporary architecture. By mid-2011, this first phase of Newhall was virtually complete and planning for the second phase was well advanced.

FIGURE 8.5
New homes by Cala Domus at Newhall, Harlow, England. Built at 39 dwellings per hectare, this phase was completed in 2006. (Steve Tiesdell)

FIGURE 8.6
New homes by Countryside Properties at Newhall, Harlow, England. Built at 52 dwellings per hectare, this phase was completed in 2008. (David Adams)

Although build costs at Newhall are about 10–15 per cent more than for conventional property in nearby suburbia, selling prices are also 10–15 per cent higher, ensuring that the developers' margins are retained. Overall project risk has been borne by the Moens. Their business model is based on the quality and success of the first phase creating strong interest in the second phase and thus increasing the value of the subsequent land parcels. It provides a good example of what might be described as 'patient equity' (see Chapter 9), where a landowner is prepared to wait for some years to reap the full financial benefit of better design and quality place-making.

Conclusions

The key message to emerge from this chapter is that landowners matter greatly in the development process. They have the potential to reduce the costs, increase the speed and enhance the quality of what is eventually built through taking a proactive rather than a reactive approach to development opportunities. In other words, those landowners who spot development potential well in advance and act to exploit it are well placed to enhance the eventual benefits both for themselves and the wider community. Design quality is central to this argument, especially as we interpret design in functional rather than simply stylistic terms.

Since good design has significant capacity to add to development value, landowners have more interest in the design quality of what will be built on their land than many of them realise. However, the broad spectrum of those who play the role of landowner in the development process means that many encounter these important issues occasionally or, in some cases, only once. This underlines the critical importance of turning to enlightened professional advisers – architects and urban designers who know how best to exploit latent place quality, and development consultants who can advise how to do so in a way that maximises financial returns. Such an approach may require embedded attitudes among many professionals to be turned on their head – emphasising the sustainable rather than the immediate and balancing the importance of cost with that of benefits. It thus behoves landowners, especially if new to development, to choose their professional advisers carefully.

Of course, what is ideal does not necessarily happen and many developments are delayed or their quality is diminished, owing to discord between those who own land and those who wish to develop its potential. There are important policy issues here, for example around the extent to which the state should explicitly encourage 'patient equity' models through the taxation system or establish more effective intervention systems so as to challenge those landowners who discourage or significantly discourage development opportunities.

Behind such consideration of how the state should treat private landowners looms the equally important question of how it should manage its own land assets. Where the state takes the view that its own surplus land should simply be sold as quickly as possible to the highest bidder, it often undermines its latent capacity to shape places for the better. For, as we shall see later on, where the state regards its land assets as a place-investment opportunity to be carefully nurtured, it can achieve better long-term returns in both financial and sustainability terms.

9 Funders and investors

Introduction

To a remarkable extent, places reflect the way in which their development was originally financed. Since construction is essentially a capital good, its cost is spread over many years, usually well into the future. Only exceptionally are developments financed from the accumulated reserves of their promoter. Instead, some measure of external funding will need to be secured and then mixed to a greater or lesser extent with any funds that the developer is willing and able to provide. The implications of this for places and place quality provide the focus of this chapter.

Whatever the exact nature of the particular relations between those who promote and those who fund any development, a transfer of power occurs in the direction of the funder. Sometimes, this transfer is explicitly and openly acknowledged, as happens, for example, when investors require developers to achieve a particular quality in the design and specification of approved developments. But more often than not, the transfer of power is implicit, taken for granted and never opened up to public scrutiny or debate. What happens instead is that places begin to mirror and reproduce the prevalent culture of finance, providing an enduring testament to the strategies, values and actions of those who fund their development. At their most influential, such cultures become ingrained within their particular epoch's approach to development, determining in a subtle and almost pernicious manner what is and is not considered achievable.

Yet whatever its apparent durability, the financial architecture of real estate development is a particularly human construct and one that can and does evolve over time. This evolution offers the opportunity to introduce new and competing agendas, such as that of sustainable property investment, which have the potential to challenge the accepted traditions of the past. Innovation in financial practices, however, can equally well generate an ever greater 'commoditisation' of place in which the built environment becomes transformed into, and primarily understood as, a specific class of financial asset. It is because such issues are so fundamental to the way places develop that this chapter is devoted to understanding development funding, development funders and the impact of both on place quality.

The next section introduces key concepts in development funding. It explains important differences between project and corporate finance and between debt and equity finance, and identifies the main forms of each. The chapter then moves on to look at strategies pursued by the most significant development funders, concentrating especially on the banks and financial institutions.[1] These two sections provide the basis for a more detailed subsequent discussion of the way in which finance capital helps to shape place. This is addressed in the third main section of the chapter, which examines the implications for places of financial volatility, product standardisation and market perception. At this point, we also show how alternative financial approaches, championed through alternative practices and developed by financial pioneers, can recast conventional notions of value and enable place-making to be reconciled with long-term financial return. The chapter ends by considering the policy implications of these issues and the extent to which they appear on the radar of policy-makers.

Development funding

Most development is financed, usually to a substantial extent, from external sources. This section provides a brief introduction to the main types of development finance. For a more detailed account, readers are strongly advised to consult texts such as Havard (2008), Isaac *et al.* (2010) and Radcliffe *et al.* (2009) which explore the various instruments used to finance development in depth. For our purposes, we concentrate on three main divisions used to delineate development finance and to which all individual instruments relate. These distinguish respectively between short- and long-term finance, between project and corporate finance and between debt and equity.

Short- and long-term finance

Short-term finance is required for the development period, and is normally arranged for a maximum of five years, to cover the costs of site acquisition, construction, professional fees and marketing. On completion, when long-term finance is raised, short-term finance is repaid. If a completed development is sold rather than let,

TABLE 9.1 Main categories of development finance

	Debt finance	Equity finance
Project finance	• Bank loans and overdrafts • Commercial mortgages	• Disposals generating profits for business expansion • Sale and leasebacks • Joint venture partnerships
Corporate finance	• Debt corporate paper	• Company share issues

long-term finance will be arranged by the investor rather than the developer. Short-term finance is usually more expensive than long-term finance, since an unfinished building provides the lender with less security than a completed development. Where short-term finance is extended to the first rent review, it is termed medium-term finance.

Project and corporate finance

If funding is raised for a specific development, and for that development alone, it is called project finance. However, developers who are large and powerful enough can access a single tranche of funding for a programme of several developments. This is called corporate finance, since it is raised by a public company while not necessarily tied to a specific project or projects. Although the distinction is sometimes blurred, it highlights how companies with the financial muscle to raise corporate finance can achieve better terms or greater flexibility than those that rely solely on project finance (Adair 1993).

Debt and equity finance

The distinction between debt and equity, which cuts across that between project and corporate finance, is equally important. Those who lend debt finance normally have no right to share in development profits but are entitled to be repaid with interest. Those who lend equity finance participate in the risks and rewards of development and are entitled to share in development profits. Three types of debt finance and four types of equity finance are outlined below.

Debt finance

As Table 9.1 shows, the main forms of debt finance are bank loans and overdrafts, commercial mortgage and debt corporate paper. The importance of bank funding to development is explained in the next section. In principle, commercial mortgages work in much the same way as residential mortgages, although, as Radcliffe *et al.* (2009: 440) explain, they have become increasingly sophisticated in operation in recent years. Commercial mortgages typically last between 10 and 25 years, although this can make them unattractive to funders at times of high inflation. Debt corporate paper provides a means for larger companies to raise substantial long-term loans, known as bonds, from the capital markets. It also enables such companies to manage cash flow through short-term IOUs known as commercial paper that are issued on the money markets. As is well explained by Havard (2008: 136–38), debt corporate paper has been used in increasingly complex ways within real estate.

Equity finance

Developers can build up their own equity by selling completed developments and using at least part of the profits for business expansion. This is the standard business model for most housebuilders. It also operates in commercial development for trader–developers who aim to secure tenants and then dispose of the completed development, fully let, to an investor. Contractual arrangements between developer and investor are again varied, but are usually set in place before development starts. The most common are forward funding and forward sale (see Havard 2008: 123–30, Wilkinson and Reed 2008: 150–56). The main difference between these is that the investor also provides short-term finance to cover the costs of construction in the former case, but not in the latter.

Sale and leaseback is another method of project-based equity finance. Under this approach, the completed development is sold by the developer to an investor on the express condition that the investor immediately grants the developer a long leasehold of say 99, 125 or 150 years. The developer then sublets the property to tenants, becoming an intermediary between investor and occupiers. This means the developer can retain at least some long-term interest in the development and so benefit from a share of rising capital value over time. A helpful explanation of the main features of sale and leaseback is provided by Dubben and Williams (2009: 150–54), with a more detailed historical account given by Darlow (1988: 288–320).

Joint ventures are created when two or more partners come together, usually on equal basis, to share risks and rewards of specific development (see Havard 2008: 142–45). Typical joint venture partners may involve:

- another developer with different profile or expertise;
- an active landowner wishing to retain an ownership interest in the development;
- a building contractor prepared to cover the cost of working capital in return for a share of development profits;
- a local authority or development agency willing to make land available (especially for urban regeneration);

- a bank, financial institution or venture capital company willing to provide finance at a preferential rate in return for a share of development profits.

Although such partnerships may be formed by deed, it is much more common to establish a joint venture company. Such companies can themselves become the vehicle to tap external development funds, such as loans, bonds or share issues.

Company share issues provide the main form of equity corporate finance. Unlike private companies, shares in public companies with a stock market listing can be traded. This enables significant equity finance to be raised through new share issues (see Havard 2008: 138–39 and Isaac *et al.* 2010: 171–72). However, developers who rely too heavily on equity finance may lose control of particular projects to the equity partner, or even face hostile takeover bids if too many voting shares are issued. Yet, in troubled times, equity finance may be more advantageous to a developer, since equity lenders share the risks of development and generally have no automatic right to payment. In contrast, developers who rely too heavily on debt finance, and in particular on bank loans, may face a financial crisis if interest rates rise steeply or unexpectedly. Developers with a high proportion of debt to equity finance are said to be highly geared.

Development funders

Banks

Banks concentrate on short-term development finance and are primarily concerned with the financial health of the developer and the likely profitability of the development. As Radcliffe *et al.* (2009: 431) explain: 'Traditionally, banks are more concerned with the "asset" base of those to whom they lend, rather than the project in hand.' This makes banks more flexible on location than other lenders, as a result of which bank lending has often been at the forefront of regeneration activity. Banks normally require themselves to be satisfied on four main grounds before lending to real estate development. These concern the track record and creditworthiness of the developer, a favourable viability study and cash flow forecast supported by independent valuation, suitable assurances that the project can be sold or refinanced on completion, and the provision of sufficient security or guarantee for the loan.

Developers may seek overdraft facilities or fixed-terms loans from banks. The former provides flexibility to draw on finance as required, but the latter has the advantage that the loan cannot be recalled by the bank before the agreed repayment date. Above a certain limit, a syndicate of several banks may be required to fund major commercial developments. The Stratford City shopping centre, located next to the Olympic Park in East London, for instance, which was opened in 2011 and comprises 175,000m² of retail and leisure space, was part refinanced on completion by a £550 million syndicated loan from a consortium of ten international banks. Syndication thus enables developers to contemplate 'mega-projects' that would not otherwise be possible.

Bank loans are usually restricted to 65–70 per cent of development value or 70–80 per cent of development cost, although this can edge up or down, dependent on economic circumstances. This funding portion is known as 'senior debt', as the lender has first claim in the event of default. An interest rate between 1–5 per cent above LIBOR (the London Interbank Offer Rate, near equivalent to base rates) tends to be charged on senior debt, reflecting the status of the borrower and the perceived risk. In bullish markets, top-up loans, known as 'mezzanine finance', may be available at higher rates of interest for up to 95 per cent of development cost.

It is sometimes argued that banks take a cautious approach to funding development. For example, from his experience of housebuilding, Calcutt (2007: 132) contends that 'Debt providers are risk averse. As it is not usually possible to share in any upside of success within the business, the best that can normally be achieved is the prompt payment of interest and full repayment of the loan. A debt provider looks on a new loan from the most pessimistic angle and needs to be assured that in the event of a default there will be sufficient assets to recover the debt.' Yet experience shows that the willingness of banks to fund property development is highly cyclical. In the UK, for example, excessive bank lending fuelled development booms in the early 1970s, late 1980s and in the middle of the first decade of the twenty-first century. Between 1988 and 1991, for example, total bank lending to real estate rose from about £15 billion to a then record of £41 billion. As Figure 9.1 shows, bank lending then dipped back to around £30 billion in 1996, before shooting ahead to reach £100 billion by 2003, and £250 billion by 2009, by which time it accounted for about half of all lending activity. Figure 9.2 shows that the growth of bank lending in those later years was fuelled by foreign lenders (notably German banks).

The 'credit crunch' experienced from 2008 signalled a virtual end of new bank lending to development, with overdrafts recalled and fixed-term loans not renewed on expiry. Yet, even by 2010, the real estate sector still accounted for about half of all corporate lending in the UK, primarily because lending to other sectors fell rapidly in the recession, while loans to the real estate sector were generally of longer maturity (Bank of England 2010). While banks may appear risk averse to individual borrowers, their repeated pattern of lending to real estate development over a period of 40 years is one of excessive feast followed by severe famine. The implications of this for place quality are discussed later in the chapter

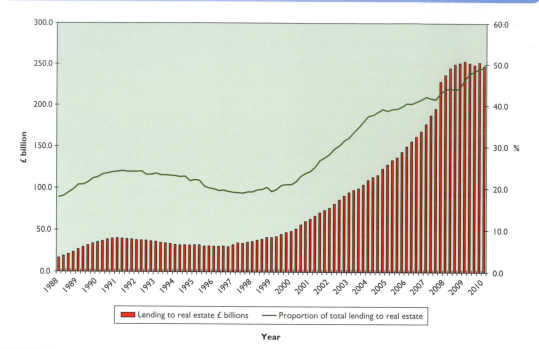

FIGURE 9.1 Bank lending to UK real estate sector 1988–2010. This highlights the rapid rise in lending from around 2000. (Bank of England)

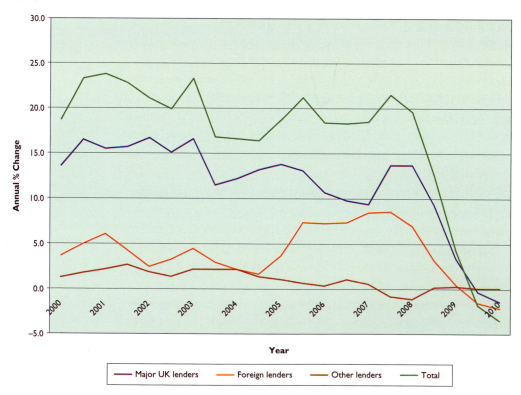

FIGURE 9.2 Annual growth in bank lending to UK real estate sector by type of lender 2000–2010. This shows how foreign lenders stoked up the later years of the development boom and reveals the dramatic impact of the 'credit crunch' from 2008. (Bank of England)

Financial institutions and other real estate investors

Whereas banks have a short- to medium-term interest in real estate funding, investors see real estate as a long-term asset to be compared financially with government securities (called gilts, because they were originally issued on gilt-edged certificates) company stocks and shares (equities) and even works of art or antiques. Funds may also be invested internationally. This means that the investment property market is therefore more closely tied to other investment markets than to the user or development markets. Major insurance companies and pension funds (known as the main 'financial institutions') dominate property investment. Over a long period of time, these institutions have thus shown a preference for investment in London and the South East (Investment Property Forum 2005). Significantly, they have no sentimental commitment to property. If property performs badly, funds will be gradually switched into alternative investments. To capture their attention, property must offer returns which, taking account of good investment practice, compare favourably with gilts and equities.

The gradual flow of investment finance in and out of real estate is thus determined as much by what happens in these other markets as in real estate itself. Although theory would suggest that returns from real estate should lie between those from gilts and equities, in the UK, real estate consistently outperformed these other two markets between 1992 and 2006, while also becoming the least volatile investment option. At its peak, the value of commercial property in the UK appreciated by 33 per cent between the second quarter of 2004 and the final quarter of 2006, attracting significant capital inflow, especially from foreign investors (Adair *et al.* 2009).

Investors are more likely to fund development when opportunities to purchase existing properties (known as 'standing investments') become rarer. Although mortgage finance, sale and leaseback and direct development have all featured within past investor approaches to funding development projects (see Adams 1994, Darlow 1988), more recent emphasis has been placed on arrangements such as forward sale and forward funding that enable investors to acquire projects from developers on completion. Significantly, investors use their financial power to ensure that any developments intended to be acquired in this way are developed in what are perceived to be prime locations and built to the highest-quality design and specification. In the UK, Guy and Henneberry (2000) argue that investor strategies privilege London over other regional markets, since they perceive that investment in the capital is less risky and more liquid than elsewhere. Adair *et al.* (2009) suggest that investors unfamiliar with the UK are even more likely to confine their activities to perceived prime assets and locations.

Ironically, however, the concept of prime real estate is ever changing in its application, as a result of which 'the Monopoly board is remade, so "prime" locations stagnate to be replaced by the new "prime"' (Jones 2009: 2379). Increasingly sophisticated analysis of real estate as a financial asset turns place simply into a trading commodity to be bought and sold from far-distant offices. As investment fund managers struggle to keep up with benchmark performances across the industry, 'portfolio churning' becomes ever more prevalent, with average holding periods for office property, for example, reduced to only about five years (Gerald Eve 2005). While financial institutions certainly see themselves as intrinsically concerned with development quality, and impose stringent requirements on developers in order to achieve this, we argue below that their narrow conception of quality impedes the potential of most such institutions to shape places more broadly.

Other development funders

Although the state can make a significant contribution to funding development, for example, through taxation incentives or by making land available, this is not considered here, as it forms an important part of Chapter 13. However, as Darlow (1988) notes, exceptionally wealthy individuals, who may include third-world politicians, international financiers, rich widows, sporting superstars and pop singers, will from time to time invest directly in real estate development. The importance of those who finance development indirectly by purchasing shares in development companies should also be recognised, and we return to their influence in the next section.

Implications for place quality

Feasts and famines

As intimated, finance does not flow evenly into real estate, but rather is concentrated at particular times and in particular locations. As Jane Jacobs (1961) argued, gradual and close-grained urban change requires a gradual but constant flow of money. Instead, however, 'Cataclysmic money pours into an area in concentrated form, producing drastic changes' (Jacobs 1961: 383). Indeed, the temporal volatility and instability in development production is exacerbated by sharp fluctuations in financial flows, which, according to Edwards (1990), help to make the development process boom prone and crisis prone.

It is essential to recognise that financial flows may drive user demand for real estate, rather than merely respond to it. According to Norwood (2004), the then booming Edinburgh housing market (see Smith *et al.* 2006 for a subsequent analysis) was fuelled by the rapid expansion of bank lending for upmarket apartments, which enabled residential developers to outbid commercial developers for any site that became available. This ready flow of finance turned residential developers into long-term gamblers ready 'to build another 22,000 apartments in the hope that Edinburgh's boom in financial services will continue for another 10 years' (Norwood 2004) (Figure 9.3).

FIGURE 9.3

Apartments under construction at Leith, Edinburgh, Scotland. Taken in 2006, this image of the apartment-building boom then underway at Leith's Western Harbour provides a powerful visual demonstration of the rapid expansion of bank lending shown in Figure 9.1. Although this scheme was subsequently completed, the subsequent collapse in bank lending on development brought the cancellation of other nearby projects and reinforced its isolated location. (Lynn Lindsay, used under the Creative Commons licence)

Much the same story was repeated across many of Britain's city centres in the buy-to-let apartment boom of that same decade. Leyshon and French (2009) show how this boom was initially driven by the liberal lending approaches of medium-sized and specialist financial services firms that had struggled to compete with global banks operating in the mainstream financial markets. In due course, however, these larger banks entered the buy-to-let market themselves, fuelling an even greater wave of speculative apartment building. When the buy-to-let bubble eventually burst in 2007, it led to significant collapse in the price of newly built flats and consequent high vacancy rates.

In the commercial sector, investment demand also prolongs development booms well beyond the point justified by user demand, again producing 'an inherent tendency towards the over-provision of space' (MacLaran 2003: 51–52). As the experience of Dublin shows (see Chapter 13), such financial exuberance can be exacerbated by public policies intended to stimulate development (Dubben and Williams 2009, MacLaran and Williams 2003). In an almost biblical sequence, financial famines usually follow financial feasts, making it difficult to promote a gradual approach to urban change. In the UK, for example, the collapse of successive development booms in the early 1970s, late 1980s and 2007–8 all led to years in which development of any type became almost impossible to fund.

This sequence happens repeatedly because, according to one investment partner interviewed by Fainstein (1994: 64), 'Banks have a herd mentality. They didn't learn the lessons of 1974. They are not run by the very intelligent.' Similar comments were reported in New York, where financial institutions with significant available cash failed to learn from previous experience and relied instead on over-optimistic revenue projections. As a result, 'Knowledgeable analysts agreed that the availability of financing [in the late 1980s] drove the market, that developers would build as long as someone was prepared to provide the necessary funds' (Fainstein 1994: 64). The re-occurrence of these trends in the first decade of the twenty-first century again showed how the power of cataclysmic finance to transform some places very rapidly can be strongly antagonistic to a more gradual process of change, both in the locations it selects and in those that it leaves altogether bereft of resources.

Product standardisation

Liquidity is an essential concern for any funder or investor in development. In practice, this means that there should normally be a ready market if it becomes necessary or desirable to sell on the development. As a general rule, the more development becomes standardised, the greater its perceived liquidity and, conversely, the more it becomes specialised, the less its perceived liquidity. Funders and investors thus believe that they have a strong vested interest in promoting standardisation, even though this may conflict with the desire of individual property users to match the space they occupy to their own particular needs. Such financial pressures for standardisation can be just as powerful in driving the design and specification of owner-occupied property as of that held by investment funds, since banks that advance mortgage funds to owner-occupiers will wish to be confident they can readily resell the property if the owner defaults.

Product standardisation is a direct result of the commodification of place. As Leinberger (2009: 50) explains in an American context, 'Wall Street is not an art auction house. Traders want the same kind of thing in high volumes . . . So when Wall Street took on real estate in the form of REITs and commercial mortgage-backed securities in the early 1990s, real estate had to commoditize what it built.' The outcome, according to Leinberger, was the consolidation of fundable US real estate development into only nineteen product types, which in the case of retail, for example, were limited to just three: the neighbourhood center, the lifestyle center[2] and the big-box anchored center.[3] Significantly, none of the 19 product types involve genuinely mixed-use development.

The requirement for standardisation in investment products is often reinforced by that for size. As Guy et al. (2002: 1183) comment from a UK perspective: 'With the continuing expansion of their portfolios, institutions are constantly looking to invest in larger and larger investment properties. This is because smaller properties have little impact on the overall performance of a portfolio and the management costs of one property with a value of £20 million are considerably less than the management costs of 10 properties of £2 million.' So it can sometimes be easier to fund more ambitious development schemes than less ambitious ones.

Product standardisation has two significant implications for place quality. First, in the US at least, the requirement for each product to be modular and stand-alone almost guarantees low-density sprawl (Leinberger 2005). Secondly, 'Like every other of the nineteen standard product types, individual neighbourhood retail centers are basically interchangeable . . . This is the reason why any suburban place in the country looks pretty much the same as any other . . . once you have seen one neighbourhood center or any other product type, you have seen them all' (Leinberger 2009: 52). Ironically, Leinberger's argument from his own experience as a real estate developer is that what he terms 'walkable urbanism' makes better long-term financial sense than the standard products favoured by financial analysts (see related evidence and discussion in Chapter 2). Nevertheless, until such arguments are more widely accepted by funders and investors, the financial pressures for standardisation will continue to undermine policy efforts to create more diverse and distinctive places.

The treadmill of shareholder value

So far, attention has focused on those who directly fund or invest in real estate development. But the influence of company shareholders, whose financial support for real estate is more indirect, can be just as important for place quality. Here, John Calcutt's (2007) account of how the top management of British housebuilders report regularly to City analysts representing their main shareholders (primarily institutional investors) is highly instructive. Calcutt recounts how presentations at these meetings by senior managers of housebuilding companies focus strongly on trading figures, past performance and future prospects, profits and margins, earnings, dividends and, especially, cash flow. Analysts who fail to be convinced by these meetings may recommend that clients reduce their shareholdings or push for management changes. The former will lessen the value of the directors' personal shareholdings and may well lead to takeover pressures. Thus, 'Paying attention to shareholder value has become something of a treadmill for directors and senior management' (Calcutt 2007: 118).

A fascinating example of this pressure can be gleaned from a transcript of a conference call held in August 2011 between the Chairman, Chief Executive and Finance Director of Persimmon, one of the UK's leading housebuilders (see Chapter 7), and nine financial analysts based in London (Persimmon plc 2011). After the Persimmon management team had presented an upbeat assessment of the company's half-year results, it was interrogated intensively by the analysts. Among the issues raised were:

- why average sales prices had fallen, and whether they would continue to do so;
- how much value had been already written down from the company's land bank and whether further write-downs were likely;

- how quickly working capital would be turned over;
- how much land had recently been acquired and where it was located.

Significantly, not a single question was asked about design or place quality, or even about customer satisfaction. Indeed, the Persimmon transcript confirms Calcutt's (2007: 120) gloomy conclusion that 'In practice investors place little weight on any corporate achievement that does not ultimately lead to increased shareholder value. Conversely, unless they impact on future value, they are not concerned by failures in design quality or social responsibility.' As this suggests, the shareholder treadmill generates intense pressure on company management teams to maximise short-term returns. However, as we argue next, this should not be confused with long-term value.

Patient equity, sustainability and urban regeneration

According to Leinberger (2001), the short-term bias of finance capital has an immense impact on the character and quality of the built environment. He argues that investment returns for most conventional development products in the US peak around year seven. In contrast, he suggests that although those from 'walkable urbanism' are far superior over the medium to long term, even though they may take longer to become established and thus underperform conventional products in the short term. The challenge for place-making is thus to create financial vehicles that can provide what Leinberger (2007) calls 'patient equity'.

Similar thinking has been applied by Adair *et al.* (2006) to urban regeneration in the UK. They argue that the regeneration process consists of three distinct phases: remediation/infrastructure provision, development and investment (Figure 9.4). As regeneration projects move through these stages, risk decreases, but so do potential returns as revenue streams become more secure and capital values more predictable. These varying and overlapping risk/return profiles provide the opportunity to meet the portfolio requirements of different types of investors. Adair *et al.* (2006) also suggest that new forms of investment vehicles are needed in order to take full advantage of this potential, and make detailed recommendations on how this might be achieved.

One excellent example of how urban regeneration can be promoted through sustainable property investment is provided by the UK-based Igloo Regeneration Fund, managed by Aviva Investors.[4] This partnership between some ten pension and life funds (mainly in the public and charitable sectors) was established to invest in environmentally sustainable and well-designed developments close to the core of the UK's top twenty cities. Working with local authorities, development agencies and other community-based partners, Igloo has marshalled the necessary funding to drive forward the development of several major urban regeneration projects such as Bermondsey Square, Southwark and Islington Wharf,

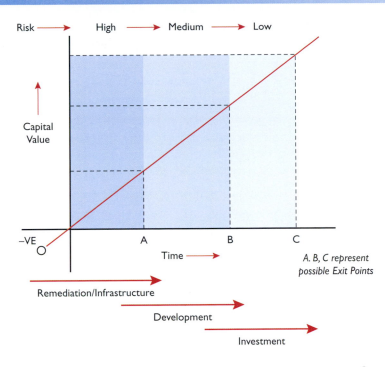

Risk ⟶ High ⟶ Medium ⟶ Low

Capital Value

–VE
O

A   B   C

Time ⟶

A, B, C represent possible Exit Points

Remediation/Infrastructure

Development

Investment

FIGURE 9.4

Regeneration phases and risk profiles. The remediation/infrastructure phase is characterised by high levels of risk, but with opportunities for specialist remediation companies to make high returns from cleaning up the land and benefiting from land value uplift. The added value from development activity is at the core of regeneration, but an unfinished and potentially unlet building still carries significant risks. Only with the completion and occupation of the development are these risks reduced. At this point, the opportunity for long-term capital appreciation in the investment market can begin to be realised. (Institutional Investment in Regeneration: Necessary Conditions for Effective Funding, Investment Property Forum, 2006)

Manchester. The projects span a range of commercial, business and residential uses, often including a significant element of mixed-use development.

Although Lützkendorf and Lorenz (2010) maintain that there is very significant global interest in 'socially responsible property investment' (SRPI), they suggest that this is held back by conceptual and technical problems. These make it difficult to prove the financial advantages of sustainable property development, rather than to merely show its risk-reduction benefits. In short, they argue that the main prerequisite to exploiting the full interest in SRPI products may well be the systematic collection of social, environmental and financial data that would enable a more sophisticated transaction base and SRPI index to be created.

The IPD Sustainability Index (IPD 2010a), launched in 2010, provides an important step in this direction, although it is likely to be some years before a reliable time series is established that will enable accurate comparison of the returns between what the index terms 'more sustainable' and 'less sustainable' properties. In this context, however, it is important to note that the IPD Regeneration Index is now well established on an annual basis and pulls together investment returns from over 500 properties located in English regeneration areas with a capital value of almost £5.5 billion.

The Regeneration Index (IPD 2010b) grew out of research originally undertaken by Adair *et al.* (2004). It demonstrates the potentially lucrative returns that can be achieved from urban regeneration (Figure 9.5), provided that investors stick with projects over the long term (even though comparative performance on an annual basis can edge above or below that across the UK as a whole, reflecting

FIGURE 9.5

Comparison of
regeneration property
returns with UK average
1999–2009. This graph
compares all commercial
property returns
1999–2009 in
regeneration areas with
the average across the UK
as a whole. Although
returns from regeneration
property appear more
volatile than the average,
the long-term trends in
both are similar. (IPD
Regeneration Index
sponsored by Argent,
Aviva and HCA)

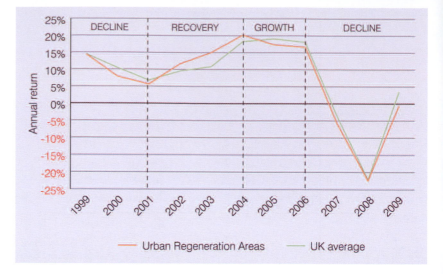

short-term property cycles). So, as both of the IPD innovations suggest, improved market information may well be the key to encouraging a more sustainable and patient approach to funding real estate development in the future and to facilitating new investment vehicles that can exploit this potential.

Conclusions

Debates around place quality often take place far removed from any understanding of the apparent logic of finance capital, but, as this chapter has shown, what is built reflects, and indeed is often driven by, what can be financed. Although the analytical capacity of real estate finance is technically far more sophisticated than it was a generation ago, this has primarily served to transform place into a financial asset, which, arguably, has exacerbated the inherent volatility of place production. Indeed, real estate development can quickly become dominated by financial analysts operating in global markets whose view of the complexities and realities of the development process in specific locations must inevitably be simplified by their own particular cultures and perceptions. The challenge for funding development in the twenty-first century will be to break out of narrowly driven perceptions of where best investment returns lie and to develop new analytical methods that enable the specific advantages of more sustainable forms of development to be best exploited.

As yet, there are only limited signs that such innovation is part of a place-led policy agenda. In Scotland, for example, although investor confidence was prioritised as a policy goal between 1999 and 2007, there was little policy analysis of exactly what actions might strengthen investor confidence, and indeed the very notion of investor confidence seems to have been accepted in uncritical terms. The important issue of investor information was hardly addressed, while no attempts appeared to have been made by the Scottish Executive to communicate with, or influence the investment priorities of, the main London-based pension funds and insurance companies (Adams *et al.* 2009a).

In contrast, it is important to acknowledge that the IPD Regeneration Index emerged out of publicly sponsored academic research, the results of which were enthusiastically taken up by the then UK Government. Essentially, the index challenged and transformed the perceptions of London-based investors towards real estate investment in regeneration areas, even if their actual investment decisions have not yet changed as much as might be justified by the index. Here lies the financial dilemma for place-makers. There may indeed, as Leinberger and others suggest, be better long-term returns to be secured from more sustainable forms of development, but the challenge is first to convince analysts that this is likely to be the case and then to promote the necessary cultural mindshift among them to ensure an actual funding shift towards sustainable urbanism.

PART 3

POLICY INSTRUMENTS

10 Shaping markets – making plans and reforming institutions

Introduction

In this chapter and the next, we look at how it is possible to create better places through shaping real estate markets. Market shaping is essentially about setting or resetting the context within which market actions and transactions take place. It is the first of four types of policy instrument which we examine in detail in this final part of the book. As in the case of the other three types of policy instrument – market regulation (Chapter 12), market stimulus (Chapter 13) and capacity building (Chapter 14) – attention is primarily focused on the impact of policy on market actors, and specifically on developers, landowners and funders in the private sector, whose strategies and actions were explored in the previous three chapters. For if we want to see more successful places created, we must not focus simply on public policy, but must critically evaluate the extent to which specific policies might shape, compel, constrain or inspire the behaviour, choices and actions of those key decision-makers closest to the problem. This approach equates to what Elmore (1987) termed 'backward-mapping', since it starts with potential impacts and works back to selecting policies.

Policies included within market shaping are those that *frame* what we call the 'decision environment' (or room for manoeuvre) of key market actors. Market shaping does not itself force any decisions upon market actors. Instead, working more subtly, it sets a context within which market actors can see benefit in meeting policy aspirations – in other words, it becomes 'worth it' for them to move in the direction intended by shaping instruments. We can identify three main types of market-shaping instruments. The first two work indirectly and are discussed in this chapter. These are the publication of plans, strategies, visions etc., which set out how the state thinks places ought to change over time, and the reform of such institutions as systems of property rights or taxation, which provide the broader framework for development. The third type of market-shaping instrument, which we term 'strategic market transformation', is discussed in the next chapter and involves direct state action that radically alters what market actors consider achievable at particular locations, normally of some scale.

These three types of instrument demonstrate in their different ways how market shaping is fundamentally concerned with joining up or integrating different decisions taken about the future of places across time and space. This may apply, for example, to the separate decision-making processes of different market actors or to the uncoordinated decisions that might otherwise be reached on adjoining sites. At the heart of market shaping is thus the conviction that the whole is potentially greater than the sum of the parts and that better integration is essential to its achievement. That is why the chapter now begins with an analysis of how real estate markets, left to their own devices, tend to induce disintegrated behaviour and create disintegrated places. On this basis, we then set out what might be expected of a more integrated approach to place-making, before then examining plans, strategies, visions etc., and institutional reform in more detail.

Challenging default urbanism

Explaining disintegrated places

Too often, real estate development creates places that function badly, impede social and economic interaction or have little visual appeal. Examples include repetitive greenfield housing estates with few facilities, short-life retail warehouses scattered around suburbia, and city-centre developments that pay no heed to their surroundings (Figures 10.1, 10.2 and 10.3). The result is what we might call '*default urbanism*' – the kind of second-rate places that emerge sporadically and spontaneously, when no one has consciously tried to do better.

Default urbanism results from *five failures of integration* in the real estate development process, namely:

- between one development site and the next, since it is often cheaper and quicker to develop sites in isolation;
- between the public and private realms, since no direct financial benefit may be thought to accrue from investing in the immediate vicinity of the development, compared to spending the same amount on additional floorspace;

FIGURE 10.1

Retail warehouse park, Dumbarton, Scotland. Here default urbanism is epitomised by low-cost forms of construction and extensive surface parking areas intended to attract shoppers from a distance. Retail warehouse parks such as this have proliferated across the UK since the 1980s. Although creating profitable development opportunities, they contribute little to local place character. (David Adams)

FIGURE 10.2

Housing development, Newton Mearns, Scotland. Here default urbanism is evident in the repetitive use of standard house types, creating an environment that could be anywhere. Developers remain reluctant to meet the full infrastructure costs of such peripheral expansion, which include new schools, roads and wastewater treatment systems. Lifestyle marketing rather than design quality is primarily used to sell such developments. (Steve Tiesdell)

FIGURE 10.3

Offices blocks on the edge of Glasgow City Centre, Scotland. Buildings such as these are designed primarily to meet commercial office floorspace requirements and are prone to rapid economic obsolescence as those requirements change. This monolithic type of default urbanism deadens the immediate streetscene and adds little to the image of the city. (David Adams)

- between use, investment and development value, since, unless the developer intends to retain ownership in the long-term, there may be little point in incurring expense that fails to produce an immediate return;
- between the additional infrastructure requirements (roads, sewerage systems, schools, hospitals etc.) generated by development and their provision, owing to the temptation to 'free ride' on whatever infrastructure already exists or is due to be built by the public sector;
- between the present and the future, since discounted cash-flow analysis prioritises present returns over future ones (especially at high interest rates), making developers suspicious of any sustainability features that do not produce immediate benefit.

Real estate developers who produce default urbanism do so because it seems entirely logical to them. Indeed, managing complexity in development requires a clear focus on what is immediate and achievable. This means paying little or no attention to potential knock-on effects, unless obliged to do so. For, as Chapters 3 to 5 made clear, real estate development is a highly risky business delivering a bulky capital good to markets that are far from perfect. Developers work hard to manage these risks. They undertake extensive preparations and often do not start on site until they have at least some commitment from end-users to buy or rent the completed space. Most stick to the products and markets they know best, hoping to learn from the mistakes of others who innovate first.[1] Above all, they try to remain on time during construction by keeping development as straight-forward as possible, consistent with the intended end-product. The rationale of the real estate developer is thus understandable, at least in its own terms. It reflects significant economic and financial deterrents to ensuring that individual developments contribute to the quality of the places where they are located and on whose vitality they ultimately depend.

Achieving integrated places

It is the responsibility primarily of governments to create an institutional framework that encourages and rewards integration within real estate development, and that deters disintegrated behaviour. For even if individual developers recognise that mounting urban congestion eventually reduces opportunities for profitable development, they may have little interest in whether their own developments contribute further to that congestion, unless required to do so. Similarly, two developers of neighbouring sites may know that they could reduce their costs, and perhaps even increase their revenues, by working co-operatively rather than in competition, but without a reliable institutional framework to promote integration, they may well default to the speedy option of developing their sites in isolation.

When governments shape markets successfully, this encourages and enables developers to do more than simply produce profitable developments – they become keen to help to create better places. This is not because they have turned unusually altruistic, but rather from a hard-headed realisation that institutional frameworks which encourage integrated and co-operative behaviour have the potential to significantly reduce risk for any individual developer. Indeed, in principle, most market actors support rather than oppose government action to shape markets because, as one interviewee in Sheffield put it, 'Developers and investors like to know what the picture is and what is happening in the long term and [whether] a place [has] got its act together' (quoted in Bell 2005: 91). Developers welcome the stability that government intervention can bring to real estate markets, even if they may express concern about particular types of intervention that impact on their individual plans.

When it is successful, market shaping can play a crucial role in breeding confidence, reducing risk and transforming developers' attitudes and behaviour towards place-making. It has the potential to ensure that individual developments come to be planned as part of a broader picture, rather than in isolation from each other. This means that the overall value of what is created, to both the local community and developers, exceeds what would otherwise have been the sum of its individual components. By helping to manage the complexity of real estate development while reducing its uncertainties, shaping markets has considerable capacity to produce all-round gains.

Yet, shaping markets is a challenging task for governments, and one with potential for failure as well as success. For example, governments are prone to information shortages, political horse-trading and pressure from powerful lobby groups (Webster and Lai 2003). To maximise the prospects of successful market shaping, two essential requirements must be met. The first is a clear articulation of how development *outcomes* which would otherwise have been produced by markets will be improved by the proposed government intervention, taking account of its likely transaction costs. The second is a clear specification of the necessary *processes* by which such preferred outcomes can best be delivered. Before we turn to exploring the three key processes of plan making, institutional reform and strategic market transformation in this chapter and the next, it is important to consider how 'plan-shaped' markets can produce better development outcomes and thus create better places than those produced if markets are left to their own devices.

As a starting point, analysis by Wong and Watkins (2009) of the desired outcomes of spatial planning in England in 2008 reveals five main policy themes:

- efficient use of land
- sustainable economic development
- environmental protection

- well-designed, resource-efficient development
- fostering sustainable communities.

Box 10.1 sets out these themes in more detail, according to Wong and Watkins' review of national policy statements. Although drawn from English experience and often contested there, these themes have resonance across much of the developed world. They reflect the optimism that shaping markets can create better kinds of places than those produced by real estate markets left to their own devices. Nevertheless, the intended outcomes of spatial planning, which Wong and Watkins (2009: 489) define in England as 'the combined effects on socio-economic and environmental changes brought by the planning system and other forces to achieve the objectives of sustainable development and sustainable communities', may be attributable, at least in part, to factors well beyond the scope of the planning system.

BOX 10.1 Key national policy themes in England 2008

Making suitable land available, and its efficient use for development in line with economic, social and environmental objectives to improve people's quality of life:

- ensuring the appropriate location of development
- encouraging an appropriate mix of development
- ensuring appropriate land supply and availability for various uses and activities
- increasing the supply of housing
- steering development towards 'brownfield' land

Contributing to sustainable economic development:

- encouraging economic growth
- increasing competition, consumer choice and competitiveness
- contributing to urban renewal
- contributing to a rural renaissance
- reducing the need to travel
- improving our local and national infrastructure

Protecting and enhancing the natural and historic environment, the quality and character of the countryside, and existing communities:

*   protecting 'greenfield land' from unnecessary development
*   preventing urban sprawl
*   environmental protection (natural and built/historic)
*   enhancing biodiversity
*   improving landscape and environmental quality
*   responding to climate change

Ensuring high-quality development through good and inclusive design, and the efficient use of resources:

*   enhancing the quality of places
*   high-quality design
*   energy reduction
*   promoting sustainable modes of travel
*   contributing to other national strategies (e.g. waste, renewable energy)

Ensuring that development supports existing communities and contributes to the creation of safe, sustainable, liveable and mixed communities with good access to jobs and key services for all members of the community

*   creation of sustainable communities
*   enhancing the quality of life
*   meeting the needs of the community
*   provision of local services
*   social inclusion
*   accessibility

Source: Wong and Watkins (2009: 488)

Drawing on the five English themes, but applying them more broadly, we can identify eight main ways in what we term '*plan-shaped markets*' aim to improve development outcomes in practice. These are set out in Box 10.2 and concern development location, product, quality, place, efficiency, horizons, consumers and production. Challenging default urbanism through shaping markets is fundamentally concerned with creating better places in one or more of these eight ways. Spatial plans, to which we now turn, are the first means to achieve this.

BOX 10.2 Outcomes in 'plan-shaped markets'

The following are eight ways in which 'plan-shaped markets' may seek to improve on outcomes produced by real estate markets, left to their own devices:

- by altering development *locations*, to promote more compact development
- by modifying development *products*, to achieve more varied places
- by transforming development *quality*, to produce environments that last longer
- by promoting developments that sustain *places*, rather than exhaust them prior to moving on elsewhere
- by enhancing development *efficiency*, through reducing demands on non-renewable resources
- by stretching development *horizons*, to take more account of the long term
- by broadening the notion of development *consumers*, to encompass local communities as well as those who purchase the products of development
- by increasing development *production*, to reduce shortages of built space.

Note: A much harder task not included in this list is that of managing development volatility by evening out the booms and slumps inherent within the real estate development process. Since development volatility is closely related to economic volatility more widely, this is a challenge more for macroeconomic management than for place shaping.

Making effective plans

The potential persuasiveness of plans

Governments regularly articulate what they think should happen to places by publishing spatial plans, strategies, visions, frameworks, policies, briefs, guidance and advice etc. What exactly is chosen from this menu varies over time and from country to country. Scotland, for example, has a national planning framework alongside a single national planning policy statement matched by strategic and local development plans prepared for different parts of the country. England, in contrast, has no equivalent planning framework at the national level. Following the

2010 election, it has abolished its regional spatial strategies, is in the process of replacing its previous series of national planning policy statements by a single document (confusingly called a national planning policy 'framework'), but otherwise will rely on local development frameworks and neighbourhood plans. We do not seek to explain in detail which types of planning document apply in the different parts of the UK, let alone in Europe and the US, since there is already a wealth of helpful references to which the interested reader can refer (see, for example, Caves and Cullingworth 2008, Cullingworth and Nadin 2006, Dühr *et al.* 2010).

We use the word 'plan' hereafter to include all such documents, for they have a common purpose: to make clear how the 'plan-maker' thinks places should change over time. Only in exceptional circumstances, however, is such change entirely driven and implemented by plan-makers. Instead, normally plans work by persuading other parties to share and to help implement the plan-maker's vision. Those parties may include other agencies or parts of government (see Chapter 6) as well as developers, landowners, funders and investors in the private sector (see Chapters 7 to 9). According to Hopkins (2001), the 'logic of making plans' derives from the valuable information they convey to such parties about interdependent decisions. Significantly, he suggests that the information contained within plans serves as an essential collective good, helping real estate markets to achieve better outcomes. On this basis, 'Plans are not inherently about government, collective choice or centralized control' (Hopkins 2001: 6) but are necessary to address uncertainty and manage complexity in real estate development.

Hopkins contends that plans have potential to improve spatial outcomes in four circumstances, which he terms the 'Four I's':

- where decisions are *interdependent*, such as where the value of land depends on road access, or vice versa;
- where decisions are *indivisible*, such as in road construction, where there is little point in building half a road to link two locations – it must either be built in full, or not at all;
- where decisions are *irreversible*, so that once a road is built, for example, it cannot be relocated or re-sized without cost;
- where decisions involve *imperfect foresight*, such where the likely numbers and type of future road users remain uncertain.

Whether or not plans succeed in shaping markets depends on what might be called their 'persuasiveness' in influencing parties not under the immediate control of the plan-maker. In Table 10.1 we identify nine key variables that determine how persuasive spatial plans are in practice. These are grouped under four main headings: substance, authority, resources and support. The more a plan is persuasive on each of these variables, the greater its chances of influencing outcomes.

TABLE 10.1 Nine key variables that determine the potential persuasiveness of plans

More persuasive	Key variable	Less persuasive
Substance		
Plans that derive from substantive analysis of socio-economic trends, including those affecting real estate markets, are more likely to include realistic proposals.	*Clear and apparent evidence base*	Plans that emerge rapidly without substantive analysis may not be taken seriously.
Where a plan's rationale derives from substantive understanding of how markets operate and can be shaped by public policy, its content is more likely to generate confidence.	*Plan's persuasive logic and rationale*	Where a plan's rationale demonstrates misunderstanding of how markets operate and can be shaped by public policy, its content is more likely to provoke criticism.
Authority		
If the plan maker is a government body with statutory powers, it is well placed to convince market actors of serious intent.	*Identity of plan maker*	If the plan maker is an entrepreneur or voluntary body, doubts may exist about long-term commitment to delivery.
Plans that are championed by successful political leaders may be taken more seriously.	*Charismatic, persuasive advocates*	Plans that have no serious political advocate may be considered of less significance.
Where plans are endorsed by higher levels of government, there is likely to be greater confidence in their survival.	*Endorsement by higher-level actors*	Where plans fail to be endorsed by higher levels of government, there will be doubts about how long they may last.
Resources		
Plan makers who can call upon significant resources to support implementation are likely to be held in high regard.	*Plan maker's capacity to marshal wider resources*	Plan makers who have access to few resources to support implementation may command little attention.
Support		
Plans that are communicated attractively are more likely to be noticed by key actors.	*Attractive communication and presentation*	Plans produced as official documents that are hard to read may tend to be left on the shelf.
The more plans engage relevant external stakeholders, the better their chances of implementation.	*Stakeholder engagement*	Plans prepared without serious stakeholder engagement may prove unrealistic, especially if

More persuasive	Key variable	Less persuasive
		significant capital investment is needed.
Plans that reflect community aspirations are more likely to be achieved without significant local conflict.	*Community support*	Plans that conflict with community aspirations may encounter significant local conflict.

BOX 10.3 Aberdeen City and Shire Structure Plan 2009–2030

The Aberdeen City and Shire Structure Plan is an ambitious long-term strategic plan intended to help diversify the economy of north-east Scotland well beyond its traditional strength in oil and gas, while enhancing the city-region's high quality of life and available stock of housing so that it can support a population of 480,000 by 2030, or about 9 per cent above the 2006 figure. About half of this growth is to be concentrated within Aberdeen itself, within another quarter taking place in two growth corridors along the main public transport routes north and south of Aberdeen (Figure 10.4).

The plan will play a significant role in shaping real estate markets in north-east Scotland over the next twenty years. Here, three examples stand out which illustrate points made in earlier chapters. First, developers are likely to focus their acquisition of building land on the settlements identified for new housebuilding, especially if market conditions there are strong. Conversely, developers will know that land purchases outside these settlements carry greater risk, since planning permission will be much harder to obtain.

Second, developers are informed in the plan that they will be expected to make significant contributions to the cost of infrastructure improvements required to support growth (including new educational, transport and water engineering systems). They will want to know what this will all cost, so that it can be reflected in any bids made for land.

Third, significant public investment in building the Aberdeen Western Peripheral Route, and in improving other major trunk roads and opening up new railway stations, will have major implications for the relative accessibility of different locations within the region, which in due course will be reflected in comparative real estate values between one location and another.

Our prime concern here is with the impact of plans on market actors, while recognising that the response of the public sector can be equally important. To illustrate this impact, in Box 10.3 we look at one region, north-east Scotland, which has experienced significant development pressure in recent decades and where planners have had to think carefully about their interaction with developers and other market actors. This highlights some of the main ways in which the Aberdeen City and Shire Structure Plan (see Figure 10.4), approved in 2009, is shaping real estate markets in the region.

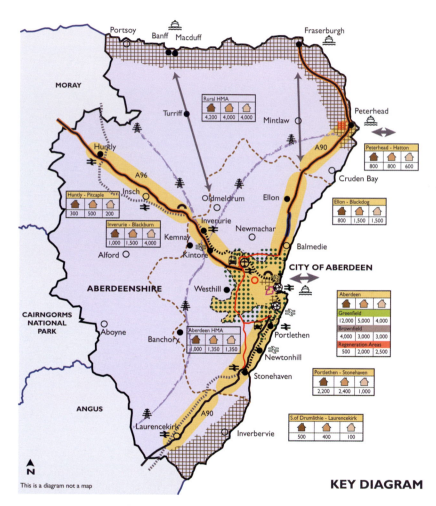

FIGURE 10.4

Aberdeen City and Shire Structure Plan 2009–2030. (Reproduced with permission from the Aberdeen City and Shire Strategic Development Authority)

KEY						
●	Towns over 3,000 people [2006]	⇌	Existing Railway Stations	⚓	Ports	
○	Towns over 1,500 people [2006]	⇌	Proposed Railway Stations	🚌	Park and Ride [Proposed Sites]	
	Strategic Growth Areas	⟷	Better Linkages	✈	Airport - Dyce	
	Local Growth & Diversification Areas		Aberdeen Western Peripheral Route	- - - -	Housing Market Area Boundary	
┼┼┼┼	Regeneration Priority Areas		A90 / A96 Improvements	🏠	Housing Allowances 2007-16	
∷∷∷	Greenbelt		Balmedie to Tipperty Dualling	🏠	Housing Allowances 2017-23	
⬭	Aberdeen City Centre	O	Haudagain Roundabout	🏠	Housing Allowances 2024-30	
▮▮▮▮▮	Crossrail Proposal	⌒	Third Don Crossing / Replacement Inveramsay Bridge	⊕	Potential Community Stadium Sites	
▬▬▬▬	Railway			▦	New Prison	
		⟷	External Sea Connections	🗼	Electricity Grid Reinforcement	

To explore how well plans shape real estate markets, we can identify six questions which draw on, but extend, the variables set out in Table 10.1. These questions, each of which we explore below, are:

- How far is the information in plans based on market analysis?
- To what extent are market actors involved in plan preparation?
- How far does information in plans change the behaviour of market actors, by encouraging them to re-think their own proposals, and/or act in a more integrated way?
- How well do plans reconcile the tension between flexibility and certainty for market actors?
- To what extent do real estate values take account of the information in plans?
- In what circumstances do plans need to be reinforced by other policy instruments?

The contribution of market analysis to plan information

If plans are to shape markets, they need to understand how markets work and how far they can be modified by planning actions. This means collecting information on how rents, prices, yields and other market variables are driven locally and evaluating how they might be affected by different planning options. Planners have traditionally collected information on people and place (for example, from the census and local surveys) and neglected real estate markets. Indeed, Healey (2006) believes that strategic spatial plans often fail to appreciate evolving market dynamics. Her research on the Cambridge sub-region suggests that this caused developers to hold back investment in the area.

Barker (2006) is amongst those who have controversially proposed that plans should do more to respond to market signals. While acknowledging that market data need to be treated with care, she identified six examples of market signals that could inform plan-making. These were property vacancies, take-up of newly built space, current construction rates, prime office rents, land values for different types of development and trends in property choices.

This kind of argument worries many planners, who remain suspicious about whether take-up rates, rents and prices are proper planning matters. They fear that any changes in planning rules to require close engagement with such information would result in market-led planning. This misses the point about plan-shaped markets, which are symbolised not by planning's simply responding to market information, but by the dynamic interaction of plans and markets, influencing each other. For example, in North Northamptonshire, local housing markets were transformed by plans that demonstrated how new housing would be linked to new retail, leisure and employment opportunities (Cowans *et al.* 2007).

The involvement of market actors in plan preparation

Plans are increasingly seen as an outcome of widespread stakeholder engagement, involving consultation with local communities, statutory agencies and infrastructure providers. This is considered an essential component of a collaborative planning process with potential to produce better-informed and more widely supported outcomes. The involvement of developers, landowners and other market actors in plan preparation needs to be handled with care, precisely because they may have a direct financial interest in the outcome of the planning process and can thus afford the best professional advice so as to advance their cause (Adams and May 1992). It is better to acknowledge this openly and establish different rules to handle engagement by market actors in plan preparation, compared to that by local communities, statutory agencies and infrastructure providers.

One tactic often used in plan-making is to encourage market actors formally to register all the preferred development proposals with the planning authority at an early stage, along with any community benefits they would be prepared to offer if development were permitted. This facilitates an open and even-handed evaluation of all such proposals and puts planners in a stronger position to negotiate and determine the combination of market proposals likely to be of most benefit to the local community.

The potential of plans to change the behaviour of market actors

Plans forewarn market actors about the future intentions of plan-makers. They may set out direct actions to be taken by the plan-maker, such as investment in new infrastructure, while also specifying the criteria by which the plan-maker will respond to any development proposals made by others. By providing such a public statement of intentions, plans can influence how market actors determine their own strategies. When more-demanding design standards were adopted in Chelmsford in the late 1990s, for example, they played a key role in subsequently raising the quality of designs submitted by private developers (Hall 2011).

Plans can also enable market actors to co-ordinate more effectively amongst themselves. Take, for example, a development brief for a major urban extension split among several builders. By specifying where the roads are to be built, where the school, health centre and other facilities are to be located, the brief facilitates co-ordination between builders, potentially at much lower transaction costs than if they had all to negotiate separately with each other.

The tension between flexibility and certainty for market actors

Market actors will pay more attention to plans which contain information that they consider to be authoritative. Authoritativeness is socially constructed, since it depends on the plan-maker's reputation for commitment and reliability, as well as the flexibility or certainty of the system itself (Alexander, 2001). In more flexible and discretionary systems (such as in the UK) the information content of plans may be less dependable than that in more rigid systems (such as in the Netherlands).

Barker (2006) argues that the British, plan-led system provides an effective balance between flexibility and certainty. This is because market actors know that development proposals made in accordance with the plan are more likely to succeed, while those that may conflict with the plan can still be considered because it is not legally binding. However, because plans can soon become out of date, they are increasingly seen in England as a type of loose-leaf file in which pages can be replaced on a regular basis, as circumstances change.

Any plan that is not regularly updated will be poorly placed to react to the ever-shifting dynamics of real estate markets. However, flexibility is a doubled-edged sword for market actors. While many owners may wish to retain maximum flexibility on their own land, they would often wish to see maximum certainty on adjoining land, so as to reduce the likelihood of negative externalities. This is an inherent problem in shaping markets and has led some to suggest that rules which facilitate externality contracts between adjoining owners may be more effective than plans and regulation in producing better urban environments (Webster and Lai 2003).

The extent to which plans are reflected in real estate values

While plans must take account of historic patterns of value, they help to determine future patterns of value. Historic patterns of value established by earlier generations and embedded in real estate markets constrain plans, since there is no simple and inexpensive way to write down what people are prepared to pay for existing property in built-up areas. This means that the ability of plans to refashion urban areas usually depends on the extent to which the plan increases land values, unless public subsidy is made available to compensate owners for any decrease in land values.

In new development locations, plans help to determine future patterns of value, and indeed create opportunities for owners to capture development value. For instance, agricultural land in the green belt is normally traded at the agricultural land prices (with perhaps some additional hope value to represent the possibility of its eventual release for development in the distant future). In contrast, land allocated for residential development will be traded at residential land prices. The difference between these two sectors can be quite staggering. For example, in 2010, the average value of a single hectare was £4 million if sold as residential building land in Oxford, compared to only £8,000 if sold as arable agricultural land in Oxfordshire (Valuation Office Agency 2010).

No intermediate market of any significance exists in the UK between land intended to remain in agricultural use and that likely to receive planning permission for residential development (Goodchild and Munton 1985). The reallocation of land from one sector of the market to another that is more valuable creates the chance for landowners to capture the difference in value between the two sectors, commonly termed development value. For example, if agricultural land is reallocated for residential development, provided that demand exists, it will immediately be traded at residential rather than agricultural land prices. In reality, it may take many years and great effort before reallocation happens and planning permission is granted. Furthermore, capital gains tax and any planning gain required by the local planning authority may reduce gross returns.

Plans thus shape real estate markets because the information they contain is soon reflected in the prices paid in individual transactions and thence in what are considered to be the underlying land values across the plan area. This makes it important for plan-makers to remember that every parcel of land has an owner and a value as well as a use, and that by assigning uses to land, plans also assign values. Planners need to think critically about the market impact of land allocations, both distributionally and in relation to the varied demands for land at different points in development cycles.

The reinforcement of plans by other policy instruments

Market conditions often determine how far plans need to be reinforced by other policy instruments that seek to regulate or stimulate development. This is shown in Table 10.2, which deliberately simplifies plans into three categories: those intended to restrict development, those intended to manage individual or incremental development and those intended to encourage integrated or collective development. Market conditions are also simplified into three categories, representing those markets that are stronger or weaker (by either time or space) and those that do not yet exist. This latter includes greenfield locations where no development has yet taken place, and brownfield locations where previous development has been exhausted.

Ironically, as Table 10.2 shows, plans are at their most effective when seeking to restrict development, provided that the plan is reinforced, as necessary, by effective regulatory power (see Chapter 12). This is exemplified by green belts, urban growth boundaries and similar containment policies. If market actors believe that restrictive planning policies cannot successfully be challenged, such policies will set the rules of the game within affected real estate markets. As a result, land values will reflect current use, even if tempered to some extent by some long-term speculative demand.

Plans that seek to manage individual or incremental development can prove highly successful in strong market conditions, especially where they facilitate

TABLE 10.2 Plan prospects according to market conditions

Market conditions	Intention of plan		
	Prevent development	Manage incremental development	Encourage integrated or collective development
Stronger markets	Plans can protect stronger markets from unwanted development, if backed by effective regulation. Development is likely to shift to next available location.	Plans can create collective confidence in stronger markets and help to secure high quality of incremental development, if backed by effective regulation.	Without effective implementation frameworks, collective action problems can undermine plans for integrated development even in stronger markets.
Weaker markets	Plans can protect weaker markets from unwanted development, if backed by effective regulation. Development may be lost to that region.	Plans alone may not generate even incremental development in weaker markets, so may require support from stimulus policies.	Without effective implementation frameworks, there may be little interest in integrated development in weaker markets.
No existing market	Plans that prevent development also inhibit market emergence.	Incremental development is unlikely, owing to 'prisoner's dilemma'* which also inhibits market emergence.	Without effective implementation frameworks, markets will not emerge to facilitate integrated development.

* See Chapter 3 for an explanation of the 'prisoner's dilemma'.

what market actors already want to do. Here, the planning challenge is relatively straightforward, making it easy for plan-makers to claim effectiveness. Landowners and developers are keen to proceed with development on their own sites and do not need to negotiate with each other to go ahead. The information contained within the plan establishes the ground rules for development. If the planning authority is expected to uphold and enforce the rules, collective confidence will be generated and externalities will potentially be resolved. Without the plan, individual developers may have been reluctant to invest, for fear of potential negative impacts from subsequent developments on neighbouring land.

In stronger markets, as the earlier Chelmsford example illustrates, plans can require and achieve high design quality on individual or incremental developments, provided that the plan is supported by effective regulatory power. In weaker markets, where plans try to achieve outcomes with which the market is reluctant to engage, even in order to produce incremental change they may need to be matched by policy instruments that stimulate demand (see Chapter 13).

Where plans are more ambitious and seek to encourage integrated or collective development, their success usually requires effective implementation frameworks that co-ordinate action between market actors to produce strategic transformation (see Chapter 11). Such frameworks are often better developed in Europe than in the UK, which is why 'Over the last ten or fifteen years, where the British have produced policies, plans and public inquiries, our European rivals have invested in transforming their cities' (Falk 2010: 39).

Reforming the institutional environment

Since markets are social rather than natural constructs (see Chapter 3), their operations reflect the context within which they are set as much as the individual choices of consumers and producers. Political, social, economic and legal institutions, for example, all structure the real estate development process. Over time, as these institutions evolve, the balance of risk and reward in development may alter. Shaping markets in this sense simply means that society pays more explicit attention to how markets are constructed, rather than entrusting this to informal change. As a result, decisive and deliberate institutional reform may from time to time be introduced, which has a significant effect on developer behaviour and development opportunities. In this section, we concentrate on two specific institutions to illustrate this: property rights and taxation systems.

Property rights reform

There would be little point in undertaking any real estate development without an effective system of property law to protect the developer from forced eviction. Real estate markets are therefore dependent on stable systems of government in which the rule of law is enforceable through the courts. Markets reflect the way in which the state chooses to structure, and occasionally restructure, its systems of property rights. Indeed, without effective property rights systems, there would be no real estate markets at all, other than in the most basic form. The way places evolve over time depends on, and points to, the particular property rights system in force at the time.

In the eighteenth century, for example, London's Mayfair and Edinburgh's New Town were hailed as pioneering forms of development which introduced the new urban concept of squares and terraces. However, from an institutional perspective, the development of Mayfair and the New Town took place only because the property rights systems in England and Scotland had by then so matured that their sophisticated landlord–tenant relationships were acknowledged and protected by law (see Chapters 2 and 3). The same principle applies today to gated communities, which have generated much controversy in the US and elsewhere (Webster 2002). What makes the 'gate' effective is not its physical strength, but the rights of those residing behind the gate to resort to law to protect their own privacy. These insights suggest that if places reflect their established systems of property rights, by modifying those systems in particular ways, it may be possible to achieve desired changes to places (Geuting 2007).

This has certainly been the recent thinking in Hong Kong, where a key policy challenge has been to encourage greater developer interest in the redevelopment of obsolete urban areas, in which numerous owners often hold property rights in the same building (for example, Figure 10.5). Multiple ownership of land or property creates significant redevelopment constraints in many countries. There are normally two conventional solutions, one private sector led and the other public sector led. The first requires a developer gradually to acquire all the property rights by private agreement. This may take considerable time and often involves working secretly through third parties. In this case, the developer can be held to ransom by the final few purchasers who demand excessively high prices for what is equivalent to the last pieces of the jigsaw. It needs only one owner to hold out to cause what is known in welfare economics as a lost opportunity (see Chapter 3). The second involves compulsory purchase of all property rights by the state, which prevents the loss of the redevelopment opportunity, but which can be highly expensive to the public purse, as well as administratively and legally complex.

In order to overcome this dilemma in Hong Kong, the Land (Compulsory Sale for Redevelopment) Ordinance was passed in 1999 to enable private developers who had acquired 90 per cent of the property rights in any redevelopment project to apply to the Lands Tribunal to force the sale of the remaining 10 per cent of property rights (Hastings and Adams 2005). This removes the advantage of holding out to the very end, and so encourages all owners to settle by negotiation. This privatised form of compulsory purchase provides an interesting example of how markets can potentially be reshaped to achieve desired policy ends (in this case, speeding up urban redevelopment) by making minor adjustments to property rights.

FIGURE 10.5 Physical obsolescence in Hong Kong. Despite a strong local property market, redevelopment of such obsolete buildings is often greatly impeded by their multiple ownership. Recent changes to property rights systems in Hong Kong provide developers with greater incentives to seek to acquire such property. (Ron Sumners)

In the US, where the courts are more protective of private property rights than in the UK, the concept of graduated density has similar intentions (Shroup 2008). This permits higher densities on larger sites, so rewarding developers who undertake land assembly. It has now been applied in several parts of the US to provide an economic imperative to promoting redevelopment through the private exchange of property rights. Similarly, in New York, public space, historic buildings and other uses of collective value are often protected from development by allowing the transfer of their development rights to nearby commercial or residential developments, which then benefit from greater height or higher density (Hack and Sagalyn 2011). Again, this illustrates how what is seen as a valuable property right in a particular institutional environment can be restructured to modify developer behaviour in support of broader policy intentions. Nevertheless, tradable development rights raise serious questions about equity and efficiency, which are addressed by Renard (2007), drawing on case studies from North America and France. More radically, property rights theorists argue that, in certain circumstances, extending the scope of property rights would be more effective than government intervention in tackling those urban externalities and public-good shortages that are seen by welfare economics as evidence of market failure (Webster and Lai 2003).

Taxation reform

The way in which real estate is taxed can also have important consequences for how places change. The three attempts made in the UK in the mid-twentieth century to capture increases in development value for the state, through some form of betterment levy or development charge, were argued to have significantly reduced the flow of land supplied for development (Goodchild and Munton 1985). More broadly, there have been extensive campaigns since the late nineteenth century to introduce land value taxation into the UK (Connellan 2004). This has been claimed by its proponents as both a fairer and more effective system of taxation than many fiscal measures currently employed, as well as one that would lead to the more efficient use of land and property.

More specifically, it is also argued that current taxation systems encourage urban vacancy and dereliction. The Urban Task Force (1999) certainly thought that the introduction of a vacant land tax, coupled with changes to the rules on VAT, corporation tax, stamp duty and local rates, would help to bring about its concept of an urban renaissance in the UK. Since taxing vacant land may discourage site assembly in strong markets and be ineffective in weak ones (Adams *et al.* 2000), the example illustrates how the potential negative impacts of institutional change need to be considered carefully alongside intended positive impacts.

Shaping markets through significant reform of taxation systems has been a long-standing theme amongst economists. As the above examples suggest, this theme has been applied only sporadically to real estate markets, although, as we discuss in Chapter 13, targeted taxation incentives have often been used on a temporary basis as a stimulus to development of specific types or in specific locations.

Conclusions

This chapter has explored two main ways in which it is possible to shape places by shaping the markets from which they emerge. As an exercise in institutional design, shaping markets seeks to rewrite the rules of the game by which real estate markets operate. This is intended to ensure integration between market actors, while transforming their attitudes and behaviour so as to create better places. By addressing the five failures of integration within real estate development, shaping markets aims to improve development outcomes in relation to location, product, quality, sustainability, efficiency, time horizons, perceived consumers and scale of production.

Of the two shaping instruments covered in this chapter, making plans is the more familiar in the British context. While plans are increasingly seen as an exercise in spatial government, we identified and explored six tests of their effectiveness as instruments to shape real estate markets. We suggested that plans are likely to be most effective as place changers when operating in strong markets and supported by the necessary regulatory power.

Some of the intentions in plans may be equally well pursued, although perhaps more subtly, by reforming the institutional environment for real estate development, primarily by making changes to property rights and taxation systems. Yet beyond these two indirect approaches to shaping markets lies the possibility of more concerted state action, especially at strategic locations. In the next chapter we therefore turn to consider more direct intervention within real estate markets, in which the state is able to take the lead in radically transforming what market actors consider achievable at specific places. As we shall see, at its most ambitious, such strategic market transformation amounts to an endeavour in market making as well as place shaping.

11 Shaping markets by strategic transformation

Introduction

Strategic market transformation is intended to deliver development of a scale beyond that attainable by any single market actor or, indeed, any informal combination of actors. It can be deployed to create entirely new places or rescue places that have fallen into decline. These typically include significant urban expansions, major regeneration projects and comprehensive city-centre improvements, although its principles are more widely applicable. Strategic market transformation involves a 'place production process' that aims to generate and capture the added value that comes from comprehensive, well-planned and integrated approaches to development, as compared to those where the future of individual plots is each determined separately.[1] This makes sustainable development financially attractive, since the greater initial investment required in place-making creates the basis for higher long-term investment returns.

Strategic market transformation produces both a wholly new or radically transformed place and a set of real estate markets spanning development, occupation and investment that reflect and underpin its vitality. Indeed, the ultimate economic test of any such transformation is whether it produces places that are attractive enough to draw in large numbers of people, whether to live, work or visit. Strategic transformation can thus be evaluated by the extent to which people are prepared to invest in new homes or businesses in the area. In short, shaping markets and making places are intrinsically and continuously interconnected.

At its core, strategic transformation resolves what are known as 'collective action' problems. Although it creates pure private goods, such as development sites available for sale, what make strategic transformation really worthwhile are better connectivity, enhanced spatial efficiency and improved urban design etc. We call these collective goods, since they are characterised by unclear property rights, which makes them neither wholly public nor wholly private.[2] Such collective goods are not easily delivered through informal market mechanisms, but normally require well-specified rules in order to determine how they are paid for, and by whom. Without special institutional arrangements, developers find it hard to charge consumers for their consumption (Webster and Lai 2003). As a result, consumers and other producers will be tempted to 'free ride' on any collective goods available, making developers reluctant to further supply the market.

The successful provision of collective goods provides an important test of strategic transformation, since it seeks to resolve collective action problems by devising institutional arrangements that are able to fund collective goods from the added value of integrated development, while still leaving individual market actors with the incentive to deliver individual development components. This requires someone to take on the important role of 'place promoter'. Such institutional arrangements, if effective, shape real estate markets and facilitate more ambitious planning by radically changing what market actors consider achievable in particular locations.

There are five main types of people or organisations[3] who can play the role of place promoter:

- *A local municipality*, common across much of Europe, where municipalities often see place promotion as an integral part of their civic mission. In this chapter, we draw on two such examples: Hammarby-Sjöstad in Stockholm and IJburg in Amsterdam.
- *A public-sector development agency*, normally accountable to central government. This is common in the UK, where new town development corporations, and subsequently urban development corporations, have been centrally involved in strategic transformation. In recent years, English Partnerships (now part of the Homes and Communities Agency) has been at the forefront of this activity. In this chapter, we draw on two examples promoted by English Partnerships: Allerton Bywater in Yorkshire and Upton in Northamptonshire.
- *A public-private development partnership*, common in many parts of the world. In this chapter, we draw on the examples of Adamstown near Dublin and Vathorst in the Netherlands.
- *A single entrepreneur or 'town founder'*. Although this is relatively rare in practice, Chapter 8 gave the examples of Robert S. Davis at Seaside in Florida, John 'Kiki' Wallace at Prospect, Colorado and Jon and William Moen at Newhall in England.[4]

- *An entrepreneurial club*, which is essentially a device to organise the production and consumption of collective goods among a variety of private-sector interests on the basis of membership contributions or fees (Webster and Lai 2003). Entrepreneurial clubs work by commodifying what might otherwise be semi-public goods, establishing a means of exclusion and then charging users a contribution or fee.[5] Webster and Lai (2003) suggest that clubs can overcome the problems of collective action and ambiguous property rights, provided that they possess a source of investment and working capital, a management capability, a constitution and a membership. In this chapter, we draw on the example of Fairfield Park in Bedfordshire (Adams *et al.* 2011a) to illustrate how it is possible to achieve strategic market transformation in this way.

Although entrepreneurial clubs, and to a lesser extent single entrepreneurs, are not unusual as a means to overcome collective action problems at greenfield sites, they rarely take on the risk of really large-scale developments. In most cases, strategic market transformations, especially at brownfield locations, are led by the public sector, which is why this chapter focuses primarily on the first three types of place promoter in the above list. Nevertheless, the principles established here are also applicable to strategic transformations led by the private sector.

The chapter presents a schematic 'event-sequence' model of the place-production process (Figure 11.1). This is based on the 'event-sequence' model of the development process presented in Chapter 5, but applied to a major part of the city instead of a single development site. Once again, the model has three main sides or phases, which in this case are labelled strategic promotion, strategic preparation and strategic implementation.

Figure 11.1 can be understood and used in a four distinct ways. First, it can be applied as an *explanatory* model or a means of emphasising key events, processes and activities from a more complex picture. Second, this enables it to serve as an *analytic* ideal or means to measure how far reality corresponds to, or differs from, the model. Third, it provides a *descriptive* model of how new places actually come about in practice. Fourth, it can be seen as a *normative* model of how the place-production process should ideally be undertaken. Although derived from eight case studies we investigated across Europe (Adams *et al.* 2011b), its potential in each of these ways could no doubt be enhanced by exploration of further case studies.

The normative concept of what constitutes a quality place occupies both the start and finish of the place-production process. In Chapter 2, we suggested that places which are designed with people primarily in mind, are well connected and permeable, of mixed use and varied density, have their own identity and distinctiveness, and are intended to be sustainable, resilient and robust, are more likely to be successful over time than those which are not. In this chapter we take these characteristics as representative of place quality, while acknowledging that

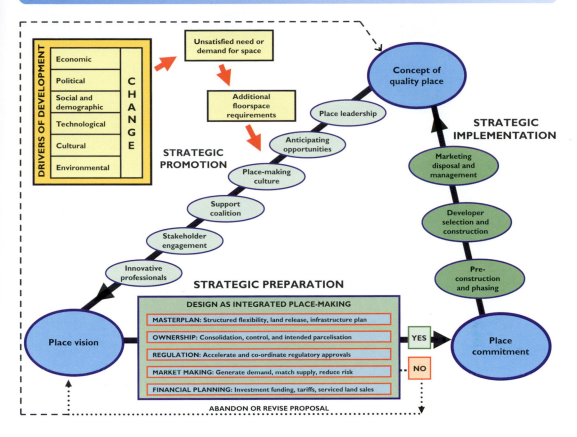

FIGURE 11.1

An event-based model of the place production process.

their meaning and value may be contested. This is because the desire to create such places often serves as a beacon of hope that sparks real commitment to the place-production process. However, even when completed, places developed to a high quality may deteriorate over time, unless they are well managed. As we shall see, a determination to maintain and enhance place quality well after the end of the production process is vital to the continued success of any place.

As Figure 11.1 suggests, on the first side of the model, the place promoter builds a broad coalition of support behind the vision of creating somewhere that functions as a sustainable, integrated and high-quality place, rather than a series of separate development projects. On the second side, all the necessary preparations are undertaken to enable the project to proceed. On the third side, the implementation process is carefully managed by the place promoter to ensure quality, distinctiveness and sustainability in all that is built. Each side must be completed before moving on to the next, but, as with the site-development process, the precise sequence of events within each side may vary. The next three sections of the chapter explain each of these sides or phases in turn. In the final section of the chapter, we summarise the key characteristics of the place-production process and evaluate the implications of such a commitment to strategic transformation for development costs, revenues and risks.

Strategic place promotion

Effective place leadership

The place-production process may indeed be inspired by the desire to create sustainable places of real quality, but it requires enthusiastic champions in order to implement such a broad concept successfully at specific locations. Effective leadership (see Chapter 6) matters because it drives forward action, breeds confidence, reduces risk and widens participation. This is the task of the place promoter, whom we can think of as a dynamic individual or set of individuals working within a supportive organisational context. Sometimes the place promoter may be a professional employee or group of employees, sometimes an elected politician or group of politicians.

Some place promoters have a high external profile and are well known. This was certainly the case at Hammarby-Sjöstad (Box 11.1 and Figure 11.2), where Stockholm's City Planner, Jan Inge-Hagström, was the driving force behind the masterplan and its implementation. Other place promoters operate in the background. For example, a succession of innovative professionals working for Projectbureau IJburg within Amsterdam's Dienst Ruimtelijke Ordening (City Planning Department) drove that project forward. The Amsterdam example demonstrates the importance of a supportive organisational context in enabling well-qualified and highly motivated people, and not constraining them, and ensuring that they are replaced if they move on elsewhere. This is why we use the term 'place promoter' to encompass both the organisation and the individuals who work within it, while fully recognising that the nature of the relations between them will vary from place to place.

BOX 11.1 Hammarby-Sjöstad, Sweden

For decades a place of low-rent industry and scrapyards, Hammarby-Sjöstad provides an excellent example of meticulously planned and executed sustainable urban regeneration, driven forward by the municipality. When complete, Hammarby-Sjöstad will contain 10,800 homes and 200,000m² of office space built by private developers, within the context of extensive physical and social infrastructure, installed by the City Council as master developer. It is linked by a tram to the T-Bana metro system and is adjacent to Stockholm's southern ring motorway. The development is considered an international exemplar of best sustainability practice for pioneering the 'Hammarby Model' of handling energy, water supplies and waste streams. A high-quality 'water cycle' recovers waste heat and other products from sewage, with methane then used to produce energy. This closed-circuit system reflects the wider environmental aims of the project, which will ensure that all flats use only 50 per cent of the energy and water of a typical Swedish development of 1990.

Development of Hammarby has taken place at a much faster pace than is experienced in speculative UK developments, with about 600–700 homes completed each year on what is a 200-hectare mixed-used waterfront development. The place vision, which was created by the late Jan Inge-Hagström, Stockholm's City Planner, and implemented with high levels of consensus, shows how widespread commitment to design excellence can produce a highly successful place. Stockholm City Council has invested about €500 million in land acquisition, reclamation and infrastructure provision, which by 2010 had already produced a return of around €3 billion of private investment.

For further information, see Adams *et al.* (2011b) and visit: www.future communities.net/case-studies/hammarby-sjostad-stockholm-sweden-1995 2015, www.hammarbysjostad.se/, http://webarchive.nationalarchives.gov.uk/ 20110118095356.

FIGURE 11.2 Hammarby-Sjöstad, Sweden. (Image by Smith Scott Mullan Associates)

Anticipating opportunities

The place-production process responds to exactly the same external drivers of change as does the real estate development process, but on a larger scale. Successful place promoters anticipate how these external drivers will create what

Jessop (see Chapter 5) calls 'conjunctural moments', reflected in what we term 'windows of development opportunity' (see Chapter 5). For example, the inclusion of IJburg as a 'VINEX' or strategic growth location in the fourth Dutch Ten Year Housing Programme (1996 to 2005) was a major spur to its development. In the UK, the then Deputy Prime Minister, John Prescott, launched a programme of sustainable Millennium Communities in 1997 and the former colliery site of Allerton Bywater readily met the requirements (Box 11.2 and Figure 11.3). Adamstown represented a joint response from South Dublin County Council and a large private developer to the then booming Irish housing market.

BOX 11.2 Allerton Bywater, Yorkshire, England

Allerton Bywater is a former colliery site six miles south east of Leeds, which was chosen in 1998 for the development of a sustainable Millennium Community with 520 new homes and 25,000m^2 of commercial development. Millennium Communities were promoted by the Deputy Prime Minister, John Prescott, as a means to 'deliver a lasting legacy of environmentally innovative and sustainable developments in diverse, challenging locations'.

Extensive dereliction and long-standing depopulation meant that Allerton Bywater was not readily attractive to private housebuilders. However, its development prospects were transformed by English Partnerships, the government agency which inherited the site from the former National Coal Board and invested £24 million on site clearance, decontamination, roads and drainage. A masterplan and design code then enabled the site to be divided into serviced land parcels, attracting housebuilders through competitive bidding. Nevertheless initial progress was slow, so English Partnerships decided to take a more 'hands on' role as place promoter, with some housebuilders replaced by others. On completion of the first phase in 2005, competitive pricing of newly built homes, along with the high quality of development, enabled an active local housing market to be established. With about half the homes built by 2010, the project has demonstrated how strategic transformation can help to reverse decline and attract population into previously unfavoured area.

For further information, see Adams et al. (2011b) and visit: www.homesandcommunities.co.uk/allerton-bywater-leeds and http://webarchive.nationalarchives.gov.uk/20110107165544.

FIGURE 11.3 Allerton Bywater, Yorkshire, England. (Steve Tiesdell)

Place-making culture

Such external pressures can easily give rise to 'default urbanism' (see Chapter 10) – the kind of second-rate places that emerge sporadically and spontaneously when no one has consciously tried to do better. Strategic transformation stands in direct opposition to default urbanism. It requires the place promoter to champion and engender an explicit culture of place-making which turns what might otherwise be a series of separate development projects into somewhere distinctive that works successfully as a whole. To achieve this, place promoters may need to challenge vested or sectional interests keen to promote their own domains, confront rules and regulations that deliver minimum standards but no more, and ensure that those in varied positions of influence and authority come to share in the emerging place vision. This requires the place promoter to build a broad coalition of support.

The support coalition

Successful places are championed by many more people and organisations than the place promoter alone. The precise list varies from one place to another but may well include prominent politicians, government bodies and agencies, professional experts, development interests, community groups and the media. These interests may be based locally, regionally or nationally, but the extent to which they are prepared to 'buy in' to any project is crucial to its success. Without a support coalition, the project may fall victim to its critics.

Stakeholder engagement

Stakeholder engagement is essential to give voice to this support coalition, to benefit from its expertise and enthusiasm and to ensure that what emerges as a place vision is one to which many others apart from the place promoter are fully committed. The development of Hammarby-Sjöstad was based on consensus between all relevant stakeholders and required numerous meetings to achieve this. At Upton, two 'Enquiry by Design' workshops proved highly effective in mobilising such broader support for the project (Box 11.3, Figure 11.4 and Chapter 6). Place promoters need well-developed communication skills in listening to, and learning from, a wide range of people beyond their own organisations.

BOX 11.3 Upton, Northamptonshire, England

In the 1960s, a New Town Development Corporation was established to expand Northampton. When the Corporation completed its work, its surplus assets passed to the Commission for New Towns, which was eventually subsumed into English Partnerships (now part of the Homes and Communities Agency). The potential development area of Upton, three miles to the south west of the town centre, was thus still in public ownership when further major expansion was proposed in the late 1990s.

With the encouragement of the then Deputy Prime Minister, John Prescott, who wanted to promote better-designed urban neighbourhoods, English Partnerships teamed up with the Prince's Foundation (a charitable trust created by the Prince of Wales to promote sustainable urbanism). Together, they ran two Enquiry by Design charrettes in 1999 and 2001. These proved catalytic in creating early consensus and partnership among relevant stakeholders and local communities that Upton should become a demonstration project in sustainable greenfield expansion.

Development commenced in 2003, with the site parcelled up into eight development blocks, according to an overall masterplan. English Partnerships invested over £24.6 million in advance infrastructure, but expects to recover at least this investment in higher receipts from serviced land. Alongside the first phase of 1,350 new homes on a 43-hectare development, a primary school, new shops and community facilities are all planned. Later phases will add a further 3,600 homes to the development. All developers are required to conform to the high expectations of the design code, with strong competition between them for land reinforcing the chances of developing Upton as a well-designed and environmentally sensitive urban exemplar.

For further information, see Adams *et al.* (2011b) and visit: www.homesandcommunities.co.uk/upton-sustainable-urban-extension, www.northamptonshireobservatory.org.uk/docs/doc_Uptoncasestudy.pdf_113342150306.pdf and http://webarchive.nationalarchives.gov.uk/20110118095356.

FIGURE 11.4 Upton, Northampton, England. (Steve Tiesdell)

Innovative professionals

Even at this early stage, place promoters often find it helpful to appoint innovative designers and facilitators with prior experience of successful place-making who are prepared to offer critical professional advice in bringing the project to fruition. Such independent consultants are often well placed to draw together all the expertise coming through stakeholder engagement so as to create a compelling vision of how the place might develop. By this point, the place-production process has reached an important stage, and the focus now shifts from strategic promotion to strategic preparation.

Strategic place preparation

On the second side of the place-production process attention focuses on what needs to be done in order to turn the place vision into a practical reality capable of implementation. Here five main tasks, each of which is examined in turn below, need to be integrated by the place promoter and all completed before implementation can begin. These are the production of the masterplan or spatial development framework, the consolidation and intended subdivision of ownership, any necessary regulatory approvals, making real estate markets, and financial planning.[6] Here, the design process plays a crucial role in integrating these five tasks, resolving conflicts, exploiting opportunities and ensuring that the focus remains firmly on place-making.

The masterplan or spatial development framework

A robust and imaginative spatial development framework is essential to creating somewhere that functions as an integrated place. This typically starts as a set of conceptual sketches, ideas and options, and develops over time into a masterplan. In this context, Tiesdell and Macfarlane (2007) make the important distinction between 'blueprint' and 'coded' masterplans. Blueprint masterplans treat a development, however large, as a single architectural project with, effectively, a single (meta) designer who prescribes a specific outcome which covers all aspects of urban space and building design. Since uncertainties over time and space make it almost impossible to stick to a closely defined product from the outset, 'coded' masterplans are far more common (both currently and historically) in managing urban development.

Coded masterplans prescribe important principles, while permitting discretion on other matters. They create a spatial development framework, which 'offers structured choice and flexibility with degrees of freedom for developers and designers', each of whom then have 'scope to contribute to the richness and variety of the resulting place' (Tiesdell and Macfarlane 2007: 408–9). Design codes (see Chapter 12) are often prepared to support and elaborate on such masterplans.

Place promoters should directly commission the masterplan and then take overall responsibility for its implementation, not delegating either of these tasks to another party. Too often in the UK, masterplans have been seen as indicative documents, produced to generate market interest rather than tied to implementation. At the Royal Docks in London, for example, over seventy separate masterplans were produced for the same site, with little practical impact. This type of masterplanning has been criticised by Falk (2011: 38) as 'an exercise in architecture on a grand scale, wasting resources rather than mobilising them'. In contrast, municipalities in Europe typically work hard with local communities and potential developers to produce a single masterplan on land they own, which is then implemented. This 'positively shapes the context within which developers act, while the incentive of infrastructure means that "design strings" can be attached' (Falk 2011: 38).

Although the best masterplans strike a balance between certainty and flexibility, to be effective they must co-ordinate strategic decisions about form and layout, land release and infrastructure provision. As intimated in Chapter 2, most contemporary masterplans adopt a form and layout structured around traditional street blocks set within interconnected street patterns. Such an approach has been characterised as 'designing cities without designing buildings' (Barnett 1974). This encourages a clear strategic focus on creating well-connected and permeable places, often as major extensions of urban centres, but leaves unresolved more detailed decisions that fundamentally influence the likely success of the urban block as a place-making device. As we therefore contend below, effective master-plans need to be related to the proposed arrangements for the subdivision or parcelisation of development areas.

The intended provision of physical and social infrastructure should be clearly specified within the masterplan. Physical infrastructure includes roads, public trans-port, open space, sewers, drainage, water and service utilities etc. Some elements such as roads and sewers are essential, while others are more discretionary. Social infrastructure covers schools, shops, nurseries, community facilities etc. Provision here typically occurs when commercially viable or triggered by a certain population threshold, both of which tend to be later than when the need first occurs. In order to ensure that the necessary physical and social infrastructure is planned and provided as an integral part of the overall development programme, it needs to be funded as part of the financial plan for the project (see below).

Ownership consolidation and parcelisation

Land ownership is a far more powerful way to deliver strategic transformation than is planning control. When deployed effectively, it can shape markets by creating certainty, enhancing confidence and reducing developer risk. Place promoters who already own, or who can acquire, the entire development area can:

- masterplan for the benefit of the area as a whole, rather than as a means of reconciling conflict between different owners;
- ensure efficient provision of collective infrastructure, if necessary by raising capital against land value;
- control the parcelisation and phasing of development areas to achieve place diversity;
- set quality standards that must be met by all developers bidding for parcels, with competitive bidding then used to select the winning developer;
- impose conditions of sale and lease to achieve high design quality and effective subsequent management.

Both Allerton Bywater and Upton were in long-standing state ownership and 'inherited' by English Partnerships. Much of Hammarby-Sjöstad was previously owned by Stockholm City Council, with the remainder acquired by compulsory purchase. Although IJburg was built on artificial islands created from the IJmeer, the city council had still to acquire the seabed from the National Land Holding Organisation. The Adamstown site was assembled and banked over several years

FIGURE 11.5
Land consolidation and distribution. Rather than creating a single product, land consolidation should be seen as a means to enable multiple participation by a diversity of developers.

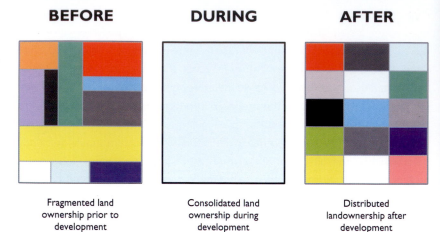

BEFORE

DURING

AFTER

Fragmented land ownership prior to development

Consolidated land ownership during development

Distributed landownership after development

by the private developers, who ultimately partnered with South Dublin County Council in the development. As these examples illustrate, ownership control turns the place promoter into a master developer (see Chapters 5 and 7) able to achieve quality of delivery and ensure provision of the necessary physical and social infrastructure.

Yet, since most large developments are usually built out as a series of smaller projects, the consolidation of land ownership is but an interim stage in the place-production process (see Figure 11.5). The intended subdivision or parcelisation of land is equally important and should be resolved as part of the masterplan. As Love and Crawford (2011: 93) argue, 'A careful parcel map, along with a set of regulatory guidelines, can and should be used as the primary tool with which to craft the character of successful new urban districts.' This is because parcelisation strategies affect the scale of developer willing to participate and so produce different outcomes. Owing to their larger operation, larger developers may need larger parcels in order to gain sufficient economies of scale. Smaller parcels attract smaller developers, increase consumer choice and reduce the impact of any one developer's proceeding slowly.

Figure 11.6 shows four common approaches to parcelisation, based on traditional urban block structures. It indicates how parcels can be defined by multi-blocks, blocks, streets or plots, with different implications for whether streets are contained within parcels and whether the seam between parcels is visible and intrusive. Smart parcelisation subdivides one large development area into different-sized parcels, encouraging a diversity of developers and designers. Love and Crawford (2011: 102) argue that smart parcelisation can produce 'greater bandwidth' that 'seeks to balance the advantages of large and flexible parcels with modest parcels that will attract capital investment at a smaller scale and create a city with more physical diversity'. The latter facilitates subsequent incremental change, and so enhances long-term resilience.

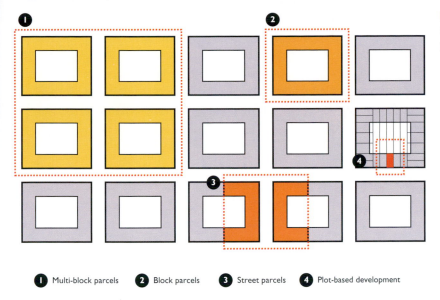

FIGURE 11.6
Four approaches to land parcelisation.

① Multi-block parcels **②** Block parcels **③** Street parcels **④** Plot-based development

Although most large developments in the UK are subdivided into multi-block or block parcels, plot-based development is popular in much of Europe. One part of IJburg, for example, employed plot-based parcelisation to ensure a mix of 4- and 5-storey narrow townhouses, 3-storey terraces and 2- and 3-storey detached, terraced and semi-detached houses, with styles ranging from mock-seventeenth century to ultra-contemporary (Figure 11.7). This highly diverse range of building types was achieved through small building plots and a strong self-procurement

FIGURE 11.7
Plot-based development at IJburg, Netherlands. (Steve Tiesdell)

culture and by setting only limited rules about overall form (such as on overall height, height of ground-floor ceiling and building line).

By making sure that each successive parcel makes its own positive contribution to the overall area, the place promoter can secure higher prices for later parcels. Effective parcelisation is both a design and a financial strategy, since it seeks to achieve a higher return per square metre from those parcels sold later.

Regulatory approvals

Delivering new places normally involves obtaining numerous regulatory approvals, often from different state agencies. The standard procedure of sequential individual approvals can have a devastating impact on project viability because the time taken can significantly lengthen the development period, increase development risk and cause 'windows of development opportunity' to be missed. Alongside this, regulatory decisions can be highly unpredictable or simply in conflict with each other. A classic example of the latter occurs when a planning authority encourages the development of shared highway space or 'home zones' but the highway authority refuses to give its approval. The challenge here is to accelerate and co-ordinate the approval process. At Adamstown (Box 11.4 and Figure 11.8), statutory declaration as a Strategic Development Zone enabled arrangements to be put in place to achieve this.

Ideally, place promoters may wish to see sequential individual regulatory approvals replaced by simultaneous multiple approvals (see Chapter 12). Alternatively, if the regulatory bodies can be persuaded to sign up to an agreed design code, then it becomes much clearer what needs to be achieved at individual developments, with those meeting the code having almost the status of deemed consent.

Making real estate markets

Strategic market transformation is so called because the scale of development normally envisaged requires the creation of wholly new real estate markets or, in the case of regeneration areas, the reinvigoration of markets that are not working at all well. If public expenditure and effort in such areas is to serve as an investment, rather than as a long-term subsidy, developers, investors and occupiers must be persuaded that flourishing real estate markets can be created where none previously existed and that such markets will move through to maturity without too much delay. By taking co-ordinated action to integrate masterplan production, ownership consolidation and subdivision, regulatory approval and financial planning, strategic market transformation radically alters what market actors think possible and so facilitates the emergence of markets whose potential would otherwise be constrained by problems of collective action.

BOX 11.4 Adamstown, Ireland

Adamstown is a new town of around 10,000 homes, along with schools and other social infrastructure and 125,000m^2 of commercial space currently under development on a 224 hectare site to the west of Dublin. A master-plan and a design code, which set the development framework, envisage Adamstown as a sustainable mixed-use, medium-density settlement with a traditional town layout.

Adamstown was designated as a Strategic Development Zone by the Irish government in 2001, which means that the public and private sectors have managed the entire development process in partnership. This has involved a simplified planning regime, with a joint project team established between the partners to co-ordinate delivery. At the peak of development in 2007, there were fifty-five separate consultants working on Adamstown, including architects, civil and structural engineers, transport consultants and urban designers. The project team provided an almost daily channel of communication between the developers, their consultants and various public-sector regulators. While such intense integration of the development regulation may be applicable only to major developments, it demonstrates what can be achieved when all parties work together in a co-ordinated way.

For further information, see Adams *et al.* (2011b) and visit: http://www.adamstown.ie/.

FIGURE 11.8 Adamstown, Ireland. (George Weeks)

Making real estate markets in such circumstances involves two main tasks. The first is to generate demand (which is one reason why place quality is so important), while matching supply flows to that demand so as to ensure that price projections can be achieved. The second is to create confidence and reduce risk, especially for those who are the first arrivals or development pioneers. Risk reduction enables faster development production (exemplified by the 600–700 new homes completed annually at Hammarby-Sjöstad) at a higher all-round quality.

BOX 11.5 IJburg, Netherlands

Built on a series of artificial islands, IJburg is a meticulously planned and executed sustainable urban extension to the east of Amsterdam, aiming to create the character, feel and amenity of the city's more established neighbourhoods. First mooted in 1965, the development was approved in principle in 1994, with island construction commencing in 1999 and roads and building starting two years later. By 2009, almost 7,000 homes had been completed. This rapid pace of development has been crucial to covering infrastructure costs. When finished, IJburg will provide 18,000 new homes for around 45,000 people, along with schools, libraries, parks, sports facilities etc.

IJburg's development has been planned and driven forward by the Municipality of Amsterdam, which bought the seabed from a national government agency and developed the masterplan in collaboration with private-sector architects, planners and urban designers. This envisaged a contemporary version of nineteenth- and twentieth-century Amsterdam, with enclosed residential rectangular housing blocks positioned adjacent to a network of canals, and with a new boulevard and tram route at its spine. Strong design control has been exercised to encourage developers to employ good architects, producing a rich variety of built environment. Although IJburg displays some quite extraordinary architecture, it is contained within a framework of well-defined streets and blocks that allows architectural variety without distracting from the place.

To deliver its vision, the Municipality invested in substantial new infrastructure, including an express tram that takes only 15–20 minutes to reach Central Amsterdam. Much of the infrastructure investment was spent on roads and bridges to ensure that IJburg is well connected to the rest of Amsterdam. Apart from some central government capital assistance towards decontamination and infrastructure, the development was intended to be self-financing, with the Municipality's investment recouped from land sales. To reduce its risk and secure developer commitment, the

Municipality entered into a pre-sale agreement with three development consortia (who, in turn, comprised 20 different development firms) to build 6,000 dwellings and some associated infrastructure. Although the price paid for the land by development consortia was later deemed to be less than could have been achieved, this agreement ensured that IJburg developed rapidly as both a new quarter of the city and an active housing market.

For further information, see Adams *et al.* (2011b) and visit: http://www.ijburg.nl/English.

FIGURE 11.9 IJburg, Netherlands. (Steve Tiesdell)

At IJburg (Box 11.5 and Figure 11.9), the market as well as the place was created from scratch by public-sector action and investment led by Amsterdam City Council. Here, the strategic planning context that selected IJburg as a major growth area, with extensive transport infrastructure then installed by the municipality, enabled developers to have confidence in the likely level of demand. This ensured a clear and consistent development programme which, intriguingly, tied developers in at an early stage through a partnership that required the private sector to buy land in advance at an agreed price. Collective action through strategic market transformation is thus essential to both making successful markets and engendering the widely held belief that they will indeed be successful. By creating valued places, rather than isolated housing estates, strategic market transformation is also a sensible long-term investment, since asset values in places that work well have greater growth potential.

Financial planning

Strategic market transformation requires significant capital investment, especially in advance infrastructure. Such investment offers a good example of how the provision of collective goods, such as new transport links, can make areas more 'ripe' for development. In Rotterdam, for example, the new waterfront location of Kop van Zuld, with its mixed-use central area, high-quality housing and eye-catching environment has been created from abandoned docks (Doucet 2010). Here, advance infrastructure investment has been critical to generating private-sector interest, for, as Cadell *et al.* (2008: xi) recount, 'Funding was secured from the central government for the iconic Erasmus Bridge, a new metro station, the extension of the tram system, and putting underground the railway lines that used to cut the area off from the adjoining residential areas . . . the early public investment in infrastructure – and the accessibility it created – convinced the private sector that it was safe to invest, starting with high-density housing and a stylish hotel.'

Commitment to early infrastructure provision matters for four main reasons:

- It ensures that the spatial development framework can be implemented.
- It provides serviced development parcels in accordance with the framework.
- It reduces private-sector commitment and risk, and so generates interest from a wider variety of developers.
- It ensures greater control on development phasing and, with multiple developer participation, allows projects to be completed quicker.

Careful financial planning is essential to ensure that infrastructure costs can eventually be recovered from the real estate values they help to create. Two approaches that have been used to achieve this are tariffs or levies and the sale of serviced land.[7]

English Partnerships pioneered the concept of a tariff or roof tax at Milton Keynes, with the figure of £18,500 to be paid on each new home built as a contribution towards overall infrastructure costs (Walker 2007). This is the approach adopted in the Community Infrastructure Levy (CIL), recently introduced in England (see Chapter 12). In Cambridgeshire, it was calculated that the infrastructure needed to support 73,000 new homes planned between 2001 and 2021 would cost about £4 billion, or nearly £55,000 per house. Of this, 57 per cent was attributable to new roads and other transport improvements, 14 per cent to health facilities, 12 per cent to utilities, 10 per cent to education and 7 per cent to open space, community facilities and other forms of infrastructure (Falk 2008). Despite interest in establishing a Milton Keynes-style tariff, progress was slow, since most of the intended development land was in private ownership, with transaction costs potentially high. This highlights the challenges involved in funding significant infrastructure provision without ownership control.

The most efficient way to cover infrastructure costs is through the competitive sale of serviced land. This is well illustrated by the example of Vathorst (Box 11.6 and Figure 11.10), where a public-private development partnership assembled the land and invested in the necessary infrastructure. At Hammarby-Sjöstad, the public sector invested €500 million primarily in land decontamination and transport infrastructure (including a tram line built early on in its development), which generated subsequent private-sector commitment of €3 billion. Costs were recovered from sales of development parcels, so the municipality achieved a financial return as well as delivering an attractive new part of the city. These examples show how land ownership offers an efficient method to price and deliver collective goods, such as improved accessibility and quality urban design (Webster and Lai 2003). This principle has been taken to its logical conclusion in Hong Kong, where the sale of development rights above and adjacent to new Mass Transit Railway (MTR) stations has become so lucrative that property-related activities contribute twice as much as user fares to MTR revenues (Cervero and Murakami 2009).

BOX 11.6 Vathorst, Netherlands

Vathorst is a sustainable urban extension to Amersfoort, intended to provide 11,000 new homes by 2018, along with a 35-hectare business park, 100,000m^2 of office space and 17,500m^2 of retail space. It has been planned around a new rail station, with ready access to Amersfoort City Centre as well as to Amsterdam and Utrecht. Solar energy, high insulation standards, district heating by waste incineration, communal recycling and internal movement primarily by bicycle and foot are all central to the vision for Vathorst.

The City of Amersfoot chose the location of Vathorst and set up the Vathorst Development Company (OBV) to promote the development. This is a joint venture company, half owned by the council and half by four private developers and a housing association. According to Studdert (2009: 43), 'The joint approach between the public and private sectors engenders trust and a shared vision because risks and benefits are shared and the local authority is empowered to engage on this basis.'

OBV assembled the land and invested in all necessary infrastructure at a cost of €772 million, which over time will be recouped from land sales. In the meantime, cash flow is supported by loans from the Dutch Municipal Bank, totalling €250 million.

The masterplan was prepared by an international urban designer appointed by OBV, who worked closely with the city planners and development partners. An expert design panel monitors quality at each stage of the development. Since private-sector partners share the vision for Vathorst and work to clear design guidance, the regulatory approval process is much faster than for comparable-sized developments in the UK.

Imaginative use is made of new canals, with 65 per cent of new houses located on the waterfront or having vistas of water. There is a balance of private and social housing at neighbourhood level. Each neighbourhood has its own architecture, density, scenery and structure. To achieve variety, developers have commissioned different architects, with no architect being responsible for more than eighty homes.

For further information see: Falk (2011), Studdert (2009) and visit: http://www.vathorst.com.

FIGURE 11.10 Vathorst, Netherlands. (Nicholas Falk)

Whatever financial model is adopted, strategic transformation is dependent on effective financial planning in order to ensure early infrastructure investment, while allowing cost recovery to be delayed until nearer the completion of the development, whether in whole or in part.

Strategic implementation

Pre-construction and phasing

Strategic transformations normally involve extensive pre-construction works, especially in reclamation and infrastructure provision. This makes careful phasing of the development essential. It normally makes sense to develop outwards from an existing thriving centre or 'hotspot' which already has a mixture of uses and is well integrated into public transport and urban movement patterns. A place promoter is more likely to achieve quality development across the project as a whole by gradually releasing parcels and insisting on high design standards from the start. The pace of release can also be managed to respond to changing market conditions and avoid any supply glut.

A carefully phased rollout matches the release of land parcels to the delivery of infrastructure. As Figure 11.11 shows, this stands in marked contrast to what might be described as the 'scattergun' approach to development, in which the parcels first built out are those purchased first by developers. With scattergun development, not even an 'invisible hand' exists to ensure overall control. Punter's (2007a) case study of Cardiff Bay is instructive here, since he shows how 'The fragmented nature of development, and its poor integration with existing communities, has undermined efforts to create a safe, attractive public realm' (p. 398). Significantly, although the development corporation could have used its all-important ownership powers to help to avert this, ownership control was rarely deployed at Cardiff Bay to ensure quality design.

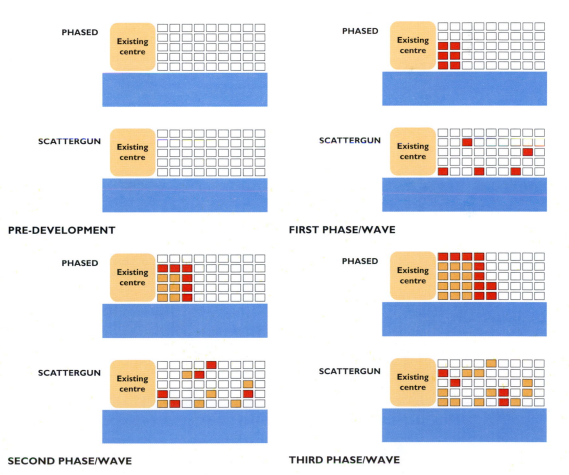

FIGURE 11.11 Contrast between phased and scattergun development. Well-phased development is economically more efficient and enables new communities to mature more quickly.

Developer selection and construction

As a general rule, the fewer the number of developers and designers involved in large development projects, the more uniform the built product. A richer, more diverse urban form promotes identity and character, but, more importantly, it permits incremental change. A conceptual diagram showing the difference between projects with single and multiple designers and developers is provided by Figure 11.12. Single-developer/single-designer and single-developer/multi-designer projects are simpler to develop and have lower transaction costs. Yet, to reproduce what Love and Crawford (2011) call the authentic character and economic diversity of the 'real' city demands a deliberate institutional decision to broaden the number and range of developers and designers involved in the build-out.

More sophisticated approaches involve a greater range and diversity of developers and designers in a project, spreading risk and encouraging competition. As master developer, the place promoter can determine the number and type of parcel developers (and indeed designers) to be involved in construction, primarily by linking smart parcelisation (see above) to competitive developer selection. In this context, Figure 11.13 shows conceptually how the phased development of one large site by a single developer differs from its simultaneous (i.e. in parallel) or sequential (i.e. in series) build-out by multiple developers. The diagram pictorially represents the increased complexity of multi-developer development, illustrating how, as the number of developers and designers increases, transactions costs are also likely to increase. Yet, multi-developer/multi-designer approaches produce

FIGURE 11.12
Designers, developers and diversity. If a single developer and a single designer are wholly responsible for all the parcels within a large development, the process will be simplified but the urban form may have little variety. Increasing the number of developers and/or designers makes the process more complex but produces a richer and more diverse urban form.

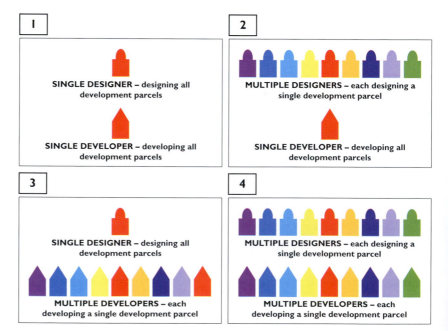

1

SINGLE DESIGNER – designing all development parcels

SINGLE DEVELOPER – developing all development parcels

2

MULTIPLE DESIGNERS – each designing a single development parcel

SINGLE DEVELOPER – developing all development parcels

3

SINGLE DESIGNER – designing all development parcels

MULTIPLE DEVELOPERS – each developing a single development parcel

4

MULTIPLE DESIGNERS – each designing a single development parcel

MULTIPLE DEVELOPERS – each developing a single development parcel

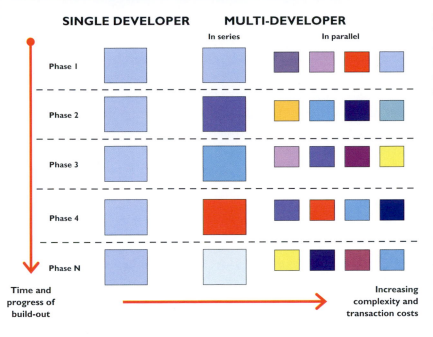

SINGLE DEVELOPER | **MULTI-DEVELOPER**

In series | In parallel

Phase 1, Phase 2, Phase 3, Phase 4, Phase N

Time and progress of build-out

Increasing complexity and transaction costs

FIGURE 11.13

The potential complexity of multi-developer projects. On the left-hand side of this diagram, the same developer takes responsibility for all the phases of a large development. In the middle, each phase becomes the responsibility of a different developer, and they work in series to build out the site. On the right-hand side of the diagram, each phase is split up into several parcels, with each being the responsibility of a different developer. Some developers secure parcels in more than one phase. This produces a richer and more diverse urban form, but the benefits of this approach have to be balanced against increased complexity and transaction costs.

long-term product benefits in the form of visually richer, more pluralistic and more diverse places. An integrated approach to development has the potential to deliver the increased value needed to justify such increased transaction costs that may be involved in creating better places.

Marketing, disposal and management

Although individual components of a place created strategically may well be marketed and sold separately, the long-term social and economic value of the place as a whole depends to a great extent on future collective action to ensure effective management and maintenance. As well-managed places mature, asset values become better established and investment returns more secure. To achieve this, management structures and institutions need to be put in place and clarified as part of the place-production process.

At Hammarby-Sjöstad, Stockholm City Council took direct responsibility for after-care, while at Upton, English Partnerships established the Upton Management Company to ensure comprehensive maintenance of the public realm by charging every unit a management fee. At Fairfield Park (Box 11.7 and Figure 11.14), a similar role is played by a residents' association. For such latter arrangements to work, the legal responsibility to pay management fees must be embedded within the contracts for sale. Indeed, the necessary resources to achieve long-term stewardship of the public realm, and reinforce a place's reputation, attractiveness and sustainability, need to be secured as part of the marketing and disposal of the component parts. To achieve this, the place promoter can and should require individual parcel developers to abide by a common scheme for future maintenance and management.

The place-production process thus ends with the creation of something quite tangible – a wholly transformed place – but with its potential to become somewhere of real quality, socially and economically as well as physically, still to be fully achieved. As this indicates, the production process arrives where it began, with the vision and determination to create a quality place. However, by this point, whether this really happens will depend on ensuring that what has been developed as a whole becomes well maintained and, indeed, well loved in the future.

BOX 11.7 Fairfield Park, Bedfordshire, England

Fairfield Park is a former NHS hospital with extensive grounds, where ten different housebuilders have created a new residential community of 1,200 new homes. Unlike so many similar developments where large sites are split up between different builders, Fairfield Park appears as an integrated development, with a common 'Victorian-style' design, well-planned roads and pathways, primary school, retail store, recreational areas and extensive landscaping. The development has a strong sense of community, and houses command a premium above similar properties nearby.

From the start, the local authority insisted on a masterplan and design code, which were both crucial in shaping the development. Two lead developers then established a joint-venture company, known as Fairfield Redevelopment Ltd, which took responsibility for infrastructure provision, before selling serviced parcels to individual developers, who built houses in accordance with the design code. The individual developers knew that the price they had paid for their respective parcels included what equated to a membership fee to cover their fair share of the infrastructure costs. House purchasers pay an annual service charge for the maintenance of the public realm to a management company, the ownership of which will be transferred to the residents once the whole development is complete. The institutional framework thus involves private contractual action by which individual housebuilders (and eventually house purchasers) share the cost of infrastructure, with incoming residents taking long-term contractual responsibility for the maintenance of common areas.

For further information, see Adams *et al.* (2011a) and visit: http://fairfield-park.com and http://webarchive.nationalarchives.gov.uk/201101071 65544.

FIGURE 11.14 Fairfield Park, Bedfordshire, England. (Steve Tiesdell)

Conclusions

Strategic market transformation requires an institutional framework to promote and manage collective action. This is because its real benefits derive from what transcends individual developments in the form, for example, of better transport connections, more efficient spatial arrangements and improved public realm. While strategic market transformation may draw on, and co-ordinate, relevant stimulus instruments (see Chapter 13), its purpose is not to tempt market actors to venture into particular locations or forms of development beyond their normal ambit.

Occasionally, various housebuilders come together in a development consortium to masterplan a large development area (usually at the insistence of the local planning authority). Such arrangements tend to be the exception, rather than the rule. Even then, the requirements of any masterplan are rarely embedded in the property rights held by each housebuilder. Too often in the UK, large development sites are soon subdivided between several housebuilders, each of whom acts as master and parcel developer on their own site. This usually results in poorly co-ordinated development and the late or under-provision of essential infrastructure. Strategic market transformation is quite different, for it is driven forward and co-ordinated by a place promoter with a clear vision for creating somewhere that functions as a well-integrated and quality place.

In most cases, strategic market transformation will initially be more costly than disintegrated forms of development, which is precisely why the case studies presented in this chapter remain the exception rather than the rule. Yet, over time, strategic transformation offers better value for money as quality places mature, while delivering more sustainable forms of development. The challenge, then, is to devise and deploy institutional and funding models that are capable of treating higher costs as an investment that can produce a higher return. Such models still require careful cost control, effective revenue enhancement and active risk management, for the larger the project, the greater the danger that control of these key variables will be lost.

Although this chapter has concentrated on models in which the role of place promoter is taken primarily by the public sector, it has identified other case studies, where private development or landed interests have assumed this role. Moreover, many of the lessons from this chapter could also be applied to smaller places, despite the focus here on larger places. For, whenever place transformation is needed, leadership, proactive vision, determination and investment are essential to both creating successful places and rescuing those that have fallen into serious decline.

12 Regulating markets

Introduction

The regulation or control of real estate is widely practised in democratic societies, affecting its ownership, use, management and development. Regulatory actions are those that compel, manage or eradicate certain activities or aspects of those activities. Ownership relations between landlord and tenants, for example, may be governed by statute so as to prevent automatic eviction at the end of a lease. Certain uses, such as night clubs, may be considered a potential public nuisance, with restrictions imposed on where and when they can operate. Management arrangements of multiple-occupied properties, for instance, may be controlled to ensure the health and safety of occupants and to minimise negative impacts on neighbours. The concern of this chapter, however, is with the regulation of real estate development and its implications for place quality.

Regulation takes many different forms, which vary according to the matter regulated and the institutional circumstances in which regulation takes place. Economists often conflate regulation with intervention and so include what we regard as market shaping, stimulus and capacity building within their definition of regulation. We take a more precise public policy approach, seeing regulation as those actions that restrict the choices available to certain actors and so limit their scope for autonomous action (while acknowledging that regulatory actions may also open up choices for other actors).

Regulation is at its most effective when it persuades actors to adapt their ideas to accord with public policy, rather than simply abandon ideas that conflict with

TABLE 12.1 Regulatory choices

Normal UK mode	Choice	Alternative mode
Public regulation by statute, universally applicable to all affected persons	Statute or contract	Private regulation by contract, applicable only to parties to contract, but enforceable by courts
Regulation that restricts detrimental action	Preventative or directive	Regulation that requires desirable action
Regulation of activities to restrict harmful impact	Activities or actors	Regulation of actors to restrict unlicensed production
Sequential regulation of different aspects of same activity	Sequential or integrated	Integrated regulation of different aspects of same activity
Regulation that seeks to manage activity	Managerial or absolute	Regulation that seeks to eradicate activity
Action may be taken against known breach of regulation	Elective or mandatory enforcement	Action automatically taken against known breach of regulation
Regulation based on case-by-case assessment	Discretionary or predefined	Regulation based on meeting common rules or standards

policy. This makes the institutional design of any regulatory environment a matter of particular concern to shaping places. Rather than provide a detailed investigation of how real estate development is regulated in specific countries, the chapter therefore sets out seven regulatory choices and considers their implications for real estate development. These are summarised in Table 12.1. Regulation of real estate development in the UK mainly takes the form shown on the left-hand column of Table 12.1, so the right-hand column serves as a basis for thinking about alternative approaches or comparing the UK with systems elsewhere.

Discussion of these seven regulatory choices is followed by more detailed examination of two specific instruments that illustrate the operation of discretionary and pre-defined regulation. The first, planning gain, reveals how discretionary regulation can become embroiled in negotiation over how financial returns from development should be distributed. The second, design codes, demonstrates the potential contribution of form-based regulation to place quality. At the end of the chapter, the potential costs and benefits of market regulation are assessed and overall conclusions are drawn.

Regulation by statute or contract

Regulation can be undertaken either by statute or by contract. Public regulation is normally imposed by statute and can involve either the removal of certain rights or the exercise of what is known as 'police power'. In the UK, development rights were nationalised in 1947, paving the way for universal regulation by planning permission. A £300 million compensation fund was established, although subsequent legislative changes meant that very little was ever paid out (Cullingworth 1980, Grant 1999, Hall and Tewdwr-Jones 2010). In the US and elsewhere, zoning regulations are regarded as an example of 'police power'. This means that certain rights or liberties are 'policed' in order to restrict actions that are considered likely to cause public harm. It is on this basis that non-residential activities are normally prohibited in residential zones. Those whose activities are limited by such police power have no right to compensation from the state, since its actions are intended to protect public welfare. This contrasts with what is known in the US as eminent domain (equivalent to compulsory purchase in the UK), in which the state is considered to have taken or appropriated some aspect of a person's property, making compensation payable. To avoid such compensation claims, land-use regulation by statute in the US is firmly based on 'police power', leaving eminent domain or 'takings' to where the whole property is required, for example, for road construction.

There is a long tradition within real estate of private regulation by contract. This can be considered a voluntary rather than coercive form of regulation, since it is entered into freely on terms that can be a matter of negotiation. Such contracts are able to control the form in which land is developed and the way in which that development is subsequently managed. For example, an owner may wish to subdivide land into development plots, while imposing some order on how development takes place, perhaps restricting uses and specifying building heights, footprints and even materials. This can be achieved by conditions or covenants in the sale or lease contracts. On a housing estate or in an apartment block, sale or lease contracts may create mutually enforceable covenants between each and every purchaser or tenant, so that any purchasers who decided to breed pigs in their garden, for instance, may find themselves taken to court by their neighbours. The extent to which regulation imposed by contract can be enforced will depend on the legal system of each country governing such matters as how far restrictive covenants are enforceable against subsequent purchasers, as well as against the original purchaser.

Although regulation by statute and contract are conceptually different, this does not mean that state regulation is limited to that undertaken by statute. In some countries such as Hong Kong, where freehold land is almost wholly owned by the state and those in possession occupy property by virtue of leases granted by the state, lease conditions provide a means to achieve public policy objectives.

The same principle applies elsewhere to land owned by the state, even in countries where most freeholds are in private ownership. So if a local authority in the UK, for example, wishes to sell or lease land for industrial development, but to restrict hours of operation because the intended factories are close to dwellings, it will often impose a condition to that effect in the sale or lease contract. A similar condition may also be imposed on any planning consent, but, crucially, the contractual relationship between the two parties established through the land sale or lease may well prove easier and faster to enforce through the courts than the planning consent. This logic raises the issue of whether and how far statutory regulation of real estate could be replaced by contractual regulation, by encouraging either more widespread contracts between private owners or greater use of land-ownership power by the state (see Lai 1998 and 2005, and Pennington 2002 for more detailed discussion of such ideas).

Preventative and directive regulation

The UK Highway Code makes reference to two important regulatory requirements upon drivers:

- 'You MUST NOT drive with a breath alcohol level higher than 35 micro-grammes/100 millilitres of breath or a blood alcohol level of more than 80 milligrammes/100 millilitres of blood' (Paragraph 95).
- 'The driver MUST ensure that all children under 14 years of age in cars, vans and other goods vehicles wear seat belts or sit in an approved child restraint where required' (Paragraph 100).

The first of these can be termed preventative regulation, in the sense that it restricts or prohibits action considered detrimental. The second amounts to directive regulation, in the sense of requiring action that is considered desirable. Preventative regulation is thus intended to prohibit an action that is seen as 'negative' in its outcome, while directive regulation seeks to achieve an outcome that is considered 'positive'. Regulations intended to prevent negative outcomes are much easier to draft and implement than are those intended to secure positive ones, which is why regulation is more often associated with the command 'Do not' rather than 'Do'.

Nevertheless, both positive and negative commands are used to regulate real estate development. In urban design, for instance, positive regulatory instruments are those that establish a predictable urban form. A prime example would be a 'build-to line', which requires all development to be built up to a defined street edge. Mandatory on each side of a street, the regulation ensures a desired three-dimensional profile for the street, which is delineated by the presence of buildings at the edge of the street. Negative regulatory instruments are those that do not

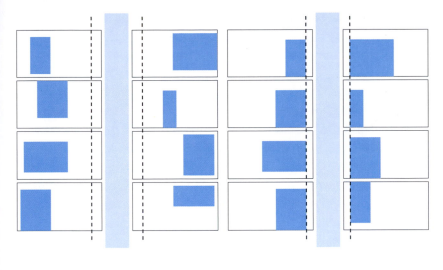

Build-behind line   **Build-to line**

FIGURE 12.1
Build-behind and build-to lines. A 'build-behind line' is a negative regulatory instrument, which produces a whole that is no greater than the sum of the parts (in this case, eight buildings and a road). In contrast, a 'build-to line' is a positive regulatory instrument, which creates synergy by producing a whole that exceeds the sum of the parts (in this case, eight buildings *plus* a street).

establish a predictable urban form. Here a prime example would be a 'build-behind line', which merely ensures that no development occurs in front of a defined line (see Figure 12.1). As a result, the edge of the street is often delineated by the absence of buildings.

Build-to lines are included in many New Urbanist form-based codes (see below). Both build-to and build-behind lines feature in the German *Bebauungsplan* (B-Plan) system (see Stille 2007). Here, the key mechanisms to control urban form include maximum building heights and site coverage. The latter operates through the *Baufenster*, which sets out the area within which any development has to be located by combining two different boundary conditions: the *Baulinie* (or line on which any building has to be located or build-to line) and the *Baugrenze* (or line identifying the maximum footprint that the building may occupy or build-behind line).

Regulation of activities or actors

Few would suggest that every medical operation should require state approval, but most would agree that entry into the medical profession should be controlled by law. In contrast, real estate activities tend to be regulated by statute, while real estate professions are left to regulate themselves. There are some exceptions to the latter case, especially in developing countries such as Malaysia, where the law provides that:

> Any person who, not being a licensed land surveyor, wilfully and falsely pretends, or takes or uses any name or title implying that he is a licensed land surveyor . . . shall be guilty of an offence against this Act and shall be liable to

a fine not exceeding five hundred ringgit for each offence and to a further penalty of fifty ringgit for each day during the continuance of such offence.
(Commissioner of Law Revision, Malaysia 2006, Act 458, Section 19)

However, in many countries, architecture is often the one built environment profession to which entry is regulated by statute along similar lines to doctors. This raises the important issue of whether those who have qualified as architects, after lengthy training and practical experience required by statute, should then find their actions subject to further regulation by local planning authorities. In other words, could it be argued that development proposals designed by registered architects should be exempt from specific regulation on much the same basis that approval is not required for individual medical operations? Of course, for this argument to hold, it would need to be accepted that architecture was primarily a matter for architects and that architects were well versed in all aspects of real estate development, including its social, economic and environmental impacts. In fact, such stances would be widely challenged by many non-architects (and indeed by many architects).

However, there might still be a case for applying the principle of 'earned autonomy', whereby developments proposed by architects who, over time, had demonstrated high levels of skill and sensitivity in urban design, could be fast-tracked through the normal regulatory processes. This would encourage developers to commission approved architects in order to benefit from greater certainty and quicker consents, and would help to promote high-quality urban design within the architectural profession. Of course, this leaves unresolved the thorny issue of who would decide which architects should be considered to have achieved 'earned autonomy' and by what means. Architecture thus provides an interesting example of opening up debate on whether the wider public interest in real estate development would be best served by the regulation of actors or activities.

Sequential and integrated regulation

A single activity may be regulated in different ways, usually by different agencies of the state. For real estate development, planning consent is often the most important form of state regulation, but it is by no means the only one. Assessment of the environment and alterations to historic buildings, for example, may have separate regulatory procedures, even if closely tied to planning consent. Other consents may be handled by different agencies and different procedures. For example, construction standards and energy efficiency may be covered by separate building regulations, road design by highway consent, fire safety by a fire certificate and the use of premises for public entertainment by a council licence. In some cases, some of these separate agencies may be consulted by the planning authority when a planning application is under consideration, but at this stage attention may focus on the principle of development, rather than on the detailed design. In due course, developers may discover that what had been agreed for planning approval needs to be amended in the light of subsequent requirements from other statutory bodies. This inevitably adds costs, causes delay and deters innovation.

Normally, regulatory conflict is neither deliberately intended nor explicitly avoided in regulatory design. Instead, what tends to happen is that different pieces of legislation add further regulatory burdens, often for good reason, but without any explicit consideration of how those burdens might be best managed as a whole, rather than as a series of separate approvals. In other words, as Barlow and King (1992: 381) comment in relation to housing development, '"regulation" does not refer to a single set of legislative decisions. Rather, regulation of most housing systems has arisen through a series of unrelated acts, bounding the market in specific ways and producing a specific competitive rationale.' In order to resolve conflict between regulatory requirements, it might be helpful to replace sequential and separate regulation by single and integrated regulation.

Managerial and absolute regulation

On 7 October 2010, the following report appeared in a local newspaper in the north of England:

> A restaurant has been shut down after council food hygiene inspectors found a cockroach infestation . . . The inspection revealed a widespread infestation, with live cockroaches found in a container full of poppadoms, on food surfaces and inside equipment. The venue was closed under the Food Hygiene (England) Regulations 2006 and the council was granted a hygiene emergency prohibition order at Teesside Magistrates' Court.
>
> (Robson 2010)

This is an example of what might be termed absolute regulation, in the sense that an activity is considered so unacceptable, in this case for reasons of public health, that it should be utterly eradicated. However, absolute regulation is much less common than what might be termed managerial regulation, where the regulator's task is to achieve a desirable amount of the regulated activity by managing production. An example of the latter would be the number of licensed drinking establishments in any particular neighbourhood. While most people may like to have a choice of where they can go for a drink locally, many would object if drinking establishments became too numerous, especially if they were allowed to open all hours. However, managerial regulation is inherently problematic, since governments, unlike markets, cannot gather or process extensive consumer information on preferred levels of supply and can be easily swayed by powerful lobbying from vested interest groups.

In real estate development, absolute regulation may apply to the demolition of historic buildings, in the sense that the preferred regulatory solution would be to prevent such destructive activity altogether. In contrast, alterations to historic buildings are normally governed by managerial regulation, which seeks to distinguish between sensitive alterations that might help to provide historic buildings with a future and those that undermine what essentially makes a building historic. As this example suggests, absolute regulation is usually much simpler to administer, since compliance and non-compliance are normally clear and unambiguous. In contrast, managerial regulation can require highly skilled regulators, such as building conservation experts, who have the necessary experience and personality to exercise their discretion with care when making finely balanced calls of judgement. This means that managerial regulation tends to be more costly and time intensive than absolute regulation.

Elective and mandatory enforcement

Without enforcement power, and the credible prospect of its use, regulations may simply be ignored. In such circumstances, market actors may gamble on the non-enforcement of regulations and steal a march on their competitors by undertaking activities that might otherwise be prohibited. In real estate development, for example, developers may surreptitiously construct larger developments than those for which they have gained approval. If this is not discovered or no action is taken, then it may encourage others to do likewise, and in due course bring the whole regulatory regime into disrepute. To restore credibility in regulation, an amnesty may be required before tighter enforcement is introduced. However, if amnesties become a regular occurrence, all credibility in the regulation system may be lost.

Enforcement is effective only when it can discover regulatory breaches, prove them in law and secure legal remedy by way of fines and/or remedial notices and then implement whatever practical action is needed in order to eliminate the breach and prevent its re-occurrence. As a general rule, the simpler the regulatory regime, the easier becomes the enforcement. The complex planning system operated in the UK makes enforcement an inherently difficult task, which over the years has been aggravated by reluctance to invest in sufficient enforcement capacity. This helps to explain why planning enforcement regimes in the UK are elective, not mandatory.

On the soccer field, mandatory enforcement is taken against certain limited breaches of association football rules, if seen by the referee. For example, if a player deliberately handles the ball, a free kick or penalty will be given to the other side, depending on where the offence took place on the field of play. But with many other offences, the referee has discretion, depending on the particular circumstances of the incident, to decide whether to blow the whistle, stop the game and order a free kick. If a free kick were deemed mandatory whatever the offence, the game would soon degenerate into a series of never-ending stops and starts, undermining its attraction as a spectacle. Although soccer referees are thus generally expected to exercise elective rather than mandatory enforcement, such an approach works only when it is seen to be consistent and fair. Otherwise, however hard they might have tried, soccer referees might find themselves the target of abuse from the crowd, and sometimes the players.

This analogy can be directly applied to regulation of real estate development, in which mandatory enforcement regimes are rare. Instead, limited enforcement resources need to be focused on tackling the most important regulatory breaches in a way that is sufficiently consistent and fair to deter further breaches. Again, the simpler and clearer the regulations, the easier this becomes to achieve.

Discretionary and predefined regulation

There is a distinct difference between regulatory approaches that consider each case on its merits and those that require all cases to meet some predefined standards or norms. The first approach is evident in the discretionary development-control systems operated in Britain and Ireland, while the second is seen in the regulatory standards that control development in most of Western Europe and North America (Booth 1996, Punter 2007b).

Although discretionary approaches may publish in advance what will be expected in individual cases (through a plan or other policy document), crucially, other relevant factors (known as 'material considerations' in the UK) may be brought into play when planning applications are submitted. This means that any plan is not considered comprehensive or binding, even if it is accorded some priority, in the UK. Discretionary approaches to regulation are therefore pragmatic and enable flexibility as circumstances change. However, they can also be resource-intensive, since case-by-case decision-making requires considerable professional expertise, supported as necessary by political oversight and judgement.

Since individual decisions are not wholly predictable but sometimes inconsistent, and can often be swayed by powerful lobby groups, it behoves market actors to invest time and effort in securing individual approvals. Increasingly, the discretionary system of development control in the UK has turned into a negotiative process, in which mutually agreed outcomes emerge from processes of bargaining, persuasion and even bluff. Such negotiation has long been applied to securing design improvements to submitted schemes and is increasingly used to extract community benefits from developers in the form of planning gain (see below). Since negotiation in a discretionary system takes place behind closed doors and normally excludes affected third parties, such as local community groups, it is often viewed with external suspicion.

Predefined approaches publish comprehensive standards, norms and zoning regulations etc., which set out in advance what is permissible. Developments that fully conform to what is expected do not require any further approval. This makes predefined approaches less resource-intensive and less open to political manipulation than discretionary ones, although significant resources and political input are likely to be needed to establish standards in the first place. Predefined approaches create greater certainty for all parties, since they deliver 'clear development rights and floor space limits and often building envelope controls' (Punter 2007b: 167). Only non-conforming developments require individual applications.

Although this produces a strong incentive for market actors to conform to published norms, it can stifle innovation and shield developers from responsibility for what is built (Ben-Joseph 2005). Despite its social and environmental flaws, sprawling suburban development in the US has generally conformed to zoning regulations, while more compact New Urbanist schemes have often required individual consideration as exceptions to the norm. Duany and Talen (2002: 262) have called for this stance to be reversed by making what they see as 'the "good" easy and the "bad" difficult'. As this suggests, regulatory procedures could themselves be designed to fast-track developments considered desirable, and to encumber those considered undesirable with more searching investigation. This might have a deterrent effect on what is proposed by developers.

According to Punter (2007b), there has been a growing convergence between discretionary and predefined regulation, at least in respect of design control. He sees evidence of this in the increased importance of published design guidance and plan policy in discretionary systems such as in the UK, and of design review in predefined systems, especially in North America.

Planning gain

Planning gain is a term commonly applied to the provision by a developer of some additional benefit, not necessarily located on the development site, which is offered to, or more usually requested by, the planning authority as an incentive or requirement for regulatory approval. While other popular names include community benefits and developers' contributions (Healey *et al.* 1992c), UK legislation formally refers to 'planning obligations' contained within a 'planning agreement', rather than to planning gain.

In England, planning obligations can be used to prescribe the nature of a development (for example, by specifying what proportion of the dwellings should be affordable), secure compensation for any consequent loss or damage (such as that of open space) or mitigate a development's impact (for example, by enhancing public transport provision) (ODPM 2005b). Crucially, they are 'intended to make acceptable development which would otherwise be unacceptable in planning terms' (ODPM 2005b: 9). This emphasises that, despite its financial characteristics, planning gain is an inherently regulatory instrument, since it constrains development proposals at particular locations. In this case, market regulation ensures that the private sector takes more responsibility for the social and infrastructure costs of development, rather than leaving these to be picked up entirely by the public purse. The exact distribution of such costs between developers, landowners and house buyers or other end-purchasers will depend on market conditions and on the size and type of the particular development (Adams and Watkins 2002). Planning gain thus contrasts with a general betterment levy or development land tax imposed on the perceived uplift in land value associated with a planning approval, but which has no direct linkage to the particular form of any development.

Although planning agreements in the UK date back to the Housing, Town Planning etc. Act 1909, until 1968 each agreement had to be approved individually by the minister. Since the late 1980s, there has been a rapid growth in their use, to the extent that by 2007–8, almost all planning approvals for fifty or more dwellings in England were accompanied by planning agreements (DCLG 2010a). This growth occurred for three main reasons. First, the huge multiplier between agricultural and residential land values, which in parts of South-East England had risen to 500 by 2010 (see Chapter 10) created ever greater opportunities for planning gain.[1] Second, tighter control of local authority capital expenditure, coupled with the privatisation of UK infrastructure providers from the mid-1980s, meant that private developers were increasingly expected to pay the costs of physical and social infrastructure that in earlier decades had been met from the public purse. Third, from the late 1990s, central government gave ever stronger encouragement to local authorities to demand affordable housing provision, in particular, through planning agreements.

By 2004–5, almost 55 per cent of the 33,000 new affordable homes built in England were delivered through planning agreements (Crook *et al.* 2006). The value of all planning obligations secured in England was estimated to have risen from about £2 billion in 2003–4 to about £4 billion in 2005–6 and about £5 billion in 2007–8 (DCLG 2010a). Almost half of the latter £5 billion figure was for affordable housing, with important contributions also made to transport, education, open space and community and leisure facilities. This scale of planning gain has turned the regulation of real estate markets in the UK, at least for major developments, into a more negotiative process in which regulators and regulated enter into a contractual bargain to determine what is actually built. This represents a significant shift from statutory regulation, as originally envisaged in British planning legislation. Real estate developers consequently complain about protracted negotiations around planning obligations, along with unpredictability and lack of transparency. From the planning authority's perspective, concerns arise about how far regulatory demands should be traded off for financial recompense. As Campbell and Henneberry (2005: 18) explain:

Planning obligations, by default, have become a financial and hence a market orientated mechanism through which the social and environmental consequences of development can be determined and their costs met. This increased market orientation of planning decisions represents a significant shift in the purpose of planning: a process that has long been justified and legitimised by its capacity to judge the appropriateness of development on non-financial grounds. The planners we interviewed in the local authority case studies found themselves between 'the rock and the hard place' of achieving often conflicting functional and financial objectives through the negotiation of planning obligations. They were unclear which took precedence.

Several European countries, including Belgium, France, Germany and the Netherlands, have similar arrangements to the UK, whereby developers build infrastructure and transfer it free to local authorities as a development obligation (Korthals Altes 2006). In North America, standard development impact fees or charges have long been commonplace (Nelson 1988). These are intended to cover the costs of providing roads, sewerage systems, schools, libraries, parks and recreational facilities to new residential areas. About 60 per cent of all American cities with a population of over 25,000 now apply development impact fees, although their scope and level can vary significantly from city to city (Nelson *et al.* 2008).

In recent years, there has been much interest within the UK in moving away from planning agreements negotiated on a case-by-case basis and towards US-style impact fees or tariffs. The success of the Milton Keynes 'roof tax' (Walker 2007), which is expected to raise £310 million in developer contributions from a single growth area, highlighted how a standardised approach can be more efficient, certain and transparent than individually negotiated planning agreements. The Community Infrastructure Levy, enacted in 2008, is likely to move area infrastructure funding in England towards a more standardised system, even though it will still leave affordable housing and site-specific planning gain to be negotiated on an individual basis. At a time of austerity, it may encourage local authorities to adopt development strategies that minimise their own financial commitment and maximise private-sector contributions, whether or not such strategies are consistent with creating more sustainable places. The levy will be charged on a per-square-metre basis on the net additional floorspace produced by any project to which it applies, so retaining the regulatory connection to the form of development (DCLG 2010b). Although the Community Infrastructure Levy may shift significant aspects of planning gain in England back from contractual to statutory regulation, it will still leave consideration of the financial implications of development as an important part of regulating markets.

Design codes

A design code is a set of rules specifying the three-dimensional form of a development and which provides a means to ensure that each plot or subdivision contributes to the intended vision for the broader place. Design codes can facilitate the regulation of development by either a landowner or a planning authority (Carmona *et al.* 2006). At Newhall in Essex, for example (see Chapter 8), a design code was prepared on behalf of the landowner so as to ensure overall place quality. It then formed part of the land sale contracts. At Fairfield Park in Bedfordshire (see Chapter 11), the development consortium took responsibility for preparing the design code as a condition of outline planning approval. It was then used as a benchmark in more detailed applications for reserved matters approvals. Both these examples show how design codes can ensure that a well-integrated place, rather than a series of separate housing estates, emerges from the efforts of different builders on component parts of the same development. They confirm that 'the real potential of codes rests in their ability to coordinate outputs from different developers/designers across large sites and to integrate different design elements with a forcefulness that other forms of guidance cannot match' (Carmona and Dann 2007: 17).

Design codes derive from the New Urbanist movement in North America and reflect its determination to challenge suburban sprawl by promoting traditional neighbourhood developments (TNDs). These developments tend to run foul of *use-based* zoning regulations and require a more imaginative regulatory approach evident in *form-based* codes. Such codes do not focus on land use but instead prioritise building type, street type or some combination of the two as the prime means of development regulation (Congress for the New Urbanism 2004, Marantz and Ben-Joseph 2011). At Seaside in Florida, Andres Duany and Elizabeth Plater-Zyberk, both founders of the Congress for the New Urbanism, pioneered coding by producing a 'simple one-page code of Seaside [which] was remarkable for its brevity and abstraction, and actually encouraged a fair amount of architectural interpretation. The code, even in its architectural details, was primarily in support of an *urban* vision' (Dutton 2000: 78). The Seaside code concentrated on specifying building types for each development plot, paying particular attention to plot size, building heights, porches, outbuildings and parking, along with the area and location for open space (Ellis 1988).

As Marantz and Ben-Joseph (2011) explain, such codes represent a *prescriptive* rather than *proscriptive* approach to development regulation. Rather than *proscribe* what is not allowed, design codes *prescribe* what is expected, often through detailed illustration, thus promoting an overall vision of a desired urban form. Crucially, design codes set out the intended qualities of street profiles and building blocks (including building lines and heights), and of the public and private spaces that determine the relationship between them. Codes may contain indicative expectations of architectural imagery and character, of building performance (including energy efficiency), and of the treatment of natural and landscaped components. As Elizabeth Plater-Zyberk contends, the positive parameters set by codes precede and frame individual design, while still leaving much to the judgement of individual designers, thus successfully combining regulatory control with scope for design freedom (see Scheer and Preiser 1994). Rouse (2003: 18) therefore argues that 'Coding could be used to mark a gradual but on-going shift in the planning system, from a reactive to a proactive model of control.'

As site-specific regulatory instruments, codes typically expand on the design vision contained in a masterplan or similar development framework and are often prepared alongside such area-based visions (Carmona 2011). They help to make the development process better integrated and more certain, especially where all relevant stakeholders work together to ensure that the design code is not produced simply by a code writer but emerges out of collective consensus. Carmona (2011) argues that design codes are particularly helpful for large sites in multiple ownership or those which are likely to be built out by different developers with different design teams over a long period of time. In such circumstances, site-specific design codes, unlike generic development standards such as highway requirements or building regulations, can significantly improve individual design and overall place quality, while speeding up regulatory consents and providing certainty to developers and the local community.

An excellent British example of the use of a design code comes from Upton in Northamptonshire (see Chapter 11), where six different builders have been responsible for the development of 1,350 new homes. The design code (Figure 12.2) was commissioned alongside a masterplan by the Upton Working Group, which operated as a collaboration between English Partnerships (the government agency that owned the land), the Prince's Foundation (a charitable trust created by the Prince of Wales to promote sustainable urbanism) and the local planning authority. The design code became the landowner's instrument for selecting housebuilders committed to delivering the quality of place envisaged in the masterplan. Although not formally adopted by the local authority, it facilitated subsequent regulatory approvals.

The Upton Design Code established a set of layout principles, specifying an interconnected street pattern with a street block structure. It detailed four character areas based on density and spatial character and established general three-dimensional massing, setting out the heights of those buildings fronting on to key streets. All streets were assigned a place within a hierarchy of four street types, namely 'urban boulevard', 'main street', 'lane' and 'mews'. Other issues covered by the code included materials, elevations and openings, the detailing of the public realm, sustainability issues and the location of affordable housing. Significantly, affordable housing was pepper-potted throughout the site, with no more than three units located together, with its external appearance indistinguishable from market housing.

7.0

FIGURE 12.2
Extract from Upton design code, Northampton, England. This extract shows how the code establishes and illustrates the main design principles applied at Upton. This particular page requires development to take the form of street-based blocks. (Homes and Communities Agency)

7.3 BLOCK PRINCIPLES

- The block layout set out in Figure 7.1 establishes the urban form of Upton and must be followed.
- The perimeter block form must be respected. There is some room for flexibility with respect to their precise dimensions and boundaries.
- Blocks cannot be combined to create larger blocks.
- The street hierarchy as set out in Chapter 6 must be respected. Street types cannot be changed.

Central Courtyard Perimeter Blocks
Figure 7.3 illustrates the character of a central courtyard perimeter block, with annotations referred below:

Figure 7.2 Central Courtyard block-plan

① Increased height to mark corner
② Access to central courtyard

Figure 7.4 Central Courtyard Block-Elevation

Figure 7.3 Central Courtyard block-axonmetric

80

03-2005

The Upton experience revealed four important benefits from the use of design codes as a means to regulate major development by several builders. First, clear ground rules that set out what is expected in design quality can transform housebuilders' thinking and make them willing to produce much better design than they normally do. Second, a design code virtually requires housebuilders to employ qualified architects, rather than simply design technicians. Third, involving local planners in writing the code simplifies the planning process and leads to faster consents. Fourth, adoption of a design code can enable smaller housebuilders more accustomed to building higher-quality developments to compete on a level playing field with volume housebuilders, who usually reduce costs by deploying standard house types.

Regulatory impacts

Regulation of real estate markets is intended to make an impact on what is developed through changing the decision-making process by which it comes about. As Table 12.2 shows, potential costs and benefits can be identified for both the processes and product of development regulation.

The process costs of development regulation tend to attract most attention. Regulation is often portrayed as a costly and inefficient means to control development, since regulators have little incentive either to reduce their information demands on applicants or accelerate their decision-making time (Allmendinger and Ball 2006, Allmendinger 2010, Ball 2008). Protracted bureaucratic procedures can often be aggravated by staff shortages and political indecisiveness. Over the years, government-sponsored reports in the UK have regularly returned to the inherent delays of development regulation, with varying recommendations made for better management (see, for example, Dobry 1975, Audit Commission 2006, Killian Pretty Review 2008). Others have suggested more radical approaches, for

TABLE 12.2 The potential costs and benefits of development regulation

	Potential costs	Potential benefits
Processes of regulation	Regulatory applications consume significant resources from both applicant and regulatory authority. Decision making can become unduly long and complex. Costs of regulation passed on to final consumer.	Efficient regulatory processes can ensure more integrated decision making during development process, so enabling potential problems to be spotted and resolved earlier, with resultant cost savings.
Products of regulation	Regulations provide no incentives for applicants to do better than the regulatory minimum. If regulators adopt 'tick box' mentality or engage in 'design by committee', quality of the final product may be impaired rather than enhanced. What is eventually built may merely reflect whichever vested interest has 'captured' the regulatory process.	The ever-present threat of regulatory refusal makes applicants unwilling to take chances. To save time and money, they at least set out to meet minimum regulatory standards.

example, replacing individual development regulation by codes of practice agreed with the development industry, or moving towards a European system where a legally binding plan automatically bestows approval on compatible development (Allmendinger and Ball 2006). Over time, Enterprise Zones, Simplified Planning Zones and other deregulation measures have sought to implement deregulatory ideas, but usually only in specific locations and for a specific time period.

Much less research has been undertaken into the potential process benefits from development regulation, partly because these are far harder to establish. However, if regulation works well, it should spot potential difficulties at an early stage of the development process and avoid subsequent resource wastage. As an example, effective integration between planning and highway authorities during regulatory analysis might identify the need for highway improvements so as to prevent local congestion occurring from a particular development. This is the kind of problem that is much cheaper and easier to resolve before development has taken place, rather than afterwards. Yet, there is little evidence so far on how far integrated regulatory processes can and do reduce long-term costs either to the developer or to the public sector, primarily because such benefits tend to remain hidden within normal working practices.

Regulation is primarily concerned with the attainment of minimum product standards. Even where it defines a variety of performance levels, as with the Code for Sustainable Homes (DCLG 2006b), performance above the minimum is a matter of voluntary compliance. If regulatory processes are seen as burdensome, applicants may concentrate their energies on at least achieving the minimal standard, rather than thinking how they might do much better. Regulations may also take some time to catch up with improved practices, which itself can act as a deterrent to innovation. Regulators who adopt a standard checklist approach, ticking off various elements of a development, may fail to spot whether the development works as a whole, and may even refuse to approval a proposal of undoubted overall quality because it fails one or two minor tests. Where members of a planning committee start to make a series of separate requests for what they believe to be individual design improvements, the end result may turn out to be more like the proverbial camel than a horse. More significantly, powerful lobby groups may capture the regulatory process and seek to turn it to their own advantage, as alleged by Pennington (2000) in the case of UK amenity and environment groups, and by Marantz and Ben-Joseph (2011) in respect of the US real estate industry. These factors may mean that the products of the regulatory process turn out to be worse than would have been the case without regulation.

The potential product benefits of development regulation are again hard to assess, primarily because they tend to remain hidden within regulatory processes. However, Hall (2011) argues strongly that the power of planning authorities to say 'no' to badly designed housing development produced a radical shift in the mindsets of housebuilders in Chelmsford (Figure 12.3). He concludes: 'The

FIGURE 12.3
Chancellor Park, Chelmsford, Essex, England. Speculative housebuilders began to produce development of this quality and diversity once Chelmsford Borough Council took a firm stand against standard house types and layouts. (Steve Tiesdell)

experience in Chelmsford showed how the gradual increase over time of both the quantity of published policy and its degree of prescription resulted in better quality of architecture and a more vibrant public realm' (Hall 2011: 91). In other words, taking a strong regulatory stand can lead to much better development outcomes. As this suggests, the precise form of regulation can often be more important than the principle of regulation itself. This chapter therefore concludes by returning to the issue of regulatory choice.

Conclusions

Regulation of real estate markets is one of four matching policy instruments and is best deployed alongside market shaping, market stimulus or capacity building. It may therefore be difficult to separate the outcomes of regulation from those of these other policy instruments. Nevertheless, the focus of market regulation is on compelling, managing or eradicating certain activities or aspects of those activities. It thus limits individual actors' scope for autonomous action, on the basis that collective gains more than outweigh any individual losses.

Although the state is the prime generator of market regulation of real estate, the long tradition of private regulation by contract is still evident today. The form that regulation takes in any particular context is highly contingent on the prevalent institutional circumstances of that context. In the UK, such circumstances largely explain why regulation of the real estate market has largely adopted the form shown by the left-hand column of Table 12.1. However, as the table suggests, explicit choices can be made in the design of regulatory systems, to the extent that radical change could be introduced to the way real estate development is regulated in the UK, without fundamentally undermining the principles of regulation. It would thus be possible to move more in the direction of contract regulation (as reflected in the growth of planning gain) or more towards a predefined system (as reflected in the increasing use of design codes). Surprisingly, debates around 'planning reform' in the UK tend not to ask these fundamental questions but concentrate instead on how the development-control system put in place in 1947 can be made to work more effectively.

Yet, as this chapter has intimated, the British approach to development control, while pioneering in its time, now stands as one of several possible methods to regulate real estate development. The contention of this chapter is that whenever planning reform is on the political agenda in the future, it needs to start by thinking from first principles about the seven regulatory choices set out in Table 12.1. Even if this were to confirm the validity of all aspects of inherited regulatory systems, it would likely be a more fruitful exercise than taking existing systems for granted and limiting discussion to how they might be speeded up or made more efficient.

13 Market stimulus

In many locations, where development is lucrative and unproblematic, all that needs to be done by the state to achieve its preferred development pattern is to shape and regulate real estate markets effectively. In other locations, where markets are thin or have failed, the state may need to promote development, rather than merely control it.[1] This involves some form of market stimulus. In this chapter, we review four main types of stimulus action that can be taken to stimulate development. The first entails direct intervention to kick-start the development process, for example by resolving physical, infrastructural or ownership constraints. The other three are more indirect and seek to change the pattern of incentives influencing whether market actors decide to undertake development at all, and, if so, the criteria by which they choose between alternative development possibilities that may differ according to location, type or timing. Stimulus instruments work by altering the outcome of financial appraisals, through impacting on development costs and revenues (price), risk and access to funding.

Stimulus instruments therefore 'lubricate' markets by making development more attractive to market actors. They have been defined by Syms and Clarke (2011: 137–38) as mechanisms 'employed by a governmental body, either central or local, or a quasi-governmental agency, to encourage an actor or group of actors, for example both public- and private-sector developers, to undertake development projects on sites, or in locations, that the actor would not otherwise consider and/or to undertake better quality development than would otherwise occur without the stimulus'. Such instruments expand the scope for autonomous action open to market actors and encourage them to venture into developments that they would otherwise consider unattractive. Testing their effectiveness must involve trying to assess what might have happened in their absence.

Syms and Clarke (2011) distinguish between stimulus instruments that promote development and those that encourage developers to invest in design and place-making. They argue that high-quality development can be achieved even in economically difficult areas by combining development- and design-stimulus instruments. Yet, too often, market stimulus is used to promote development, irrespective of design considerations. At best, this means that opportunities to improve place quality are lost, but more often it encourages disintegrated development that leads to a significant deterioration in place quality.[2]

Market stimulus is often associated with urban regeneration and with a policy approach that has been labelled as entrepreneurial or leverage planning (Brindley *et al.* 1996), since it seeks to lever private-sector investment into thin markets by making public-sector finance available as an enticement. This has been much practised in the UK, the US and elsewhere since the late 1970s as a response to deindustrialisation and urban decline. In its most ardent form, it came to be associated with the term 'property-led urban regeneration' (see, for example, Healey *et al.* 1992, Imrie and Thomas 1993, Turok 1992).

Property-led urban regeneration has been widely criticised for three main reasons. First, it often produced what was alleged to be the wrong kind of development – hotels and convention centres, for instance, rather than factories and decent homes for local people. Second, it was thought to benefit the urban rich rather than the urban poor. Third, it directed significant public-sector resources towards the property-development industry, which was considered by many to represent poor value for public money, compared to other potential regeneration strategies. In some cases, this served to distance investment markets from user markets through tax breaks that stoked up investment demand for new developments in places where user demand was still weak, making the chances of any future development without state support even less likely. Property-led urban regeneration thus fell out of favour from the mid-1990s, even to the extent that some regeneration strategies began to neglect property altogether.

Such criticisms make it essential to approach stimulus instruments with caution and carefully assess their potential social impact, value for money and implications for place-making. Nevertheless, it would be mistaken wholly to discard state support for property development, since new shops, offices, factories and homes create hard economic assets that improve urban competitiveness, as well as providing well-paid jobs in the construction industry. In regeneration areas, for example, the hardest task is often to help private-sector pioneers to overcome risk perceptions and other institutional barriers to initial developments. Such barriers can create a first-mover disadvantage in the sense that it is safer and easier to be among the second, not the first, wave of businesses moving into such areas. At Denver, Colorado, Weiler's (2000) study demonstrated the importance of public-sector support (in this case through a $1 million revolving loan fund) in encouraging pioneer businesses to move into the neglected Lo-Do area close to the city centre and kick-start its revival. Since cities with a more modern property stock have a competitive advantage, the core debate where real estate markets are thin or have failed often concerns how and to what purpose stimulus instruments should be deployed, rather than whether they should be used at all.

Direct state actions

Since 1981, all but 6 of the 130 coalmines then existing in England have closed, with the loss of 193,000 jobs (National Audit Office 2009). This scale of deindustrialisation, and the extensive dereliction it brought, called for a strategic response. The National Coalfields Programme, established by the UK Government in 1996, had by 2010 spent £521 million on the physical regeneration of 107 coalfield sites, levering in a further £1 billion of private investment (Homes and Communities Agency 2011). This stimulus package helped to reclaim 2,700 hectares of brownfield land, and generated around 2,700 new homes and over 1 million square metres of new employment floorspace. (About half of the former coalfield lands were considered unsuitable for development and will instead provide valuable open space.) One illustration of this direct state stimulus to regeneration is the former Shirebrook Colliery in Derbyshire (Box 13.1 and Figure 13.1), which has been transformed into the site of a major new business park and housing development (Figure 13.2).

BOX 13.1 Shirebrook, Derbyshire, England

The closure of Shirebrook Colliery in the early 1990s left a devastated local economy and an extensive area of derelict land. In 1996, ownership of the 130-hectare site passed to English Partnerships, the government agency responsible for the National Coalfields Programme (NCP). The site was then passed on in 1999 to the East Midlands Development Agency, who between 2000 and 2008 invested some £38 million of NCP funding to reclaim the site and prepare it for the development of a 38-hectare business park and around 850 new homes. Work included extensive reclamation of the former colliery site and its associated spoil heaps, along with expansion of the adjacent sewage treatment works. The reclamation works involved around 2 million cubic metres of earthworks, including the excavation of around 150,000 cubic metres of limestone rock with which to cap the development plots. A 1.5km link road was built to access the new development. A new drainage channel and balancing ponds were created to remove the Shirebrook itself from a culvert and re-establish it as a natural watercourse, with footbridges provided to connect new paths and tracks.

The new Brook Park Business Park was chosen by Sports Direct as the location of its new central headquarters. Occupying around 25 hectares, this £80 million development will comprise around 120,000m² of ware-

FIGURE 13.1 Shirebrook Colliery, taken in 2007, Derbyshire, England. (Phil Sangwell, used under the Creative Commons licence)

FIGURE 13.2 Brook Park Business Park taken in 2010, Derbyshire, England. (East Midlands Development Agency)

housing, 15,000m² of office space and a retail training centre, creating about 1,800 jobs. Direct state action in reclaiming the colliery site for private-sector development was an essential precursor to this investment. As a form of market stimulus, such action was markedly different from the city centre property-led urban regeneration of the late 1980s and early 1990s. At Shirebrook, state intervention in resolving critical land development constraints transformed the environmental and economic fortunes of an area in severe decline following colliery closure.

The National Coalfields Programme is an exceptional example of how direct state intervention can be used to stimulate new development in locations that would otherwise be avoided by market actors. The task of coalfield regeneration demanded national action to reclaim derelict and contaminated land, undertake environmental improvement, provide access roads, drains and sewers and make serviced plots available to private developers at prices that reflect the future potential of the land, rather than its past history. Although few forms of direct state action match the scale and ambition of the National Coalfields Programme, the principle of bringing land up to a point at which the private sector will invest, by undertaking advance reclamation, landscaping and infrastructure provision, is widely applicable and, indeed, has been put into practice by many different state agencies at locations large and small. A stimulus instrument is therefore defined by its purpose rather than its scale, with small-scale actions to promote development potentially being just as effective as large-scale ones.

An essential part of development stimulus is often to take brownfield land that is deemed unattractive by the private sector, undertake whatever work is necessary to make it attractive, and then market it for private-sector development. This can prove to be an expensive activity, so tight cost control is crucial in keeping the public subsidy to a minimum and achieving value for money. The acquisition and disposal of land more generally, whether or not linked to reclamation work or infrastructure provision and/or undertaken in regeneration areas, provides a powerful instrument by which the state can directly influence development. We therefore explore this in more detail.

Land acquisition and assembly

Some countries have long experience in direct state management of overall land supply. One example is the Netherlands (see Louw 2008, Needham 1997, Verhage 2003), where traditionally almost all development land passed through public ownership, with acquisitions normally taking place voluntarily.[3] As the Dutch case highlights, where development land would otherwise be in short supply, the state can play an important role in lubricating markets by purchasing land for subsequent onward sale to developers. This principle has been widely applied elsewhere, although usually on a far more targeted basis than in the Netherlands. One important focus for such direct intervention is where development is constrained by multiple or fragmented land ownership.

Multiple ownership of even small sites can be endemic in urban areas, proving highly problematic to development (see Chapter 5). Without state intervention, development cannot proceed unless agreement is reached with each owner. In a private market, the last owner to settle is thus in the strongest position to drive a hard bargain with any developer who has already bought out all other owners. Compulsory purchase by the state provides a potentially effective means to accelerate the development of land in multiple ownership by taking over and assembling all the different individual interests into the single ownership of a local authority or other state agency.

In theory, where development is impeded by multiple ownership, local planning authorities in the UK are well empowered to acquire land by compulsory purchase, and then to sell to whichever developer willing to implement planning policies makes the highest offer. However, in practice, most local authorities regard compulsory purchase as a last resort. There are three reasons for this, which limit its effectiveness as a stimulus instrument. The first is administrative and legal. Compulsory purchase is a lengthy and cumbersome procedure with no certain outcome (see Winter and Lloyd 2006, for example, for a brief summary of what is involved in making a compulsory purchase order for regeneration in England). Substantial opposition may be generated. If objections are received, local authorities must make a strong case at public inquiry to show that the particular planning purpose is in the public interest and cannot be achieved without compulsory acquisition. The Secretary of State certainly does not confirm every order submitted, and even confirmed orders may subsequently be overturned by the courts (Riley 2009).

The second reason is political and ideological. Many local authorities, by no means all of a right-wing persuasion, regard compulsory purchase as an undue interference in private land markets. They do not consider it to be a legitimate role of local government to support certain private interests above others, whether such action enables planning policies to be implemented or not.

The third, and perhaps the most important reason, is financial. Compulsory purchase is simply a very expensive business. Disposed owners are entitled to claim compensation not merely to cover the loss of land and property but also to meet legitimate costs of disturbance, together with any reasonable bills that they incur in instructing surveyors, solicitors or other professional advisers to handle their case. It is therefore not surprising that financially constrained local authorities are reluctant to incur such costs. Indeed, most authorities are prepared to undertake compulsory purchase for planning reasons only when persuaded to do so by a particular developer who agrees in advance both to purchase the land from the authority as soon as compulsory acquisition is complete and to reimburse the authority in full for any expenses incurred.[4]

Although compulsory purchase was widely used in the UK to promote slum clearance and city-centre redevelopment in the immediate post-war period, by the mid-1990s it had largely fallen into disuse, except for transport schemes (Adams 1996). After the Urban Task Force (1999) reinvigorated the urban agenda in England, there was renewed interest in using compulsory purchase to promote urban regeneration. The American courts and many state legislatures remain reluctant to authorise use of eminent domain (the American equivalent of compulsory purchase) for similar purposes in the US. In the UK, some commentators have suggested that land readjustment, which is widely practised elsewhere as a means to encourage co-operative land assembly, could, in certain cases, provide an alternative to the highly complex process of compulsory purchase (Adams *et al.* 2001b, Dixon 2001, Lichfield 2002).

Urban land readjustment has been defined as the consolidation of adjoining plots 'by a government agency for their unified planning, servicing and subdivision with the sale of some of the new plots for cost recovery and the redistribution of other plots to the landowners' (Archer 1989: 307). Most commonly used at the urban fringe, this system of land pooling and replotting originated in Germany in the early twentieth century (Doebele 1982), was widely applied as the basis of urban planning in Japan (Sorensen 1999 and 2000) and has since been adopted in many other countries, including Korea, India, Indonesia, Nepal, Palestine/Israel, Taiwan, Thailand and Malaysia (Archer 1989 and 1992, Home 2007, Lin 2005). The system enables fragmented and irregularly shaped plots to be consolidated to create serviced and usable parcels. Land is then redistributed to the original landowners, with public infrastructure costs borne collectively by the increase in development value. As a development stimulus, land readjustment thus connects land assembly, disposal and infrastructure provision with a method to distribute the financial benefits of development between landowners and public agencies (Home 2007).

An edited volume by Hong and Needham (2007) chronicles recent experiences with land readjustment in China, Germany, Israel, Japan, the Netherlands and the US. In China, for example, an experimental form of land readjustment demonstrated how resident participation reduced potential conflict and enabled local people to benefit from a better-planned environment with good infrastructure and service provision (Li and Li 2007). From the Dutch perspective, van der Krabben and Needham (2009) argue the theoretical case for urban land readjustment in cases where renovation and redevelopment take place alongside each other, where original owners wish to participate in development and where the full costs of infrastructure provision cannot necessarily be covered through municipal acquisition.

Urban land readjustment thus offers landowners much greater opportunity than compulsory purchase to share in the financial benefits of redevelopment, even if they, rather than the municipality, must bear significant redevelopment risk. Since compulsory purchase is so complex, lengthy and uncertain, Adams *et al.* (2001b) have proposed a bespoke form of land readjustment for the UK, termed an 'urban partnership zone'. This would combine owner participation, a joint-venture corporate structure and simplified planning procedures to resolve multiple land ownership in circumstances where wholesale compulsory purchase is unlikely or inappropriate.

Land disposal

Making its own land available for development by others is potentially one of the most important stimulus instruments in the state's armoury. Nevertheless, a conflict can soon arise between maximising the immediate financial return to the public purse and securing development of a type and quality most likely to enhance the long-term value and attractiveness of the particular place in which it is located. In Exeter, for example, the city council entered into agreement with one of the UK's largest developer/investors to redevelop council-owned land for a major city-centre retail-led project. Despite significant local controversy, this was approved in 2003, with the development completed in 2007. However, as Campbell *et al.* (2009: 19) argue, 'In the Exeter case by breaking up the redevelopment into a number of smaller schemes the Council could have secured a redevelopment outcome which would have been better for the local economy, with the attendant social and economic implications for the least advantaged, as well as being more environmentally and aesthetically sensitive.'

As this suggests, local authorities do not always see their landholdings as a significant resource that can be deployed creatively to shape places for the better. Indeed, financial deficits and audit requirements mean that authorities are often under great pressure to rationalise their land and property holdings, maximising sales to cover short-term revenue gaps. A typical manual written to help UK local authorities realise latent value from their property holdings recommends that they should 'rationalise the asset base, release capital and reduce revenue' (4ps and Deloitte 2008: 5) but makes no attempt to explore how surplus public land can be used strategically to help enhance place quality.

It is therefore no wonder that other public agencies with land to sell, such as hospitals or the military, tend to concentrate on maximising capital receipts from surplus sites, even if this brings them into conflict with local planning policy. However, Clark (2003) contends that the pursuit of the highest price and maximum planning value may amount to 'wasting the peace dividend', since surplus military land then becomes too expensive to redevelop for local needs. Instead, she commends the Swedish approach, where economic reconstruction takes priority over maximising the financial returns from sale, allowing local authorities to acquire surplus sites at current use, consult widely to match future uses to local needs, and keep subsequent sale profits.

One way to stimulate better-quality development is to release surplus public land on a competitive basis in which financial return and design quality are seen as equally important determinants of the competition (Tolson 2011). This requires the design merit of competition entries to be evaluated separately from the financial bid, and an explicitly weighted formula to be used to derive an overall assessment of each bid. In Hong Kong, what is known as 'two envelope fee bidding' is generally used to evaluate development competitions, with the design and financial bid submitted separately in different 'envelopes'. However, even this formalised evaluation system has its drawbacks, since research has shown that financial bids vary much more than designs, with the result that the lowest financial bid is always likely to win the competition, irrespective of its design merits (Drew *et al.* 2004).[5] An alternative approach, often used in the UK, is to separate the development competition into at least two rounds, one of which is used to evaluate design merits, with the other then a simple financial competition between all entrants whose designs are considered of high enough quality (Fisher *et al.* 2007). As these issues highlight, although the disposal of public land may serve as an immediate development stimulus, the chances of also creating successful and sustainable places are highly dependent on the terms and conditions on which any disposal takes place.

Price-adjusting actions

Price-adjusting stimulus actions are those that impact on projected costs and revenues in a development appraisal. They take three main forms: development grants, tax incentives and project bonuses. The first two involve an immediate cost to the state, through either expenditure incurred or tax revenue foregone. The third operates as a deregulatory incentive, enabling developers to realise more of the development potential of their sites. Each of these is now discussed in turn.

Development grants

Development grants provide a direct public subsidy to encourage private-sector development either in particular locations, such as regeneration areas or declining regions, or of particular types, such as affordable housing or small industrial units. Preferably, they should provide the minimum additional sum needed in order to turn financially unattractive, but desirable, developments into attractive ones. It is never easy to calculate this with precision, especially since development appraisal itself is methodically inexact, with minor changes in important variables having potentially significant impacts on the overall outcome. The inevitable danger is that individual development grants become over-generous, so reducing the amount of private investment that can be levered into a particular area for a given level of public subsidy (the 'leverage ratio'). To achieve better value for public money, it is necessary to establish and monitor complex entitlement rules, which even allow the state to 'claw back' what eventually turns out to have been excessive public subsidy.[6] However, the more such rules conflict with the principle of making incentives simple and transparent, the more counter-productive they can become in deterring interest from developers.

In the UK, grants have long been made available by central government to subsidise specifically approved developments in regeneration areas. However, this tradition was largely brought to an end by the European Commission in 1999, which ruled that such grants amounted to illegal state aid to individual companies. This coincided with the desire among relevant government agencies to switch development support from a subsidy model to an investment model. It reflected concerns that grant subsidy may simply redistribute development that might otherwise have been undertaken elsewhere and/or by other developers. In the US, bidding wars between cities to attract apparently mobile capital investments have been mercilessly exploited by site consultants who act as brokers playing one city off against another in order to extract the most advantageous subsidy packages for their clients. Markusen (2007) calls for substantial reform of such practices in order to 'rein in the competition for capital' between American cities and ensure that whatever public costs are incurred are clearly outweighed by public benefits.

Taxation incentives

While development grants are individually negotiated and approved development by development, taxation incentives are applicable to all developments of the class to which they apply. Unlike grants, which primarily reduce the costs of development, taxation incentives can affect either costs or revenues. Taxation incentives provide exemptions from national taxation systems and are less closely targeted than development grants, with consequent potential displacement or deadweight loss. This means that some of the developments would have taken place anyway without the taxation incentive, so at least part of the resources expended on the incentive produce no actual welfare gain.

Taxation incentives can take the form either of a tax break to encourage desirable development or a tax penalty to discourage undesirable development. The former are more much popular and well used than the latter. For example, real estate tax credits are widely used in the US to promote investment in historic buildings (Pickard and Pickerill 2002). In the UK, land remediation relief encourages landowners to remediate their contaminated or derelict land (Syms and Clarke 2011). There are few examples of tax penalties on undesirable development, although the Civic Trust's (1998) proposal for a greenfield development tax in the UK offers a theoretical illustration of how imposing a tax penalty on one particular type of development might act as a stimulus to other development types.

Dublin provides one of the most prominent recent examples of the use of tax incentives to stimulate development. Here, the Irish Government introduced a package of tax breaks in 1986 to promote the regeneration of designated areas within Dublin and elsewhere, which lasted in one form or another until 2008. The package included a varied array of capital allowances, double rent allowances, rates remission, income tax relief, investment property tax relief and reduced corporation tax rates (MacLaran and Williams 2003). Different parts of the package stimulated demand for new development, while others encouraged its supply (see Chapter 5). The overall package was estimated to have cost IR£367–461 million nationally by 1996 alone, but by then to have generated around IR£1.7 billion of new development, of which IR£1 billion were concentrated in Dublin (Dubben and Williams 2009).

According to McGreal *et al.* (2002), without the stimulus, the extent of development that happened in Dublin over a ten- to fifteen-year period would otherwise have taken decades to achieve. New locations and markets such as the International Financial Services Centre were established, even though this partially displaced office activity elsewhere in Dublin. A newly rejuvenated cultural, artistic and environmental quarter was created at Temple Bar, where tax breaks funded property refurbishment. McGreal *et al.* (2002) suggest that the Dublin package was most effective in attracting end-users (especially new residents), which helped to kick-start the demand for apartments. Leverage ratios for residential development were six times those for commercial development (Dubben and Williams 2009).

Institutional property investors were much less impressed than other actors, owing to their tax-neutral status and perception of added risk in regeneration. As a result, new commercial developments appealed more to individual investors who saw them as a relatively short-term tax shelter. This itself created political controversy. By 2010, with the Irish economy and its banking sector in serious trouble, many expressed concern in retrospect that the stimulus package had artificially boosted commercial office development in Dublin. This was thought to have helped to overheat both the property market and the broader economy, contributing to the severe economic decline experienced by Ireland at the end of the first decade of the twenty-first century. As this suggests, property markets that become over-dependent on taxation incentives may experience damaging long-term effects.

Project bonuses

Project bonuses provide a development stimulus by waiving specific regulatory restrictions in exchange for higher-quality development or other community benefits. In part of Hong Kong, for example, a two-tier plot ratio system has been operated in which more floorspace than normal is allowed on larger sites with better ancillary servicing facilities (Tang and Tang 1999). This principle is also applied in New York, where developers who improve a subway station, create open space, provide affordable housing, preserve a historic building or create a cultural facility can all claim additional floorspace bonuses (Hack and Sagalyn 2011). Where development is otherwise constrained by regulatory restrictions, project bonuses can potentially add more to marginal revenues than to marginal costs, so stimulating development and providing funds to pay for public goods. In such circumstances, 'One of the central tasks of an urban designer is ensuring that the collective goods being sought are in balance with the resources that flow from the project' (Hack and Sagalyn 2011: 258).

Risk-reducing actions

As a general principle of development appraisal, the greater the perceived risk involved in a proposed development, the lower the projected capital value. This is because capital value is calculated by multiplying expected net annual income by the inverse of the initial yield. The riskier the perceived development, then the higher the initial yield, thus the lower the income multiplier.[7] Where two projects have exactly the same income stream, developers will normally prefer the one perceived to be less risky, since it will have a higher initial capital value. Actions that reduce perceived risks in regeneration areas can thus provide an important development stimulus.

In a world where many future events are possible, uncertainty refers to a lack of knowledge of all possible outcomes and the impossibility of specifying their likelihood. Risk refers to specific calculations of the likelihood of each possible outcome taking place. An important function of markets in a modern economy (including real estate markets) is to convert uncertainty into risk (van der Krabben 1995). Yet, Guy and Henneberry (2000: 2405) pose an important question by asking 'Are "risk weightings" simply a product of objective science, or might the agency of risk analysts – for example, their more intimate knowledge of the London market – play some role in the relative weighting of risk between London and the regions?' In other words, if risk is as much socially as economically constructed, as Guy and Henneberry argue, public agencies may have more scope than they realise to stimulate development by challenging risk perceptions about regeneration areas. Four types of confidence-building measure are relevant here, each discussed in turn below.

Accurate market information

Until research was undertaken by Adair *et al.* (2004), it was generally presumed that investment returns from regeneration property were poor, as compared to benchmarks set by overall property returns. However, according to Adair *et al.* (2004: 4):

> The results stemming from this study show that investment property in regeneration areas can out-perform national and local benchmarks. The analysis demonstrates that over the long-term perspective regeneration areas offer significant investment opportunities. These findings challenge perceptions regarding investment returns. The message to major institutional investors from this research is the need to reconsider strategies regarding the potential of property within regeneration areas.

As a result of this research, English Partnerships (now part of the Homes and Communities Agency) collaborated with Investment Property Databank (IPD) and others to produce an annual IPD Regeneration Index, which compares the returns on retail, office, industrial and now residential property in English regeneration areas with those across the UK as a whole (see Chapter 9). Although the detailed picture varies from year to year, it has become clear that regeneration areas offer lucrative opportunities for real estate investors, especially if property is acquired early enough in the regeneration process to take advantage of the financial uplift as the area matures. This highlights the importance of accurate information in matching perceived risks to real returns and thus providing a development stimulus.

Policy certainty and stability

The second type of confidence-building measure capable of stimulating development through risk reduction is policy certainty and stability. A feasible masterplan or development framework for a regeneration area, for instance, which market actors consider likely to be implemented, creates confidence about what is likely to happen at particular locations and, crucially, at adjoining locations. In other words, policy certainty helps to contain the risk exposure of developers by providing reassurance against the threat of negative externalities that might otherwise subsequently arise on land neighbouring any proposed development. As the example of Adamstown showed in Chapter 11, once a masterplan or development framework is in place, simplified planning processes that ensure rapid approval of compliant development (while rejecting manifestly non-compliant development) also help to create a more secure and predictable investment environment.

Demonstration projects and environmental improvements

Demonstration projects, such as museums, leisure centres or even government offices, can show public-sector commitment and convince the private sector that an apparently run-down area has a positive and prosperous future. Manchester's Museum of Science and Industry, for example, which opened in the Castlefield area in 1983, proved to be an important early catalyst for the regeneration of its surrounding area. Strategic landscaping, environment improvement and public realm investment, undertaken as a precursor to development, can also generate confidence in the determination of the public sector to achieve substantial regeneration. These messages may be reinforced by place-marketing campaigns and general promotion activity. Such clear demonstration of public commitment to an area's future is usually linked to the type of direct state action to resolve physical, infrastructural or ownership constraints to development, discussed earlier in the chapter.

Holistic place management

Town Centre Management (TCM) schemes and Business Improvement Districts (BIDs) can reduce development and investment risk by the collective commitment of local authorities, businesses and other key players to the effective management and enhancement of an area as a whole. They seek to make places more attractive, accessible, cleaner, lively and safer to the extent that those urban centres in which numerous different interests own and operate property can then compete more effectively with out-of-town centres, which are usually owned and well managed by a single landlord. This can help to stimulate further development, since, by tackling negative externalities and promoting positive ones, active management of places generates greater confidence in their long-term future, protects and enhances real estate asset values and so reduces perceived investment risk.

In the UK, TCM originated in the late 1980s and spread rapidly during the 1990s in response to the development of regional shopping centres and other forms of out-of-town retailing. This was encouraged by central government, but usually driven forward by local authorities in partnership with retailers and local businesses. TCM sought to promote the vitality and viability of traditional centres by public realm improvements, pedestrianisation, better security and litter control, special events, marketing promotions and so on. 'Vitality is a measure of how lively and busy a town centre is and viability is a measure of its capacity to attract on-going investment, for maintenance, improvement and adaptation to changing needs' (Scottish Executive 2006: 9). Holistic management was thus intended to reinforce the centre's immediate consumer appeal and its longer-term investment potential. By 2010, some 600 towns and cities across the UK had established some form of place-management initiative.

Although TCM in the UK has been widely supported by local authorities and certain national retailers such as Boots, Marks & Spencer and Sainsburys, support and contributions from the private sector have been wholly voluntary. This has created a 'free riding' problem, where some local business have been prepared to contribute financially to management costs but others have refused to do so, while still enjoying the benefits of active place management. This has diminished the potential of TCM, while causing local friction and frustration. BIDs provide a potential solution to this dilemma. They share many of the characteristics of TCM schemes, but have a limited lifespan (five years in the UK) and can be established only when supported in a ballot by the majority of businesses in an area. Once so established, all businesses in the area must pay the BID levy.

BIDs originated in Canada in the 1960s and expanded significantly across North America in the 1990s, to the extent that, by the turn of the century, there were about 1,500 North American BIDs, varying substantially in size, format and character. New York is seen as the established centre of activity in the US, with the city home to over 130 BIDs, including the most ambitious such organisation in the US, the Times Square BID (Figure 13.3) (Lloyd *et al.* 2004). In the UK, the concept was commended by the Urban Task Force (1999) and introduced by legislation in England in 2003 and Scotland in 2006. Following initial pilots, BIDs have become well established across the UK, with around 120 successfully established by 2010. They extend the concept of active place management well beyond town and city centres, to include business parks and industrial estates. Peel *et al.* (2009) argue that BIDs represent a marked departure from the relatively more organic and voluntary relationships evident in TCM, since they reflect a more privatised arrangement based on contractual relationships, evident especially in contractual service level agreements between BIDs and local authorities.

FIGURE 13.3
Times Square, New York, USA. The Times Square Business Improvement District (now known as the Times Square Alliance) was formed in 1992 as a partnership between the City of New York and local businesses. It has since transformed the image and fortunes of Times Square through redevelopment, public realm improvements, enhanced security, brand marketing and related activities. (David Adams)

Tax Increment Financing districts (TIFs), like BIDs, originated in North America in the 1950s, and appear likely to take hold in the UK. Almost all American states have adopted legislation to establish TIFs, with Chicago, which alone has over 130 TIF districts, seen as one of the leading advocates in the field.[8] While BIDs rely on annual income from business levy, TIFs seek to capture the value uplift from regeneration and put it to work to make that regeneration happen. To achieve this, the property tax base of a TIF district is frozen at the start of the project, with all subsequent increases used to fund infrastructure investment and regeneration costs. These are often initially covered by bonds issued against the expectation of future tax increases. In the US, TIFs are 'widely seen as an effective tool with a proven track record. Overall, TIF schemes in the US have generated billions of dollars of investment – creating more jobs, more affordable housing and better public spaces' (British Property Federation 2008: 9).

If this seemingly painless method to fund regeneration without calling on public expenditure sounds too good to be true, it probably is. This is because devoting all future tax increases to cover substantial bond repayments is a bit like an individual directing all future salary increases to repay an excessively large personal mortgage. In the latter case, there is nothing left to cover inflation in food and household costs, let alone enjoy an extra night out or a better holiday. With TIFs, there may be nothing left to maintain the standard of local schools or other local services, which may be especially worrying if service demands increase as population rises (Carroll 2008). This highlights how the unintended social impacts of any development stimulus need to be considered well in advance. Moreover, 'Since most US cities are using TIFs, businesses can play them off against each other to boost the handouts they receive simply to operate profit-making enterprises. Now that TIFs are so widespread, cities find it hard to attract new development without tax breaks' (British Property Federation 2008: 9). Much care is therefore needed in any international transfer of the TIF model, so as to ensure true development stimulus without the negative social impacts.

Capital-raising actions

Capital-raising actions are those that provide or facilitate access to development finance, where private-sector capital is either not available or needs to be reinforced in some way. At a simple level, loan guarantees may be provided by the state to enable market actors to borrow from the banks for projects that might otherwise be considered to carry a high level of risk, and thus a high interest rate even if funding were available at all. In the US, federal and state loan guarantees have been widely used as a stimulus to promote the redevelopment of brownfield sites (De Sousa 2008).

Revolving loan funds provide another illustration of capital-raising stimulus actions. These are used extensively to fund the restoration of historic buildings in the US and elsewhere and may well combine public funds with those raised on a voluntary or charitable basis. Once established, a revolving loan fund makes use of interest and capital payments on old loans to issue new ones and is thus a self-replenishing source of funding. One of the most active revolving funds in the US is Preservation North America, which was responsible for the acquisition and resale of some 300 historic properties in the last two decades of the twentieth century (Pickard and Pickerill 2002).

Although locally important, these capital-raising actions are small-scale, as compared to the potential of public-private development partnerships, in which the state moves beyond the general promotion of development and enters into specific contractual arrangements with one or more private-sector partners, agreeing to share the risks and rewards of development. Such arrangements have grown significantly in importance in recent decades and have extended beyond single-project partnerships between public agencies and private developers, to encompass a variety of multi-project partnerships. The latter involve some form of longer-term collaboration between the public and private sectors, which enables a series of developments to be undertaken over a number of years (Adams 1994). The most common contribution of public authorities to public-private partnerships comes from landholdings or other fixed assets. These can then be used as a capital-raising instrument to provide security for debt finance raised by a joint-venture vehicle formally established to pursue the development partnership. Importantly, such arrangements provide the public sector with the opportunity to invest in regeneration, rather than merely to subsidise it.

One good example is Blueprint, a joint-venture company established between English Partnerships, the East Midlands Development Agency and Igloo, widely recognised as a socially responsible real estate investment fund. The public sector partners contributed around £17 million in property assets and some cash to secure a 50 per cent equal stake in the partnership. A similar sum was contributed by the private-sector partner, with the total equity then matched by £14.5 million of debt finance (Ebbs 2009). Early developments included a £50 million award-winning extension to Nottingham Science Park, intended to provide research and development users with flexible space from 100m^2 to 2,000m^2.

Conclusions

Whenever public agencies are faced with development scarcity, they experience a strong temptation to press the stimulus button. As this chapter has demonstrated, there are a wide variety of stimulus instruments that can be deployed to kick-start development where it is in short supply. But, crucially, not all are equally effective, economically or socially. Indeed, four unintended consequences exist with any stimulus instrument, which raise important questions about whether such instruments provide value for money or are socially just.

The first of these is what might be called 'deadweight loss', where any real benefits produced are outweighed by the cost. This may be disguised in any economic appraisals undertaken by the agency responsible for the stimulus, for example, by exaggerating the number of jobs created or failing to include indirect costs, such as the salaries of agency staff. The second unintended consequence is where stimulus creates merely a 'displacement' of activity that would have taken place with other companies or in other locations. Here, the concern expressed by the European Union about the potentially anti-competitive impact of development subsidies is particularly relevant. Third, stimulus packages may have unintended externalities or spill-overs, which may harm vulnerable social and economic groups beyond the development itself. The viability of local restaurants, for example, may well be put into jeopardy by a nearby major new retail and leisure complex with its own food court, whose development is assisted by a stimulus package. Finally, there is strong evidence from Dublin and elsewhere that long-term stimulus packages are at least partly capitalised into land values, to the benefit of landowners and investors.

Where concerns arise, it is usually where public agencies display naïveté and indeed ignorance about the real estate development industry. When they are promised a shiny new development in an economically depressed region, it is understandable why many local politicians pull out all the stops to make sure that the development happens. Policy certainty and accurate market information may be just as effective in attracting development, but less likely to catch the local headlines. In the end, however, most real estate development companies are not philanthropic organisations, but instead well used to striking a hard bargain in order to maximise their own profits. Often, public authorities suffer significantly from their often unsophisticated understanding of the development industry.

What this chapter suggests is the need for public agencies to apply stimulus interests selectively from a position of power. In the development process, ownership of land bestows considerable resource power and enables the holder to influence the development outcome significantly. In this context, those stimulus instruments that deploy public land ownership as an investment within some form of development partnership hold most prospect of securing value for public money as well as making sure that development meets the needs of a broad range of social groups and not just the urban rich. This calls for public agencies to resist the temptation to sell off their own landholdings for immediate capital gain and instead to use them strategically and with ingenuity so as to help create better places in less prosperous areas as much as in buoyant ones.

14 Capacity building

Introduction

An essential challenge for planners is to help to create places that better meet people's needs and aspirations. Too often, this end is obscured by excessive concentration on the means, with the result that many planners and politicians mistakenly believe that the production or regulation of plans completes the planning task. In reality, places come about as political power engages with the dynamics of real estate development,[1] which is why planners working for public agencies are essentially engaged in shaping, regulating and stimulating real estate markets. Indeed, what is required is not for planners to *become* market actors, but rather for them to *realise* that they already are market actors, intricately involved in market construction and reconstruction, and to develop their capacity and confidence to act accordingly.

Since policy instruments intended to create better places through influencing real estate markets are only as effective as the individuals and organisations charged with their delivery, this chapter concentrates on building planners' capacity in four crucial areas: market-shaping cultures, mindsets and ideas; market-rich information and knowledge; market-rooted networks; and market-relevant skills and capabilities. Capacity building is deliberately identified here as a separate policy instrument, even though it is intended to support market shaping, regulation and stimulus. To be successful, it requires careful thought and explicit attention, and often consumes significant time and resources. It is primarily an investment in people, with considerable potential for long-term returns (Elmore 1987). Indeed, enhancing planners' capacity to act in the world is an important part of building their confidence to succeed as place-makers, rather than as plan-makers.

Capacity building enables actors to operate more effectively within their own opportunity space, while influencing the opportunity space of other actors to wider advantage. Across the full spectrum of development actors, each may have potential to enhance their capacity for place-making in different ways. Speculative housebuilders, for instance, may well have much to learn about how creating integrated places rather than just housing estates can be deployed to add financial, as well as environmental and social, value to their developments. Although, for the sake of brevity, this chapter focuses on what might be done to enhance the effectiveness of planners, where relevant, attention is also drawn to the need for capacity building among other development actors. Indeed, many of the principles set out below could be applied more widely across the development spectrum.

Market-shaping cultures, mindsets and ideas

Planners who wish to build their capacity as market actors and place-makers must often start by looking afresh at their own cultural perspectives, mindsets or ways of thinking. Taking many different forms, cultural mindsets emerge, develop and are sustained in varied ways. They provide an important means of editing and processing information and so establish how 'things' are perceived, interpreted and appraised. Embedded mindsets may unhelpfully reinforce 'conventional wisdom', inhibiting the development of new ideas. 'Loft living', for example, became an emergent market in the 1980s and early 1990s, but the prevailing conventional wisdom was that people did not want to live in former industrial units with bare brickwork and exposed wooden floorboards and pipework. Overturning cultural mindsets involves what Landry calls a mindshift, which he describes as 'the process whereby the way one thinks of one's position, function and core ideas is dramatically re-assessed and changed. At its best it is based on the capacity to be open-minded enough to allow this change to occur' (Landry 2000: 52). Openness to, and anticipation of, change is thus an essential characteristic of successful planners.

Mindshifts challenge and change the cultural perspectives of decision-makers and so enhance their receptivity to new ideas. Civic leaders, for example, may come to see a new tram-line as a place-shaping opportunity, rather than merely a means of transport, and thus strive to exploit its potential accordingly. Mindshifts can be 'difficult, unsettling and potentially frightening' (Landry 2000: 53) because they confront the 'linearity' and 'box-like thinking' which Landry identified as characteristic of property developers, planners and accountants. Challenging default urbanism (see Chapter 10), for example, requires innovative and integrated thinking, as well as innate determination.

For planners working in the public sector, an important cultural mindshift is to see themselves as active participants in development, communicating vision and championing innovation, rather than external controllers of development. In particular, capacity building helps planners to visualise that their task is one of making places rather than simply plans, and of achieving desirable change rather than merely resisting undesirable change. This may challenge inherited professional or organisational cultures, which are seen to emerge from professional education, expertise and socialisation, and provide 'a predisposition to frame situations and problems in particular ways, that is, to analyse them according to specific categories, to synthesise them into specific structures, and to represent them in specific verbal, graphic, or numerical ways' (Fischler 1995: 21).

As Harvey (1989b) has observed, each profession sees the world through its own cultural lens. So, in viewing any particular street scene, architects may appreciate architectural design, visual rhythms and historical references, while real estate developers see buildings in terms of rents per square foot, planning or zoning regulations, set-backs and height limitations. Effective place-making involves working across culturally embedded barriers to create a holistic or rounded vision of what makes places function well. So, creating an 'ideas bank' about successful practices and places, for example, that demonstrates what is achievable in particular circumstances can encourage mindshifts among developers and funding agencies as well as among professional advisers.

Although 'changing the culture of planning' became an important policy theme in the UK and elsewhere in the first decade of the twenty-first century, it often confused the pursuit of organisational speed and efficiency with the transformation of cultural attitudes and mindsets. In the UK, for example, culture change in planning became heavily linked to the Labour Government's broader programme for administrative modernisation based upon the concept of 'managerialism' in the delivery of public services (Shaw and Lord 2007). In the end, 'changing the culture of planning' was largely indecipherable from the broader planning reform agenda. This lack of focus caused one senior planning practitioner, in giving evidence to the Scottish Parliament, to claim that 'when we first heard of and started debating the concept of culture change, all the planners thought that it was an issue for the developers and communities, whereas all the communities thought that it was an issue for the developers and the planners, and so on' (Hartland 2006). Real cultural change involves a more fundamental appreciation of the central role of planners as place-makers.

Market-rich information and knowledge

To create better places requires information and knowledge about place quality and how it can be influenced through market and development processes. This demands both background knowledge of 'the rules of the game' by which such processes function as well as quite specific information about their practical operations. Market-rich information and knowledge enhances the confidence of planners and empowers them to consider a wider range of policy alternatives, such as enabling redevelopment through restructuring property rights, rather than by direct government intervention.

Planners have traditionally been strong in collecting information on people and place (for example, from the census and local surveys), but much weaker in obtaining that for real estate markets. There has indeed been some suspicion about whether prices, values and ownership are proper planning matters, reflecting the fear that too close a knowledge of such information would soon result in a market-led style of planning. Yet, the annual IPD Regeneration Index shows how reliable market statistics can be used to test, demonstrate and reinforce the success of urban regeneration policies (see Chapter 9). As regeneration initiatives further highlight, planners can play an important role in reducing development risk. This requires a rounded appreciation of risk and of how risk reduction can be achieved through better-integrated development.

A wide range of statistical time series on the performance of property markets at the national, regional and, increasingly, local levels, are now available to be accessed from both public and private-sector sources, and these, together with the more qualitative market reports published by most leading property agents, can provide planners with a rich information base about market performance. Better market information can enable planners to understand more clearly how 'windows of development opportunity' open and close unevenly between places and create the confidence to take advantage of this.

Such initial information needs to be reinforced by better understanding of the motives and behaviour of private-sector implementation agents in order to recognise which landowners, developers and investors are most likely to share policy agendas and which are likely to be more hostile (see Chapters 7 to 9). More detailed knowledge of the real estate industry can also help to secure better contractual bargains, whether in relation to planning gain or development subsidies.

Market-rooted networks

Plan-shaped markets emerge not from remote pronouncements by planners, but from their close engagement with other market actors – presenting, hearing, arguing and exchanging views about how places should develop in future. This is why, according to Hopkins (2001: 38), a planning vision represents 'a normative forecast: a desired future that can work if people can be persuaded that it can and will come true'. Capacity building is thus about enhancing relations across the development spectrum so that planners working for public agencies are well connected with other professionals and with those working within the development industry. Such connections need to be characterised by mutual respect rather than domination by one side or another. At their best, they can generate a powerful coalition of shared interests to drive place-making forward, in which market priorities and policy intent shape and influence one another. While it remains essential to maintain the probity of government decision-making, it is also important to promote mutual learning and sharing of experience between the public, private and voluntary sectors so as to break down barriers between them. This can occur through both informal networks and formal organisations.

An informal network has been defined as 'An extended group of people with similar interests or concerns who interact and remain in informal contact for mutual assistance or support.'[2] People spontaneously form social and business networks, and are variously embedded within social webs and clusters.[3] These networks are inevitably selective and partial, since people tend to link to other like-minded people and are often most influenced by those to whom they are closest, whether as friends, neighbours or colleagues. Referring to this as 'embeddedness', Granovetter (1985: 490) explains how the concept highlights 'the role of concrete personal relations and structures (or "networks") of such relations in generating trust and discouraging malfeasance. The widespread preference for transacting with individuals of known reputation implies that few are actually content to rely on either generalized morality or institutional arrangements to guard against trouble.'

Planners working for public agencies can often be reluctant or ineffective in network collaboration with those working in the private sector, partly because of suspected conflicting values and partly to protect themselves from undue commercial influence. Yet, without the benefit of informal debate and shared intelligence across the sectors, it becomes difficult for planners to know how best to shape, regulate and stimulate real estate markets. Moreover, reflecting Granovetter's (1973) belief in the strength of weak ties, planners are likely to benefit more from breadth than depth in their informal networks. Market-rooted networks may thus better help planners to understand how market actors think if they provide relatively loose connections across a broad range of such actors, rather than strong links to one or two particular developers.

Networks that promote trust and mutual commitment play a crucial role in building social capital and improving society's efficiency by providing greater potential for collective action (Putnam 1993). Social capital has long been recognised as an economic resource (see Coleman 1990, Putnam 2000). A distinction is commonly made between 'bonding' and 'bridging' forms of social capital. As Putnam (2000: 22–23) explains, bonding capital exists in networks that are, by choice or necessity, inward looking and tends to reinforce social isolation, exclusive identities and homogeneous groups. By contrast, bridging capital exists in networks that are outward looking and encompasses social diversity.

Trust potentially provides an efficient alternative to reliance on contracts, guarantees, insurances and safeguards as a means to cope with market imperfections. According to Macauley (1963: 58), for example, 'businessmen often prefer to rely on "a man's word" in a brief letter, a handshake, or "common honesty and decency" – even where the transaction involves exposure to serious risks'. Vulnerability thus remains an essential component of trust, since, irrespective of how far trust 'alleviates the fear that one's exchange partner will act opportunistically . . . the risk of opportunism must be present for trust to operate' (Bradach and Eccles 1989: 104). This explains why, at least at a personal level, trust is seen as dependent on relative proximity to the person to be trusted (Brien 1998) and knowledge of their likely motivations (Hardin 2006) and capabilities (Larson 1992).

Overcoming potential distrust between public and private sectors is an important aspect of capacity building. This challenge is well illustrated by Tait's (2009) analysis of a particular development dispute between local planners and a housebuilder. In this case, he attributed the breakdown of trust to the housebuilder's perception of planners as unreliable and incompetent and to the planners' view of the housebuilder as aggressive, prone to cutting corners and unconcerned for wider values. In both cases, distrust was based not merely on previous, direct experience of the other party, but also on perceptions of what they represented. More widely, Höppner (2009) explored the extent of trust in the institution of regulatory planning by looking at whether participants in the planning process trust planning committees. This she found to be dependent on the extent to which participants believed members of the planning committee to be competent, honest, open, fair, reliable, reciprocating, respectful and committed. Trust is built when these qualities are central to behaviour and decision-making.

Since informal networks tend to emerge and develop spontaneously, their vitality depends more on individual commitment than on overt management. However, as Lowndes and Wilson (2001) argue, explicit institutional design can play a crucial role in building social capital and providing a more formalised context for mobilising the influence of organised interests and individual citizens within the democratic process.[4]

At a local level, formal organisations such as city-centre partnerships and design review panels enlarge the pool of available resources and create synergies. At a national level, place-making has been championed by organisations such as Architecture + Design Scotland (A+DS) and the Commission for Architecture and the Built Environment (CABE) in England, which have successfully brought together national representatives of a broad range of development interests to identify key agendas in delivering better places.[5] Such organisations are able to act as a conduit for governmental resources (such as authority, expertise and finance), which distinguishes them from informal networks. Capacity building thus requires formal organisations as well as informal networks in order to ensure a groundswell of support across the sectors in favour of place-making initiatives and in opposition to the unchallenged acceptance of default urbanism.

Market-relevant skills and capabilities

Developing human capital involves enhancing the skills and abilities of key individuals and organisations. This is an important capacity-building action which facilitates more effective operation of market shaping, regulation and stimulus. It may include such activities as continuous professional development, on-the-job training, exposure to good or innovative practice, expert seminars, field visits, and job swaps or secondments. Where particular skills are deficient in an organisation and cannot easily be developed among existing staff, capacity building may need to include targeted recruitment.

In this context, professional institutes and other accreditation bodies can play an important role in identifying certain areas of knowledge and capabilities as expected learning outcomes from professional education. For example, one important area of practical knowledge that is increasingly seen as central to planning education is (what is perhaps mistakenly called) 'development economics'. In the RTPI's (2004: 11) revisions to its guidance on the content of academic planning education, typical graduates in spatial planning were expected to: 'Understand the relationship between market processes, built form, different development models and patterns of movement, evaluate the economic and financial implications of alternative development strategies and consider how best to generate and capture added value for both particular interests and the wider community.'

Yet, this is a good illustration of where it is necessary to distinguish between shallow and substantive skills. It can be 'a dangerous thing' if planners gain only limited awareness of development economics, since this may merely reinforce acceptance of market-led planning, in which planners develop a more sympathetic understanding of developers' calculations but do not have the expertise to challenge them fundamentally. As effective market actors, planners need the confidence to be able to negotiate financially on level terms with developers, and this requires substantial knowledge, not shallow awareness of development economics.

In the past decade, the importance of developing skills and capabilities for place-making and regeneration has attracted much attention, especially in the UK. The challenge has been 'to consider place shaping, making and management as a set of inter-linked activities best undertaken through a common philosophy and approach, joint working between professionals, and the development and application of shared generic skills and knowledge' (Roberts 2009: 438). The Urban Task Force (1999) made recommendations to redress the uneven and segmented skill base in urban development and promote multi-disciplinary professional engagement. It argued that rigid divisions between professions were institutionalised in professional education and accreditation systems and that such barriers should be broken down by more broadly based programmes and courses with an emphasis on generic problem solving and multi-disciplinary working.

More broadly, Salamon (2002: 16–17) argued that public-sector managers needed better *enablement* skills in order to reach out to multiple stakeholders. Specifically, he highlighted the need for three particular types of skills:

- Activation skills – these help to mobilise and activate involvement by those beyond government so as to achieve real partnership in problem solving.
- Orchestration skills – these help to create effective networks, especially by persuading participants to act in concert and achieve public objectives.
- Modulation skills – these help to set the framework of rewards and penalties to elicit co-operative behaviour. Salamon illustrates this by the concept of 'enoughmanship', which refers to persuading developers to invest in run-down areas that they otherwise might avoid by providing just enough incentive, but without unduly subsidising profits.

The Egan Review of *Skills for Sustainable Communities* (2004), which supported the Urban Task Force's focus on cross-disciplinary learning with a strong vocational element, identified ten important generic skills for sustainable place-making. These were:

- inclusive visioning
- project management
- leadership in sustainable communities
- breakthrough thinking/brokerage
- team/partnership working within and between teams, based on a shared sense of purpose
- making it happen, given constraints
- process management/change management
- financial management and appraisal
- stakeholder management
- analysis, decision-making, learning from mistakes, evaluation.

Significantly, the Egan Report matched each of these generic skills to a specification of the behaviours and knowledge required in order to make them effective. The report emphasised that 'generic skills development must be honed, practised and enhanced by working in a variety of projects, in a variety of jobs, within multi-disciplinary teams, in the public and private sectors with people who already demonstrate some or all of the skills' (Egan 2004: 69).

An alternative perspective to the development of generic skills came from the ODPM's (2002) publication of *The Learning Curve*. This made the important distinction between three main types of learning. It noted that the first of these, 'formal learning', consumed significant time for professionals, practitioners and civil servants both in terms of initial education and subsequent continuing professional development training. 'Action learning', or learning through doing, was the second type identified, in which day-to-day work experiences and interaction with other people and organisations provide an important setting in which to try out new skills and resolve new problems. The third type of learning identified in the report is that of 'social learning' by observing others. The extent to which people develop important skills and areas of knowledge in this almost unnoticed form of learning is often underestimated. Building capacity in human capital may well involve all three types of learning.

Although these and other studies helped to enlighten the range and diversity of skills needed for place-making, each tended to produce a separate list of what might be required, rather than to develop a workable typology of particular skills into broad but well-defined types. An important exception to this approach was the categorisation devised by Taylor *et al.* (2004) for the Scottish Centre for Regeneration. This moved beyond the mere listing of likely skills, to develop an organised fourfold division into strategic, practical, process (or people) and specialised skills (Figure 14.1). While strategic skills initiate and promote change, process skills enable change and practical skills deliver change. All are essential in successful place-making. This division thus provides a workable framework that facilitates a more comprehensive approach to skill development, especially as it has been supported by a useful online learning pack.[6]

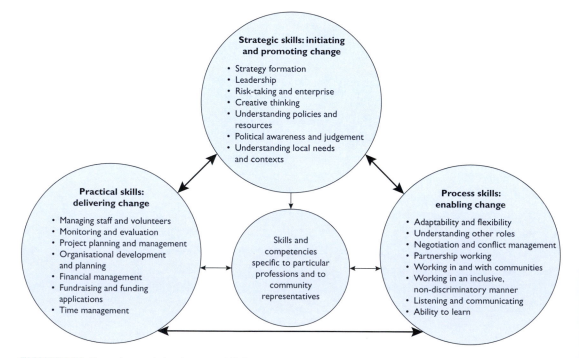

FIGURE 14.1 Strategic, practical and process skills for regeneration. (Adams *et al.*, 2006)

Conclusions

Planners already operate as market actors, even though they may need to recognise this more clearly and build their capacity to do so effectively. The four types of capacity-building instruments reviewed in this chapter point to a much broader notion of what it means to be a planner than was understood in many previous accounts of planning. Once the focus moves on from the production or regulation of plans to the making of places, it becomes essential for planners to engage with a much broader range of outlooks and disciplines in order to achieve success.

This is reflected at various points throughout the chapter. Place-making calls for planners to benefit from changed perspectives on their role and function, seeing themselves as active participants in development, rather than as external controllers of development. This requires them to invest in both informal networks and formal organisations so as to help them build trust between varied stakeholders and facilitate their connections to different forms of development expertise. Significantly, fresh mindsets and broader networks need to be reinforced by more varied information than was traditionally collected by planners, especially in relation to how market trends can be influenced by planning action. Finally, if planners are to make a central contribution to sustainable place-making, and on occasion to take a leading or co-ordinating role, then much greater emphasis could be placed on developing their broader skills and capabilities, so that multidisciplinary approaches become an essential element of planning work. The importance of this agenda should not be underestimated, for capacity building among planners, and indeed among development actors more generally, is as crucial in delivering better places as are market shaping, regulation and stimulus.

15 Conclusions

The challenge of institutional reform

How can more integrated development and more successful places be achieved? The exemplar case studies in this book suggest that, as far as 'first-order' design is concerned (see Chapter 2), much is already known about how best to produce sustainable forms of development, at least in the architectural, construction and engineering sense. Instead, the real challenge is one of 'second-order' design, and specifically that of restructuring institutional processes so as to modify the decision environments of individual development actors. Second-order design is more highly path-dependent than first-order design, since institutional processes become deeply embedded in regimes of established laws and procedures, in cultural customs and conventions and in the working practices of relevant organisations (Jepperson 1991).

To break out from conventional approaches to managing and developing places, which have emerged and been refined over many decades, is much more difficult than creating a fresh approach from scratch, when no inherited baggage has to be cleared away. Two main implications flow from this. First, the challenge of producing more integrated development and more successful places is essentially one of institutional creativity. Second, this challenge is inherently problematic because effective institutional reform will always be opposed both by those who feel secure and comfortable with their current ways of working, irrespective of the results these produce, and by vested interests able to extract significant personal gains that would be threatened by effective reform. So, while noting that powerful voices will always contest reform, both explicitly by lobbying against it and implicitly by seeking to undermine it, this final chapter highlights five priorities for 'second-order' design that could significantly enhance the prospects for delivering better-integrated development and more successful places

Outcomes matter

To those not involved in the development or place-production processes, what matters most is the outcomes they produce, rather than necessarily how they are achieved. Successful outcomes create sustainable forms of development that last for generations. Unsuccessful outcomes create significant problems that often have to be remedied at considerable expense within a generation. Yet, the inherent risks of real estate development create a necessary focus, among those responsible for its production, on delivering products on time and within budget. In recent decades, this emphasis on managing production has spread to spatial planning to such an extent that, according to Allmendinger (2011), while the emphasis may have been on hitting processing targets, the result has been to miss the point.

As we argue in Chapter 10, the point of spatial planning is to change development outcomes to such an extent that, as far as development location, product, quality, place, efficiency, horizons, consumers and production are concerned, the results are noticeably different than those which would have been produced by real estate markets, left to their own devices (see Box 10.2). This means that the central focus of spatial planning should be on place-making rather than on plan-making or the regulation of plans made by others. Despite the importance of these latter activities, they do not exist in a vacuum unrelated to some broader concept of place or to the particular institutional framework through which more sustainable places can be delivered.

This emphasis on place takes a broad-minded approach to the definition of planning and planners, recasting the activity and profession as essentially concerned with the delivery of quality outcomes, rather than merely with the efficient management of operational processes. It challenges those who take a reductionist view of spatial planning, constructing it simply as a regulatory activity which impedes efficient production. This is deliberately done by those who wish to promote deregulation, in the erroneous belief that this will assist economic development. Instead, once spatial planning concentrates on achieving the delivery of better places, rather than merely on the publication of plans or operational agreements, the more beneficial its likely contribution to social and economic development. The first necessary reform is thus to challenge embedded institutional cultures that portray planning as essentially concerned with regulatory processes and instead to re-establish that its fundamental purpose is about changing market outcomes and delivering better places.

Reforming processes

Nothing said so far should be taken to imply that processes can be ignored – indeed the whole tenor of much of this book has been about improving processes in order to deliver better-quality outcomes. More integrated forms of development, for example, require effective governance processes that join up separate decisions about the future of places taken across time and space. In Chapter 6, for example, we explored the importance of these processes in relation to governance capacity, and looked specifically at issues around leadership, stakeholder engagement and the importance of adequate powers, resources and expertise.

In Chapter 11, we applied these lessons to explain the creation of such exemplar places as Hammarby-Sjöstad, IJburg, Newhall and Upton. This helped us to develop a model of the place-production process that encapsulates what might ideally be involved in undertaking strategic urban transformations. Such lessons can also be applied at the more mundane and limited end of place-making, for example in relation to a small housing development, for without effective governance processes, the chances of creating somewhere less successful are greater than those of creating somewhere more successful. The 'tragedy of spatial planning' is that it has had to operate too often without effective governance processes, thus opening itself up to criticism when unwanted outcomes result. In most such instances, what is often needed is not less planning, but a different form of planning.

Reconstructing markets

There is nothing natural or immutable about real estate markets. As we argued in Chapters 3 to 5, the way real estate markets operate reflects the particular institutional characteristics of the society, culture and legal framework within which they are located. If real estate markets are socially constructed, it follows that they can be socially reconstructed. In part, this happens implicitly all the time as individuals and organisations make fresh choices and set off in different directions. It also happens explicitly when powerful market actors such as developers, landowners, funders and investors re-appraise their strategies so as to capture and direct such market movements to their own advantage. The argument in this book is that planners are also essentially market actors and that their agenda is (or at least should be) to promote plan-shaped markets, rather than market-led planning.

To achieve this, planners should be able to take some of the risk out of the development process (and certainly not add to it), stretch the thinking of other market actors from the short into the medium and long term and engage with market dynamics to take advantage of windows of development opportunity. All this tends to run counter to the way many planners see themselves as either referees who are there to ensure that no fouls are committed or as spectators who watch the match from the side-lines. It may take a considerable change in culture for most planners to see themselves as active market participants, daily engaged in a game of very high stakes, who, like all other participants, are seeking to change the rules in their favour. So, while planners may be located within the processes of governance, their field of action is centred on the processes of markets.

Market engagement and reconstruction thus demand that planners are able to mobilise the processes of governance so as to change what other market actors think is possible in particular locations. Again, case studies earlier in the book, such as Raploch (Chapter 6), Aberdeen and Aberdeenshire (Chapter 10) and Allerton Bywater (Chapter 11) show what can be achieved when explicit thought is given to how planning actions can modify market thinking and reconstruct market process to help deliver more integrated development and more successful places.

Re-stocking the tool-box

In Chapter 6, we quoted the epigram attributed to Mark Twain that 'If your only tool is a hammer, all your problems are nails.' If regulatory instruments are all that planners have available, their problems and actions become reduced primarily to the speed by which regulatory decisions can be made. In the final section of the book, we outlined a wide variety of instruments intended to shape, regulate and stimulate real estate markets while building the capacity to do so. Which of these, or indeed which combination of these, are appropriate in particular cases to achieve more integrated development depends on the specific circumstances of those cases. It has to be admitted, however, that many planners find the contents of their tool-boxes rather limited. At an individual level, the most rational response may well be to narrow the definition of planning problems, so that it is at least possible to claim some success with the instruments actually available.

It is not feasible to resolve this narrowing of planning at the individual or, necessarily, at the local level. What is instead required is a more fundamental debate about how the creation of successful places requires a well-stocked tool-box so as to enable the judicious deployment of the appropriate instruments in the appropriate circumstances. In some cases, what may principally be needed is active project leadership by the state, using its powers and expertise to change market outcomes, without any great resource commitment. In other instances, more direct intervention in the development process may be necessary.

As we have argued throughout the book, land ownership has a potentially more powerful influence on place-making than has planning control. There are many circumstances in which it can helpful for the state to consolidate and then distribute land rights within a development area, or at least set processes in train that enable this to be undertaken efficiently by private-sector actors. In the context of consistent concerns that the UK fails to build enough new homes, it is noticeable that European systems which endow municipalities with a broader range of planning instruments and encourage them to engage in active development promotion do not seem to have the same difficulties as the UK in housing supply (Oxley *et al.* 2009).

Investing in place

It is clear from the examples of Hammarby-Sjöstad, IJburg, Newhall and Upton and of many similar cases around Europe that, while effective place-making is initially more costly, it is likely to produce higher long-term returns, financially, socially and environmentally. An essential cultural change necessary to enable more successful places to be delivered is to begin to see place-making as an investment, and, indeed, as an investment worth making. While this approach embodies and reflects the broad concept of sustainable development, it requires new models of funding in both the public and private sectors that enable place-making investments to be made now on the basis that significant returns will flow in the medium to long term.

To those who recoil from such commitment, it should be borne in mind that, over time, the state already makes numerous individual investments in the physical and social infrastructure of place, such as in roads and educational facilities, at considerable cost but at a lower return than might be achieved with explicit spatial co-ordination. Additionally, significant recurrent resources are devoted to employing professional expertise, such as planners and highway engineers, and maintaining associated regulatory systems, irrespective of how well they contribute to place-making. So, taking an integrated view of all relevant public expenditure might well conclude that better value for money can be achieved by a comprehensive re-evaluation and redirection of the various ways in which the state already invests in place.

Some final questions

To draw together this chapter, and indeed the book, we end with five questions that we believe need to be addressed by researchers and practitioners alike if better-integrated development and more successful places are indeed to be delivered in future. These are:

- To what extent are governance processes to manage change in the built environment really focused on delivering better places?
- Are such processes effective enough to support this focus?
- How far do planners actively and explicitly seek to reconstitute real estate markets?
- What essential policy instruments are missing from the tool-box generally available to planners?

- To what extent do governments see place-making as a potentially lucrative investment opportunity able to deliver value for money for the public purse?

In the end, thorough analysis and debate around questions such as these are essential to shaping places more effectively and delivering more sustainable forms of development.

Notes

Chapter 1

1   The case study of Raploch presented in Chapter 6 is one of many such examples that demonstrate how effective place making is an inclusive activity able to fulfil a social justice agenda.

Chapter 2

1   New Urbanists 'envision dense, mixed-use neighborhoods with walkable streets, civic amenities, defined open spaces, and if possible, connections to transit . . . Much of the architectural designs are based on local building types and attempt to respect local ecological conditions' (Dutton 2000: 11).
2   It should be noted that this claim is not without controversy and is contested by some economists, such as Gordon and Richardson (1989).

Chapter 3

1   It should be noted that certain titles, such as those for leases of seven years or less, are not regarded as substantial enough to be registered. Since such unregistered interests are capable of 'overriding' or binding registered ones, purchasers should make enquiries of vendors and inspect the land, rather than rely simply on the information contained in the Land Registry.

Chapter 4

1   Although the phrase 'location, location, location' is often attributed to Harold (later Lord) Samuel, founder of Land Securities (see Chapter 7) and is still mistakenly ascribed to him

on the Land Securities website, its origin goes back at least to the Chicago Tribune in 1926, which carried a classified real estate advertisement with the words 'Attention salesmen, sales managers: location, location, location, close to Rogers Park' (Saffire 2009).

2   A recession is generally regarded as a fall in gross domestic product lasting two or more quarters (or at least six months). In the UK, GDP first fell in the second quarter of 2008 and continued falling until the third quarter of 2009, when it began to rise again. However, it did not return to the pre-recession figure until the second quarter of 2010.

Chapter 5

1   The Leadership in Energy and Environmental Design Neighborhood Development rating system was developed jointly by the Congress for the New Urbanism and the US Green Building Council (see Marantz and Ben-Joseph 2011).

2   In Hong Kong, the term 'resumption' is used in the same way as the American term 'eminent domain' to cover what is called compulsory purchase in the UK. Both 'resumption' and 'eminent domain' reflect the theoretical view that property rights derive from the state and can therefore be reclaimed by the state, when justified on a strict interpretation of the public interest.

3   'An option is an agreement that allows a developer to buy land at an agreed, fixed price by serving notice on the owner at any time within a specified period, normally two years. A conditional contract is one that does not take effect until a specific event occurs, usually the granting of planning permission' (Goodchild and Munton 1985: 70).

4   A charrette is an intensive and time-limited exercise, normally involving the active participation of relevant stakeholders and interest groups, which seeks to generate visionary and creative design solutions through understanding different viewpoints, exploring alternative ideas and resolving perceived constraints.

5   There have been few attempts to apply Jessop's insights to real estate development, although his collaboration with Ngai-Ling Sum has produced a series of papers on cultural political economy, including work on urban entrepreneurial strategies (see, for example, Jessop and Sum 2000). Readers who wish to apply Jessop's theories in real estate research are strongly advised to develop a more extensive understanding of the strategic-relational approach than is possible here, by consulting the original sources directly.

Chapter 6

1   Although it can be argued that the UK Parliament has ceded sovereignty over certain matters upwards to the European Union, in theory this could be reversed if Parliament voted to withdraw from the EU.

2   The financial provisions of the Town and Country Planning Act 1947 intended to capture any 'betterment' between the value of land with planning consent compared to that in its existing use, were watered down by the incoming Conservative Government, and eventually abolished.

3   It is not possible within the space available to explore in any detail the variety of thought *within* neo-liberalism. However, as Gamble (2009: 71) emphasises 'There has never been one neo-liberalism' He distinguishes at least three main strands. The first, market fundamentalism, seeks to remove as many impediments to market operations as possible. The

second, which he labels the anarcho-capitalist strand, aims to privatise all state activities, including defence and law enforcement. The third, which he calls the social market strand, believes that the state should create the right institutional environment in which markets can flourish, including welfare safety nets, investment in human capital and environmental protection. Each of these strands would present a different analysis of the case for and against a planning system. The survival of the UK planning system in the neo-liberal era can be attributed to the dominant influence of the third strand above the other two within everyday environmental politics.

4   Although this statement is attributed to Mark Twain, it is not actually found in his published writings. Kaplan (1964: 28) popularised the concept in his 'law of the instrument' in which he stated 'Give a small boy a hammer, and he will find that everything he encounters needs pounding'. Maslow's (1966: 15) own variant argued that 'if all you have is a hammer, everything looks like a nail'. For further information, see http://en.wikipedia.org/wiki/Law_of_the_instrument (accessed 6 June 2011).

5   See Chapter 5, note 4.

Chapter 7

1   It is far more common in Continental Europe than in the UK for the roles of master developer and infrastructure provider to be separated from that of parcel developer. A good example is provided by 'aménageurs-lotisseur' in France, whose role is to assemble sites, subdivide them into development parcels and install the necessary infrastructure (see Booth 1991).

2   We discuss developer risk further and consider its implications for place making in Chapter 10.

3   Real Estate Investment Trusts now exist in more than 25 countries around the world, including the UK, USA, France, Germany and Japan. Although arrangements vary country by country, there are three common features. First, the bulk of the income/profit must come from property ownership and investment, not development. Secondly, most of that income or profit must be distributed to shareholders. Thirdly, although shareholders may well be taxed on any dividends etc. that they receive, REITS themselves pay no tax on income or capital gains, thus avoiding what would otherwise be double taxation (Goodchild 2008).

4   The term 'speculative' is used here to refer to development that is initiated before the purchaser is known. It contrasts with development that is pre-sold to, or directly commissioned by, a purchaser. Hence (almost) all speculative developers operate in the private sector, but not all private developers operate speculatively.

5   There is also evidence that when quite different design approaches are offered to the consumer, they can also sell well. Newhall in Essex (see Chapter 8), with its strong contemporary feel, is a case in point.

6   http://webarchive.nationalarchives.gov.uk/20110107165544 (accessed 30 August 2011)

7   In April 2011, a much slimmed-down CABE merged with the Design Council as a result of the Coalition Government's financial cuts. The 'Building-for-Life' initiative was retained, although the annual awards process did not take place in 2011, while responsibilities were clarified.

8   A second edition of this book with some updated material was published in 2001.

Chapter 8

1   For further details, see www.morayestates.com/index.asp.
2   These figures represent only 26 per cent of vacant and derelict land in Scotland and the same proportion of previously developed land in England, confirming that the majority of brownfield land in the UK is in private, mixed or unknown ownership.
3   www.ernestcooktrust.org.uk/estates/bucks/hartwell.html (accessed 13 September 2011).
4   www.seasidefl.com/communityHistory2.asp (accessed 14 September 2011).
5   www.prospectnewtown.com/story.html (accessed 14 September 2011).
6   For further details of Newhall, see: http://webarchive.nationalarchives.gov.uk/201101 18095356.

Chapter 9

1   The chapter does not consider the role of the state in offering grants and subsidies to help fund development (especially in regeneration areas), since this is dealt with in Chapter 13. By implication, the chapter is therefore primarily concerned with development markets that can function effectively without financial support from the state.
2   Leinberger (2009: 108) defines a lifestyle center as 'pseudo-Main Street; a two-lane street with 'teaser" parking on one or both sides of the street, regional and national stores built up to the sidewalks, and a sea of surface parking surrounding the place where most of the customers park. It is Disneyland in nature – a suburban theme park – but it begins to provide a sense of community in an otherwise sterile suburban place.'
3   A good example of a North American big-box anchored center is the Freemont Village Shopping Centre, at Port Coquitlam in British Columbia, Canada. It will provide 65,000m^2 of lettable retail floorspace with over 1,000 car parking spaces, to be developed from 2011 on a 20 hectare out-of-town site located at a major highway intersection. Although containing a variety of smaller stores, the centre will be anchored by its main draw: a large, freestanding 14,000m^2 Walmart store.
4   See www.igloo.uk.net/.

Chapter 10

1   Free-riding on the innovation of others is thought to confer what is known as 'second mover advantage' (see Geroski and Markides 2005).

Chapter 11

1   As this implies, we use the word 'place' in this chapter to refer to an urban area of some scale, and not, for example, to a small collection of buildings or to an urban square.
2   In the case of pure public goods, one person's consumption is not lessened by the consumption of another at the same time (making the goods non-rival), while it is impossible to restrict anyone's consumption by preventing access (because they are non-excludable). Goods that are wholly non-rival and non-excludable are pure public goods, of which national defence, clean air and open countryside are commonly cited as obvious examples. Conversely, goods that are wholly rival and excludable are pure private goods, which are easily traded in markets. Webster and Lai (2003) argue that pure public goods are a theoretical fiction and cite in support Coase's (1974) investigation of

how lighthouses around the British coast were funded by harbour fees, not by the government.

3 Some might refer to these as 'delivery vehicles'.

4 Although we illustrate the concept of a town founder by reference to individual landowners, the role may well be played by a single large development company.

5 To illustrate the concept of an entrepreneurial club, it is helpful to compare a public park open to all and a private park, such as those which occupied the centres of many London squares, surrounded by a fence with a gate that can be unlocked only by a key given to residents who contribute to the upkeep. Today's gated communities operate along much the same lines and have been analysed by Webster (2002) drawing on the theory of club goods, derived from Buchanan (1965) and Olson (1965).

6 Although all five tasks are included in the 'ideal' model of place production, one or more may be absent in practice. This does not automatically prevent the creation of quality places, but it does make it harder.

7 Tax Increment Financing (see Chapter 13) could provide a third way.

Chapter 12

1 Of course, this argument depends on the extent to which any planning gain requirements are widely known and reflected in land transaction prices. Moreover, severe house price falls, as witnessed in parts of the UK during the recession of 2008–9, can undermine the delivery of previously agreed planning gain on sites that had earlier been acquired by developers in better times.

Chapter 13

1 Readers interested in the concept of market failure are referred back to Chapter 3. The converse problem of government failure was discussed briefly in that chapter and more extensively in Chapter 6.

2 For brevity, this chapter concentrates only on development-stimulus instruments. Readers wishing to explore design-stimulus instruments are recommended to consult Syms and Clarke (2011).

3 During the 1990s, as private housing development became more profitable in the Netherlands, municipalities found themselves in competition from private developers for building land, as a result of which the traditional Dutch model of land supply became less prevalent (Verhage 2003).

4 This is known as a 'back to back' agreement since the developer stands ready to complete the sale from the local authority on the day after the compulsory purchase order takes effect. For an example of an important city centre back to back agreement, which was contested as far as the House of Lords, see *Standard Commercial Property Securities Limited and others* v. *Glasgow City Council and others* [2006] UKHL 50.

5 In theory, this problem could be resolved by changing the relative weightings of the two envelopes, although some experimentation might be required before the most appropriate weightings became clear.

6 A converse danger occurs if development grants are accompanied by continuing employment subsidies, in which case no economically sustainable activity may ever be established. In that case, any withdrawal of subsidies may result in the closure of the enterprise and the vacancy of the development.

7 Take, for example, two investments, each with the same annual income of £5 million. The first is perceived to be high risk, so a 12.5% initial yield is assigned to it. The second is lower risk and has a 6.25% initial yield. Capital value is the income multiplied by the inverse of the yield, i.e. 8 in the first case but 16 in the second. So the first investment is considered to be worth £40 million and the second £80 million.

8 The fiscal autonomy of cities in the USA (unlike those in the UK) has contributed significantly to the rapid growth of TIFs and the resultant intense competition between them.

Chapter 14

1 In the sense that structure and agency dimensions are embedded in both political power and the dynamics of real estate development (see Chapter 5 and 6), the way places change and develop thus also reflects the constant interaction between political, economic and social structures and the aspirations and efforts of people and communities.

2 www.thefreedictionary.com/network.

3 In the context of place, social networks can range from the very informal (such as a group of friends who campaign on a one-off basis against a particular development proposal) through the semi-formal (such as a neighbourhood watch scheme in which encouraging 'eyes on the street' normally has some organisational support) to the truly formal (such as a local civic society with a formal constitution and membership).

4 In this context, the Scottish Government's (2010a) initiative to promote short-term exchanges of planning and development staff between public- and private-sector employers provides a good example of how network development and shared understanding can be fostered by policy initiative.

5 CABE was established in 1999 as the UK Government's independent advisor on architecture, urban design and public space. As a result of the Coalition Government's financial cuts, it merged with the Design Council in 2011, when its role was significantly reduced. Architecture + Design Scotland was established in 2005 with a similar remit to CABE north of border (although at a lesser scale), which it continues to discharge.

6 www.communitiesscotland.gov.uk/stellent/groups/public/documents/webpages/scrcs_020047.pdf (accessed 2 December 2011).

References

4ps and Deloitte (2008) *The Estate We're In: Driving Better Value from Property*, London: 4ps.

Adair, A. (1993) 'Financing of property development', pp. 50–76 in Berry, J., McGreal, S. and Deddis, B. (eds) *Urban Regeneration: Property Investment and Development*, London: E and F N Spon.

Adair, A., Berry, J., Deddis, W., Hirst, S. and McGreal, S. (1998) *Assessing Private Finance: The Availability and Effectiveness of Private Finance in Urban Regeneration*, London: Royal Institution of Chartered Surveyors.

Adair, A., Berry, J., Gibb, K., Hutchison, N., McGreal, S., Poon, J. and Watkins, C. (2004) *Benchmarking Urban Regeneration*, London: Royal Institution of Chartered Surveyors.

Adair, A., Berry, J., Haran, M., Lloyd, G. and McGreal, S. (2009) *The Global Financial Crisis: Impact on Property Markets in the UK and Ireland*, Jordanstown: University of Ulster.

Adair, A., Berry, J., McGreal, S., Hutchison, N. and Allan, S. (2006) *Institutional Investment in Regeneration: Necessary Conditions for Effective Funding*, London: Investment Property Forum.

Adams, D. (1994) *Urban Planning and the Development Process*, London: UCL Press.

Adams, D. (1996) 'The use of compulsory purchase under planning legislation', *Journal of Planning and Environmental Law*, 275–85.

Adams, D. and May, H. (1991) 'Active and passive behaviour in land ownership', *Urban Studies*, 28: 687–705.

Adams, D. and May, H. (1992) 'The role of landowners in the preparation of statutory local plans', *Town Planning Review*, 63: 297–323.

Adams, D. and Payne, S. (2011) '"Business as usual"? – Exploring the design response of UK speculative housebuilders to the brownfield development challenge', pp. 199–218 in Tiesdell, S. and Adams, D. (eds) *Urban Design in the Real Estate Development Process*, Oxford: Wiley-Blackwell.

Adams, D. and Tiesdell, S. (2010) 'Planners as market actors: rethinking state–market relations in land and property development', *Planning Theory and Practice*, 11: 187–207.

Adams, D. and Tiesdell, S. (2011) *Smart Parcelisation: Reconciling Development and Design Priorities*, Paper presented to ACSP Conference, Salt Lake City, USA, October 2011.

Adams, D. and Watkins, C. (2002) *Greenfields, Brownfields and Housing Development*, Oxford: Blackwell.

Adams, D., Watkins, C. and White, M. (eds) (2005) *Planning, Public Policy and Property Markets*, Oxford: Blackwell.

Adams, D., Allmendinger, P., Dunse, N., Houston, D., Tiesdell, S., Townend, J., Turok, I. and White, M. (2003) *Assessing the Impact of Planning, Housing, Transport and Regeneration Policies on Land Pricing*, London: Office of the Deputy Prime Minister. Available at www.communities.gov.uk/documents/corporate/pdf/142754.pdf.

Adams, D., Baum, A. and MacGregor, B. (1985) 'The influence of valuation practices upon the price of vacant inner city land', *Land Development Studies*, 2: 157–73.

Adams, D., Baum, A. and MacGregor, B. (1988) 'The availability of land for inner city development: a case study of inner Manchester', *Urban Studies*, 25: 62–76.

Adams, D., Croudace, R. and Tiesdell, S. (2009a) *Discovering Property Policy: An Examination of Scottish Executive Policy and the Property Sector*, London: Royal Institution of Chartered Surveyors. Available at www.rics.org/site/download_feed.aspx?fileID=5753&fileExtension=PDF.

Adams, D., Croudace, R. and Tiesdell, S. (2011a) 'Design codes, opportunity space and the marketability of new housing', *Environment and Planning B*, 38: 289–306.

Adams, D., Croudace, R. and Tiesdell, S. (2012a) 'The notional property developer as a policy concept', *Urban Studies*. http://usj.sagepub.com/content/early/2012/01/05/00420980 11431283

Adams, D., Disberry, A., Hutchison, N. and Munjoma, T. (1999) *Do Landowners Constrain Urban Redevelopment?* Aberdeen Papers in Land Economy 99–01, Department of Land Economy, University of Aberdeen.

Adams, D., Disberry, A., Hutchison, N. and Munjoma, T. (2000) 'Mind the gap! Taxes, subsidies and the behaviour of brownfield owners', *Land Use Policy*, 17: 135–45.

Adams, D., Disberry, A., Hutchison, N. and Munjoma, T. (2001a) 'Ownership constraints to brownfield redevelopment', *Environment and Planning A*, 33: 453–77.

Adams, D., Disberry, A., Hutchison, N. and Munjoma, T. (2001b) 'Managing urban land: the case for urban partnership zones', *Regional Studies*, 35: 153–62.

Adams, D., Disberry, A., Hutchison, N. and Munjoma, T. (2002) 'Vacant urban land: exploring ownership strategies and actions', *Town Planning Review*, 73: 395–416.

Adams, D., Leishman, C. and Moore, C. (2009b) 'Why not build faster? Explaining the speed at which British housebuilders develop new homes for owner occupation', *Town Planning Review*, 80: 291–314.

Adams, D., Leishman, C. and Watkins, C. (2012b) 'Housebuilder networks and residential land markets', *Urban Studies*, 49, 705–20.

Adams, D., May, H. and Pope, T. (1992) 'Changing strategies for the acquisition of residential development land', *Journal of Property Research*, 9: 209–26.

Adams, D., Russell, L. and Taylor-Russell, C. (1995) 'Market activity and industrial development', *Urban Studies*, 32: 471–89.

Adams, D., Tiesdell, S. and Weeks G. (2011b) *Delivering Better Places in Scotland: Learning from Broader Experience*, Edinburgh: Scottish Government. Available at www.scotland.gov.uk/Resource/Doc/336587/0110158.pdf.

Adams, D., Watkins, C. and White, M. (eds) (2005) *Planning, Public Policy and Property Markets*, Oxford: Blackwell.

Albrechts, L. (2003) 'Planning and power: towards an emancipatory planning approach', *Environment and Planning C: Government and Policy*, 21: 905–24.

Albrechts, L. (2006) 'Shifts in strategic spatial planning? Some evidence from Europe and Australia', *Environment and Planning A*, 38: 1149–70.

Alexander, A. (2009) *Britain's New Towns: Garden Cities to Sustainable Communities*, Abingdon: Routledge.

Alexander, E. R. (2001) 'A transaction costs theory of land use planning and development control: towards an institutional analysis of public planning', *Town Planning Review*, 72: 45–75.

Allmendinger, P. (2010) *Transaction Costs, Planning and Housing Supply*, London: Royal Institution of Chartered Surveyors.

Allmendinger, P. (2011) *New Labour and Planning: From New Right to New Left*, Abingdon: Routledge.

Allmendinger, P. and Ball, M. (2006) *Rethinking the Planning Regulation of Land and Property Markets*, London: Office of the Deputy Prime Minister.

Allmendinger, P. and Haughton, G. (2007) 'The fluid scales and scope of UK spatial planning', *Environment and Planning A*, 39: 1478–96.

Amin, A. (2005) *Cities in the Cultural-Economy*, Paper presented at ESRC Planning and Development Seminar Group Workshop on Institutions, Markets and Governance, University of Sheffield, January 2005.

Amin, A. and Thrift, N. (2003) *The Cultural Economy Reader*, Oxford: Blackwell.

Antwi, A. and Henneberry, J. (1995) 'Developers, non-linearity and asymmetry in the development cycle', *Journal of Property Research*, 12: 217–39.

Archer, R. W. (1989) 'Transferring the urban land pooling/readjustment technique to the developing countries of Asia', *Third World Planning Review*, 11: 307–31.

Archer, R. W. (1992) 'Introducing the urban land pooling/readjustment technique into Thailand to improve urban development and land supply', *Public Administration*, 12: 155–74.

Arnstein, S. R. (1969) 'A ladder of citizen participation', *Journal of the American Institute of Planners*, 35: 216–24.

Article 13 (2006) *CSR Best Practice: Urban Splash*. Available at www.article13.com/A13_ContentList.asp?strAction=GetPublication&PNID=1246 (accessed 22 September 2011).

Audit Commission (2006) *The Planning System – Matching Expectations and Capacity*, London: Audit Commission.

Balchin, P. N., Bull, G. H. and Kieve, J. L. (1988, 4th edn) *Urban Land Economics and Public Policy*, London: Macmillan.

Balchin, P. N., Bull, G. H. and Kieve, J. L. (1995, 5th edn) *Urban Land Economics and Public Policy*, London: Macmillan.

Ball, M. (1983) *Housing Policy and Economic Power*, London: Methuen.

Ball, M. (1998) 'Institutions in British property research', *Urban Studies*, 35: 1501–17.

Ball, M. (1999) 'Chasing a snail: innovation and housebuilding firms' strategies', *Housing Studies*, 14: 9–22.

Ball, M. (2008) *UK Planning Controls and the Market Responsiveness of Housing Supply*, Working Papers in Real Estate and Planning 13/08, School of Real Estate and Planning, Henley Business School, University of Reading.

Ball, M., Le Ny, L. and Maginn, P. J. (2003) 'Synergy in urban regeneration partnerships: property agents' perspectives', *Urban Studies*, 40: 2239–53.

Ball, M., Lizieri, C. and MacGregor, B. D. (1998) *The Economics of Commercial Property Markets*, London: Routledge.

Bank of England (2010) *Trends in Lending: September 2010*, London: Bank of England.

Barker, K. (2003) *Review of Housing Supply: Securing our Future Housing Needs – Interim Report – Analysis*, London: HMSO.

Barker, K (2004) *Review of Housing Supply – Delivering Stability: Steering Our Future Housing Needs, Final Report – Recommendations*, London: Office of the Deputy Prime Minister.

Barker, K. (2006) 'Planning policy, planning practice, and housing supply', *Oxford Review of Economic Policy*, 24: 34–49.

Barlow, J. (1999) 'From craft production to mass customisation: innovation requirements for the UK housebuilding industry', *Housing Studies*, 14: 23–42.

Barlow, J. and King, A. (1992) 'The state, the market and competitive strategy: the housebuilding industry in the United Kingdom, France and Sweden', *Environment and Planning A*, 24: 381–400.

Barnett, J. (1974) *An Introduction to Urban Design*, New York: Harper and Row.

Barras, R. (1984) 'The office development cycle in London', *Land Development Studies*, 1: 35–50.

Barras, R. (1985) 'Development of profit and development control: the case of office development in London', pp. 93–105 in Barrett, S. and Healey, P. (eds) *Land Policy: Problems and Alternatives*, Aldershot: Gower.

Barras, R. (1994) 'Property and the economic cycle: building cycles revisited', *Journal of Property Research*, 11: 183–97.

Barrett, S., Stewart, M. and Underwood, J. (1978) *The Land Market and the Development Process*, Occasional Paper 2, School for Advanced Urban Studies, University of Bristol.

Beauregard, R. A. (2005) 'The textures of property markets: downtown housing and office conversions in New York City', *Urban Studies*, 42: 2431–45.

Bell, D. (2005) 'The emergence of contemporary masterplans: property markets and the value of urban design', *Journal of Urban Design*, 10: 81–110.

Bemelmans-Videc, M.-L., Rist, R. C. and Vedung, E. (2007) (eds) *Carrots, Sticks and Sermons: Policy Instruments and their Evaluation*, London: Transaction Publishers.

Ben-Joseph, E. (2005) 'On Standards', pp. 1–14 in Ben-Joseph, E. and Szold, T. (eds) *Regulating Place: Standards and the Shaping of Urban America*, New York: Routledge.

Bentley, I. (1999) *Urban Transformations – Power, People and Urban Design*, London: Routledge.

Blakely, E. J. and Snyder, M. G. (1997) *Fortress America: Gated Communities in the United States*, Washington, DC: Brookings Institution Press and Cambridge, MA: Lincoln Institute of Land Policy.

Bloxham, T. (2009) Letter to the Editor, *Estates Gazette*, 12 October.

Booth, P. (1991) 'Preparing land for development in France: the role of the aménageur-lotisseur', *Journal of Property Research*, 8: 239–51.

Booth, P. (1996) *Controlling Development: Certainty and Discretion in Europe, the USA and Hong Kong*, London: UCL Press.

Bourne, L. S. (1967) *Private Redevelopment of the Central City*, Research Paper 112, Department of Geography, University of Chicago.

Bradach, J. L. and Eccles, R. G. (1989) 'Price, authority and trust: from ideal types to plural forms', *Annual Review of Sociology*, 15: 97–118.

Bramley, G. (1993a) 'Land-use planning and the housing-market in Britain: the impact on housebuilding and house price', *Environment and Planning A*, 25: 1021–51.

Bramley, G. (1993b) 'The impact of land-use planning and tax subsidies on the supply and price of housing in Britain', *Urban Studies*, 30: 5–30.

Bramley, G. and Kirk, K. (2005) 'Does planning make a difference to urban form? Recent evidence from Central Scotland', *Environment and Planning A*, 37: 355–78.

Bramley, G. and Leishman, C. (2005) 'Planning and housing supply in two-speed Britain: modelling local market outcomes', *Urban Studies*, 42: 2213–44.

Bramley, G., Bartlett, W. and Lambert, C. (1995) *Planning, the Market and Private Housebuilding*, London: UCL Press.

Branson, A. (2010) 'Interview transcript: Tom Bloxham, Urban Splash', *Regeneration and Renewal*, 7 April. Available at www.regen.net/news/995219/Interview-transcript-Tom-Bloxham-Urban-Splash/?DCMP=ILC-SEARCH (accessed 22 September 2011).

Brenner, N. and Theodore, N. (2002) 'Cities and the geographies of actually existing neoliberalism', *Antipode*, 34: 349–79.

Bridge, G., Butler, T. and Lees, L. (eds) (2011) *Mixed Communities: Gentrification by Stealth?* Bristol: Policy Press.

Brien, A. (1998) 'Professional ethics and the culture of trust', *Journal of Business Ethics*, 17: 391–409.

Brindley, T., Rydin, Y. and Stoker, G. (1996, 2nd edn) *Remaking Planning*, London: Routledge.

British Property Federation (2008) *Tax Increment Financing: A New Tool for Funding Regeneration in the UK?* London: British Property Federation.

Brown, H. J., Phillips, R. S. and Roberts, N. (1982) 'Landownership and market dynamics at the urban periphery: implications for land policy design and implementation', pp. 119–47 in Cullen, M. and Woolery, S. (eds) *World Congress on Land Policy*, Lexington, MA: Lexington Books.

Buchanan, J. (1965) 'An economic theory of clubs', *Economica NS*, 32 (125): 1–14.

Cadell, C., Falk, N. and King, F. (2008) *Regeneration in European Cities: Making Connections*, York: Joseph Rowntree Foundation.

Calcutt, J. (2007) *The Calcutt Review of Housebuilding Delivery*, London: Department for Communities and Local Government.

Cameron, G. C., Monk, S. and Pearce, B. J. (1988) *Vacant Urban Land: A Literature Review 1976–86*, London: Department of the Environment.

Campbell, H. and Henneberry, J. (2005) 'Planning obligations, the market orientation of planning and planning professionalism', *Journal of Property Research*, 22: 37–59.

Campbell, H., Tait, M. and Watkins, C. (2009) *Making Space for Justice?* Paper presented at Association of Collegiate Schools of Planning Conference, Crystal City, VA, 2009.

Carmona, M. (2009a) 'Sustainable urban design: definitions and delivery', *International Journal for Sustainable Development*, 12: 48–77.

Carmona, M. (2009b) 'The Isle of Dogs: four development waves, five planning models, twelve plans, thirty-five years, and a renaissance . . . of sorts', *Progress in Planning*, 71: 87–151.

Carmona, M. (2011) 'Design coding: mediating the tyrannies of practice', pp. 54–73 in Adams, D. and Tiesdell, S. (eds) *Urban Design in the Real Estate Development Process*, Oxford: Wiley-Blackwell.

Carmona, M. and Dann, J. (eds) (2007) 'Design codes', *Urban Design*, 101, Winter: 16–35.

Carmona, M., de Magalhaes, C. and Edwards, M. (2001) *The Value of Urban Design*, London: Commission for Architecture and the Built Environment.

Carmona, M., Marshall, S. and Stevens, Q. (2006) 'Design codes, their use and potential', *Progress in Planning*, 65: 209–89.

REFERENCES

Carmona, M., Tiesdell, S., Heath, T. and Oc, T. (2010, 2nd edn) *Public Places, Urban Spaces: The Dimensions of Urban Design*, London: Architectural Press.

Carrithers, D. F. and Peterson, D. (2006) 'Conflicting views of markets and economic justice: implications for student learning', *Journal of Business Ethics*, 69: 373–87.

Carroll, D.A. (2008) 'Tax increment financing and property value', *Urban Affairs Review*, 43: 520–52.

Caves, R. and Cullingworth, J. B. (2008, 3rd edn) *Planning in the USA*, London: Routledge.

Cervero, R. and Murakami, J. (2009) 'Rail and property development in Hong Kong: experiences and extensions', *Urban Studies*, 46: 2019–43.

Chapin, F. S. and Weiss, S. F. (eds) (1962) *Urban Growth Dynamics*, New York: John Wiley.

Cheshire, P. (2006) *Segregated Neighbourhoods and Mixed Communities*, York: Joseph Rowntree Foundation.

Cheshire, P. (2008) 'Reflections on the nature and policy implications of planning restrictions on housing supply. Discussion of "Planning policy, planning practice, and housing supply" by Kate Barker', *Oxford Review of Economic Policy*, 24: 50–58.

Cheshire, P. (2009) *Urban Containment, Housing Affordability and Price Stability – Irreconcilable Goals*, SERC Policy Paper 4, Spatial Economics Research Centre, London School of Economics.

Cheshire, P. and Hilber, C. (2008) 'Office space supply restrictions in Britain: the political economy of market revenge', *The Economic Journal*, 118: F185–F221.

Cheshire, P. and Sheppard, S. (1989) 'British planning policy and access to housing: some empirical estimates', *Urban Studies*, 26: 469–85.

Chisholm, M. and Kivell, P. (1987) *Inner City Waste Land*, Hobart Paper No. 108, London: Institute of Economic Affairs.

Christie, H., Smith, S. J. and Munro, M. (2008) 'The emotional economy of housing', *Environment and Planning A*, 40: 2296–312.

Ciochetti, B. and Malizia, E. (2000) 'The application of financial analysis and market research to the real estate development process', pp. 135–65 in DeLisle, J. and Worzala, E. (eds) *Essays in Honor of James A. Graaskamp: Ten Years After*, Boston, MA: Kluwer Academic Publishers.

Civic Trust (1988) *Urban Wasteland Now*, London: Civic Trust.

Civic Trust (1998) *Housing and Regeneration: How a Greenfield Levy Can Help*, London: Civic Trust.

Clark, C. (2003) 'Defence estate: are we wasting the peace dividend?' *Town and Country Planning*, 150–54.

Clarke, L. (1992) *Building Capitalism*, London: Routledge.

Coase, R. H. (1937) 'The nature of the firm', *Economica*, 4: 386–405.

Coase, R. H. (1960) 'The problem of social cost', *Journal of Law and Economics*, 3, 1–44.

Coase, R. H. (1974) 'The lighthouse in economics', *Journal of Law and Economics*, 7: 357–76.

Coiacetto, E. (2009) 'Industry structure in real estate development: is city building competitive?' *Urban Policy and Research*, 27: 117–35.

Coleman, J. S. (1990) *Foundations of Social Theory*, Cambridge, MA: Harvard University Press.

CABE (Commission for Architecture and the Built Environment) (2007) *Housing Audit – Assessing the Design Quality of New Homes Housing in the East Midlands, West Midlands and the South West*, London: Commission for Architecture and the Built Environment.

Commissioner of Law Revision, Malaysia (2006) *Laws of Malaysia, Act 458 Licensed Land Surveyors Act 1958 (Incorporating all amendments up to 1 January 2006)*, Kuala Lumpur: The Commissioner of Law Revision.

Competition Commission (2008) *The Supply of Groceries in the UK – Market Investigation*, London: Competition Commission.

Competition Commission (2010) *The Groceries Market Investigation (Controlled Land) Order*, London: Competition Commission.

Condon, P. M. (2008) *Design Charrettes for Sustainable Communities*, Washington DC: Island Press.

CBI (Confederation of British Industry) (2005) *Planning Reform: Delivering For Business*, London: CBI.

CBI Scotland (2004) *Planning for Growth: The Business Agenda for Planning Reform*, Glasgow: CBI Scotland.

Congress for the New Urbanism (2004) *Codifying New Urbanism: How to Reform Municipal Land Development Regulations*, Chicago: American Planning Association.

Connellan, O. (2004) *Land Value Taxation in Britain*, Cambridge, MA: Lincoln Institute of Land Policy.

Couch, C. and Fowler, S. (1992) 'Vacancy and recent structural change in the demand for land in Liverpool', pp. 100–13 in Healey, P., Davoudi, S., O'Toole, M., Tavsanoglu, S. and Usher, D. (eds) *Rebuilding the City*, London: E and F N Spon.

Cowans, J., Robinson, D. and Meikle, J. (2007) *Large-Scale Housing Growth in North Northamptonshire – Challenges and Opportunities*, London: Town and Country Planning Association.

Cowell, R. (2004) 'Community planning: fostering participation in the congested state?' *Local Government Studies*, 30: 497–518.

Crook, A. D. H., Monk, S., Rowley, S. and Whitehead, C. M. E. (2006) 'Planning gain and the supply of new affordable housing in England – understanding the numbers', *Town Planning Review*, 77: 353–73.

Cullingworth, J. B. (1980) *Environmental Planning 1939–1969 Volume 4: Land Values, Compensation and Betterment*, London: HMSO.

Cullingworth, J. B. and Nadin, V. (2006, 14th edn) *Town and Country Planning in the UK*, London: Routledge.

Dale, P., Mahoney, R. and McLaren, R. (2010, 2nd edn) *Land Markets and the Modern Economy*, London: Royal Institution of Chartered Surveyors.

Darlow, C. (ed.) (1988, 2nd edn) *Valuation and Development Appraisal*, London: Estates Gazette.

Dawkins, C. J. (2000) 'Transaction costs and the land use planning process', *Journal of Planning Literature*, 14: 507–18.

Dawson, E. and Higgins, M. (2009) 'How local authorities can improve design quality through the design review process: lessons from Edinburgh', *Journal of Urban Design*, 14: 101–14.

De Magalhães, C. (2001) 'International property consultants and the transformation of local property markets', *Journal of Property Research*, 18: 99–121.

De Sousa, C. (2008) *Brownfields Redevelopment and the Quest for Sustainability*, Oxford: Elsevier.

DellaVigna, S. (2009) 'Psychology and economics: evidence from the field', *Journal of Economic Literature*, 47: 315–72.

Denman, D. R. and Prodano, S. (1972) *Land Use: An Introduction to Proprietary Land Use Analysis*, London: Allen and Unwin.

DCLG (Department for Communities and Local Government) (2006a) *Design Coding in Practice: An Evaluation*, London: DCLG.

DCLG (2006b) *Code for Sustainable Homes: A Step-Change in Sustainable Homebuilding Practice*, London: DCLG.

DCLG (2007) *Housing Green Paper: Homes for the Future: More Affordable, More Sustainable*, Cm 7191, London: The Stationery Office.

DCLG (2008) *Spatial Plans in Practice: Supporting the Reform of Local Planning*, London: DCLG.

DCLG (2009) *Live Table 209 House Building: Permanent Dwellings Completed, by Tenure and Country*, London: DCLG.

DCLG (2010a) *The Incidence, Value and Delivery of Planning Obligations in England in 2007–08, Final Report*, London: DCLG.

DCLG (2010b) *The Community Infrastructure Levy: An Overview*, London: DCLG.

DETR (Department of the Environment, Transport and the Regions) and CABE (Commission for Architecture and the Built Environment) (2000) *By Design: Urban Design in the Planning System: Towards Better Practice*, London: DETR and CABE.

Dixon, T. (2001) *Land Pooling for Major Development Projects: A Discussion Paper*, London: Urban Villages Forum.

Dixon, T. (2009) 'Urban land and property ownership patterns in the UK: trends and forces for change', *Land Use Policy*, 26S: S43–S53.

Dixon, T., Abe, H. and Otsuka, N. (2010) *Cities in Recession: Urban Regeneration in Manchester (England) and Osaka (Japan) and the Case of 'Hardcore' Brownfield Sites*, Findings in Built and Rural Environments, London: Royal Institution of Chartered Surveyors.

Dobry, G. (1975) *Review of the Development Control System*, Final Report, London: HMSO.

Docherty, I. and McKiernan, P. (2008) 'Scenario planning for the Edinburgh city region', *Environment and Planning C: Government and Policy*, 26: 982–99.

Doebele, W. A. (1982) 'Introduction', pp. 1–10 in Doebele, W. A., *Land Readjustment: A Different Approach to Financing Urbanization*, Lexington, MA: Lexington Books, D.C. Heath and Co.

Doucet, B. (2010) *Rich Cities with Poor People: Waterfront Regeneration in the Netherlands and Scotland*, Netherlands Geographical Studies 391, Utrecht: Koninklijk Nederlands Aardrijkskundig Genootschap.

Drew, D. S., Tang, S. L. Y. and Lui, C. K. (2004) 'Balancing fee and quality in two envelope fee bidding', *Engineering, Construction and Architectural Management*, 11: 159–75.

Duany, A. and Talen, E. (2002) 'Transect planning', *Journal of the American Planning Association*, 68: 245–66.

Dubben, N. and Williams, B (2009) *Partnerships in Urban Property Development*, Oxford: Wiley-Blackwell.

Dühr, S., Nadin, V. and Colomb, C. (2010) *European Spatial Planning and Territorial Cooperation*, London: Routledge.

Dunse, N. and Jones, C. (2002) 'The existence of office submarkets in cities', *Journal of Property Research*, 19: 159–82.

Dunse, N., Dehring, C. and White, M. (2007) *Urban Parks, Open Space and Residential Property Values*, London: RICS.

Dutton, J. A. (2000) *New American Urbanism: Re-forming the Suburban Metropolis*, Milan: Skira.

Ebbs, N. (2009) *Urban Regeneration and Social Sustainability Workshop: Socially Responsible Investment and Blueprint/Igloo*, Presentation given at Oxford Brookes University, February 2008.

Edwards, M. (1990) 'What is needed from public policy?' pp. 175–85 in Healey, P. and Nabarro, R. (eds) *Land and Property Development in a Changing Context*, Aldershot: Gower.

Egan Review (2004) *Skills for Sustainable Communities*, London: Office of the Deputy Prime Minister.

Ellis, J. (1988) 'Codes and controls', *The Architectural Review*, 1101: 79–84.

Elmore, R. F. (1987) 'Instruments and strategy in public policy', *Policy Studies Review*, 7: 174–86.

English Partnerships (2003) *Towards a National Brownfield Strategy*, Warrington: English Partnerships.

English Partnerships (2007a, 2nd edn) *Urban Design Compendium Volume 1*, Prepared by Llewelyn-Davies for English Partnerships and The Housing Corporation, London: English Partnerships.

English Partnerships (2007b) *Urban Design Compendium Volume 2: Delivering Quality Places*, Prepared by Roger Evans Associates for English Partnerships and The Housing Corporation, London: English Partnerships.

European Union (2004) *Final Report of the Working Group on Urban Design for Sustainability*, Vienna: Austrian Federal Ministry of Agriculture, Forestry, Environment and Water Management.

Evans, A. W. (1985) *Urban Economics*, Oxford: Basil Blackwell.

Evans, A. W. (1991) 'Rabbit hutches on postage stamps: planning, development and political economy', *Urban Studies*, 28: 853–70.

Evans, A. W. (2004a) *Economics and Land Use Planning*, Oxford: Blackwell.

Evans, A. W. (2004b) *Economics, Real Estate and the Supply of Land*, Oxford: Blackwell.

Evans, A. W. and Hartwich, O. M. (2007) *The Best Laid Plans: How Planning Prevents Economic Growth*, London: Policy Exchange.

Evans, R. (2003) 'Redefining suburbs: Newhall, Harlow', *Urban Design Quarterly*, 86: 31–35.

Evans, R. (2008) 'Newhall, Harlow', *Urban Design Quarterly*, 108: 37–39.

Fainstein S. S. (1994) *The City Builders*, Oxford: Blackwell.

Falk, N. (2008) *Beyond Ecotowns: The Economic Issues*, London: URBED.

Falk, N. (2010) 'Rebuilding the common wealth of our towns and cities', *New Start*, November: 37–40.

Falk, N. (2011) 'Masterplanning and infrastructure in new communities in Europe', pp. 34–53 in Adams, D. and Tiesdell, S. (eds) *Urban Design in the Real Estate Development Process*, Oxford: Wiley-Blackwell.

Ferrari, E., Henneberry, J., Leahy Laughlin, D., Tait, M., Watkins, C. and McMaster, R. (2011) *Behavioural Change Approach to the Housing Sector*, London: Department for Communities and Local Government.

Fischler, R. (1995) 'Strategy and history in professional practice: planning as world making' pp. 13–58 in Liggett, H. and Perry, D. C. (eds) *Spatial Practices*, London: Sage.

Fisher, P. (2005) 'The property development process: case studies from Grainger Town' *Property Management*, 23: 158–75.

Fisher, P. (2010) 'The role of pre-letting in office property development in the UK', *Planning Practice and Research*, 25: 117–39.

Fisher, P., Robson, S. and Todd, S. (2007) 'The disposal of public sector sites by development competition', *Property Management*, 25: 381–99.

Florida, R. (2002) *The Rise of the Creative Class*, New York: Basic Books.

Flyvbjerg, B. (1998) *Rationality and Power: Democracy in Practice*, Chicago: University of Chicago Press.

Gamble, A. (2009) *The Spectre at the Feast: Capitalist Crisis and the Politics of Recession*, Basingstoke: Palgrave Macmillan.

Garrod, G. and Willis, K. G. (1999) *Economic Valuation of the Environment: Methods and Case Studies*, Cheltenham: Edward Elgar.

George, R. V. (1997) 'A procedural explanation for contemporary urban design', *Journal of Urban Design*, 2: 143–61.

Gerald Eve (2005) *Holding Periods: Analysis for UK Office Investors*, London: Gerald Eve.

Geroski, P. and Markides, C. (2005) *Fast Second*, San Francisco: Jossey-Bass.

Geuting, E. (2007) 'Proprietary governance and property development: using changes in the property-rights regime as a market-based policy tool', *Town Planning Review*, 78: 23–39.

Giddens, A. (1984) *The Constitution of Society*, London: Polity.

Glaeser, E. L. and Gyourko, J. (2003) 'The impact of building restrictions on housing affordability', *Federal Reserve Bank of New York Economic Policy Review*, June: 21–39.

Glaeser, E. L., Gyourko, J. and Saks, R. E. (2005) 'Why is Manhattan so expensive? Regulation and the rise in housing prices', *Journal of Law and Economics*, 48: 331–69.

Golland, A. and Boelhouwer, P. (2002) 'Speculative housing supply, land and housing markets: a comparison', *Journal of Property Research*, 19: 231–51.

Goodchild, B. and Karn, V. (1997) 'Standards, quality control and housebuilding in the UK', pp. 156–74 in Williams, P. (ed.) *Directions in Housing Policy: Towards Sustainable Housing Policies for the UK*, London: Paul Chapman Publishing.

Goodchild, R. (2008) 'REITs – a global phenomenon', *Journal of Property Investment and Finance*, 26: 280–81.

Goodchild, R. and Munton, R. (1985) *Development and the Landowner: An Analysis of the British Experience*, London: George Allen and Unwin.

Gordon, P. and Richardson, H. (1989) 'Gasoline consumption and cities – a reply', *Journal of the American Planning Association*, 55: 376–79.

Gore, T. and Nicholson, D. (1991) 'Models of the land-development process: a critical review', *Environment and Planning A*, 23: 705–30.

Graaskamp J. A. (1970) *A Guide to Feasibility Analysis*, Chicago: Society of Real Estate Appraisers.

Granovetter, M. (1973) 'The strength of weak ties', *American Journal of Sociology*, 78: 201–33.

Granovetter, M. (1985) 'Economic action and social structure: the problem of embeddedness', *American Journal of Sociology*, 91: 481–510.

Grant, J. (2007) 'Vision, planning and democracy', pp. 39–57 in Hopkins, L. D. and Zapata, M. A. (eds) *Engaging the Future: Forecasts, Scenarios, Plans and Projects*, Cambridge, MA: Lincoln Institute of Land Policy.

Grant, M. (1999) 'Compensation and betterment', pp. 62–75 in Cullingworth, B. (ed.) *British Planning – 50 years of Urban and Regional Policy*, London: Athlone.

Guy, S. and Henneberry, J. (2000) 'Understanding urban development processes: integrating the economic and the social in property research', *Urban Studies*, 37: 2399–416.

Guy, S., Henneberry, J. and Rowley, S. (2002) 'Development cultures and urban regeneration', *Urban Studies*, 39: 1181–96.

Hack, G. and Sagalyn, L. (2011) 'Value creation through urban design', pp. 258–81 in Adams, D. and Tiesdell, S. (eds) *Urban Design in the Real Estate Development Process*, Oxford: Wiley-Blackwell.

Hall, P. and Tewdwr-Jones, M. (2010, 5th edn) *Urban and Regional Planning*, London: Routledge.

Hall, P. and Ward, C. (1998) *Sociable Cities: The Legacy of Ebenezer Howard*, Chichester: John Wiley and Sons.

Hall, T. (2011) 'Proactive engagement in urban design – the case of Chelmsford', pp. 74–91 in Adams, D. and Tiesdell, S. (eds) *Urban Design in the Real Estate Development Process*, Oxford: Wiley-Blackwell.

Hamilton, W. H. (1932) 'Institutions', in Seligman, E. R. A. and Johnson, A. (eds) *Encyclopaedia of the Social Sciences*, 8: 84–89.

Hardin, R. (2006) *Trust*, Cambridge: Polity Press.

Hartland, R. (2006) *Evidence to Scottish Parliament Communities Committee*, Communities Committee Official Report 25 January 2006, Edinburgh: Scottish Parliament. Available at www.scottish.parliament.uk/business/committees/communities/or-06/co06–0302. htm (accessed 3 January 2011).

Harvey, D. (1989a) 'From managerialism to entrepreneurialism: the transformation of urban governance in late capitalism', *Geografiska Annaler Series B*, 1: 3–17.

Harvey, D. (1989b) *The Urban Experience*, London: Blackwell.

Hastings E. M. and Adams, D. (2005) 'Facilitating urban renewal: changing institutional arrangements and land assembly in Hong Kong', *Property Management*, 23: 110–21.

Haughton, G., Allmendinger, P., Counsell, D. and Vigar, G. (2010) *The New Spatial Planning: Territorial Management with Soft Spaces and Fuzzy Boundaries*, Abingdon: Routledge.

Havard, T. (2008, 2nd edn) *Contemporary Property Development*, London: RIBA Enterprises.

Healey, P. (1991) 'Models of the development process: a review', *Journal of Property Research*, 8: 219–38.

Healey, P. (1992a) 'An institutional model of the development process', *Journal of Property Research*, 9: 33–44.

Healey, P. (1992b) 'Development plans and markets', *Planning Practice and Research*, 7: 13–20.

Healey, P. (1992c) 'The reorganisation of the state and the market in planning', *Urban Studies*, 29: 411–34.

Healey, P. (2006) 'Relational complexity and the imaginative power of strategic spatial planning', *European Planning Studies*, 14: 525–46.

Healey, P. (2007) *Urban Complexity and Spatial Strategies: Towards a Relational Planning for our Times*, Abingdon: Routledge.

Healey, P. (2010) *Making Better Places*, Basingstoke: Palgrave Macmillan.

Healey, P. and Barrett, S. M. (1990) 'Structure and agency in land and property development processes: some ideas for research', *Urban Studies*, 27: 89–104.

Healey, P., Davoudi, S., O'Toole, M., Tavsanoglu, S. and Usher, D. (eds) (1992) *Rebuilding the City: Property-led Urban Regeneration*, London: E and FN Spon.

Healey, P., McNamara, P., Elson, M. and Doak, J. (1988) *Land Use Planning and the Mediation of Urban Change*, Cambridge: Cambridge University Press.

Heim, C. E. (1990) 'The Treasury as developer-capitalist? British new town building in the 1950s', *Journal of Economic History*, 50: 903–24.

Hellman, L. (1995) 'A century of development', *Building Design*, 1236: 5.

Hendershott, P., MacGregor, B. and White, M. (2002) 'Explaining real commercial rents using an error correction model with panel data', *Journal of Real Estate Finance and Economics*, 24: 59–87.

Henneberry, J. and Rowley, S. (2002) 'Developers' decisions and property market behaviour', pp. 96–114 in Guy, S. and Henneberry, J. (eds) *Development and Developers*, Oxford: Blackwell Science.

Henneberry, J., McGough, T. and Mouzakis, F. (2005) 'Estimating the impact of planning on commercial property markets', pp. 105–23 in Adams, D., Watkins, C. and White, M. (eds) *Planning, Public Policy and Property Markets*, Oxford: Blackwell.

Henneberry, J., Lange, E., Moore, S., Morgan, E. and Zhao, N. (2011) 'Physical-financial modelling as an aid to developers' decision-making', pp. 219–35 in Adams, D. and Tiesdell, S. (eds) *Urban Design in the Real Estate Development Process*, Oxford: Wiley-Blackwell.

Heywood, A. (2000) *Key Concepts in Politics*, Basingstoke: Palgrave Macmillan.

Hilton, C. (2007) 'Making it happen in Liverpool', *Urban Design*, 103, Summer: 27–29.

Hodgson, G. M. (1988) *Economics and Institutions*, Cambridge: Polity Press.

Home, R. (2007) 'Land readjustment as a method of development land assembly: a comparative overview', *Town Planning Review*, 78: 459–83.

Homes and Communities Agency (2010) *Previously-Developed Land that may be Available for Development: Results from the 2009 National Land Use Database of Previously-Developed Land in England*, Warrington: Homes and Communities Agency.

Homes and Communities Agency (2011) *National Coalfields Programme*. Available at www.homesandcommunities.co.uk/ourwork/national-coalfields-programme (accessed 2 December 2011).

Hong, Y. and Needham, B. (eds) (2007) *Analyzing Land Readjustment, Economics, Law, and Collective Action*, Cambridge, MA: Lincoln Institute of Land Policy.

Hood, C. (1983) *The Tools of Government*, Chatham: Chatham House Publishers.

Hood, C. and Margetts, H. Z. (2007) *The Tools of Government in the Digital Age*, Basingstoke: Palgrave Macmillan.

Hooper, A. (1992) 'The construction of theory: a comment', *Journal of Property Research*, 9: 45–48.

Hooper, A. and Nicol, C. (1999) 'The design and planning of residential development: standard house types in the speculative housebuilding industry', *Environment and Planning B: Planning and Design*, 26: 793–805.

Hopkins, L. D. (2001) *Urban Development: The Logic of Development Plans*, Washington, DC: Island Press.

Höppner, C. (2009) 'Trust – a monolithic panacea in land use planning?' *Land Use Policy*, 26: 1046–54.

Howlett, M. (1991) 'Policy instruments, policy styles, and policy implementation: national approaches to theories of instrument choice', *Policy Studies Journal*, 19: 1–21.

Hudson, J. and Lowe, S. (2009, 2nd edn) *Understanding the Policy Process: Analysing Welfare Policy and Practice*, Bristol: The Policy Press.

Imrie, R. and Thomas, H. (1993) 'The limits of property-led regeneration', *Environment and Planning C*, 11: 87–102.

Investment Property Forum (2005) *The Size and Structure of the UK Property Market*, London: Investment Property Forum.

IPD (2010a) *IPD Sustainability Property Index*, London: IPD.

IPD (2010b) *IPD Regeneration Index*, London: IPD.

Isaac, D., O'Leary, J. and Daley, M. (2010, 2nd edn) *Property Development Appraisal and Finance*, Basingstoke: Palgrave Macmillan.

Jackson, C. and Watkins, C. (2005) 'Planning policy and retail property markets: measuring the dimensions of planning intervention', *Urban Studies*, 42: 1453–69.

Jackson, C. and Watkins, C. (2007) 'Supply-side policies and retail property market performance', *Environment and Planning A*, 39: 1134–46.

Jacobs, J. (1961) *The Death and Life of Great American Cities*, New York: Vintage Books.

Jepperson, R. L. (1991) 'Institutions, institutional effects and institutionalism', pp. 143–63 in Powell, W. W. and DiMaggio, P. J. (eds) *The New Institutionalism in Organization Analysis*, Chicago: University of Chicago Press.

Jessop, B. (1996) 'Interpretative sociology and the dialectic of structure and agency: reflections on Holmwood and Stewart's *Explanation and Social Theory*', *Theory, Culture and Society*, 13: 119–28.

Jessop, B. (2001) 'Institutional (re)turns and the strategic-relational approach', *Environment and Planning A*, 33: 1213–35.

Jessop, B. (2007) *State Power*, Cambridge: Polity.

Jessop, B. and Sum, N.-L. (2000) 'An entrepreneurial city in action: Hong Kong's emerging strategies in and for (inter) urban competition', *Urban Studies*, 37: 2287–313.

Jones, C. A. (2009) 'Remaking the monopoly board: urban economic change and property investment', *Urban Studies*, 46: 2363–80.

Jones, C. and Watkins, C. (2009) *Housing Markets and Planning Policy*, Oxford: Wiley-Blackwell.

Jones, H. (2000) 'This is magnificent! 300,000 houses a year and the Tory revival after 1945', *Contemporary British History*, 14: 99–121.

Kaiser, E. J. and Weiss, S. F. (1970) 'Public policy and the residential development process', *Journal of the American Institute of Planners*, 36: 30–37.

Kaplan, A. (1964) *The Conduct of Inquiry: Methodology for Behavioral Science*, San Francisco: Chandler Publishing.

Karadimitriou, N. (2005) 'Changing the way UK cities are built: the shifting urban policy and the adaptation of London's housebuilders', *Journal of Housing and the Built Environment*, 20: 271–86.

Kelbaugh, D. (2002) *Repairing the American Metropolis: Common Place Revisited*, Seattle, WA: University of Washington Press.

Kelbie, P. (2008) 'Brighter future for notorious sink estate' *Observer*, 27 January: 25.

Keogh, G. and D'Arcy, E. (1999) 'Property market efficiency: an institutional perspective', *Urban Studies*, 36: 2401–14.

Killian Pretty Review (2008) *Planning Applications: A Faster and More Responsive System, Final Report*, London: DCLG.

King, A. (1975) 'Overload: problems of governing in the 1970s', *Political Studies*, 23: 284–96.

Kivell, P. T. and McKay, I. (1988) 'Public ownership of urban land', *Transactions of the Institute of British Geographers*, 13: 165–78.

Kollewe, J. (2011) 'Persimmon's former Saint closes door on a life in housebuilding', *Guardian*, 21 April 2011. Available at www.guardian.co.uk/business/2011/apr/21/john-white-persimmon-homes-friday-interview/print (accessed 21 September 2011).

Korthals Altes, W. K. (2006) 'The single European market and land development', *Planning Theory and Practice*, 7: 247–66.

Lai, L. W. C. (1998) 'The leasehold system as a means of planning by contract', *Town Planning Review*, 69: 249–75.

Lai, L. W. C. (2005) *Planning by Contract: The Leasehold Foundation of a Comprehensively Planned Capitalist Land Market*, London: Institute of Economic Affairs, and Oxford: Blackwell.

Landry, C. (2000) *The Creative City: A Toolkit for Urban Innovators*, London: Earthscan.

Larson, A. (1992) 'Network dyads in entrepreneurial settings: a study of the governance of exchange relationship', *Administrative Science Quarterly*, 37: 76–104.

Le Goix, R. and Webster, C. J. (2008) 'Gated communities', *Geography Compass*, 2: 1189–214.

Leinberger, C. B. (2001) *Financing Progressive Development*, Center on Urban and Metropolitan Policy, The Brookings Institution and Joint Center for Housing Studies, University of Harvard.

Leinberger, C. B. (2005) 'The need for alternatives to the nineteen standard real estate product types', *Places*, 17 (2): 24–29.

Leinberger, C. B. (2007) *Back to the Future: The Need for Patient Equity in Real Estate Development Finance*, The Brookings Institution Research Brief, Washington, DC: The Brookings Institution.

Leinberger, C. B. (2009) *The Option of Urbanism: Investing in a New American Dream*, Washington, DC: Island Press.

Leyshon, A. and French, S. (2009) '"We all live in a Robbie Fowler house": The geographies of the buy to let market in the UK', *The British Journal of Politics and International Relations*, 11: 438–60.

Li, L.-H. and Li, X. (2007) 'Land readjustment: an innovative urban experiment in China', *Urban Studies*, 44: 81–98.

Lichfield, N. (2002) 'Land assembly in the urban renaissance', *Town and Country Planning*, 71: 10–13.

Lichfield, N. and Darin-Drabkin, D. (1980) *Land Policy in Planning*, London: George Allen and Unwin.

Lin, T.-C. (2005) 'Land assembly in a fragmented land market through land readjustment', *Land Use Policy*, 22: 95–102.

Llewelyn-Davies (1996) *The Re-use of Brownfield Land for Housing: A Preliminary Study of Strathclyde*, London: Joseph Rowntree Foundation.

Lloyd, M. G., McCarthy, J., McGreal, S. and Berry, J. (2004) 'Business improvement districts, planning and urban regeneration', *International Planning Studies*, 8: 295–321.

Louw, E. (2008) 'Land assembly for urban transformation – the case of 's-Hertogenbosch in The Netherlands', *Land Use Policy*, 25: 69–80.

Love, T. (2009) 'Urban design after Battery Park City: opportunities for variety and vitality', pp. 208–26 in Krieger, A. and Saunders, W. S. (eds) *Urban Design*, Minneapolis: University of Minnesota Press.

Love, T. and Crawford, C. (2011) 'Plot logic: character-building through creative parcelisation', pp. 92–113 in Adams, D. and Tiesdell, S. (eds) *Urban Design in the Real Estate Development Process*, Oxford: Wiley-Blackwell.

Lowndes, V. and Wilson, D. (2001) 'Social capital and local governance: exploring the institutional design variable', *Political Studies*, 49: 629–47.

Luttik, J. (2000) 'The value of trees, water and open space as reflected by house prices in the Netherlands', *Landscape and Urban Planning*, 48: 161–67.

Lützkendorf, T. and Lorenz, D. (2010) 'Socially responsible property investment – background, trends and consequences', pp. 193–238 in Newell, G. and Sieracki, K. (eds) *Global Trends in Real Estate Finance*, Oxford: Wiley-Blackwell.

Lynch, K. (1960) *The Image of the City*, Cambridge, MA: MIT Press.

Lyons, M. (2007) *Place-Shaping: A Shared Ambition for the Future of Local Government*, Enquiry into Local Government Final Report, London: The Stationery Office.

Macaulay, S, (1963) 'Non-contractual relations in business: a preliminary study', *American Sociological Review*, 28: 55–67.

MacLaran, A. (2003) 'Masters of space: the property development sector', pp. 7–62 in MacLaran, A. (ed.) *Making Space: Property Development and Urban Planning*, London: Hodder Arnold.

MacLaran, A. (2010) *End of the Fifth Development Boom*, Dublin: Savills.

MacLaran, A. and Williams, B. (2003) 'Dublin: property development and planning in an entrepreneurial city', pp. 148–71 in MacLaran, A. (eds) *Making Space: Property Development and Urban Planning*, London: Hodder Arnold.

MacLaran, A., MacLaran, M. and Malone, P. (1987) 'Property cycles in Dublin: the anatomy of a boom and slump in the industrial and office property sectors', *Economic and Social Review*, 18: 237–56.

Maclennan, D. and Whitehead, C. (1996) 'Housing economics – an evolving agenda', *Housing Studies*, 11: 341–44.

Macmillan, S. (2006) 'Added value of good design', *Building Research and Information*, 34: 257–71.

Marantz, N. J, and Ben-Joseph, E. (2011) 'The business of codes: urban design regulation in an entrepreneurial society', pp. 114–36 in Adams, D. and Tiesdell, S. (eds) *Urban Design in the Real Estate Development Process*, Oxford: Wiley-Blackwell.

Markusen, A. (ed.) (2007) *Reining in the Competition for Capital*, Kalamazoo, MI: W. E. Upjohn Institute for Employment Research.

Marriot, O. (1967) *The Property Boom*, London: Hamish Hamilton.

Marshall, T. (2004) (ed.) *Transforming Barcelona*, London: Routledge.

Martin, L. and March, L. (1972) *Urban Space and Structures*, Cambridge: Cambridge University Press.

Maslow, A. H. (1966) *The Psychology of Science: A Reconnaissance*, New York: Harper and Row.

Massey, D. and Catalano, A. (1978) *Capital and Land: Land Ownership by Capital in Great Britain*, London: Edward Arnold.

McGreal, S., Berry, J., Lloyd, G. and McCarthy, J. (2002) 'Tax-based mechanisms in urban regeneration: Dublin and Chicago models', *Urban Studies*, 39: 1819–31.

McGregor, M. (2011) 'City regeneration pioneer Tom Bloxham in "decline" warning', BBC News Online, 17 April. Available at www.bbc.co.uk/news/uk-england-manchester-12987618 (accessed 22 September 2011).

McNamara, P. F. (1983) 'Towards a classification of land developers' *Urban Law and Policy*, 6: 87–94.

Meen, G. (1998) 'Modelling sustainable home ownership: demographics and economics', *Urban Studies*, 35: 1919–34.

Millington, A. F. (2000) *Property Development*, London: Estates Gazette.

Monk, S. and Whitehead, C. (1999) 'Evaluating the impact of planning controls in the UK – some implications for housing', *Land Economics*, 75: 74–93.

Montgomery, J. (1998) 'Making a city: urbanity, vitality and urban design', *Journal of Urban Design*, 3: 93–116.

Morphet, J. (2011) *Effective Practice in Spatial Planning*, Abingdon: Routledge.

Moss, G. (1981) *Britain's Wasting Acres: Land-use in a Changing Society*, London: Architectural Press.

Nabarro, R. and Richards, D. (1980) *Wasteland*, London: Methuen.

National Audit Office (2009) *Regenerating the English Coalfields*, Report by the Comptroller and Auditor General, House of Commons 84, 2009–2010, London: The Stationery Office.

NHPAU (National Housing and Planning Advice Unit) (2010) *Public Attitudes to Housing 2010*, Titchfield: NHPAU.

Needham, B. (1997) 'Land policy in the Netherlands', *Tijdschrift voor Economische en Sociale Geografie*, 88: 291–96.

Needham, B. (2006) *Planning, Law and Economics*, London: Routledge.

Nelson, A. C. (ed.) (1988) *Development Impact Fees: Policy Rational, Practice, Theory, and Issues*, Chicago: American Planning Association.

Nelson, A. C., Bowles, A. K., Juergensmeyer, J. C. and Nicholas, J. C. (2008) *A Guide to Impact Fees and Housing Affordability*, Washington, DC: Island Press.

New Economics Foundation (2005) *Clone Town Britain*, London: New Economics Foundation.

New London Architecture (2006) *The Great Estates: Sustainable Development over the Centuries*, London: NLA.

Newman, P. and Kenworthy, J. (2000) 'Sustainable urban form: the big picture', pp. 109–20 in Williams, K., Burton, E. and Jenks, M. (eds) *Achieving Sustainable Urban Form*, London: E and F N Spon.

NextGeneration (2008) *Developing Homes for Climate Change*, London: NextGeneration.

NFU (2011) 'NFU Responds to New Government Planning Regime', Press Release 2 March, Stoneleigh: NFU.

Norton-Taylor, R. (1982) *Whose Land Is It Anyway? How Urban Greed Exploits the Land*, Wellingborough: Turnstone.

Norwood (2004) 'Boom based on the banks', *Estates Gazette*, Issue 424, 6 December.

NWRA and RENEW Northwest (2007) *Economic Value of Urban Design*, Liverpool: Amion Consulting.

ODPM (Office of the Deputy Prime Minister) (2003) *Sustainable Communities: Building for the Future*, London: ODPM.

ODPM (2005a) *Affordability Targets: Implications for Housing Supply*, London: HMSO.

ODPM (2005b) *Circular 05/2005: Planning Obligations*, London: HMSO.

ODPM Neighbourhood Renewal Unit (2002) *The Learning Curve: Developing Skills and Knowledge for Neighbourhood Renewal*, London: ODPM.

Olson, M. (1965) *The Logic of Collective Action*, Cambridge, MA: Harvard University Press.

Osbourne, D. and Gaebler, T. (1992) *Reinventing Government – How the Entrepreneurial Spirit is Transforming the Public Sector*, London: Penguin Books.

Oxley, M. (2004) *Economics, Planning and Housing*, Basingstoke: Palgrave.

Oxley, M., Brown, T., Nadin, V., Qu, L., Tummers, L. and Fernández-Maldonado, A.-M. (2009) *Review of European Planning Systems*, Titchfield: National Housing and Planning Advice Unit.

Pan, W., Gibb, A. G. F. and Dainty, A. R. J. (2007) 'Perspectives of UK housebuilders on the use of offsite modern methods of construction', *Construction Management and Economics*, 25: 183–94.

Parr, J. B. (2007) 'Spatial definitions of the city: four perspectives', *Urban Studies*, 44: 381–92.

Participation and Sustainable Development in Europe (2005) *Mediation Vienna International Airport Factsheet*. Available at www.partizipation.at/fileadmin/media_data/Downloads/Praxisbeispiele/mediation_vienna_airport_engl.pdf (accessed 20 June 2011).

Pavlov, A. (2004) *Land Values and Sustainable Development*, London: Royal Institution of Chartered Surveyors.

Payne, S. L. (2009) 'The Institutional Capacity of the UK Speculative Housebuilding Industry', PhD Thesis, Department of Urban Studies, University of Glasgow. Available at http://theses.gla.ac.uk/853/.

Peace, L. (2009) 'Financing and changing business models for housing', pp. 56–71 in Commission for Architecture and the Built Environment, *Who Should Build our Homes? Six Experts Challenge the Status Quo*, London: CABE.

Pearce, B. J., Curry, N. R. and Goodchild, R. N. (1978) *Land, Planning and the Market*, Occasional Paper 9, Department of Land Economy, University of Cambridge.

Peel, D., Lloyd, G. and Lord, A. (2009) 'Business improvement districts and the discourse of contractualism', *European Planning Studies*, 17: 401–22.

Pennington, M. (2000) *Planning and the Political Market: Public Choice and the Politics of Government Failure*, London: Athlone.

Pennington, M. (2002) *Liberating the Land: The Case for Private Land Use Planning*, London: Institute of Economic Affairs.

Persimmon plc (2011) *Final Transcript Half Year 2011 Persimmon Plc Earnings Conference Call: 23 August 2011*, London: Thomson Reuters Streetevents.

Pickard, R. and Pickerell, T. (2002) *Real Estate Tax Credits and other Financial Incentives for*

Investing in Historic Property in the United States, Research Paper 4.17, London: RICS Foundation.

Prince's Foundation for the Built Environment (2007) *Valuing Sustainable Urbanism*, London: Prince's Foundation for the Built Environment.

PRP, URBED and Design for Homes (2008) *Beyond Eco-towns: Applying the Lessons from Europe*, London: PRP Architects Ltd.

Pryce, G. and Levin, E. (2008) 'Beyond reason', *RICS Residential Property Journal*, September/October: 16–17.

Punter, J. (2003) *The Vancouver Achievement: Urban Planning and Design*, Vancouver: UBC Press.

Punter, J. (2007a) 'Design-led regeneration? Evaluating the design outcomes of Cardiff Bay and their implications for future regeneration and design', *Journal of Urban Design*, 12, 375–405.

Punter, J. (2007b) 'Developing urban design as public policy: best practice principles for design review and development management', *Journal of Urban Design*, 12: 167–202.

Punter, J. (2009) 'An introduction to the British urban renaissance' pp. 1–31 in Punter, J. (ed.) *Urban Design and the British Urban Renaissance*, London: Routledge.

Punter, J. (2011) 'Design review: an effective means of raising design quality?' pp. 182–98 in Adams, D. and Tiesdell, S. (eds) *Urban Design in the Real Estate Development Process*, Oxford: Wiley-Blackwell.

Putnam, R. D. (1993) *Making Democracy Work: Civic Traditions in Modern Italy*, Princeton: Princeton University Press.

Putnam, R. D. (2000) *Bowling Alone: The Collapse and Revival of American Community*, London: Simon and Schuster.

Radcliffe, J., Stubbs, M. and Keeping, M. (2009, 3rd edn) *Urban Planning and Real Estate Development*, London: Routledge.

Rayner, G. and Gemmell, C. (2009) 'Tahir Zaman, controversial developer: MPs' expenses', *Daily Telegraph*, 15 May. Available at www.telegraph.co.uk/news/newstopics/mps-expenses/5326677/Tahir-Zaman-controversial-developer-MPs-expenses.html (accessed 26 August 2009).

Relph, E. (1976) *Place and Placelessness*, London: Pion.

Renard, V. (2007) 'Property rights and the transfer of development rights: questions of efficiency and equity', *Town Planning Review*, 78: 41–60.

Rhodes, R. A. W. (1994) 'The hollowing out of the state: the changing nature of the public service in Britain', *Political Quarterly*, 65: 138–51.

Rhodes, R. A. W. (1996) 'The new governance: governing without government', *Political Studies*, 44: 652–67.

Rhodes, R. A. W. (1997) *Understanding Governance: Policy Networks, Governance, Reflectivity and Accountability*, Buckingham: Open University Press.

Riley, J. (2009) 'Well-being and the democracy of compulsory purchase', *Journal of Place Management and Development*, 2: 230–39.

Roberts, P. (2009) 'Shaping, making and managing places: creating and maintaining sustainable communities through the delivery of enhanced skills and knowledge', *Town Planning Review*, 80: 437–53.

Robertson, D., Smyth, J. and McIntosh, I. (2008) *Neighbourhood Identity: People, Time and Place*, York: Joseph Rowntree Foundation.

Robson, D. (2010) *Redcar Restaurant had Cockroach Infestation*. Available at www.gazettelive.co.uk/news/teesside-news/2010/10/07/redcar-restaurant-had-cockroach-infestation-84229–27421915/#ixzz16I7chDYr (accessed 25 November 2010).

REFERENCES

Ross Goobey, A. (1992) *Bricks and Mortals*, London: Century Business.

Rouse, J. (2003) 'Born in the USA and heading to a growth area over here', *Housing Today*, 28 November, 18–19.

RTPI (Royal Town Planning Institute) (2001) *A New Vision for Planning*, London: RTPI.

RTPI (2003) *Education Commission Final Report*, London: RTPI.

RTPI (2004) *Policy Statement on Initial Planning Education*, London, RTPI.

RTPI (2007) *Opening up the Debate: Exploring Housing Land Supply Myths*, London: RTPI.

Saffire, W. (2009) 'Location, location, location', *New York Times Magazine*, 26 June. Available at www.nytimes.com/2009/06/28/magazine/28FOB-onlanguage-t.html (accessed 29 October 2011).

Salamon, L. (2002) *The Tools of Government*, Oxford: Oxford University Press.

Samuels, W. (1995) 'The present state of institutional economics', *Cambridge Journal of Economics*, 19: 569–90.

Savills (2007) *Investing in Place*, London: Savills.

Scheer, B. C. and Preiser, W. (1994) *Design Review: Challenging Urban Aesthetic Control*, New York: Chapman and Hall.

Scott, P. (1996) *The Property Masters*, London: E and F N Spon.

Scottish Executive (2006) *Scottish Planning Policy 8: Town Centres and Retailing*, Edinburgh: Scottish Executive.

Scottish Government (2009) *Draft Guide on Development Viability*, Scottish Government, Edinburgh.

Scottish Government (2010a) *Scheme of Staff Development Pilot: Project Summary Report*, Edinburgh: Scottish Government. Available at www.scotland.gov.uk/Topics/Built-Environment/planning/modernising/cc/projectsummary (accessed 6 January 2011).

Scottish Government (2010b) *Scottish Vacant and Derelict Land Survey 2009*, Edinburgh: Scottish Government.

Scottish Government Council of Economic Advisers (2008) *First Annual Report*, Edinburgh: Scottish Government.

Shaw, D. and Lord, A. (2007) 'The cultural turn? Culture change and what it means for spatial planning in England', *Planning Practice and Research*, 22: 63–78.

Shiel, L. and Smith-Milne, D. (2007) *Best Practice in Establishing Urban Regeneration Companies in Scotland*, Edinburgh: Scottish Government.

Shroup, D. (2008) 'Graduated density zoning', *Journal of Planning Education and Research*, 28: 161–78.

Simmonds, R. (2006) 'The cost of bad design', pp. 7–31 in *The Cost of Bad Design*, London: Commission for Architecture and the Built Environment.

Skelcher, C. (2000) 'Changing images of the state: overloaded, hollowed-out, congested', *Public Policy and Administration*, 15: 3–19.

Smith, N. (1996) *The New Urban Frontier: Gentrification and the Revanchist City*, London: Routledge.

Smith, S. J., Munro, M. and Christie, H. (2006) 'Performing (housing) markets', *Urban Studies*, 43: 81–98.

Smithson, A. (1968) *Team 10 Primer*, Cambridge, MA: MIT Press.

Sorauf, F. J. (1957) 'The public interest reconsidered', *Journal of Politics*, 19: 616–39.

Sorensen, A. (1999) 'Land readjustment, urban planning and urban sprawl in the Tokyo metropolitan area', *Urban Studies*, 36: 2333–60.

Sorensen, A. (2000) 'Land readjustment and metropolitan growth: an examination of suburban land development and urban sprawl in the Tokyo metropolitan area', *Progress in Planning*, 53: 217–330.

Stille, K. (2007) 'The B-plan in Germany', *Urban Design*, 101 (Winter): 24–26.

Studdert, P. (2009) 'Building new communities through local partnerships', pp. 32–54 in Commission for Architecture and the Built Environment, *Who Should Build Our Homes? Six Experts Challenge the Status Quo*, London: CABE.

Sweeting, D. (2002) 'Leadership in urban governance: the Mayor of London', *Local Government Studies*, 28: 3–20.

Symes, M. and Pauwels, S. (1999) 'The diffusion of innovations in urban design: the case of sustainability in the Hulme development guide', *Journal of Urban Design*, 4: 97–117.

Syms, P. and Clarke, A. (2011) 'Good design in the redevelopment of brownfield sites', pp. 137–58 in Adams, D. and Tiesdell, S. (eds) *Urban Design in the Real Estate Development Process*, Oxford: Wiley-Blackwell.

Syms, P. (2004) *Previously Developed Land*, Oxford: Blackwell.

Tait, M. (2009) *Building Trust in Planning: Understanding the Contested Legitimacy of a Planning Decision*, Paper presented at ACSP Conference, Crystal City, VA.

Tang, B.-S. and Tang, R. M. H. (1999) 'Development control, planning incentive and urban redevelopment: evaluation of a two-tier plot ratio system in Hong Kong', *Land Use Policy*, 16: 33–43.

Taylor, P., Turok, I., Kirkpatrick, D. and Rosengard, A. (2004) *Skills and Competencies for Community Regeneration: Needs Analysis and Framework*, Research Report 42, Edinburgh: Communities Scotland.

Thaler, R. H. and Sunstein, C. R. (2008) *Nudge*, London: Penguin.

The Prince's Foundation for the Built Environment (2007) *Valuing Sustainable Urbanism*, London: The Prince's Foundation.

Tibbalds, F. (1992) *Making People Friendly Towns*, Harlow: Longman.

Tiesdell, S. and Adams, D. (2004) 'Design matters: major house builders and the design challenge of brownfield development contexts', *Journal of Urban Design*, 9: 23–45.

Tiesdell, S. and Allmendinger, P. (2005) 'Planning tools and markets: towards an extended conceptualisation', pp. 56–76 in Adams, D., Watkins, C. and White, M. (eds) *Planning, Public Policy and Property Markets*, Oxford: Blackwell.

Tiesdell, S. and Macfarlane, G. (2007) 'The part and the whole: implementing masterplans in Glasgow's New Gorbals', *Journal of Urban Design*, 12: 407–33.

Tolson, S. (2011) 'Competitions as a component of design-led development (place) procurement', pp. 159–81 in Adams, D. and Tiesdell, S. (eds) *Urban Design in the Real Estate Development Process*, Oxford: Wiley-Blackwell.

Tu, C. C. and Eppli, M. J. (1999) 'Valuing New Urbanism; the case of Kentlands', *Real Estate Economics*, 27: 425–51.

Turok, I. (1992) 'Property-led urban regeneration: panacea or placebo?' *Environment and Planning A*, 24: 361–79.

UCL and Deloitte (2007) *Shaping and Delivering Tomorrow's Places: Effective Practice in Spatial Planning*, London: RTPI.

UK Government (2009) *World Class Places: The Government's Strategy for Improving Quality of Place*, London: Department for Communities and Local Government.

Unsworth, R. (2007) '"City living" and sustainable development: the experience of a UK regional city', *Town Planning Review*, 78: 725–47.

Urban Task Force (1999) *Towards an Urban Renaissance*, London: E and F N Spon.

Uthwatt Report (1942) *Expert Committee on Compensation and Betterment*, Final Report, Cmnd 6386, London: HMSO.

Valuation Office Agency (2010) *Property Market Report: January 2010*, London: VOA.

van der Krabben, E. (1995) *Urban Dynamics: A Real Estate Perspective – An Institutional Analysis of the Production of the Built Environment*, Center for Economic Research, Tilburg University.

van der Krabben, E. (2009) 'A property rights approach to externality problems: planning based on compensation rules', *Urban Studies*, 2869–90.

van der Krabben, E. and Needham, B. (2009) 'Land readjustment for value capturing: a new planning tool for urban redevelopment', *Town Planning Review*, 79: 651–72.

Vedung, E. (2007) 'Policy instruments: typologies and theories', pp. 21–58 in Bemelmans-Videc, M-L., Rist, R. C. and Vedung, E. (eds) *Carrots, Sticks and Sermons: Policy Instruments and their Evaluation*, London: Transaction Publishers.

Verhage, R. (2003) 'The role of the public sector in urban development: lessons from Leidsche Rijn Utrecht (The Netherlands)', *Planning Theory and Practice*, 4: 29–44.

Vigar, G. (2009) 'Towards an integrated spatial planning?' *European Planning Studies*, 17: 1571–90.

Vigar, G., Healey, P., Hull, A. and Davoudi, S. (2000) *Planning, Governance and Spatial Strategy in Britain: An Institutional Analysis*, Basingstoke: Macmillan.

Walker, J. (2007) 'Tariffs for infrastructure delivery – building better communities through a "business plan" approach', *Town and Country Planning*, Tomorrow Series Paper 7.

Wallace, A. (2008) 'Knowing the market? Understanding and performing York's housing', *Housing Studies*, 23: 253–70.

Walters, D. (2007) *Designing Community: Charettes, Masterplans and Form-Based Codes*, Oxford: Architectural Press.

Weber, R. (2002) 'Extracting value from the city: neoliberalism and urban redevelopment', *Antipode*, 34: 519–40.

Webster, C. (2001) 'Gated cities of tomorrow', *Town Planning Review*, 72: 149–70.

Webster, C. (2002) 'Property rights and the public realm: gates, green belts and gemein-schaft', *Environment and Planning B*, 29: 397–412.

Webster, C. and Lai, W. C. L. (2003) *Property Rights, Planning and Markets: Managing Spontaneous Cities*, Cheltenham: Edward Elgar.

Weiler, S. (2000) 'Pioneers and settlers in Lo-Do Denver: private risk and public benefits in urban redevelopment', *Urban Studies*, 37: 167–79.

Weiss, S. F., Smith, J. E., Kaiser, E. J. and Kenny, K. B. (1966) *Residential Developer Decisions*, Center for Urban and Regional Studies, University of North Carolina.

Wellings, F. (2001) *Private Housebuilding Annual 2001*, London: Credit Lyonnais Securities Europe.

Wellings, F. (2006) *British Housebuilders: History and Analysis*, Oxford: Blackwell.

Whitehead, C. (2009) 'Land supply and the planning system', pp. 8–31 in Commission for Architecture and the Built Environment, *Who Should Build Our Homes*, London: CABE.

Wilkinson, S. and Reed, R. (2008, 5th edn) *Property Development*, London: Routledge.

Willis, K. G. (1980) *The Economics of Town and Country Planning*, London: Granada.

Winter, P. and Lloyd, R. (2006) 'Regeneration, compulsory orders and practical related issues', *Journal of Planning and Environmental Law*, June, 781–804.

Wong, C. and Watkins, C. (2009) 'Conceptualising spatial planning outcomes: towards an integrative measurement framework', *Town Planning Review*, 80: 481–516.

Zukin, S. (1989) *Loft Living: Culture and Capital in Urban Change*, New Brunswick, NJ: Rutgers University Press.

Index

Page numbers in **bold** refer to illustrations.